HISTORY, LITERATURE, AND
THE WRITING OF THE CANADIAN PRAIRIES

HISTORY, LITERATURE, AND THE WRITING OF THE CANADIAN PRAIRIES

edited by
ALISON CALDER and
ROBERT WARDHAUGH

UNIVERSITY OF MANITOBA PRESS

University of Manitoba Press
Winnipeg, Manitoba R3T 2N2 Canada
www.umanitoba.ca/uofmpress
Printed in Canada on acid-free paper.

Cover Design: Kirk Warren
Text Design: Sharon Caseburg

Selections from *Marsh Burning* by David Arnason are reprinted from *a/long prairie lines* by permission of David Arnason and Turnstone Press.

Selections from *Sightings* by Walter Hildebrandt are reprinted by permission of Walter Hildebrandt.

Library and Archives Canada Cataloguing in Publication

   History, literature, and the writing of the Canadian Prairies /
Alison Calder and Robert Wardhaugh, editors.

Includes bibliographical references.
ISBN 0-88755-682-5

   1. Canadian literature (English)—Prairie Provinces—History and criticism. 2. Prairie Provinces—In literature. I. Calder, Alison C. (Alison Claire), 1969-
II. Wardhaugh, Robert Alexander, 1967-

PS8131.P7H57 2005   C810.9'9712   C2005-901133-5

The University of Manitoba Press gratefully acknowledges the financial support for its publication program provided by the Government of Canada through the Book Publishing Industry Development Program (BPIDP); the Canada Council for the Arts; the Manitoba Arts Council; and the Manitoba Department of Culture, Heritage and Tourism.

Support for the publication of this book was also provided by The University of Western Ontario, J.B. Smallman Fund.

CONTENTS

ACKNOWLEDGEMENTS

We would like to thank Dave Carr and Pat Sanders from the University of Manitoba Press for all their hard work in assembling this book. Additional thanks go out to all contributors for their continuing patience throughout this endeavour.

We would also like to thank two research assistants, Bryan Rosati at the University of Western Ontario for his work in compiling the bibliography, and Taryn Plett at the University of Manitoba for her skilled proofreading.

HISTORY, LITERATURE, AND
THE WRITING OF THE CANADIAN PRAIRIES

INTRODUCTION

When Is the Prairie?

by Alison Calder and Robert Wardhaugh

What does the question "When is the prairie?" mean? This collection takes as its starting point the assumption that the Canadian prairies exist both in space and in time, and that the intersection of these two concepts produces something distinctive, a region perhaps. Many examinations of Canadian prairie literature and history have focussed on the environment, particularly on the impact of the prairie landscape on European settler/invader culture. Much of the earlier scholarship emerged from the primal moment of contact between Europeans and the "new" land, and built its discourse around the narrative of the dominant western European settler society that followed. Until recently, reading available historical and literary sources, it has been possible to believe that the Canadian prairies began in 1850 or so, when the beginnings of intensive agricultural practices came to the West. It has also been possible to believe that the Canadian prairies have ended, or at least that time has ceased to pass here, judging by representations of the prairies in much literature and popular culture, and that we are permanently frozen in a rural, agricultural scene alternately coloured by the grainy, sepia tones of the Dirty Thirties or by the romanticized, golden glow of a nostalgic small-town sunset. But the prairies are still going strong, and its continued unfolding is observed and represented by environmentalists, journal-keepers, creative writers, historians, geographers, and archivists, to name but a few. Traditionally, prairie geography has been seen to determine history. This collection brings together ten essays by current scholars who argue instead that on the plains, geography, history, and culture are inextricably linked, and that only by considering all these facets at once can we begin to understand the diverse cultural landscapes of the place.

Great Plains topography is popularly perceived as absolute: absolutely flat, absolutely treeless, absolutely boring. It is also seen as absolute in the sense of being both unchanging and unchangeable, for better or worse. In *The Nature of the Place: A Study of Great Plains Fiction* (1995), Diane Dufva Quantic writes that "since the Puritans first looked into the forest, American writers have been exploring the meaning of place and the human community, but on the plains and prairies, this relationship seems especially significant, perhaps because the landscape is so sparse that, to some observers, it seems non-existent; by its very absence, landscape overwhelms."[1] Robert Thacker concludes his study of Canadian and American prairie fiction, *The Great Prairie Fact and Literary Imagination* (1989), by asserting that "from Castañeda's sixteenth-century exploration narrative to contemporary writers, prairie writing attests that the land does, without question, speak louder than the people."[2] These studies focus on how the land speaks the people, how it shapes human history and culture. The question that our collection asks is, instead, how do the people speak the land? In what ways do we write ourselves onto the prairie space, and what are the implications of those inscriptions? If, as Robert Kroetsch argues, "the fiction makes us real,"[3] then what reality is being depicted? Given that representations not only reflect but also shape a place, how are writers, creative and scholarly, representing the prairie, and what do these representations mean?

The value of interdisciplinary scholarship in understanding these questions is seen within the interdisciplinary nature of the literature and history itself. The category "Canadian prairies" came into being as a consciously constructed space, an entity deliberately produced in order to fulfill specific economic and imperial needs. While the area had appeared in explorer and surveyor literature as inhospitable, it was deliberately reconstructed through advertising as paradisal farmland in order to facilitate immigration and settlement, which were necessary to establish British claim to the Canadian West. Doug Francis points out that this deliberately manufactured image of the prairie as "fertile belt" predated actual experience of the area, writing that "even before Canadians had had an opportunity to assess the potential of the land in the North West in order to judge its intrinsic value for agricultural settlement, there existed in the mind of powerful eastern commercial, political, and expansionist interests an image of the North West."[4] Francis also emphasizes the effects of the mutually reinforcing spheres of politics and art: not only did romanticism emerge in the mid-nineteenth century as "a strong force which inspired individuals and nations to open up new vistas of exploration," but it also shaped artistic depictions of those vistas, as paintings of the West "reveal[ed] less a West actually seen than the romantic image of the West in the painter's eye before he actually saw the West."[5] From their beginnings, then, the post-contact Canadian prairies were tied up in questions of representation that combined historical and literary/artistic considerations. Literary and historical scholarship, on the other hand, has most often looked at these considerations in isolation, perhaps owing to a discipline-bound academic system that tacitly encourages the intellectual separation of literature and history. We argue for an imbrication of the multiple and contending disciplines and discourses, an opportunity to view time and place together to see how literature, history, and geography are both mutually supporting and mutually challenging perspectives.

LITERATURE

Until very recently, literary critics have privileged the prairie environment in their identification of the forces that shape writings from the prairies. The development of a tradition of Canadian prairie literary criticism is relatively young. Although Edward McCourt's *The Canadian West in Fiction* first came out in 1949,[6] it was not until 1968 that Henry Kreisel's influential essay "The Prairie: A State of Mind" appeared. The essay suggested the need always to consider the prairie landscape when attempting to understand the region's literature and people, asserting that "all discussion of the literature produced in the Canadian west must of necessity begin with the impact of the landscape upon the human mind."[7] In this essay, Kreisel focusses his argument on literature set in a much earlier historical moment, such as W.O. Mitchell's *Who Has Seen the Wind*, Sinclair Ross's *As for Me and My House*, and Martha Ostenso's *Wild Geese*. The effect of this retrospective focus is to construct a generalized prairie reality that is actually specific to a particular historical moment, as seen in the article's closing passage:

> For though much has changed in the west, much also still remains unchanged.... On a hot summer day it does not take long before, having left the paved streets of the great cities where hundreds of thousands of people now live, one can still see, outlined against the sky, the lonely, giant-appearing figures of men like Caleb Gare or the Ukrainian farmer in my story. And on a winter day one can turn off the great superhighways that now cross the prairies and drive along narrow, snow-covered roads, and there it still lies, the great, vast land-sea, and it is not difficult to imagine Philip Grove in his fragile cutter, speaking softly to Dan and Peter, his gentle, faithful horses, and preparing them to hurl themselves once more against that barren sea, those drifts of snow.[8]

The appealing image of the unchanging prairie that Kriesel invokes is only possible, however, if one ignores the very visible signs of change that have irrevocably altered the actual prairie. Kriesel's vision yearns for a timeless and authentic prairie, a "real" one here displaced by the modern world of highways and cities.

Kreisel's essay was followed by two book-length studies: Laurie Ricou's *Vertical Man/Horizontal World: Man and Landscape in Canadian Prairie Fiction* (1973) and Dick Harrison's *Unnamed Country: The Struggle for a Canadian Prairie Fiction* (1977). These two studies sought to consolidate Canadian prairie writing as a field of study and to establish a distinct canon; it is a measure of their influence that they are still widely consulted and cited. Ricou's study establishes Canadian prairie writing within a context of international modernism and existentialism, arguing that the prairie landscape functions as an analogue to the terrifying emptiness of the modern world.[9] Harrison's work focusses on describing a prairie literary tradition, taking a 1690 poem by Henry Kelsey as a starting point. For Harrison, there seems to have been no pre-contact prairie history: he writes that "like all unsettled territory it [the prairie] had no human associations, no ghosts, none of the significance imagination gives to the expressionless face of the earth after men have lived and died there."[10] Settlement gives meaning to this place.

Both Ricou and Harrison, like Kreisel, work retrospectively, identifying themes in early literature and then tracing them forward. Ricou takes Wallace Stegner's memoir *Wolf Willow*, itself a retrospective narration, as a paradigmatic text, remarking that it provides "the right verbalization" of the prairie environment.[11] The emphasis on *Wolf Willow* has some peculiar effects. It provides a vision of prairie history that is at once frozen at a particular moment (at the "belated and almost symbolic frontier" of Stegner's childhood[12]), and is also over: there is no future in Stegner's vision of the stagnant town of Whitemud. The extent to which the particulars of prairie history are subsumed into a generalized timelessness is clear when Ricou explains the terseness of seventeenth-century explorer Henry Kelsey's journals by saying that "the prairie farmer is often as laconic, especially about landscape aesthetics, as Kelsey seems to have been."[13] This model does not differentiate among the cultural, physical, or economic conditions of the two men, though nearly 300 years separates them. Harrison acknowledges increasing urbanization and the development of agribusiness on the prairies, arguing that "a sense of the prairie as past haunts contemporary fiction,"[14] which he sees as compulsively revisiting the past in order to reimagine and reunderstand it. But while Harrison recognizes human culture as changing, the geography of the region remains static, as he writes that "the austere face of the prairie has not changed that much since Henry Kelsey first saw it."[15] This moment of contact resonates to this day, as "the incongruities of that first response to the plains have never been overcome."[16] However, Harrison's assessment differs significantly from that of Ricou, who saw geography assuming primacy over history, where landscape has the same impact on the human imagination regardless of historical location or material conditions. Harrison's reading, while still evoking a timeless and ahistorical landscape, is more nuanced: it is not necessarily the land itself, but rather the initial literary and historical representations of it, with which subsequent generations must wrestle.

American scholars are also interested in the Canadian prairie, in the context of a generalized North American Great Plains. Thacker's *The Great Prairie Fact* preserves the primacy of an ahistoric prairie landscape, writing that "on the prairie, the great fact *is* the land itself, and it has ever been so since Castañeda's first European incursion."[17] However, Thacker argues against a simple environmental determinism, arguing that Great Plains "fiction combines the geography, history, sociology, and ultimately epistemology of prairie adaptation within its compass."[18] Such writings, interdisciplinary in nature, thus demand an interdisciplinary response. Thacker's argument is not taken up in Quantic's *The Nature of the Place*, however, which closely resembles the much earlier *Vertical Man/Horizontal World* in its arguments (down to its use of gender-exclusive language), as when Quantic lists some "distinctive characteristics" of the environment that are used by writers: "isolated, barren farmyards, sod houses buried in the ground, and flat towns hidden by trees or lost in space."[19] Strangely, Quantic's study examines no contemporary texts at length, instead locating what she sees as the coherence of Great Plains once again in the attempt to articulate the moment of settlement and subsequent rural life, and reiterating earlier critics' conclusions that geography, "the land itself," dominates representations of the plains to the exclusion of other factors, such as literary "convention."[20]

Up to the late 1990s, critics of Canadian prairie literature, with the exception of Thacker, seem to have constructed a category of "Canadian prairie writing" in which landscape dominates culture and geography effaces history. The creative writers themselves, however, have repeatedly brought history, geography, and literature together. In his influential essay "On Being an Alberta Writer" (1980), Robert Kroetsch urges the adoption of an "archaeological method" of fiction that would allow the Canadian prairies to become fully present in writing:

> It is a kind of archaeology that makes this place, with all its implications, available to us for literary purposes. We have not yet grasped the whole story; we have hints and guesses that slowly persuade us towards the recognition of larger patterns. Archaeology allows the fragmentary nature of the story, against the coerced unity of traditional history. Archaeology allows for discontinuity. It allows for layering. It allows for imaginative speculation.[21]

Whereas Wallace Stegner located his childhood town of Whitemud at the end of history, and therefore viewed Whitemud as a dying place, Kroetsch reconfigures the criteria, arguing that it is a "coercive" history, not the prairies, that are at an end. Kroetsch's project of rewriting the past and interrogating the idea of "history," as he does in his long poem *Seed Catalogue* and his novel *Badlands*, to name but two examples, has been hugely influential in the prairie writing community, as seen in even a small list of prominent authors who address similar themes in diverse ways: Rudy Wiebe, Dennis Cooley, Andy Suknaski, Lorna Crozier, Aritha van Herk, Kristjana Gunnars, Guy Vanderhaeghe, and Louise Halfe. These authors do not use historical sources naïvely, but with the knowledge that, as Kroetsch writes, they "both record and invent these new places called Alberta and Saskatchewan."[22] The results are metafictional, metahistorical documents that interrogate their sources even as they reinscribe them. Recently, creative nonfiction writers such as Sharon Butala, in *Wild Stone Heart: An Apprentice in the Fields* (2000), Trevor Herriot, in *River in a Dry Land: A Prairie Passage* (2000), and Warren Cariou, in *Lake of the Prairies: A Story of Belonging* (2002), have begun to engage in a project of deep mapping, a genre that combines history and geography with culture to produce a portrait of a single area over time. As Susan Maher writes, "inspired by paradigm shifts across disciplines, these writers build stories using intricate, often paradoxical, webs of cause and effect, loss and gain, natural and cultural forces, and deep time and human time."[23] The challenge to scholars is to develop a discourse as flexible as the writing itself.

In *Making it Home: Place in Canadian Prairie Literature* (1998), Deborah Keahey explictly writes against literary criticism that privileges geography over history, but also cautions against reading writings from the prairie provinces as though they were exclusively determined by culture. She argues, "place must instead be reimagined as a creation of the social, psychological, and cultural relationships that people have to particular landscapes or physical spaces."[24] But what does this reimagined place look like? Recent work in literary regionalism has begun to move in a new direction by redrawing regional boundaries, pointing to interconnections among regions, and by challenging the notion of the region itself. David Jordan emphasizes the need to historicize regional studies in *New World Regionalism* (1994), "because prevailing perceptions of the relation between the New World and the Old have shifted over time, as have perceptions of our relation to the natural environment, and even of the relation between fiction and the world it purportedly represents."[25] Similarly, the editors of *A Sense of Place* (1997) point to the need to re-examine ideas that equate the regional with the static and the unchanging, and, instead, to understand the regional as a process continually changing in response to local and global currents.[26] In her article in that collection, "Reassessing Prairie

Realism," Alison Calder argues for a recognition of the political implications of the category "prairie writing," asking, "what does it mean that we usually read and teach a literature that places the prairies solely in the context of the past?"[27] Essays in *Toward Defining the Prairies: Region, Culture, History* (2001), edited by Robert Wardhaugh, move towards the interrogation of geography, history, and literature by bringing together essays by historians and literary scholars that examine the construction of the prairies in both literature and history, though these examinations remain largely separate.[28] At the same time, however, there is a countermove within the prairie region itself that attempts to reinforce regional boundaries by generating a distinct prairie literature written by "prairie writers" and intended for a "prairie audience." This insistence on regional distinction is partly motivated by market forces, as prairie writing becomes a cultural product to be commodified: for it to retain its value in the market, it must be identifiably "prairie." This desire to simultaneously break down and construct regional boundaries points to the conflicted and contradictory impulses imbedded within any discussion of the region, and to the need to develop ways of reading that recognize that the prairies are both place and no-place, unique and generic.

The most significant task facing scholars in the area of Prairie literary studies today is to diversify the field. Perhaps because the moment of settler contact with the prairie environment has long been seen as the originary moment of prairie culture, Aboriginal writers and scholars have been almost completely silenced within the field. This collection also reflects that exclusion. Of all the proposals we received in our call for papers on prairie topics, not one was on a text by an Aboriginal author. Yet Aboriginal writers such as Louise Halfe, Thomas King, Maria Campbell, Marvin Francis, and many others create significant writings about the region, reflecting regional experiences not found in other texts. If we seek to understand prairie writings in part to understand our regional culture, then as academics we need to look to Aboriginal writers and scholars and to examine why our field has become so narrow. Otherwise, we risk obsolescence.

HISTORY

Historians in Canada have also struggled with the concept of region. They have articulated yet resisted region, through the desire for a broader "national" interpretation, a "national" history. Throughout the nineteenth and twentieth centuries, the prairie environment posed seemingly insurmountable obstacles to the commercial success of the fur trade, the expansion of the British Empire, the resistance to American annexation, the construction of the railroad, the process of settlement, the development of an agricultural frontier, and ultimately, the building of an industrial-urban society. The drive for nation, however, proved triumphant. The history of the "forging" of the Canadian West, through some of the earliest historical accounts at the end of the nineteenth century by Donald Gunn, Alexander Begg, and George Bryce, is depicted as a struggle of man against nature and the progress of "civilization." In the process of creating a western society, newcomers to the prairies were beset by a seemingly endless series of unforgiving challenges. The story told by historians mirrored that of their literary counterparts: it was a tale of conquering and taming the landscape—the triumph of the human spirit and condition.

Yet, the antagonistic landscape remained unconquered. The "classic" works that followed by such Canadian historians as A.S. Morton, A.R. Lower, Donald Creighton, G.F.G. Stanley, and W.L. Morton focussed on the "romantic period" of prairie history, dominated by pioneers, North-West Mounted Police, and railways. Even works dealing with the Riel Rebellion, the wheat economy, and the emergence of the farm protest movements were depicted within the framework of nation-building and ultimately as part of a national success story. "The history—and therefore the image—of the West that Morton created," Francis argues, "was one which saw the region as attempting to be like, not different from the rest of Canada. He argued in fact that the West had been germane to the Canadian experience and that its history could be seen as a miniature replica of the nation itself."[29] Debates as to the nature of the new society may have offered a diverse range of approaches, such as F.J. Turner's frontier thesis, Louis Hartz's model of fragmentation, and the metropolitan-hinterland Laurentian thesis, but all became grounded within the confines of Canadian nationalism.

From the late 1960s to the early 1980s, prairie historians resisted and challenged these centralist metanarratives, and began focussing attention on the western region as a time and place in and of itself. W.L. Morton accepted the validity of the Laurentian thesis, and the argument that the metropolitan centres of central Canada formed a commercial, political, and cultural empire that dominated and exploited its hinterlands such as the West, but he resisted the negative image of western Canada it implied. Instead, he attempted to create a new self-image in the minds of prairie dwellers through an appreciation of "their" history, an understanding of "their" myths. He saw a natural link between the historian and the poet. Both were mythmakers, "only the historian has neglected his job of making myths in this decadent, analytical age."[30] Prairie historians joined their literary counterparts in expressing "the mythic West"; the prairies had become a mental construct, a "state of mind," in Kreisel's words.[31] A generation of prairie writers who were, literally, "children of the West" set out on a search for their own distinct roots, a search for home.[32] Morton discovered that "the history of the West was shaped more by people's perception of themselves than by the region's topography."[33] In the works of two Manitoba writers, W.L. Morton, "the boy from Gladstone," and Margaret Laurence, "the girl from Neepawa," the vision of prairie writer and prairie historian came together.[34]

Sentiments of regional alienation (and western exceptionalism) were strong on the prairies during this period and the success of the multidisciplinary Western Canadian Studies conferences demonstrated that the region had indeed become a distinct field of study. The conference series lasted from 1969 to 1987 and also made clear that writers and historians were on the same page. In resisting the two-nations concept of Canada, historians embraced the "Limited Identities" approach authored by Ramsay Cook and popularized by J.M.S. Careless.[35] They urged a "multicultural" understanding of the nation. The emergence of social history led to a move away from politically and economically dominated understandings of the past and toward the inclusion of race, gender, ethnicity, and class. The emphasis on diversity opened many new historical avenues of inquiry. In the process of challenging the metanarratives, historians successfully cleared the way for new, multiple understandings of the prairie West. Gerald Friesen's *The Canadian Prairies: A History* (1984), along with Douglas Francis and Howard Palmer's *The Prairie West: Historical Readings* (1985), clearly reflected these trends. J.R. Miller confidently announced that "the new preoccupations represent substantial progress in the writing of western Canadian history and give reason for optimism about the future of the genre."[36]

But the energy and excitement among historians, so necessary to reconstruct previous understandings of the region, gradually diminished. As Bill Waiser asserts, in the last two decades "the public profile of Prairie scholarship seems to have slipped."[37] Historians failed to claim the ground they had so recently cleared. The gap was filled instead with a plethora of micro-studies. As Francis points out, "at times one has the impression that the historians of western Canada have assumed that the best way to understand the evolution of their region is to compile study upon study of the most intricate and minute historical detail."[38] Some critics charged that the domination of social history together with an emphasis on region had led to the collapse in Canada of a "national history."[39] If this was the case, it certainly was not replaced by a "regional history." Historians failed to consider new methods of interrogating, understanding, and representing the past; old definitions of region were challenged but new ones were not offered. Francis took the lead from such literary figures as Margaret Laurence, W.O. Mitchell, Wallace Stegner, Rudy Wiebe, Eli Mandel, and Robert Kroetsch in advancing the argument that writing on the prairies had shifted from that of an actual physical landscape to a mental landscape, a region of the mind. "The mythic West," he claimed, "has moulded a western Canadian identity in a way that earlier images of the West could not do, because the West has been freed from its restrictions to geographical locale or historical era to become a state of mind where it can take on universal meaning." But while Francis was prepared to view the prairie West as a mythic region, a fusion of fact and fiction, historical "truth" and literary licence, he would go no further in challenging these myths, these "dominant images." Instead he concluded that as a result of this "inward journey of self-discovery ... their images have become as much a part of the West as the prairie landscape itself."[40] But if we accept these myths to be more "real than reality," why are they not subject to the same historical scrutiny? Is it not necessary to "demythologize" the prairie?

Recently, some historians have returned to the study of the prairie region to offer new ways of conceptualizing time and place.[41] Gerald Friesen now argues that the forces of provincialism, communication technology, cultural change, and globalization have transformed regional constructs in the Canadian West to the point that a new definition of the prairies is necessary. That new definition shatters old notions of region and as a result, he argues, "prairie" is no longer an applicable or useful concept with which to discuss the area.[42] "The West has taken a new shape in recent decades," Friesen writes, ". . . the old two-region vision of western Canada—the Prairies and the Coast—has been superseded by a single economic and social experience. Now we have one West, extending from the Lake of the Woods to Vancouver Island."[43]

Friesen's contentious arguments are clearly intended to urge Canadians to reimagine the Prairie region. The traditional perception of the West has been shaped by history but these perceptions now may stand in the way of perceiving the region clearly, particularly in the context of the post-1945 era, which has so radically transformed the area. But as Waiser points out, "ironically, this same warning could easily be turned on its head and applied to the historical writing about the Prairies—that perceptions of the region may have stood in the way of understanding and explaining the past. In other words, how historians have seen the West may have been as important as the historical record in telling the region's history."[44]

The restructuring of the West is part of Friesen's desire to create "a new version of national history." The world is changing so rapidly, he writes, that "time and space, the fundamental dimensions of life, are not only under siege but have been annihilated, leaving us bewildered and without a pole star." Works of history are designed to offer a "sense of perspective" so Friesen offers a new lens with which to view not only the history of the prairies, but the history of Canada. Over the course of Canadian history, he argues, "common people have experienced four constructions of the dimensions of time and space." These constructions are correlated with "four dominant communication systems": the oral-traditional world of pre-contact Aboriginal people; the textual-settler household of immigrants, the print-capitalism of the nineteenth and twentieth centuries; and the screen-capitalism that has emerged in the last few decades. Friesen's arguments build on the communication theories of Harold Innis, but the "perception of time and place" remains bound by traditional historical structures, such as nationalism. Ultimately, he wishes to "provide assurances of continuity" in the face of challenges arising from "the apostles of poststructuralism and the postmodern."[45] He returns the challenge by arguing that there is little use in debating "borders" and "boundaries" when there is no centre. It is these "apostles" who are offering some of the most invigorating challenges and new ways of understanding the prairie region. They are, however, not historians.

Canadian historians of the West have fallen far behind the innovative work of their American counterparts. The "New Western History," which forced a complete rethinking of the history of the American plains twenty years ago, has failed to produce a parallel in Canada. There have been no attempts to reconceptualize the region through ambitious works of synthesis, such as Friesen's tome that appeared in the mid-1980s. Colin G. Calloway's *One Vast Winter Count: The Native American West before Lewis and Clark* (2004) serves as a fine example of the innovative work being done in the United States. The American West is portrayed less as a fixed place than as a web of historical processes, connections, and continuities. The region's spatial and temporal dimensions are stretched, the result being a history with radically different emphases, where the pre-contact period is elevated from a mere prelude to a central place in the story. While forcefully challenging our beliefs as to the traditional regional boundaries, Calloway also challenges the conventional ways of telling the region's stories. The result is a much more open-ended history of the early American West in which two interpretations—Aboriginal and non-Aboriginal—exist side by side, competing with one another, occasionally overlapping but ultimately remaining worlds apart. "Struggles for the West were—and still are—not just about who should own and occupy the land but also about what the land should mean, the kind of lives that should be lived there, and, ultimately, the kind of stories it would hold."[46] Calloway balances indigenous and Euro-American perceptions and purposes, compelling readers to continuously shift their point of view.

It is perhaps "time" for prairie historians in Canada to re-examine their most fundamental approaches. Such an examination may involve stepping outside the boundaries of these traditional structures and working without "assurances of continuity." While historians may not have the same latitude as novelists, poets, and literary critics to play with such structures as time and place, they can at least test the boundaries. Time is a complex phenomenon. If historians can accept that place is a mental construct, a perception of the viewer, can they not accept the same of time? Our standard notions of time (and notions of standard time) are undoubtedly historical constructs that differ considerably from those held by other groups, such as the Aboriginal peoples prior to contact. How have these constructs meshed with other understandings of place to create the prairie?

HISTORY, LITERATURE, AND THE WRITING OF THE CANADIAN PRAIRIES

This book brings together ten essays by Canadian, American, and European academics, and ranges from discussions of individual literary works to historical constructions of region. The writers were asked to address the question "When is the prairie?" and the essays are united through their considerations of time and place and the complex relationship between the two. Some essays concentrate on the ways that particular creative writers interrogate history and history making in their works; others focus on the ways that history making is itself a creative act. All point to interdisciplinary inquiry as a productive process. At a time when the Canadian prairies are undergoing extensive cultural, economic, and political transformation, it is necessary to offer new theoretical frameworks for understanding the area. Together, the essays in this collection point in that direction.

What do the articles collected in this anthology offer? One suggestion is that prairie writers are indeed focussing on alternate models of time. Several articles in this anthology centre on decisions made by authors to resituate the prairie in a geological time frame, a recontextualization that both contests traditional models of prairie history that privilege the explorer or settler moment, and also seeks to deconstruct narratives of patriarchal, white authority. Traditional ways of looking at the prairies tend to focus on the progress of human settlement, reading the region through human contact and privileging the forward motion of technological advancement. By recontextualizing human occupation of the prairie into a much larger background, these geological models interrogate anthrocentric perspectives and consequently emphasize the human connection to the environment, rather than human alienation from it. These new models also see the prairie as a thing apart from humans, existing for itself and not for what it reveals about the human condition or human progress. In offering a new "beginning" for the prairie, one not bound by human history, these models recontextualize the prairie as an ecosystem unto itself, which humans participate in but do not dominate.

At the same time, writers are extending the traditional boundaries of the "prairie" region to include its geographical contrasts like the mountains and the foothills, the parkland and the Shield. Some of the essays in this collection detail the methods employed by various writers to explore how these diverse areas fit or do not fit into the "imagined" region, suggesting that the prairie exists both as an empirical landscape and as a concept, an imagined reality whose coherence is located not only in a particular geography, but also in another, less tangible site. Traditional models have defined regions geographically. But what is gained if we look at region from a new perspective, defining it through treatment of time, for example? What new avenues of scholarship might this response suggest? One of the arguments made by regional studies such as *A Sense of Place* is the need to view regions in relation to each other. If, as the essays in this collection suggest, creative writers and historians in non-prairie landscapes like the Alberta foothills respond to the intersections of time and space in ways similar to their counterparts on the prairie, then it is possible to assert that the impact of the prairie environment, so long held to be a governing factor in the region's cultural development, might be no more important here than elsewhere. Or, to rephrase the point, the prairie environment determines literature, history, and identity to exactly the same extent as does the mountain, the seashore, or the urban streetscape. Focussing on questions of *when* rather than questions of *where* allows a reconfiguration of a region usually thought of as fixed. As Curt Meine writes, "the prairie is not and cannot be present except in its transformed and ever-changing state; the prairie that our ancestors experienced is gone."[47] The question yet remains as to where, precisely, a coherent prairie may be sited, as an ostensibly stable landscape is revealed to be, in Aritha van Herk's words, "an upthrust and earthquake prairie."[48]

Such regional reconfiguration opens this collection of essays. In "The Tantalizing Possibility of Living on the Plains," Frances W. Kaye addresses the question "When is the prairie?" by suggesting that we must look at the issue from a vast, geological time scale. She points out that while the prairie existed long before human settlement, it is a brittle environment, both environmentally and culturally, and we may be at the end of a certain kind of rural prairie existence. Kaye's article examines Sharon

Butala's novel, *The Fourth Archangel*, a portrait of a town in crisis, to eval-
uate the coping strategies evinced by Butala's characters. Kaye argues we
must re-evaluate the concept of "progress," as this way of moving into the
future has turned out to be profitable only for big business, and disastrous
for many prairie dwellers. She reads Butala's novel alongside the conditions of life in the empirical prairie to argue for the urgency of a community-based prairie culture; otherwise, she argues, the question we have to
answer will not be when *is* the prairie, but when it *was*. Regional reconfiguration is also offered by Claire Omhovère's examination of the "great ice
prairie" of Alberta glaciers in "The Melting of Time in Thomas Warton's
Icefields." In interrogating Wharton's blend of fiction and history, natural
and supernatural, Omhovère emphasizes that "geographical space may
not only shape the imagination, but may also be constructed by it."
Wharton's glacier challenges traditional spatial-temporal relations: it
encapsulates history and memory (sometimes literally) *in* space, but that
space is constantly in flux. The function and meaning of the place change
through time, a transition manifest in the transformation of Wharton's
glacier from isolated site of exploration to tourist destination. Omhovère
illuminates Wharton's linkage of artistic production to geological time,
highlighting the presence in the text of erratics, temporal/spatial discontinuities that jolt the character, or the text, from silence to articulation.

Nina van Gessel uncovers a similar focus on geology in her essay,
"Autogeology: Limestone and Life Narrative in Carol Shields's *The Stone
Diaries*." Traditional models of autobiography stress the formation of a
complete, linear narrative that presents a unified subject. In contrast, van
Gessel demonstrates the complex ways in which limestone functions in
the novel as a geological analogue for Shields's project. The novel's protagonist, Daisy Goodwill, an historian of sorts, seeks to recover her life.
Memories and incidents appear as fossils to be examined. Shields's narrative is marked by accretion and stratification, literary and geological; as in
Icefields, *The Stone Diaries* is studded with "irregularities," or erratics. Such
irregularities disrupt linear temporality, as parts of Daisy's life are replayed
from different angles, and parts are left out entirely. Heidi Slettedahl
Macpherson extends van Gessel's argument that the lacunae in Daisy's
narrative may be an attempt to represent a gendered concept of time. In
"The Coyote as Culprit: 'Her-story' and the Feminist Fantastic in Gail
Anderson-Dargatz's *The Cure for Death by Lightning*," Macpherson

examines the strategies Anderson-Dargatz uses to rewrite history through the stories of the disenfranchised, which are located both in artifacts and in oral stories. Focussing on the ways the novel presents space and time as contested sites, Macpherson sees one of the novel's fundamental conflicts as the disjunction between "male power (the facility to order and classify, including the right to name history through the lens of war and economic upheaval) and women's cyclical time, indicated through the (always violable) body."

The postmodern has been read by some literary critics as functioning in a kind of no-time, a space without fixed anchors. Contrarily, Russell Brown and Dennis Cooley argue separately that postmodernism in prairie writing is very definitely, and importantly, linked to particular historical moments. Brown, in "Robert Kroetsch, Marshall McLuhan, and Canada's Prairie Postmodernism," argues that the history of Canadian literary postmodernism can be productively reread in light of Robert Kroetsch's 1966 novel *The Words of My Roaring*. Kroetsch's postmodern use of myth in this novel, suggests Brown, is properly read as a response to a particular moment in prairie social history: the emergence of Alberta Social Credit leader William Aberhart as a powerful media presence. Brown points out that both Kroetsch and Marshall McLuhan "came to maturity in a region that was experiencing, to an extreme degree, severe disruptions of drought and economic depression along with the powerful rhetoric of apocalyptic evangelism and populist politics." Brown thus resituates Canadian literary postmodernism in a specific historical context: instead of appearing as a product of a borrowed internationalism, postmodernism emerges as a particular response to the intersections of environment, culture, time, and place. In "Documents in the Postmodern Long Prairie Poem" Dennis Cooley playfully examines the presence of documents in the postmodern long prairie poem, arguing that interpolated documents function to "site," "cite," and "sight" the poems. While the transformation of these documents into poetry thus releases the documents into a play of literary meaning, they do not give up their historical status: they are never entirely divorced from their specific local contexts. He contends that the ties these documents maintain to their specific contexts impart a kind of authenticity to these long poems, constituting a genuinely local, rather than universal, expression.

Two essays examine Margaret Laurence from entirely different angles. In "A Timeless Imagined Prairie: Return and Regeneration in Margaret Laurence's Manawaka Novels," Debra Dudek argues that the Manawaka novels should be contexualized as works that contribute to a revisionary Canadian literary modernism. These works reimagine the region and nation out of repressive social structures through the liberated female individual. According to Dudek, "the imagined prairie that appears is a timeless and timely place grounded in the mythic and the local, a place of both return and regeneration." Laurence's heroines incorporate their prairie pasts into their modern presents and are able to imagine transformed, hopeful futures. They avoid modernist trappings by imagining their prairie pasts as a regenerative place contained within their bodies. Their inner geography contains the regenerative prairie, and each heroine is connected to another and to each other through this communal past. Discussing Laurence from another angle, Sarah Payne analyzes how Laurence's home town, Neepawa, has constructed itself as a site of literary tourism, arguing that imaginative literature and heritage tourism play a significant role in the reconstruction of particular prairie localities. In "Reconstructions of Literary Settings in North America's Prairie Regions," Payne explores why issues of heritage, tourism, and identity, influenced by the writings (and places) of such authors as Willa Cather and Margaret Laurence, should be seen as essential features defining contemporary studies of literary tourism in the North American plains. Such a study demonstrates the cross-cultural differences in national identity and heritage between the declining small towns of the Canadian prairie and the American plains. Payne points to the ways in which history is manipulated into heritage and then employed for present-day cultural purposes to provide interpretations of the region.

The two other essays in this collection offer analyses of how the influence of time, and the differing conceptions of it, affect the construction both of histories and of individual and regional identities. In "The 'Precarious Perch' of the 'Decent Woman': Spatial (De)Constructions of Gender in Women's Prairie Memoirs," S. Leigh Matthews examines how gender is (de)constructed within the space of the Canadian West, the physical space of the female body, and the textual space in which memoir writers represented their lived experiences. Time is central because of the distinction made between the cultural moment of experience within the geographic space of the prairies, and the cultural moment in which the experience is re-presented within textual space. The link between these two cultural moments, Matthews argues, occurs at the site of the female body, which is both inscribed upon (by being confined to the performance of what was deemed appropriately feminine behaviour at the time of settlement) and inscribing (through the representation of resistance to such confinement in the act of writing). In "Time's Grip along the Athabasca in the 1920s and 1930s," Cam McEachern explores the role of space and time in understanding the story of the Athabasca River as well as the area's relationship to the prairie region and the rest of the nation. By analyzing the memoir of an alpine climber in the 1920s, McEachern argues that the popular idea, which linked this "end-of-prairie" with the surrounding space, was "Liberalism, and more specifically the ideology's implicit, subconscious attitude toward time." The effects of "Liberal time" on the Athabasca country, however, would not enjoy the same success as in the southern prairies. "In the interwar years," McEachern argues, "white, Christian, masculine, utilitarian, liberal individualism put a poorly inked stamp on the region again and again, and the ideology's requisite sense of time was diluent."

The essays in this collection offer a basis for looking at the writing of the Canadian prairies in a way that is both flexible and rigorous, one that emerges from the writing itself. Scholars have traditionally focussed on the twin axes of the geographic and the human, an approach crystallized in the oft-repeated image of a vertical human attempting to dominate a horizontal world. By adding a third axis, time, to the diagram, these interdisciplinary scholars reorient thinking about the prairies and the region's writers. Reading the words of these creative writers, historians, and critics, we are led to the same realization about the prairies that Sharon Butala comes to when she walks in a coulee near her home in her memoir *Wild Stone Heart* (2000): the knowledge that the land she loves is "at once both place and time."[49]

ENDNOTES

1. Diane Dufva Quantic, *The Nature of the Place: A Study of Great Plains Fiction* (Lincoln: University of Nebraska Press, 1995), 67.

2. Robert Thacker, *The Great Prairie Fact and Literary Imagination* (Albuquerque: University of New Mexico Press, 1989), 224.

3. Robert Kroetsch, "A Conversation with Margaret Laurence, " in *Trace: Prairie Writers on Writing*, ed. Birk Sproxton (Winnipeg: Turnstone, 1986), 19–30.

4. R. Douglas Francis, "Changing Images of the West," in *The Prairie West:*

Historical Readings, ed. R. Douglas Francis and Howard Palmer (Edmonton: University of Alberta Press, 1985), 718.

5. Ibid., 720.

6. Edward McCourt, *The Canadian West in Fiction* (1949; Toronto: Ryerson Press, 1970).

7. Henry Kreisel, "The Prairie: A State of Mind," in *Trace: Prairie Writers on Writing*, 6.

8. Ibid., 17.

9. Laurie Ricou, *Vertical Man/Horizontal World: Man and Nature in Canadian Prairie Fiction* (Vancouver: University of British Columbia Press, 1973).

10. Dick Harrison, *Unnamed Country: The Struggle for a Canadian Prairie Fiction* (Edmonton: University of Alberta Press, 1977), ix.

11. Ricou, *Vertical Man*, 111.

12. Wallace Stegner, *Wolf Willow: a history, a story, and a memory of the last plains frontier* (New York: Penguin, 2000), 22.

13. Ricou, *Vertical Man*, 9.

14. Harrison, *Unnamed Country*, 185.

15. Ibid., 28.

16. Ibid.

17. Thacker, *Great Prairie Fact*, 224 (italics in original).

18. Ibid., 5–6.

19. Quantic, *Nature of the Place*, 165.

20. Ibid., 169.

21. Robert Kroetsch, "On Being an Alberta Writer: Or, I Wanted to Tell Our Story," in *Towards a Canadian Literature*, vol. 2, ed. D. Daymond and L. Monkman (1980; Ottawa: Tecumseh, 1985), 585.

22. Ibid., 584.

23. Susan Naramore Maher, "Deep Mapping the Great Plains: Surveying the Literary Cartography of Place," *Western American Literature* 36, 1 (2001): 4.

24. Deborah Keahey, *Making it Home: Place in Canadian Prairie Literature* (Winnipeg: University of Manitoba Press, 1998), 7.

25. David Jordan, *New World Regionalism: Literature in the Americas* (Toronto: University of Toronto Press, 1994), 3.

26. Christian Riegel and Herb Wyile, eds., *A Sense of Place: Re-Evaluating Regionalism in Canadian and American Writing* (Edmonton: University of Alberta Press, 1977).

27. Alison Calder, "Reassessing Prairie Realism," in *A Sense of Place*, 51.

28. Robert Wardhaugh, ed., *Toward Defining the Prairies: Region, Culture, and History* (Winnipeg: University of Manitoba Press, 2001).

29. Francis, "Changing Images," 641.

30. As quoted in Carl Berger, *The Writing of Canadian History: Aspects of English-Canadian Historical Writing since 1900* (Toronto: University of Toronto Press, 1976), 252.

31. Eli Mandel, "Writing West: On the Road to Wood Mountain," *Canadian Forum* LVII: 28. Dick Harrison calls the Prairie "a territory within the psyche" (*Unnamed Country*, 189).

32. Francis, "Changing Images," 641.

33. R. Douglas Francis, *Images of the West* (Saskatoon: Western Producer Prairie Books, 1989), 194.

34. For a discussion of the relationship between Margaret Laurence and W.L. Morton, see Peter Easingwood, "Margaret Laurence: Prairie Fiction and Prairie History," in *Revisions of Canadian Literature* (1984).

35. The term "limited identity" in this context was first used by Ramsay Cook to describe challenges to a national identity posed by such forces as ethnicity, class, gender, and region. J.M.S. Careless popularized the term. See Ramsay Cook, "Canadian Centennial Celebrations," *International Journal* XXII: 659–663; J.M.S. Careless, "'Limited Identities' in Canada," *Canadian Historical Review* L, 1: 1–10.

36. J.R. Miller, "Farewell to 'Monks, Eunuchs and Vestal Virgins': Recent Western Canadian Historical Writing," *Journal of Canadian Studies* 20, 3 (1985): 165.

37. Bill Waiser, "Introduction: Place, Process, and the New Prairie Realities," *The Canadian Historical Review* 84, 4 (December 2003): 511.

38. Francis, "Changing Images," 629.

39. J.L. Granatstein, *Who Killed Canadian History?* (Toronto: HarperCollins, 1998).

40. Francis, *Images of the West*, 193–194.

41. See also Sarah Carter, *Capturing Women: The Manipulation of Cultural Imagery in Canada's Prairie West* (Montreal: McGill-Queen's University Press, 1997); Catherine Cavanaugh and Randi Warne, *Telling Tales: Essays in Western Women's History* (Vancouver: University of British Columbia Press, 2000); John Herd Thompson, *Forging the Prairie West: The Illustrated History of Canada* (Don Mills: Oxford University Press, 1998); and Jeremy Mouat and Catherine Cavanaugh, eds., *Making Western Canada: Essays on European Colonization and Settlement* (Toronto: Garamond Press, 1996).

42. Gerald Friesen, "Defining the Prairies: or, why the prairies don't exist," in *Toward Defining the Prairies*, 13–28.

43. Gerald Friesen, "Introduction," in *The West: Regional Ambitions, National Debates, Global Age* (Toronto: Penguin, 1999).

44. Waiser, "Place, Process," 509–510.

45. Gerald Friesen, *Citizens and Nation: An Essay on History, Communication, and Canada* (Toronto: University of Toronto Press, 2000), 3–7, 219.

46. Colin G. Calloway, *One Vast Winter Count: The Native American West before Lewis and Clark* (Lincoln: University of Nebraska Press, 2003), 13; reviewed by Pekka Hämäläinen for *H-AmIndian* (March, 2004).

ALISON CALDER and ROBERT WARDHAUGH

47. Curt Meine, "Reimagining the Prairie: Aldo Leopold and the Origins of Prairie Restoration" in *Recovering the Prairie*, ed. Robert F. Sayre (Madison: University of Wisconsin Press, 1999), 144.

48. Aritha Van Herk, "Prairie as Flat as . . . ," in *A Frozen Tongue* (Sydney, Australia: Dangaroo, 1992), 127.

49. Sharon Butala, *Wild Stone Heart* (Toronto: HarperCollins, 2000), 131.

THE TANTALIZING POSSIBILITY OF LIVING ON THE PLAINS

by Frances W. Kaye

Ravenscrag is old rock, Precambrian, picturesque as any landscape garden with aesthetically crafted ruins. Like Rocher Percé to the east or the Alberta Badlands to the west, it is eroded fantastically, a remnant that has been glaciated and bared again. The Cypress Hills are a fragment of old rock on the Plains, survivor of the glaciers that scooped out their U-shaped valleys but did not obliterate the hills or the woodland plants and animals now islanded there. Dinosaur bones come out of the ground like rocks with frost, and the sparse upland grass does not hide the projectile points nor stone hammers that lie upon the hillsides, blending, like the tipi rings, into the rock-strewn ground. These High Plains, which travellers have sometimes claimed were barren, throb with a history that predates history, ossified. The tectonic plates that crawl like turtles across the earth's mantle carry their shell of fossil forests from warmer latitudes and warmer times up here where the sun slants even at noon as it beats upon your head in prairie July.

Kansas inventor of eco-history James Malin kept asking to what state conservationists wished to restore the prairie. Figs and palm trees and roving dinosaurs? Or glaciers and the rivers of rock and sand they carried with them? Or the grass and buffalo and people of the tipi rings? Does grass have rights? Do people?

The Cypress Hills were the last prairie frontier, the final act in the conflict between the farmer and the rancher, the plough and the grass, a final act in the drama that Columbus began and that would have begun without him, when some European marshalled the technology to move beyond the sea. Except that if there is no single past, no before, there is also no single future, no permanent after, no final act. Climaxes and successions succeed each other. All environments are fragile. One degree turns glaciers around. A few centimetres set deserts on the march. One volcano changed the whole globe. But the High Plains are brittle. There are no tolerant limits. If you bulldoze a patch of forest on the Niagara peninsula of Ontario or in Oregon, it'll come back pretty quickly. Do the same thing on the High Plains, leave the area strictly alone, and in a hundred years your great-grandchildren will be able to define the patch pretty clearly. The tipi rings in the Cypress Hills are hundreds of years old, but they have not been displaced. Long-term change, short-term stasis. And right now, crisis.

Crisis is nothing new, either. Paul Martin and other anthropologists, calculating the demise of the megafauna, the mastodons and rhinoceroses and so on, at about the same time that a wave of humans streamed over the land bridge from Asia and down into the centre of the continent, have calculated that the human hunters hunted out the game. Or perhaps their animals brought with them microbes to which the mastodons had no resistance, and so they perished.[1] Certainly there was a crisis sometime not terribly long ago in geological terms, 10,000 years ago, more or less. Maybe it was the glaciers, maybe the people, but there was a crisis. Even more recently, another invasion disrupted the ecology of the region and replaced it with another, perhaps a climax ecology. The introduced horses, *sunka wakan* of the Lakotas, escaped from the Spanish and moved rapidly north, both on their own and through trade among the people who lived there. Horses thrived on the High Plains, as they should have, for horses evolved here, as the fossil record clearly shows. In a hundred years, between about 1650 and 1750, horses had become a part of the culture of almost all the Plains peoples, who transformed themselves from farmers timidly hunting along the river valleys of the plains to "a lordly and dangerous society of fighters and thieves, hunters and priests of the sun."[2]

Mounted buffalo hunters put pressure on the great migratory herds of shaggy beasts, *tatanka*, the Lakotas called them, and the people of the horses based their economies more and more on buffalo hunting. The need to feed increasing horse herds led riders to fire the prairie to improve the grass—and also, unintended consequence, to drive the trees back to the wettest river valleys. According to New Western historian Richard White, the struggle of grass versus trees grew into a struggle between horse-riding men and fire-building women.[3] (But the trees and grass had always fought, fire and rainfall their weapons, just as the boreal forest had fought the deciduous trees on the ecotone north of the prairies.)

Exactly how this new ecology would have worked had it lasted is unclear, especially with the addition of a market—an insatiable market—for buffalo robes and buffalo-hide leather. Would the technology of the horse and the ever-improving rifles have led to a desert of grass, barren of buffalo? Or would the buffalo and mounted hunters have reached an equilibrium and spun off another equilibrium between grass and trees? Another crisis intervened and so the question is moot. Humans, then 10,000 years later horses, then 200 years later Euro-Americans, bringing their spotted cattle, *pte gleska*, and their ploughs. This later crisis coincided with the end of the buffalo as free-ranging members of the ecology. Certainly the people of the spotted cows could not have grazed their herds or strung their fences or tended their fields if the buffalo still migrated in shaggy rivers across the Plains. And without the buffalo, the mounted buffalo hunters also lost their climax culture, that of the horse, Sun Dance, and buffalo.

For only fifty years the spotted cow people lived with sporadic crises, droughts, and fences, and more and more sod ploughed under and planted. Broad-scale Euro-American settlement on the Great Plains commenced in the 1870s, climaxed around the period of World War I, and was waning fast even before the crash of 1929 and the ensuing drought and depression. Since then, farms have grown larger, towns and populations smaller. Some of the most brittle land was seeded back to grass to keep it from blowing. Some was never ploughed. Some is still farmed, and the dust blows off newly turned fields, grit on the windowsills and dust clouds up into the upper atmosphere. Farm consolidation and abandonment, of course, is not unique to the Great Plains. My home county in New York State first attracted Euro-American settlement after the American

Revolution, after the New Hampshireman, Colonel Sullivan, had burnt the Onondaga and Cayuga villages, laid waste their peach orchards. By the 1830s the rural population had peaked and was following the Erie Canal west to the Genessee country and beyond. When we walked through the heifer pasture and up to the blueberry meadows where the hawks soared, we were walking through third-growth forest and through the quarry where the foundation of the "new" addition of our house had been hewed by our neighbour's grandfather. Across the valley on Bald Hill, an abandoned house still blows with signs of habitation, but in the state forests, taken back, like the central counties of the Dust Bowl, during the Depression, only lilac bushes and the rock-walled holes mark the farmyards and cellars of abandoned houses. Brucellosis and the dairy buy-back have long since emptied the heifer pasture, but I imagine the blueberries and hawks remain. And the county has once again surpassed its 1850 population. People live there and work at the two colleges or some of the local commerce or manufacture, much of it created by the technological capabilities inhering in the land grant university.

Nor are blowing dust or the sick yellow delta in the milo field new to the Great Plains. Our soils are wind-borne loess, laid down by winds that scoured the fine grains from the Rockies. Or they are glacial till, boulders and all, carried along by the glaciers and the great streams of glacier melt. American historian James Malin reminded us that the profile dear to soil scientists, soil formed by the weathering of the bedrock nurtured by the humus of the progressively more complex plants that lived and died in the nascent soil, soil created in situ, is not the soil of the Great Plains. Malin also referred, again and again, to travellers' accounts of dust storms, especially on newly burned land, before any of the western prairies were ploughed.[4] The plough that broke the Plains may have defined the particular nature of the dust storms of the 1930s, but it did not introduce blowing dust to the Plains. We are a restless place, from the soil up. The great sandhills of Nebraska and Saskatchewan are only the most recent evidence of the wind, moving great dunes, aggregating great dunes—and threatening to move them on again.

The technology of the people conjectured to have hunted the megafauna was flint projectile points mounted on wood, and the projectile points remain. What they meant in the context of their culture, no one now knows, and perhaps it will remain unknowable. The technology of the horse, buffalo, and Sun Dance culture remains—if not intact, certainly documented by anthropologists and reimagined by the dancers. The technology of the people who brought the plough and the spotted cow is manifest on the Plains. The circles of the centre pivots patchwork within the lines of the square survey fixed by the Land Ordinance of 1785, antedating both the American Constitution and the Dominion of Canada. Railroads and highways create the towns and shelter belts that are the new linear groves that once followed the rivers. In most parts of the world, cities are determined by geography, by harbours or the confluence of rivers. But the cities of the Plains were created first—and geography followed. Both Lincoln, Nebraska, and Regina, Saskatchewan, were chosen as the sites of capital cities for political and economic reasons. New Jersey poet Edgar Guest could fairly reasonably, if fatuously, assert that "only God can make a tree," but in the grasslands the trees followed the city builders who followed or beckoned hither the railroads. The plough turns the earth wrong side up; the irrigation pumps pull water wrong side up and the sprinklers toss it down again. But wrong, once more, is a convention. Does it have any effective meaning? Does grass have rights? Do people have rights?

From Colorado up through Saskatchewan, pronghorns soar over fences and graze fields as nonchalantly as the spotted cows. Coyotes patrol the outskirts of cities and do not scruple to eat a domestic cat or two. A hayfield in eastern Nebraska that has been planted to brome will gradually go back to big and little bluestem, Indian grass and switch grass and needle grass, at least if a creek or slough has preserved a little native stock so the rhizomes can migrate, little by little, into the field. My birdfeeder is part of a string of artificial habitats that have lured cardinals west of the Missouri, and red-bellied woodpeckers live in the trees that surcease of prairie fires has enabled and eat my suet. My neighbour's milo field lies snug under its stubble, the soil protected as well by the spotted cows turned into the field all fall after the crop was taken out. For sixteen years this field has seen milo and cattle, except the year of the Payment in Kind program, when it raised only weeds. The anhydrous ammonia tipped into it in the fall runs off and eventually lodges in our well. We cover the rhubarb and lettuce when the neighbour sprays herbicide.

It would be easy to play our neighbour as the heavy—the big John Deere tractor loafing diesel fumes as he goes home to lunch, passing a petition the first year we were here to close down the little village school because the cost of accommodating a child who used a wheelchair might raise taxes too high. A big landowner, a successful farmer, bent on passing to his children a farm homesteaded by ancestors a century ago and carried on and added to. Stress. Our neighbour fought constantly with his mother on how to operate the farm, how to change the land use. I do not know what either said. But when it came to blows, there was Mother at the foot of the stairs, and now our neighbour is serving time for second-degree murder while his wife and son manage the farm. It would be easy to say that the greed of land abuse, the greed of monocropping and drenching the earth with poisons, the greed that would refuse ramps to a child in a wheelchair (that would suggest, in fact, that the child should have his legs amputated so he could be fitted with prostheses and taught to climb stairs) is a monstrous greed. It would be easy to say that ploughing the breast of mother earth is fundamentally akin to pushing one's mother down the stairs, but such a metaphoric reading is itself cramped and cruel, no better than scapegoating. My neighbour is a perfectly nice guy. The pathology of crisis is inherent in the culture of crisis. What does our culture offer to counteract greed?

In her novel *The Fourth Archangel* Sharon Butala calls the little prairie town Ordeal.[5] And its slightly larger neighbour, taking up the services one by one, is Crisis. For this novel is set in the apocalypse as well as the Cypress Hills. King Wheat has dominated Canadian prairie agriculture. The development of short-season Marquis wheat that could be planted and mature in the short prairie summers coincided with the first world war and a great European demand for wheat, as well as with wet years on the prairies that made ploughing and planting seem reasonable. After the war, prices fell and rain slowed down. The bust hit the Prairies in the 1920s and persisted through the thirties until rain and war coincided. The Prairies and the Plains export almost all the grain they grow, some directly, like wheat, and some indirectly, like milo transformed into beef in feedlots and slaughterhouses. Most of the corn grown in Nebraska during the irrigation boom of the 1970s was exported to feed a hungry world, but, with export subsidies and aid programs, it undercut the cost of production on the small farms of the Third World, and sent small farmers to the cities or to labour on plantations producing export rather than subsistence commodities, rubber or coffee, or, increasingly, coca for cocaine, a highly profitable export crop.

Ordeal's ordeal is a microcosm for all of us, from those of us on the eastern and metropolitan edges of the Plains to those like Butala, in southwest Saskatchewan, the purest remnant of High Plains country. Compared to Third World farmers, who have been displaced by drought and civil war and who are starving, massacred, perishing of AIDS, tuberculosis, and cholera in the cities of Africa or Latin America, or compared to Blackfeet, Pawnees, Lakotas, or other Plains peoples conquered and dispossessed, contemporary farmers and townspeople on the Great Plains are not hurting. The bank forecloses. We lose the farm and move to the city. Dad gets a job on the third shift at Kawasaki and Mom goes back to school and the kids learn the pecking order of a school that plays regular football instead of six-man. Or we keep the farm and Mom drives 100 kilometres each way in the clunker to work at McDonald's on the interstate so there's a reliable trickle of cash income, and the kids go away to college and none of them ever comes back. And then the grammar school closes and the little main-street shops close and the high school in the next town over is forced by state law to consolidate and the kids who are left ride the bus fifty kilometres each way.

That's Ordeal's ordeal, except the distances are already longer and Swift Current and Maple Creek are already the only towns that seem likely to survive and more and more you have to drive to Medicine Hat or to Regina or Saskatoon for a big purchase like a car or even farm machinery. But Ordeal is fighting for its life and fighting in a number of ways at cross-purposes with each other. The Heartland Center for Leadership Development, a rural planning think-tank for the Plains, has developed a list of twenty characteristics that are enabling Nebraska communities to survive and prosper.[6] Ordeal has a strange mixture of them. Among the keys is the acceptance of women and people under forty in leadership positions. Here Ordeal is in good shape. Community pride and cooperative spirit are present. The schools and the churches are not in good shape. Even though Alma Sheridan, the very old-time schoolmarm, is let go, the school stresses conformity and obedience rather than inventiveness and problem solving. The mainline churches are tired and the charismatics are more visible but are isolated from the community. The businesses seem to lack any economic development program, and they are not very aware of their competitors in other towns. They seem to accept their gradual demise as a given, like the weather. But there are glimmers.

Butala's main point-of-view character is Amy Sparrow, a potter, a young widow in a town of old widows, the rare child who has returned to Ordeal, to the house where she grew up, after college. Amy befriends young Jessie Sheridan, city girl, who has married her farm-boy husband and moved to the country, where she finds herself lost and bewildered, understanding neither her in-laws nor the economic and social ordeal of southwestern Saskatchewan. Amy is a community leader and, an artist by training and temperament, she has the devotion to quality and imagination that is crucial to small-town survival. She energizes Jessie and her husband, Val, and thus secures continuing young leadership. Leadership also comes from the community of widows who form a secret but powerful network of social action. The good but somewhat colourless mainstream pastor is killed by what almost seems to be a phantom train, coming down abandoned tracks (symbol of the disintegration of the political and economic structure of the province) in the fog. His place is taken, surprisingly enough, by the Pentecostal preacher, Uriel Raven, a man who has lived his life firmly believing he was chosen by God as a prophet. Finally there is the unlikely saviour of the town's economy, Melody Masuria, the town's teenaged good-time girl, who has a revelation and joins Raven's flock, soon spouting stigmata. In the face of this Sign, Raven wrestles with his god and emerges into the new humility of being simply one of the people, finally joining a political rally by asking the blessing on its beginning.

There is a dreamlike quality to the novel. Published in 1992, it is set in the year 2000 and is deliberately apocalyptic. Events are more portent than plot, and names, as in Butala's earlier allegorical novel, *Luna*, are significant. Amy Sparrow's lover is Neil Locke, a biologist who has come to the magnificence of the Cypress Hills. Neil, who has, with some justification, left his wife, Faith, brings to mind the non-hero of an earlier Saskatchewan novel, Neil Fraser of Edward McCourt's *Music at the Close*. The earlier Neil, a would-be poet who is failed by all the institutions of the society, especially the university, which had the greatest obligation to him, dies in World War II. He hopes that his hero's death will provide his son a romantic dream, refusing to realize that such a dream would be as pernicious as his own dreams that led him to betray his best friend, his wife, and the land itself. Neil Locke's dooming cynicism is the converse of the earlier Neil's perverse romanticism, but it also represents the failure of nineteenth-century liberalism—the legacy of John Locke—to come up with a land ethic befitting the High Plains, the people who now inhabit the area, or Neil Locke himself. Neil reads the nineteenth-century explorers of the Cypress Hills and the Palliser Triangle, the arid grasslands of Canada's southern prairies, and tries to imagine what he conceives of as the natural prairie, before the coming of the people of the plough and the spotted cow. Uriel Raven and his congregation erect a huge cross nearly in Neil's yard, and though a tornado takes the cross and returns to Neil some peace and quiet, he chooses to abandon Ordeal and Amy's commitment to the community, to pack his books and leave without saying goodbye. Locke is not sufficient for the land or the community.

Uriel Raven, named for the mysterious fourth archangel and Raven, the trickster hero of the arctic rim peoples, is far more problematic. Uriel, who must have had every reason to expect to be an equal archangel, is forgotten, while the reputations of his more famous cousins, Michael, Gabriel, and, improbably, Lucifer, continue to burnish. Uriel Raven finds his soul and his relationship to the community when he finds that it is not he but the girl who is chosen, who spouts stigmata. Ravens, unlike British philosophers, are at home on the Plains, and it is a flock of their close cousins, the crows, that bespot the premier at the rally opened by Uriel, and give him the sign that the people cannot.

Yet post offices, branch lines, schools close. Fewer and fewer people are needed on the land as farmers leave or fail or sell out. The land concentrates in the hands of a few. There are not enough shoppers to keep the stores open and so they close. And the people who are left, looking for more choice, more variety, drive to larger towns. Prairie towns were platted in response to a transportation network of railroads and horse-drawn wagons. They are perishing in a transportation network of automobiles and airplanes. In Nebraska's sandhills, the ranchers have their own planes and landing strips. They can shop in Dallas or Houston or Minneapolis or Denver. And so they do. And the towns like Hyannis and Mullen and Sergeant get smaller and poorer. Sergeant has recently, very reluctantly, dismissed a doctor with fraud convictions or licence suspensions in three states. He was all they could get, and they desperately wanted to keep a doctor, any doctor. But not at the price of his killing people. It's technology that renders these High Plains areas more efficient for capital, less efficient for humans. But technology is neutral—what counts is how a culture accommodates to its technology. Neither archangels nor neo-Lockians suffice.

The previous great technological innovation to hit the Plains, the horse, also made for great inequities in wealth. The owner of a good buffalo horse could kill more buffalo than someone with a slow horse or no horse at all. More kills meant more robes for the traders, more meat to use or barter or give away, and more wealth to exchange for more good horses for sons or poor relations who could gain still more wealth for the family. Among the Pawnees and Lakotas and Blackfeet, and most other buffalo peoples, rituals of community evened out the wealth again. A man with a good buffalo horse was expected to provide meat for the various ceremonies that honoured the buffalo and guaranteed that future buffalo would continue to offer themselves to the people for food. In addition, the successful hunter was expected to provide meat to the poor, to those with no hunter to hunt for them, for generosity was the mark of a good leader, a good man or woman. The Lakotas marked births and comings of age and other events of note with giveaways of things and horses. To have many fine horses was good; to give them away was better. In part, such redistribution was simple good sense. The horse and buffalo people moved often. They raided and were raided by other peoples. Someone with too many goods or without ponies could slow down and endanger the entire group.

The buffalo were the material as well as the spiritual mainstay of the long-time Plains peoples. Systematic slaughter of the herds was more successful than outright warfare in forcing the Lakotas and Blackfeet and Crees and other Plains peoples to treaties and reserves. Among the Lakotas and Blackfeet particularly, some people quickly made the transition from hunting to herding but, largely through government intervention in both countries, such successes were short-lived, and in the United States much reservation land was quickly confiscated by either lease or purchase. Now reserve towns are a special case of the desolated plains town. Unemployment often exceeds seventy-five per cent and what few jobs there are, are typically in band and federal offices. People leave in droves for the cities, and still there are housing shortages on the reserves and the treaty payments and lease payments are so small as to be useless, unless there are mineral rights involved. The needs are the same as in the white Plains towns but more acute, and the responses are also similar.

An enormous spiritual renaissance, like the Ghost Dance, comes from both desperation and renewal. The Sun Dance flourishes again—two summers ago there were seventy-five Sun Dances on Pine Ridge alone. Women take on significant leadership positions, restating the importance of White Buffalo Calf Woman and rechannelling it in the Fancy Shawl Dancers and Hoop Dancers of the north. The Sarcee are born again as the Tsuu T'ina and use their location southwest of Calgary to thrive on both recreation and administration, their magnificent new building in the form of a beaver dam and lodge housing not only the tribal council but also a number of federal and Treaty Seven offices. From apparent ruin, they are re-erecting a nation in which pragmatic and spiritual reinforce each other.

Such reinforcement is lacking in both Ordeal and in the real High Plains towns on which it is based, regions from which the Sun Dance people and culture were deliberately "cleansed" by treaties. Lacking, but not absent. It is the women and the preachers who provide the community ethic in Ordeal, an alliance that has its roots in the particular development of capitalism in eighteenth- and nineteenth-century North America and western Europe. The model holds that men are acquisitive in the public sphere; women and preachers create a sense of community and mutual love in the private sphere. Women's suffrage came in part out of the sense of woman as public housekeeper, women moving out of the house to clean up the messes male chicanery had made in the public sphere. The best-known voice of Prairie suffrage, Nellie McClung, came explicitly out of this tradition of maternal activism, and although Saskatchewan leaders like Violet McNaughton were more explicitly egalitarian, they could not help being affected by the rhetoric and reasoning McClung and other maternal feminists wielded most effectively. Ordeal's women, therefore, come out of a tradition that is community-minded across North America and has traditionally been opposed to the acquisitive public tradition. Jessie Sheridan, novice, isolated from the community in every way, at first can only stand by her man, angry at him, at herself, at the land itself, at the drought, at the light, white heads of the wheat. Her husband is no tight-lipped Ross character, unable to express his fears or his worries to his wife. Once Jessie has attended the first farm rally and begun to understand, her husband explains their debt to her. When they lose their cattle and equipment and all but the original homestead quarter, Jessie understands and takes the usual role of a farmwife in hard times—she volunteers for the commute to a bigger town, where she can find a job, provide some solvency, tide them over so they can stay on the land. Fast food, convenience stores. But something. And being Canadians, not Americans, Jessie and her husband do not have to worry about health insurance.

Vera, the MLA, also offers a conventional role, one that makes economic and political sense but offers no new philosophy. She, unlike the premier, is a politician who speaks the truth, as her name indicates, but takes a male role, as her name also, more punningly, indicates. She speaks tenaciously for the people who want their farms, their town, their branch line, their post office. The distinctively Saskatchewan political ethic is community-minded, Co-operative Commonwealth Federation and New Democrat Party. But it is not enough and does not prevail against the smooth and citified premier, who is not at home with the farmers in the way Vera is, despite his advantage of gender in a predominantly male society.

Amy Sparrow, another bird, is the central figure in the fight for community. Like Jessie, her economic decision is significant. She is a potter, turning out souvenirs for dinosaur-watching tourists, perhaps gifts for people in the town, and sculpture of her own, art with no audience and no market, yet ungainsayable. She is the entrepreneur of a microbusiness. She is not creating jobs, except her own, but she is supporting herself, providing clientele for the shops and post office. Like her namesake, she lives sparingly, driving an old half-ton and growing her own garden, wearing cheap cotton dresses. Ordeal is hers both by birth and by choice. She grew up on her parents' farm, left for college, and came back. After her husband's death in a car accident, she stays on the farm, lovingly haunted by her father and her husband, and works as a potter. The combination of the land base, the microbusiness, and a Canadian social safety net enable her not only to stay in Ordeal but also to become an organizer of the crucial protests that, while they do not seem to affect decisions in Ottawa and Regina, do provide community solidarity. At the first farm rally Jessie learns for the first time that she and Val are on the verge of losing their farm. The second farm rally brings two other community forces into action and unites the chastened Pastor Raven with the community he had never really noticed before. Amy learns from Neil, especially from his studies of the human ecology of the grasslands, but most of what she learns strengthens her in her sense of what she does *not* want. She loves Neil, even expects to marry him, at the same time she realizes that she can neither leave her house nor bear to have him live with her there. Neil's cynicism and selfishness—though it is in many ways a saving selfishness—alienate him from the community and eventually from Amy, friend and love.

The second farm rally brings action from the village's solidarity committee, the widows. Meticulously but secretly organized, the widows are the women who have tended to community functions throughout their lives. Although only one or two can actually remember the exhaustive suffrage campaign that brought women's suffrage to Saskatchewan in 1916, they borrow a tactic from the radical suffragettes and chain themselves—and the premier—to the railings of their threatened post office. Like the original suffragettes, whose demonstrations and subsequent arrests, hunger strikes and subsequent force-feeding attracted attention, the widows dramatize their point and help solidify the community. People recognize, without necessarily being able to articulate it to themselves, that they *do* have power, that they can—even if only momentarily and in a sort of jest—seriously discomfit the political powers that be.

And then there is Melody Masuria, young and beautiful, the girl who makes herself available to all the young men. In reaction to her father's beating her as a whore, Melody leaves home and converts to Raven's band of Pentecostalists. When she develops stigmata, she has Raven call an American televangelist, and soon hundreds of eager seekers descend on the town before Melody is whisked away by the televangelist. Raven's cross is splintered by a tornado and Raven himself assumes a more human and accessible character. Amy realizes, however, that Melody's stigmata and the evangelist's merchandising of it will bring tourists to the girl's hometown, provide the economic engine to allow survival if not resurrection. Who needs to bring back the buffalo if one can produce the simulacrum of a saint? Melody has made the town visible and valuable to the continental media, but quite unwittingly she has presented a solution that goes beyond tourism. The transportation revolution that has wrecked towns like Ordeal by providing paved roads to schools, stores, and grain elevators in larger towns is giving way to a communications revolution. With telephones and modems and fax machines, Ordeal is once more capable of being the centre of a meaningful circle, though it will be continental rather than regional. Closing the post office reflects not only the death of the town but the relative decline in importance of the postal service and written communication in general. As Canadian prairie historian Gerald Friesen points out, rural growth in some parts of Alberta seems to be fuelled by telecommuters who provide business services to metropolises too far away for ordinary commuters. Although increases in agricultural productivity have not stemmed the population drain of the rural West, they do provide income for the service industries such as nursing homes that can support small-town residents.[7] Hundreds of satellite channels and virtually unlimited computer bulletin boards are accessible to Ordeal even as the post office closes. Melody's actions are unintended and largely unrecognized, but they are prophetic, tying Ordeal to the continental communications network. The same media that take her stigmata out to the continent can also provide jobs in communications and computers. Programming, research, even management jobs are already migrating from the cities and silicon valleys of North America to the Third World—they can migrate to the Plains as well as long as there are communities there with the self-awareness to welcome them.

The Great Plains is a land of violent climatic extremes, and southwest Saskatchewan can undergo differences of eighty degrees Celsius or more in a single year. It is also a land of many microclimates. A single section may easily contain croppable land, grazable land, swamp, and rocky hillside. Thus it is a land that must be micromanaged. The spotted cows and their descendants, as Don Gayton points out, are not as good at range management as the buffalo were.[8] They are lazy and graze too heavily near water holes and water tanks. Nor do they disturb the ground the way the buffalo did, give it a good aeration. In order to be efficient grazers, cattle also must be micromanaged, rotated carefully through a series of small pastures augmented by systematic burns or other perturbations of the grass. As High Plains agriculture becomes less and less labour-intensive, we become more and more aware that what it really needs is more management and fewer machines. Because this means that productivity per person would have to drop, farm income must be replaced with part-time income, not from off-farm employment, as is already the case for most farm families, but with on-farm employment using the communications revolution. Agricultural labour elasticity used to be provided, at the expense of women and children, by farm families of many children who could be pressed into the labour force during heavy work periods and allowed to go to school in light seasons. Such large families are no longer feasible, but that does not mean labour elasticity is unattainable. Nor can agricultural productivity continue to come from fossil fuel, fossil water, and largely fossil fertilizers. The huge inputs of gasoline, diesel, and petrochemical fertilizers and herbicides are not sustainable either economically or physically. Wes Jackson's Land Institute exploits the microclimates of its 800 acres on the Smokey Hill River in Kansas to develop perennial grain crops that can be harvested year after year without planting and without irrigation—and hence without the damage to the land caused by tillage, wind and water erosion, and the depletion of surface and ground water.

On the eastern side of the Plains and among the archipelago cities along the interstates and Trans-Canada Highway, the problem is different. Small towns like mine are swallowed up by the cities that create the jobs that absorb the people pushed or pulled out of the rural areas. My son's school, truly a model of innovation and flexibility, of individual attention and inclusiveness, efficient without economies of scale, becomes invisible to the city planners of the neighbouring metropolis who imagine white flight and tax havens as the only reasons to choose an alternative to the progressive metropolitan system. Margaret Laurence, when she returned to Canada, settled in the small town of Lakefield, Ontario—not the Plains, to be sure, but rural, and sharing the rural problems of the deserted village and the swallowed village. Like the mediaeval monastery, the small town, Laurence believed, might serve as a sanctuary for ideals of community in an age that favoured power. Kathleen Norris comes to the same conclusion from quite different premises in her appreciation of the Benedictine monasteries of North Dakota,[9] reminding me of the time my four-year-old son and I stayed with a friend there, the two of us among seventy Benedictine priests and friars in a community where the food on the table came from the monastery garden, and the ploughland and pastureland was worked by the Brothers. Geography did not call forth these monasteries—they were created by culture, and while their European form may seem incongruous to the High Plains, their community-based ideal both enables and naturalizes them.

Many of the problems and promises of the Great Plains are simply those of rural North America writ large and exaggerated by our large spaces, our relative lack of cities, and our brittle environment. As Butala reminds us in an article written for the *Globe & Mail's West* magazine, agriculture is not a pacifist sport.[10] Fertile crescents worldwide turn to desert as irrigated soil wicks up salts from underground and poisons the soil, just as a houseplant grows a white mineral crust from frequent watering. Myths can pacify us for slaughter or save us. Culture can bring our creation or destruction, which are themselves invisibly and implacably linked, just as Einstein's equation predicts for the physical universe. Although the Pawnees were always an agricultural people, they depended heavily on hunting and gathering and, even in the dog days, on the buffalo hunt. When introduced technology, the horse, altered their lifestyle, they adapted by countering the consolidation of wealth with generosity. Euro-Americans were also changed greatly by introduction of new horse technologies, but culture furthered consolidation of wealth. We see this in the loss of the commons—which, as Irene Spry has suggested, reached its apogee in the North American systems of reserves and reservations for Aboriginal peoples.[11] The ideology of the loss of the commons is that private enterprise best serves the land and, by best serving the individual, best serves the community—the heart of free enterprise theory. The Pawnee or Lakota giveaway, however, rests on the ideology that the community is stronger when no individual is impoverished or weak. And despite material poverty and the infighting that accompanies it, that ideal is still powerful on reserves and reservations.

The culture, the ideology, of community, makes a good case for itself as the appropriate response to the current human and environmental crisis of the Great Plains. If we cannot create more pseudo-saints to promote tourism (or even more shootouts like the one in Waco, Texas, where T-shirt vendors raked in $1000 a day before the final inferno with quickly printed David Koresh-wear),[12] we can plan for community. We must have universal health insurance that is not tied to employment in order to take the human—though not the economic—risk out of entrepreneurship and microbusinesses. We must have suitable, sustainable agriculture that respects not only microclimates but also sustainable input of fuel, fertilizer, and water. We must have labour-intensive management that is sensitive to the needs of wildlife—flora and fauna—as well as agricultural soil, water, grass, and other resources. And we must have on-farm employment through communications technology to subsidize such management and hence the protection of both natural resources and low food prices. Alternatives like monster hog-confinement operations simply are not economically or

40

ecologically viable. The existence of cities like Regina and Lincoln, as well as of the monasteries, located to fit cultural rather than geographical needs, shows that culture is perfectly capable of building and sustaining such human infrastructures, while computer technologies suggest the present means. Tourism, whether eco-tourism or a quest for saints and messiahs, also offers the on-farm, on-land income necessary to fund a culture community. We must reduce agricultural output so that we are not dependent on export markets that themselves displace sustainable agriculture from other parts of the globe by artificially undercutting the prices of staples. And we must keep our schools both as the foci of community and the replicators of the rural culture and indigenous culture we must borrow and invent to provide the ideological background for renewable community in a brittle environment.

Do people have rights? Does grass have rights? The whole idea of rights presupposes a community that is willing to recognize and guarantee rights. They are based on fear and convenience as well as on more noble passions. If we who are of the Prairies want to maintain a way of life recognizably like the small towns and mixed farming and ranching agriculture we have now, we have to recognize the rights of both the people and the grass. The land will survive us, whatever we do. Humans are, after all, only one of the cyclic perturbations that have marked this area, and by no means the most impressive. The people of the spotted cow are a tiny blip, no more consequential in the great scheme of geological time than one good volcanic eruption. We humans are, however, quite important to ourselves. The land will survive us as it survived the dinosaurs. But we will not survive our ecological niche. Thus, it behooves us to respect the land, lest it cast us away as small micro-organisms to be burnt off mother earth with a good fever.

ENDNOTES

1. Paul Martin, "The Discovery of America," *Science* 179 (1973): 969–973. Cited in Don Gayton, *The Wheatgrass Mechanism: Science and Imagination in the Western Canadian Landscape* (Saskatoon: Fifth House, 1990). See also *Morning Edition*, National Public Radio, 25 November 1999.

2. N. Scott Momaday, *The Way to Rainy Mountain* (Albuquerque: University of New Mexico Press, 1968), 7.

3. Richard White, "The Cultural Landscape of the Pawnees," *Great Plains Quarterly* 2 (1982): 31–40.

4. James C. Malin, *History and Ecology: Studies of the Grassland*, ed. Robert P. Swierenga (Lincoln: University of Nebraska Press, 1984), esp. pp. 3–67, 105–26.

5. Sharon Butala, *The Fourth Archangel* (Toronto: HarperCollins, 1992).

6. "What Does it Take to Survive?" *Lincoln Journal Star*, 6 April 1993, C11–12.

7. Gerald Friesen, *The West: Regional Ambitions, National Debates, Global Age.* McGill Institute Books (Toronto: Penguin, 1999), 47, 31.

8. Gayton, *Wheatgrass Mechanism*, 99–108.

9. Kathleen Norris, *Dakota: A Spiritual Geography* (New York: Ticknor & Fields, 1993).

10. Sharon Butala, "Vanishing Species," *West (Globe & Mail)*, June 1990, 23–30.

11. Irene Spry, "The Tragedy of the Loss of Commons in Western Canada," in *As Long as the Sun Shines and the Water Flows: A Reader in Canadian Native Studies*, ed. Ian A.L. Getty and Antoine S. Lussier (Vancouver: University of British Columbia Press, 1983), 203–228.

12. *Weekend Edition*, National Public Radio, 27 March 1993.

THE MELTING OF TIME IN THOMAS WHARTON'S *Icefields*

by Claire Omhovère

Hornbook #99
   "The question is always a question of trace. What remains of
what does not remain?"
                     Robert Kroetsch, "The Poetics of Rita Kleinhart"

Published in 1995, Thomas Wharton's first novel *Icefields*[1] addresses the question "When is the Prairie?" by exploring the memories preserved in the remnants of the great ice sheet that once covered the western side of the North American continent and shaped the geography of the Prairies.[2] Staging the historical ruptures through which visions of the glacier have evolved, *Icefields* presents the living landscape as the result of a changing interference between the human gaze and its geographical environment. To do so, Wharton inflects the fixity of spatial representations, giving them a temporal slant characteristic of the interrogation that is the theoretical backbone of the present collection. Indeed, what comes to the fore in *Icefields* is not so much a distrust of history as a desire to observe how landscapes are historically as well as artistically produced in the analogies we draw between what our eyes see, and what they have seen (or read) before. It could then be contended that "without memory, there is no landscape."[3] Thus, addressing newness becomes profoundly problematic:

> The borderline work of culture demands an encounter with 'newness' that is not part of the continuum of past and present. It creates a sense of the new as an insurgent act of cultural translation. Such art does not merely recall the past as social cause or aesthetic precedent; it renews the past, refiguring it as a contingent 'in-between' space, that innovates and interrupts the performance of the present.[4]

Unlike rivers and their dumbfounding Heraclitean properties, glaciers combine linear and cyclical displacement through time. Melting as it advances or retreats, the glacier's flow suggests that temporality can be iterative: the past becomes projective, and interrupts "the performance of the present" when it emerges to be re-envisioned.[5] The glacier could, therefore, figure the disjunctive "time-lag" that cultural studies theorist Homi Bhabha sees at the core of the post-colonial experience.[6] Contrary to the homogenous seriality of historical time, Bhabha posits the contramodernity of the post-colonial, an iterative temporality that opens onto the articulation of cultural difference.[7] In this essay, I will therefore address the question of how imaginary and geographical spaces are presented as related processes, the glacier acting as a metaphorical frame that unframes and transforms the deposits from the past.

APPROACHING THE SITE

Set in the Athabasca valley, *Icefields* opens in August 1898 when Doctor Edward Byrne, a member of a Royal Geographical Society exploration team, falls into a crevasse; it ends in June 1923 when the ice walls that had trapped him finally reach the terminus of the glacier. After a twenty-five-year vigil, Byrne hopes to ascertain if the winged figure he glimpsed down in the depths of the glacier was truly an angelic spirit or a mere chance design of the ice. The novel, however, extends well beyond the temporal span of its central narrative. Through a series of flashbacks, it stretches across three generations, braiding together adjacent plot lines. It thus recounts the arrival of the first British explorer, Sexsmith, in the last period of the fur trade when the area was still vastly unmapped. In the yet unnamed valley, Sexsmith and Viraj, his East Indian servant, come into contact with Athabasca, the last descendant of the Snake people who used to live there. When the British lord returns to England, he leaves behind his servant with Athabasca, and the valley gradually opens to European settlement. Among the newcomers, Trask quickly recognizes the picturesque assets of the area, and its potential for tourism once it can be reached by rail. In a few decades, the chalet he builds by the hot springs fills with visitors and climbers like the dashing Freya Becker, a young woman determined to try her mettle on the surrounding rock faces. Within three generations, "the great ice prairie" (50), on which the Snake people feared to tread, evolves from a holy ground to a playground for the tourists boarding the entrepreneur's "rattling motor-coaches" (271). Ironically, the ice-crawlers seem to have deprived both the Aboriginal people and the glacial site of their totemic attributes. At first, Shelley's lines are still thought appropriate enough to be quoted among Trask's guests—"The glaciers creep / Like snakes that watch their prey, from their far fountains."[8] But, by the end of the novel, the Romantic vision has been converted into marketing hype advertising the nearby caves of ice and the sunny pleasure dome the developer built over the hot springs (253).

Starting from Hugh Stutfield and J. Norman Collie's account of the expedition, which took them to Jasper along with Edward Byrne in 1898,[9] Wharton blends facts and fiction, revisiting the conventions of the historical novel to give them an intriguing geographical twist. The Collie and Stutfield exploration is resituated on the fictitious Arcturus Glacier. Similarly, a man bearing the same name as the author of *Tay John* works as a trail guide for Trask.[10] In a liminal note to his readers, Wharton disarms possible critics of his distortion of historical truth and claims the plenipotency of the fiction writer: "Any resemblance to actual events, locales, persons, or glaciers, living or dead, is entirely coincidental." Having been advised not to assimilate the fictive with the real, but having been granted that there may be such a possibility, the reader turns the page and discovers a series of coincidences: first, two maps combine the space of the real Athabasca valley and Wharton's inventions in their ambiguous 'legends.' Then, each of the headings of the novel's five sections consists of a term that, on a literal level, does refer to glacial formations but, on a metaphorical level, to the organization of narrative material, signalling a constant slippage between geography and fiction. The section entitled "Névé" thus introduces the reader to layers of accumulated narratives. The "Moraine" section refers to geological debris as well as to narrative fragments. "Nunatak" corresponds to a vantage point on the glacier and to the observations Byrne compiles there. "Ablation zone" culminates with the death of Freya Becker. Finally, "Terminus" locates narrative resolution at the point where the glacier itself ends. Whereas it is now accepted that imaginary constructs along with narrative conventions do inform the writing of history, we are less accustomed to the idea that geographical space may not only shape the imagination but may also be constructed by it.[11] The author's overt rejection of a "mimesis of product" is in fact undercut by his covert acknowledgement of a "mimesis of process," to use Linda Hutcheon's fine distinction in her analysis of historiographical metafiction.[12]

The glacier therefore provides Wharton with a setting, a vocabulary, and a literary fund of metaphors. But its function as a structural trope allows him to conflate space and time, and refine the equation by which we commonly assess the passing of time as a spatial displacement. Better than the sundial making uniform time into space or the clepsydra converting the instant into a trickle of vanishing seconds, the ice records time in the traces it inscribes on the landscape, all the while preserving the memory of its passing in an accumulation of past layers. As a "time-machine," the ice is therefore both a history and a memory (217). However, the glacier's solid flow, its cyclical melting and crystallization, destabilize the fixity of traditional time-space representations. Glacial dynamics remind the observer that, far from being a static object to behold, the landscape is subjected to erosion, and is produced through time,[13] as are cultural representations of the landscape.

FROZEN VISIONS

Although the introductory map records the presence of only one icefield, its singularity is diffracted into the several points of view concurring in elaborating the plural narrative of *Icefields*. Simultaneously, a constellation of visions both precedes and screens the focalizers' perceptions, dispelling even further the emergence of a prevailing, unifying view. Actual sight is invariably occulted by imaginary visions. Thus the "lone sighting" (18), which posited Mount Brown as the highest peak on the continent and prompted the Collie and Stutfield expedition, was preceded for the first explorer by his dream of a silver grizzly bear (24), and another of the Grail (41). Both instances, however, lead to misconstructions of the new environment. The black bear his Métis guide eventually kills for Sexsmith has none of the grizzly's heroic attributes he fantasized for himself (53). Sexsmith nevertheless inscribes the precedence of his vision on the landscape and bestows the name of "Arcturus"[14]—the Greek compound literally means Bear (*arktos*) Watcher (*ouros*)—onto the glacier that led him to the high plain of ice. As for the Grail itself, when Sexsmith reaches it, he is unable to connect the silver cup he saw in his dream with the geological bowl he has just stepped on:

> Blue, silver. What is it?
> He pours the remains of his tea into the hole, hacks at it with the point of the alpenstock. Crystalline shards fly out.
> Ice.
> He understands now that he is walking across a bowl of ice on the top of the world. The glaciers have been spilling from its brim.
> Nothing. A dreary waste of ice. (181)

For Sexsmith, the landscape is apt to be inscribed with metaphors, but inapt to generate a signification. The "blank, wordless space in the atlas" (29) that fascinates him so much is replete with memories of the Oriental splendours that lie beyond the Northwest Passage and recur obsessively in the literature of the British Empire. Venturing into unchartered land, Sexsmith clings to the reassurance of memorized texts. He thus greets the Snake woman Athabasca with Macbeth's bewildered question to the Weird Sisters: *"Are you aught that man may question?"* (35). As he enters the valley, the rhythm of Caliban's speech in the third act of *The Tempest* supersedes the cadence of his own feet on scree (27). But the iambic pentameter is not quite attuned to the rough terrain, and when Sexsmith trips and falls, "sinking into rock, drowning" (27), he owes his life to the agility of Viraj, who, Ariel-like, rescues him from the abyss.[15]

The pre-eminence of past visions also comes to the fore when Byrne falls into the crevasse:

> The white figure lay on its side, the head turned away from him. Its huge wings were spread wide, one of them cracked obliquely near the tip, the broken pinions slightly detached.
> One arm was also visible, outstretched, in the semblance of some gesture that Byrne felt he had seen before, but could not

> interpret. A remembered sculpture, or one of Blake's hovering,
> pitying spirits. (11)

Literary precedents are, in Byrne's case, rapidly superseded by a reminiscence from his own past, "A magnificent, impossible figure from a long-forgotten childhood dream" (13). Byrne's fall is occasioned by a slipping foot as much as by a slip in the signifying chain. On the glacier, he mistakes what he sees for the sea, "frozen waves" and "aquamarine" ice (11). The crevasse becomes coextensive with a gap in his memory. And it will take him the next twenty-five years to retrieve from oblivion the linguistic pun that condensed these frozen waves with his dead mother's wave on a Dublin beach (272).

More than the blank on the colonizers' map, the constant slide between land and language,[16] therefore, opens chasms under the colonizers' feet. In fact, the terrain is far less treacherous than the tropes used to describe it: "the tree leans out over the abyss, gnarled, *like a tortured soul on the verge of a final leap. 'Unsightly,'* Sibelius mutters" (107, my emphasis). To construct space into a legible landscape, the railroad magnate uses a code that turns the failure of his gaze into an aesthetic response. Above the gorge, he teeters on the brink of the sublime, and this brutal shift from landscape to inscape[17] would have caused his fall if it had not been for Trask's immunity to romantic rapture and his immediate reaction. Rather than the gaping chasm, it is an emotion constructed by countless European paintings that made Anton Sibelius lose his sense of balance. Prior to this scene, we are told that the "avenues and spires of ice" he saw on a painting in George Simpson's office impressed him so much that he conceived the dream of erecting a city in the Athabasca valley (105). What the financier assumed to be a genuine rendering of the Rockies was, in fact, a representation of the artist's native Alps, as Wilhelm Streit later acknowledged in his own journal (230–231). Unable to render the quality of the light in the Canadian Rockies, and urged by the governor of the Hudson's Bay Company to produce the commissioned work, Streit finally painted the mountains of his homeland using the conventions with which he was familiar.

In the novel, what the colonizers see never quite matches what they are shown. When Sexsmith first arrives in the valley, two Stoney brothers bring him their adopted sister to guide him up to the icefield. Athabasca's body bears the evidence that the Snake people experienced themselves as extensions of the land: her face is painted blue and, on her palm, she has the tracks of the rivers and streams. But a cooking stone has left a reddish scar on the map of her hand, blurring the location of the icefield (36). The lacuna on Athabasca's palm does not merely duplicate the blank on the Europeans' map. Its opacity blocks the elaboration of the colonial map on which "the reinscription, enclosure and hierarchization of space [provide] an analogue for the acquisition, management and reinforcement of colonial power."[18] The blur, as opposed to a blank, which can always be filled, undermines the transparency of the colonial map. As such, it frustrates the colonizers' "vigorous demand for narrative" and is immediately interpreted as a wish to deceive:[19] *The burn on the girl's palm*, Sexsmith said. *If her map is accurate, we're just below it now. I want to know what's up there, what she is hiding from us*" (43). Under Sexsmith's scrutiny, Athabasca's otherness both as an Aboriginal and as a woman resorbs itself into the racial stereotype that posits her as unpredictably predictable and surmises a hidden significance beyond the cultural nonsense she offers.[20]

The burn on Athabasca's palm is as unreadable to the foreign eye as the single print left by the Snake people in the snow (48), or the overnight offensive of the Swan glacier: "the two steel rails twisted around each other like twining snakes" (85). With brutal precision, the ice defeats at once the double tracks of colonization and the penetration of western binaries, the "stereotomy"[21] positioning the inside as distinct from the outside. On Athabasca's palm, the outside coincides with the inside, space with the subject, form with content, and signifier with signified. The burn conceals nothing except a "space of burning, eternal light" (100) for those who will risk the climb to the "great ice prairie" (50).

Characters who, like Byrne, contemplate from a distance the dazzling sliver of snow above the Arcturus glacier merely run the risk of momentary snow blindness (100). But those who are daring enough to go to see beyond the veil that shrouds the mountains are struck by a blindness that is merely figurative in Sexsmith's case but lethal for Freya Becker. Down in the valley, the snow pattern she sees on the side of Mount Meru reminds her of what climbers call "Parvati's curtain" in the Himalayas (193). Although the Hindu goddess embodying the power of Nature belongs to a different set of references from the Greek myths sustaining Western culture, the punishment Freya incurs for lifting Mother Nature's veil retains strange Oedipal overtones. The young woman who set off on the climb of Mount Meru laden with collapsible tripod, Panoram portable, mirror, and field glasses vanishes when the summit cornice collapses (207). Although she fell 300 metres, Freya does not die instantly:

> She was brushing snow from her wool jacket, and looked vaguely perplexed, like someone who had misplaced her reading glasses.
> *I'm fine*, she said when she was aware of his approach. *Just cold*.
> He saw the streak of snow stained red at her feet. She looked past his shoulder as if blind. (209)

The blindness that precedes Freya's death is given further resonance in the snapshots salvaged from the film cartridge. The photograph can freeze Byrne's figure (213), but it captures nothing of the icefield, which, by an effect of the glare, remains "a dark amoeboid blur to one side" (212). On another picture taken by Trask's chalet, Arthur the Bear also stands "frozen onto film," and, yet, it remains out of focus. It is difficult, then, to ascertain if it is the movement of its held-out front paws or the obscure intent of the animal's gesture that blurs the photograph (225). As in Sexsmith's encounter with the "frozen hilarity" of the black bear's carcass, the projection of the human gaze onto the animal and, by metonymic extension, the space it stands for, creates a "comic incongruity": at its best, mimesis turns into mimicry. At its worst, the blurred photographs retain an *unheimlich* residue pointing out a presence heterogenous to representation in the bear as well as in the icefield.

Icefields therefore contrasts natural space and cultural landscape. The icefield threatens the human gaze with blindness and defeats any representation other than the oracular symbol of its burning light. As opposed to the icefield, which the gaze fails to frame, the landscape of Arcturus glacier is culturally inscribed with scores of visions and images projected on it by the colonizers' gaze. Envisioning what the ice inscribes rather than what its surface reflects therefore requires a change in perspective and a shift from the instant that arrests the eye to the duration of the observation, from the vision of ice to the narrative of ice.

A FLOWING FRIEZE

Byrne belongs to the group of characters who, like Viraj and his daughter Sara, have never set eyes on the icefield, and have thus avoided its blinding light. In the shelter he built on the nunatak, Byrne assesses from a static point the flow rate of the glacier in order to locate the point of resurgence of his past. His intimacy with the glacier causes the distance between human observer and exterior space to diminish. After years of scrutiny, it becomes harder and harder to distinguish between Bear Watcher and the man who watches it, the doctor's notebooks filling with transcriptions of the glacier's traces:

> Stones, fragments of a lost continent, lie scattered in the dirty snow of the till plain. A shattered palette at my feet, the mad artist having just stalked away. Grey breccia flecked with acid green and primrose yellow. Pock-marked slabs into which powder of burnt sienna has been ground. The many-coloured constellations of lichen growth: rocks splattered with alizarin crimson and cadmium orange. The purple and white veins of limestone.
>
> The enchantment of these mute fragments is undeniable. The bewitching garden of signs. Down among the cool stones, one might not perceive the burning rays of sunlight reflected from lingering patches of summer snow, until it is too late. (140–141)

The correspondence European art first established between what the human eye encompasses and the view framed on canvas dissolves under Byrne's scrutiny. The hierarchy between foreground and background, the resulting effect of depth, is disrupted as the viewer is not placed in front of and outside the painting but inside it, somewhere in its middle ground. The flattening caused by this shift in the viewer's position makes it difficult to assess the difference between near and far. Because it is no longer envisioned as a distanced, composed spectacle,[22] the landscape loses its coherence and becomes loose elements. Its content is ground down into pure form, colour chords, the vibration of natural pigments.[23] Nonfigurative as the landscape may now seem, Byrne nevertheless still reads it as a combination of signifiers pointing out the presence of some subject or intention.[24] In its obvious absence, therefore, it depends on him to organize the motif into a motive.

In a way, Byrne wrestles with the very conundrum that Sexsmith eluded in his blindness. This indifferent space allows the watching eye, or the speaking subject, no stable position from which to fathom its radical otherness: "The sparsity of the landscape draws me to it," acknowledges Byrne (152). Leaving his secure position as an outside observer, Byrne becomes an active interpreter, and lets the "glacier's writing" guide him (143). The lines inscribed by the slow flow of the ice take him through

space and time from the emptiness of the present landscape to petroglyphs carved by prehistoric hands:

> There are human figures, crude and distorted, but recognizable
> in various poses: fighting, hunting, giving birth. And other fig-
> ures, more like animals. Interweaving among the human shapes.
> And curving lines like the traceries of braided streams. Circles.
> Arrows. Lines of force.
> He traces a frieze along the flank of the cabin-sized boulder.
> Confusing everything is the presence of glacial scars. Undevi-
> ating straight lines. They lure his linear mind's eye into following
> them, away from the human carvings. (144)

The curves traced by human hands stand in contrast with the linearity
of glacial history. They do not make sense insofar as they lack an orienta-
tion and an apparent sequence. However, far from being lacunae waiting
to be filled with interpretation, they impose themselves as a system of signifiers—alphabet, or dictionary (146)—with its own law of composition.
As such, these inscriptions allow a reinscription, and these traces provide
a matrix for further tracing: first Byrne attempts to write his own story in
the clay using similar stick figures (145). Then, with the help of Rawson, a
young poet who works as a trail guide for Trask, the two men retrace a
frieze, which, along the vector of glacial striations, articulates the random
carvings into a narrative sequence. Despite Byrne's awareness that their
construct is indeed totally artificial, the story of the river-woman that the
scientist and the poet make out on the boulder operates as a suture
between the past of the valley—the fate of Athabasca, who survived the
massacre of her tribe before vanishing into the setting sun—and future
events. The frieze could also be read as a foretelling of Freya Becker's
death, her passage through rock, and her resurgence as water in Rawson's
memory, even after the glare of the icefield took away her smouldering
vitality (183).[25] Seen as mere "scratches," the petroglyphs "have nothing
to do with [Byrne's] presence, they do not anticipate him, prophecy him,"
as he duly reminds himself (147). But read as signifiers, they branch out
into the past and the future, including Byrne and Rawson in a flowing
frieze of stories, which stems from the everlasting transmission and transformation of narrative material between ethnic groups:

> *The early tribes of humans, once simple hunters and gatherers, were*
> *forced into a nomadic existence, into the unknown, and they needed new*
> *tools for the journey. New ways of thinking. New words.*

> Byrne sets down his pen. Stories. They took their stories with
> them, to remind them who they were. And there were the tales
> brought back by those who scouted ahead. They moved through
> stories. (197)

Writing a pamphlet for Trask's guests, Byrne stops short with the sudden
realization that newness has been occurring before and after Columbus
blundered into the New World, ever since inherited stories have been
translated into another culture, thus creating new, because hybridized,
narratives.[26]

The ice-maiden motif presents such a hybridized configuration: Aboriginal Wendigo superstitions[27] (35) have aggregated and transformed
folktales from northern Europe as, for instance, Andersen's *Snow Queen*
(187) associating women with ice and projecting female attributes upon
the glacier.[28] All the female characters in the novel share some of the
characteristics of the ice maiden, whether it be diffident Sara in her "icy
stronghold" (124) or Arctic Freya (113), who comes back to haunt Rawson
as meltwater (225). In spite of her affinity with fire and tropical vegeta-
tion, even Elspeth, the chalet's housekeeper, fleetingly reminds Byrne of
the wings that almost enfolded him in the crevasse (166).

One reason for such an assimilation may be that, contrary to the men
who explore the valley, settle it, blast the mountain open, and frantically
turn the remnants of the Ice Age into a tourist haven (103), these women
seem impervious to historical progress. They share the resilience of glaciers; they remain and recur as ice periods do. Sara's ageless face reminds
Byrne of his own grandmother and stories heard in childhood (14). To
him, Sara is always "this youthful ancient woman" (22), her skin like
parchment (44), her memory the repository of Viraj's tales, Sexsmith's
poetry, and Athabasca's native stories (48). Sara's timelessness is shared
by her daughter, who is so much like her mother that, for a brief
moment, Byrne believes the woman of twenty-five years ago has come to
greet him (263).

But one could also argue that, for the male characters who warily
approach them, these ice maidens retain the double edge of primal identi-
fications in which kissing lips both heal and devour.[29] Rawson therefore
knows that his wishful dream of a domestic(ated) Freya, neither fairy nor
vampire,[30] but homely wife, negates the ambivalent attraction he felt for
her (227). Even in dream fantasies, the male gaze fails to hold these

women still, their appearances and disappearances remaining beyond the men's control. When Byrne wakes up from a nightmare, he remembers how his mother's ice-blue corpse twitched back to life on the examination table. Despite his father's reassurance that the body would go back to "its proper state of lifeless immobility," the woman got up and walked out into bright sunlight (246). Byrne's nightmare finds a sequel in the reminiscence that surges from his past and disrupts the narrative present while he stands by the glacier's terminus. It is as if the woman he now sees had stepped out of his dream onto the seashore that superimposes itself upon the tarn in which he is dipping his hand. The phantasm, Byrne realizes, is neither Freya nor Sara, but an intact memory of his mother waving to him. When Byrne turns back to face her, the figure suddenly dissolves in "the fierce sunlight" (272).

Byrne's nightmare and hallucination thus articulate a pattern that was first traced in the frieze of petroglyphs. The story of the river-woman disappearing into the sun does not merely help Byrne recapture the past. This narrative kernel articulates something of the unspeakable loss that left him stranded in time at the age of eleven: "Next to the clock he places a sea urchin shell, the only surviving relic from his childhood" (156–157). As an alternative time-marker, the empty shell belies the stubborn ticking of chronological time. The urchin—mollusk and/or child—metaphorically condenses the sea and orphanhood, thus pointing out the moment when Byrne's life was arrested in time. No longer staring into the void materialized in the urchin's empty shell, Byrne receives from her a sign that is both a greeting and a farewell, an acknowledgement of their separation. Byrne takes this epiphany as a gift from the glacier's meltwater: "A day long forgotten, given to him now in its fullness" (272). It closes the crevasse's gap and signals the end of his vigil: "There is no longer any reason for him to be there" (272).

The subtle blending of landscape and inscape, the ultimate convergence between geological and individual time, could be read as a forceful demonstration that Wharton's novel moves away from the traumatic discontinuities of post-colonial history.[31] In this respect, Byrne's character is an obvious foil to the covetousness of past explorers such as Sexsmith and the greed of present developers exemplified by Trask. And yet, Byrne's ultimate sense of belonging is not obtained at the cost of difference: he does not appropriate the landscape, neither does he merge with it in blissful indifference. Rather, he becomes *part of* the landscape, "he blends in with the rocks" (271). Camouflage here denotes the possibility of becoming inconspicuous while remaining distinct from the surroundings. In this respect, Byrne must be distinguished from O'Hagan's Tay John, who achieves a mythical unity with the landscape, "becomes the landscape,"[32] but at the cost of his own life. When the glacier suddenly lets the resurgence of Byrne's past flow out, the recognition that follows remains a missed encounter. And the melting of time lets a sign of difference subsist.

ERRATICS

> Glacial ice is not a liquid, nor is it a solid. It flows like lava, like melting wax, like honey. Supple glass. Fluid stone. . . . There are ice quakes that shift the terrain, unpredictable geysers of meltwater that carry away ice aiguilles and other landmarks. And of course the evidence of flow, acts of delicate, random precision: shards of rock are plucked by the ice from their strata, carried miles downstream, and left lying with fragments from another geological age. (159)

Glacial sites are a challenge to the linearity of history. In *Icefields*, the erratic consequently becomes a paradigm for reading the landscape and the text alike. The erratic points out the role of two factors somehow undermining the predictability of both: one is error, the other displacement, and these two notions are relevant to the novel's denouement.[33]

Readers have no choice but to revise their interpretation of Byrne's vision as a figment of his imagination, or unconscious, when the winged shape he saw down in the crevasse ends its erratic progress under Trask's eyes. The developer glimpses the sculpted pinnacle emerging from the glacial spur just before it crashes down and disappears in the meltwater tarn (260–261). Because the narrative is narrowly funnelled through Trask's perceptions, we are denied the searching gaze that would settle the question of the origin and nature of the sculpture. At first, only rational explanations are suggested: the action of the water and the sun (259), or the hand of a construction crew member (260). Once he is back at the chalet, a third possibility comes to Trask's mind, but he finds it so odd that he will not let himself think about it, thereby denying readers the confirmation of Byrne's wildest hypotheses. No one will ever know for sure if

Trask saw an ice sculpture carved by Aboriginal people in ancient times, or if he was given the ultimate evidence of the existence of angels: "No, he decides, he won't be turning this into one of his incredible tales to entertain guests at the chalet" (261). Trask's reaction is all the more surprising as we are well aware of his incredible talent for turning art into cash. His musing hints at a possible revelation but conceals everything about its content. The reader's desire to see and read the sculpture is teased and trapped in the folds of the interpretative veil that is suddenly lowered. Trask's silencing nevertheless suggests that the upsurge of the past presents the spectator with something so unprecedented that attempts at rationalizations ring hollow. His predicament in addressing the singularity of the sculpture—the sculpture's oddness might well become his own in people's minds (261)—parallels Rawson's failure to write about Freya: "I tried, but nothing came close. I didn't have a language for something I'd never encountered before" (240). What remains is an evocation of movement, as the swift italic slant Rawson associates with Freya (121 and 152). Similarly, Trask's narrative leaves us with the glimpse of a fugitive form and no content. But the sight that was wasted on him, and denied to us, generates the very speculation through which readers get enmeshed in the writing of the story.[34]

The sculpture's appearance and disappearance is a beckoning sign that amplifies the ironic anecdote of the Wing and Sons piano. The monumental instrument was pushed into Avernus chasm after the one and only performance of an avant-garde piece by the French composer Michel Barnaud (233). Nothing will remain of this masterpiece, or perfect hoax, except for a few scattered ivory keys "found later in the summer by hikers.... Often they are mistaken for the teeth of mammoths" (233). Most would dismiss their gross error with a complacent laugh. But nothing will be retrieved of Barnaud's art except for this erratic evidence, which initiates an exchange of jokes, summer anecdotes, even tall tales for the best raconteurs.

The way disappearance induces the production of stories finds an enigmatic symbol in the circulation of a small stone among the novel's narrators. Before Athabasca leaves Viraj and her young daughter, she gives them the cooking stone that left the scar on her palm. The gesture is prefigured in her gift to Viraj of a piece of ice, "like a blue-green diamond," which is so cold that it burns his hand, and he lets it drop (45). The gift of the stone, which, unlike ice, neither breaks nor melts but endures, is echoed in a tale turning Sara's mother's disappearance into a parable: in the fable Viraj tells, an Indian woman abandoned her husband, also a storyteller, but she left him with one green eye of the same colour as the exquisite cloth she weaved: *"The storyteller leaned forward and pointed to his green eye. He said,* Look closely and tell me if you see her." (49)

Later in the novel, the small stone reappears. Its shape has altered with the passing of time: it is no longer flat but egg-shaped; its colour is the same as the storyteller's eye, and this time, it sits in Elspeth's palm (267). The son of an American tourist found it on the till plain and shared his treasure with her. Wise Elspeth senses that gifts cannot be capitalized, that their symbolic value depends on their being exchanged within the group and between communities.[35] That is why she asks Byrne to take the stone back to the glacier's terminus: "That's where it belongs. For all the other boys to find" (267). When Byrne returns the stone to the glacial debris, a gleam catches his eye and he discovers an orchid that has miraculously grown out of the remains of the specimen box he lost at the time of his accident twenty-five years before.

In *Icefields*, the circulation of the erratic therefore materializes what remains after the past has melted into the present. Like the ice sculpture, the small stone leads to a revision of the past, which does not amount to a reconstruction saturating the lacunae and silences of post-colonial history. In *Tay John*, the violence of colonial contact resulted in a "strangled articulateness"[36] encapsulated in the stone that choked Red Rorty or the snow that filled Ardith Aeriola's mouth, as if the landscape itself had rebelled against being appropriated by a foreign tongue. But in *Icefields*, the stone that is picked up, handed over, and returned to the landscape to be found again leaves an indelible trace on the astonished characters who momentarily hold it. The stone, like the orchid blooming among the devastation of the terminus, allows the narrator to speak, launching the old story into fresh retellings. Wharton then observes how the imagination operates in two distinct ways by (re)producing images that disfigure the colonial space when its otherness is not acknowledged, this process resulting in violence. But he also insists that the creative imagination receives an imprint from geography whenever its space is read for the signifiers that will grant the subject an existence as a distinct interpreter. From then on, the discontinuity of post-colonial history is no longer perceived as debilitating.

"When is the great ice prairie?" is therefore a central question posed by Wharton in *Icefields*. Reaching beyond this singular novel, I would tentatively answer 'everywhere': in the boulders, rubbing stones, tipi rings, and stone hammers[37] that dot the Prairies and erratically recur in its literature. Such landmarks insistently recall the brutal wiping out of First Nations people. But in Wharton's novel, as well as in texts by Kroetsch or van Herk, erratics also point out a genealogy of the Prairie landscape in which the homogenous linearity of Empire gets disrupted by the scansion these signs of displacement inscribe. Stones rising from the depths of van Herk's memory and her father's Battle River fields,[38] stone hammer lost and found in the summer wheat, rings of stones circled by the plough,[39] these erratics are stubbornly mispronounced "erotic"[40] because they signal that an intimacy is achieved with the landscape through years of back-breaking work and scrupulous attention. For these Albertan writers, interacting with the landscape need not revive the violence and/or the blind fusion of archaic fantasies. Instead, they approach the Prairie with the patience of lovers and a fierce awareness of its precious singularity.

ENDNOTES

1. Thomas Wharton, *Icefields* (Edmonton: NeWest Press, 1995). Further references to the novel will appear directly in the text.

2. Cf. R. Cole Harris, ed., *The Historical Atlas of Canada. From the Beginning to 1800* (Toronto: University of Toronto Press, 1987), Plate 1, "The Last Ice Sheets, 18 000–10 000 B.C."

3. My translation of "Sans souvenir, pas de paysage." Michel Pical, "Lecture(s) du paysage," *Lire le paysage—lire les paysages, C.I.E.R.E.C. Travaux KLII* (Saint Etienne: Presses de L'Université de Saint Etienne, 1982), 309, the translation is mine.

4. Homi Bhabha, *The Location of Culture* (London and New York: Routledge, 1994), 7.

5. Ibid., 177.

6. Ibid.

7. Ibid., 245: "The problem of the articulation of cultural difference is not the problem of free-wheeling pragmatist pluralism or the 'diversity' of the many; it is the problem of the not-one, the minus in the origin and repetition of cultural signs in a doubling that will not be sublated into a similitude."

8. Percy Bysshe Shelley, "Mont Blanc," section IV.

9. The book they wrote together, *Climbs and Explorations in the Canadian Rockies* (London: Longmans, Green and Co, 1903), is listed by Wharton in the

Acknowledgements along with Yoshiro Kagami, "Edward Byrne: A Life in Ice," *Journal of Alpine Exploration* 2, 6 (1951).

10. Howard O'Hagan did spend a few years in his youth working as a tour guide, but it was in Banff. He later came to Jasper to work for the Canadian National Railroad. See the biographical note in Howard O'Hagan, *Tay John*, Afterword by Michael Ondaatje (1939; Toronto: McClelland and Stewart, 1989).

11. See, for instance, "The Geographical Imagination: Knowledge and Critique," in Gillian Rose, *Feminism and Geography: The Limits of Geographical Knowledge* (Cambridge, Oxford: Polity Press, 1993), 62–85.

12. Linda Hutcheon, *Narcissistic Narrative* (1980; London: Methuen, 1984), 5. On the analogy between the actual landscape and the novel, see Joel Martineau, "Landscapes and Inscape in Thomas Wharton's *Icefields*," *Open Letter* 10, 2 (Spring 1998): 41–49.

13. According to the *O.E.D.*, the term "landscape" did not appear in English until the sixteenth century, when it was borrowed from the Dutch as a painter's term. It originally implied the framing of a portion of land from the point of view of a static observer. Although the landscape can move with the observer, as when it is seen from a train's window, it is rarely perceived as having a movement of its own. W.H. New points out that the term "landscape" therefore implies the distinction maintained by "the philosophical tradition that separates 'objective world' from 'viewing subject'" (*Land Sliding: Imagining Space, Presence, and Power in Canadian Writing* [Toronto: University of Toronto Press, 1997], 10). For a detailed analysis of the concept of landscape in various languages, see Jeanne Martinet, "Le paysage: signifiant et signifié," in *Lire le paysage—lire les paysages*, 61–67. Martinet shows that the concept of "landscape" implies a coherent vision isolating significant units in the amorphous expanse of space. Languages such as Montagnais relying on other senses than vision to apprehend space have no concept equivalent to the Dutch *landschap*, the English *landscape*, or the French *paysage*.

14. *The Collins English Dictionary*. Arcturus is also the name of the brightest star in the constellation Boötes.

15. On this occasion, the lines that come to Sexsmith's mind are from *Henry IV*, Part I, Act IV, scene i: "I saw young Harry with his beaver on / His cushes on his thighs, gallantly armed / Rise from the ground like feathered Mercury / And vaulted with such ease into his seat / As if an angel dropped." The sudden shift from *The Tempest* to *Henry IV* seems to have been prompted by the analogy between the mediaeval helmet and the buffalo cap on Viraj's head.

16. To the stalemate of the post-colonial "gap" between imported language and lived environment, W.H. New opposes the dynamic notion of a "slide" between land and language: "the language is at once an impediment to communication and the very means of communication, a site of paradox, a ground at once of exhaustion and creativity" (*Land Sliding*, 11).

17. Martineau, "Landscapes and Inscape," 48. The term "inscape" was coined by Gerard Manley Hopkins "to refer to the inner beauty of natural forms as they reveal themselves to the observer. The concept has been extended to embrace

the notion of the observer's mental landscape, or what might be described as the metaphorical terrain of the mind."

18. Graham Huggan, "Decolonizing the Map: Post-Colonialism, Post-Structuralism and the Cartographic Connection," *Ariel* 20, 4 (October 1989): 115.

19. Homi Bhabha links the colonizer's demand for narrative to the power politics of the gaze: "The natives' resistance represents a frustration of that nineteenth-century strategy of surveillance, the confession, which seeks to dominate the 'calculable' individual by positing the truth that the subject has *but does not know*" (*Location of Culture*, 99).

20. Drawing on Lacan's analysis of the function of the veil in *Le Séminaire, livre IV, La relation d'objet* (Paris: Seuil, 1994), 151, Homi Bhabha argues that the colonizer's negation of cultural difference is analogous to the fetishist's denial of sexual difference, and the subsequent misconstruction of an absence of penis as the veiled presence of the Phallus. The racial stereotype then performs the same function as the fetish (*Location of Culture*, 75–76).

21. Bhabha, *Location of Culture*, 186.

22. For a discussion of "the unmoving gaze from afar," which the Enlightenment identified with "dispassionate cognition," see Martin Jay, "Photo-unrealism: The Contribution of the Camera to the Crisis of Ocularcentrism," in *Vision and Textuality*, ed. Stephen Melville and Bill Readings (Durham: Duke University Press, 1995), 355.

23. Cf. Thomas Wharton, "The Country of Illusion," in *Fresh Tracks: Writing the Western Landscape*, ed. Pamela Banting (Victoria: Polestar Book Publishers, 1998), 304: "The object that I would like you to take note of, on the front of this postcard, is a large boulder, an erratic. It's really somewhat difficult to see, camouflaged as it is by the stippled grey mud flat where it sits, equally stippled and grey, and overshadowed, in accordance with the conventions of postcards, by the peaks and the glacier that fill the top half of the frame and are the real subject of the photograph."

24. I am using Lacan's distinction between the sign (which represents something for somebody) and the signifier (which represents a subject for another signifier). See *Le Séminaire, livre XI, les quatre concepts fondamentaux de la psychanalyse* (Paris: Seuil, 1973), 144.

25. Byrne and Rawson isolate the following narrative fragments: "*Woman, in a river? Escapes battle, massacre of her people by enemy tribe. Runs away to (from forest?), lives with rocks, standing stones. The rocks stand in a ring. Erratics? She walks between two of them. Then a space, nothing. / Further along the carving the woman reappears (or is it in fact the same one?) A single line spirals around her. She faces the other way now (?), going up into the sun*" (147).

26. Homi Bhabha defines hybridization as the translation of elements from one culture to another. But with their rearticulation, cultural symbols split and become "less than one and double." For instance, Bhabha analyzes the colonial appropriation of the English Bible by Indian natives: "If, on one side, its authority, or some symbol or meaning of it, is maintained—willy-nilly, less than one—then, on the other, it fades. It is at the point of its fading that the

metonymy of presence gets caught up in an alienating strategy of doubling or repetition" (*Location of Culture*, 116 and 119).

27. In *Strange Things, The Malevolent North in Canadian Literature* (Oxford: Clarendon Press, 1995), 64, Margaret Atwood notes that the Wendigo can be either male or female, and that it is one the most cross-pollinated motifs in Canadian literature.

28. See, for instance, the tall tale of the Swan glacier rushing down in flowing skirts to kiss men in their sleep (85).

29. Julia Kristeva, *Polylogue* (Paris: Seuil, 1977), 205–208. This archaic motif comes to the fore in Atwood's analysis of the male attraction for the "cold, savage, alluring, female power of the North" (*Strange Things*, 101). Robert Kroetsch, in "The Veil of Knowing," in *The Lovely Treachery of Words: Essays Selected and New* (Toronto: Oxford University Press, 1989), 185, also refers quite explicitly to pre-Oedipal fantasies when he writes: "The Great Mother [in *The Double Hook* and in *Tay John*] with her doubled and doubling lure ... darkens the veil into a knowledge that both men and women try to, and try not to, read."

30. Freya is associated with both (see pp. 119 and 174).

31. Albertan writer Aritha van Herk is another case in point. She gives several twists to the post-colonial gap in her "CrowB(e)ars and Kangaroos of the Future: The Post-Colonial Ga(s)p," *World Literature Written in English* 30, 2 (Fall 1990): 42–54. In *Places Far from Ellesmere, a geografictione, explorations on site* (Red Deer: Red Deer College Press, 1990), the fractured lines of geography provide van Herk with an alternative map countering the imperial grid that disfigured the Prairie into a repetition of symmetrical, identical units. I analyze van Herk's poetic use of geography in "Aritha van Herk's Tesselated Territory," *Etudes canadiennes / Canadian Studies* 47 (1999): 177–190.

32. Wharton, "Country of Illusion," 310.

33. Both notions are present in the word "erratic": the prefix of the Latin verb *errare* is related to the Gothic forms *airze* ("error") and *airzjan* ("led astray") in the etymology given in the *O.E.D.*

34. Cf. Kroetsch, "Veil of Knowing," 192: "Canadian writing, by that trope of concealment, reveals to the reader a readerly predicament, that is, in Roland Barthes's terms, writerly. The reader reading Canadian becomes the reader writing the writer, then writing the reader."

35. See Jean Baudrillard's analysis of the symbolic exchange in *L'Echange symbolique et la mort* (Paris: Gallimard, 1976).

36. Northrop Frye, *The Bush Garden* (Toronto: House of Anansi Press, 1971), 220.

37. Robert Kroetsch, "Stone Hammer Poem," in *Completed Field Notes: The Long Poems of Robert Kroetsch* (Toronto: McClelland and Stewart, 1989), 3:

> It is a stone
> old as the last Ice Age, the retreating / the
> recreating ice,
> the retreating buffalo, the retreating Indians

38. Aritha van Herk, *Places far from Ellesmere*, 34. Aritha van Herk and Brian Stanko, "De-binarizing the Erotic Kroetsch," *The New Quarterly: New Directions in Canadian Writing* 18, 1 (Spring 1998): 136.

39. Robert Kroetsch, "The Moment of the Discovery of America Continues," in *The Lovely Treachery of Words*, 2.

40. Robert Kroetsch, *A Likely Story: The Writing Life* (Red Deer: Red Deer College Press, 1995); "I Wanted to Write a Manifesto," 41–64, and "The Poetics of Rita Kleinhart,"171–216.

AUTOGEOLOGY

Limestone and Life Narrative in Carol Shields's *The Stone Diaries*

by Nina van Gessel

Carol Shields's 1993 Pulitzer award-winning *The Stone Diaries* is not an autobiography, although the casual reader might be forgiven for thinking that it is. After all, its chapter titles—"Birth, 1905," "Childhood, 1916," "Marriage, 1927," and so forth—denote the conventional stages of the self-representational journey. Furthermore, the family tree that prefaces the text and the photographs that punctuate it are elements commonly associated with the autobiographical, rather than novelistic, narration of a life. At the same time, however, *The Stone Diaries* repeatedly thwarts the reader's expectations of conventional autobiography. "[W]ritten on air, written with imagination's invisible ink,"[1] Daisy Goodwill's reconstruction of her life begins with an eye-witness account of her own birth and violates the open-endedness of the genre by progressing right up to, and even beyond, her death. Further, the first-person narration characteristic of life writing is more often displaced by a third-person point of view, drama-tizing the autobiographical subject's (usually obscured) dual position as nar-rator and protagonist. That subject is traditionally understood to be pro-moting noteworthy feats executed in the public realm: canonical authors of autobiography chronicle their professional or intellectual accomplishments in a bid to immortalize themselves as worthy representatives of their age.[2] However, *The Stone Diaries* evinces Shields's interest in the "unrecorded lives of good citizens."[3] This anti-heroic, female-centred response to an historically androcentric genre depicts a woman whose life merits neither "distinguished honors" nor "outraged condemnation," whose obituary cites achievements not achieved (344). Shields herself has remarked, "In some ways I see this as the antithesis of the Nineteen[th] Century novel, where characters struggle to find themselves—and she doesn't find herself."[4] If the failure of Daisy's quest for self-actualization disputes the closure inherent in the Victorian novel, still more does it contest the conventions of autobiography, which dictate that the author discover a "meaningful pattern in the flux of past experience in order to arrive at an understanding of *him* self as unique and unified."[5]

The Stone Diaries, then, substantiates Linda Hutcheon's observation that the postmodernist text both "uses and abuses" literary tradition as it contests the authority of that tradition.[6] More specifically, the novel's incorporation of autobiographical trappings ironically inflects its interrogation of the complacent stability, seamlessness, and ostensible referentiality of the genre's canonical texts.[7] A life narrative, *The Stone Diaries* suggests, does not emerge titled and bound; its neat packaging is deceptive, stamping the illusion of completeness on a text that is in fact not product but process. Further, autobiography bears no privileged relation to "truth," being merely a narrative, or composite of narratives, arbitrarily assembled from the fossils of the past. *The Stone Diaries* reveals autobiography to be a fusion of science and artistry, and a function of accretion and erosion, like the limestone that supports, physically and economically, the novel's assorted locales. And Shields demonstrates that, like that fossil-embedded mineral, autobiography threatens life with ossification. It is only through the metamorphosis of life into a dynamically indeterminate *story* that the transformation of life into static *stone* can be avoided.

During the first quarter of the novel, the mineral that furnishes the novel's central metaphor is the dolomitic limestone underlying the region around Winnipeg, the city that has been home for the past two decades to the American-born Shields. Situated as it is on the margins of the Canadian prairie, the area offers a fitting site for Shields's postmodern play with genre, for, as Hutcheon notes, postmodernism treats the periphery as more than simply a zone of transgression. Rather, "[t]he margin or the

border is the postmodern space par excellence, the place where new possibilities exist."[8] When, at the age of eleven, Daisy leaves Winnipeg with
her father, Indiana limestone replaces its Manitoban counterpart as both
the increasingly lucrative source of Cuyler Goodwill's income and the
novel's central metaphor for life narrative. Almost sixty years later, during
Daisy's visit to Scotland, it is the "coded dots of life" (310) embedded in
the ancient stone of the Orkney Islands that metaphorically evoke the
autobiographical text. However, the young Daisy's recognition that "the
absent are always present" aptly describes the place of Canadian limestone
in the novel (90). Though ultimately submerged by other geographical
formations, that prairie limestone remains a vital layer—the bedrock—of
Shields's densely stratified metafictional project.

HISTORY AND FOSSILS

The Stone Diaries' revision of conventional models of autobiography
invokes the challenge to the "traditional causal, closed, linear nature of
narrative history" by theorists of historiography.[9] Michel Foucault and
Hayden White, among others, have demonstrated that historical narratives do not yield unmediated, transparent access to the past. Rather, "our
knowledge of the past is something constructed (or even re-constructed)"
through "its documents, through its traces in the present."[10] As White
puts it, "In the unprocessed historical record and in the chronicle of
events which the historian extracts from the record, the facts exist only as
a congeries of contiguously related fragments."[11] Assembling these fragments into a coherent narrative, the historian makes sense of history "in
the same way that the poet or novelist tries to make sense of it, i.e. by
endowing what originally appears to be problematical and mysterious
with the aspect of a recognizable, because it is familiar, form."[12] Facts,
White emphasizes, do not speak for themselves. Rather, "the historian
speaks for them, speaks on their behalf, and fashions the fragments of the
past into a whole whose integrity is—in its *re*presentation—a purely discursive one."[13]

In *The Stone Diaries*, Daisy assumes the historian's role as she seeks to
construct—and, as White would say, make sense of—her own life story.
Already as a child she is intuitively aware that "the meaning of the past is
not coherent, continuous, or unified—until we make it so"[14]: "if she was

going to hold on to her life at all, she would have to rescue it by a primary act of imagination, supplementing, modifying, summoning up the necessary connections" (76). Bewildered by a present marked by disorder and alienation, the adult Daisy possesses even more strongly a "long[ing] to bring symmetry to the various discordant elements" of the past (23). Those discordant elements, what Hutcheon terms "traces" and White "fragments," are the detritus of Daisy's domestic life. "[L]etters, newspaper articles, speeches, lists, historical accounts, scientific jargon, definitions, photographs, recipes, conversations, obituaries, wedding announcements, telephone conversations" are all faithfully reproduced among the novel's pages.[15] The distillation of the past into White's "congeries of fragments" is a central theme throughout. Surveying the drawerful of quotidian articles that is all that remains of Daisy's possessions following her hospitalization, her daughter Alice wonders, "How is it possible, so much shrinkage?" (323). The miniature pyramid Cuyler Goodwill erects in his old age looms over a buried time capsule intended to preserve for posterity select items "representative of the times": a postage stamp, pressed leaf, newspaper headline, fennel seeds, his first wife's wedding ring (182). When Magnus Flett returns to his ancestral home in the Orkneys, he carries with him a few mementoes of nearly five decades in Canada, including some samples of the prairie limestone he had quarried.

The Stone Diaries invokes the geology of the Canadian prairies to represent the "fragment[s] from the past" (174) from which Shields's characters seek to craft their historical narratives. These fragments are figured as fossils analogous to those embedded in the prairie limestone, the "gastropods, brachiopods, trilobites, corals and snails" that provide its rich texture and inspire the sobriquet "tapestry stone" (25). Hence, for example, the narrator's assertion that "childhood is what anyone wants to remember of it. It leaves behind no fossils, except perhaps in fiction" (148). Hence too the account of how Cuyler Goodwill subjects the young daughter he has only just met to an "assault of unsorted recollections" (90) on the train between Winnipeg, Manitoba, and Bloomington, Indiana: "He talked to fill the frightening silence and to hold back the uncertainty of the future, but chiefly he talked in order to claim back his child. He felt, rightly, that he owed her a complete accounting for his years of absence. Owed her the whole of his story, his life prised out of the fossil field and brought up to the light" (91). His act of narrative excavation here evokes an earlier incident in which, inspired by a "naturalist's curiosity," he had literally dug up interesting fossils to take home to his wife (25).

Cuyler's compulsion to uncover the fossils of history, figurative as well as literal, is symptomatic of the (thwarted) yearning for certainty Shields explores throughout the novel. Harold Hoad, Daisy's first husband, is tormented by a hunger for details of his father's suicide, a hunger he perceives as emasculating in its neediness but which he is impotent to resist: "Wasn't this unseemly, unhealthy, grotesque, this unnatural slavering after documentation? Wasn't this, well, unmanly?" (110). Later, "laps[ing] into an amicable nostalgia," Daisy's children devote entire afternoons to "acts of retrieval" (175) in an image that validates the narrator's speculation that childhood's fossils manifest themselves in fiction, that is, subjective memory: "This nostalgia of theirs is extraordinary, each of them feels the richness of it. On and on they'll talk; a whole afternoon will disappear while they take turns comparing and repeating their separate and shared memories and shivering with pleasure every time a fresh fragment from the past is unearthed" (174–175). Daisy herself marvels at the apparently insatiable hunger for facts that characterizes their "documentary age" (330).

The phrase "acts of retrieval" thus yokes two of the novel's central motifs: the geological excavation of fossils or, more broadly, the limestone that encases them, and the analogous act of unearthing facts from the historical field. Daisy, as "[s]omeone who's learned to dig a hole in her own life story" (263), metaphorically pursues her paternal ancestors' work in the prairie quarries of Stonewall and Tyndall. Her exertions are also linked to those of her beloved niece, Victoria, who, with another biologist, seeks evidence of early plant life in the fossil-rich stone of the Orkneys. "[S]crambl[ing] like insects on the plates of outcropping rock, and scrap[ing] with their tiny tools at the surface of the hidden world" (301), they look for traces of a primitive flower or even of bacterial presence. The scientists' aspirations of joining these "coded dots of life" (301) into a coherent chronicle of the earth's geological history mirror Daisy's quest to forge an autobiographical narrative from the fossil fragments of her life. And the evident failure of their scientific expedition—the reader learns only that "with fewer than half a dozen days remaining, they had turned up nothing" (301)—reflects Daisy's inability to craft a conventional, unified life narrative.[16]

Victoria and Lewis's scientific quest, then, exemplifies a hunger for fossils/facts prevalent throughout the novel. But if much of Daisy's life is set against the backdrop of a "documentary age," it is only through a process of fabrication that those facts can be assembled into historical or life narrative, as White's earlier comments suggest. The union of objectively real fact and imaginatively crafted fiction constitutive of such narratives is loosely mirrored in the fusion of science and artistry evident in the fossil-embedded limestone. The label "tapestry stone" attests to the aesthetic appeal of the Tyndall stone, its "unique lacy look" and textured shading. The stone's multicoloured hues—it appears as both "a light buff mixed with brown" and, Daisy's favourite, "a pale gray with darker gray mottles (25)—are not the work of a divine paintbrush, as Cuyler is fond of pointing out, but rather of a complex sequence of geological forces unleashed several hundred million years ago. (The rainbow that inspires Cuyler's creation of the tower commemorating his first wife also offers science—the refraction and dispersion of light through droplets of water—in the guise of the artist's canvas [57].) The life narrative Daisy constructs is loosely analogous to the limestone and the rainbow. It too unites elements of what we commonly, if reductively, associate with the scientific and artistic realms, whereby the former implies that which is objectively verifiable, or extra-discursive, and the latter suggests the effects of subjective imagination. The empirically "true" fossil fragments of Daisy's life are embellished, aestheticized:

> She enlarges on the available material, extends, shrinks, reshapes what's offered; this mixed potion is her life. She swirls it one way or the other, depending on—who knows what it depends on?— the fulcrum of desire, or of necessity. She might drop in a ripe plum from a library book she's reading or something out of a soap opera or a dream. Not often, but occasionally, she will make a bold subtraction. (282–283)

This compulsion to transform historical fact into narrative through judicious supplementation and deduction motivates Daisy through much of a century. It is only in the final years of her long life that the ceaseless spinning of narrative threatens to become too burdensome:

> All she's trying to do is keep things straight in her head. To keep the weight of her memories evenly distributed. To hold the chapters of her life in order. She feels a new tenderness growing for certain moments; they're like beads on a string, and the string is wearing out. At the same time she knows that what lies ahead of her must be concluded by the efforts of her imagination and not

by the straight-faced recital of a throttled and unlit history. Words
are more and more required. (340)

Daisy is aware of the imaginative effort required to conjoin her life's fragments, but senses that the strength necessary for those efforts is fading,
that the string/narrative she weaves is fraying. In the novel's final chapter,
that string has evidently worn through completely in places. Here the narrative collapses into an unruly heap of fragments: obituaries, assorted lists,
gravestone inscriptions, menus, recipes, snippets of reflection and conversation. Although Daisy resists total ontological disintegration with her
plaintive refrain, "I'm still here ... I'm still here, oh, oh" (352), the con-
nective tissue of embellishment and imagination is no longer accessible.

That the union of fact and fiction comprising Daisy's life narrative until
these final pages is a troubled one is evident in the frequent challenges to
her dependability. "Maybe now is the time to tell you that Daisy Goodwill
has a little trouble with getting things straight; with the truth, that is," we
are told midway through the text (148). She is, we learn,

> not always reliable when it comes to the details of her life; much of
> what she has to say is speculative, exaggerated, wildly unlikely. . . .
> Daisy Goodwill's perspective is off. Furthermore, she imposes the
> voice of the future on the events of the past, causing all manner of
> wavy distortion. She takes great jumps in time, leaving out impor-
> tant matters. . . . Sometimes she looks at things close up and some-
> times from a distance, and she does insist on showing herself in a
> sunny light, hardly ever giving us a glimpse of those dark premo-
> nitions we all experience. And, oh dear, dear, she is cursed with
> the lonely woman's romantic imagination and thus can support
> only happy endings. (148–149)

In so blatantly undermining the authority of the autobiographical voice,
Shields dismantles the contractual model of self-representation proposed
by Philippe Lejeune, according to which the authorial signature under-
writes the referentiality of the text.[17] Daisy's recognition of the unrepresentability, the unknowability, of her experience is profoundly detrimental
to her sense of identity; it informs such reflections as, "What she lacked
was the kernel of authenticity, that precious interior ore that everyone
else around her seemed to possess" (75) and her final, poignant "I am not
at peace" (361). Nonetheless, that recognition does have some positive
implications for the narration of her experience, as we shall see later.

PRAIRIE LIMESTONE: ACCRETION AND STRATIFICATION

The issue of referentiality is further problematized by the multiplicity of versions that collectively comprise Daisy's narrative. If that narrative is metaphorically akin to the prairie limestone in its metaphorical melding of art and science, the two forms, literary and geological, are also both a function of accretion and stratification. In one of his "mythopoetic" speeches (86), Cuyler describes the process whereby the sedimentation of shells of "billions and trillions of little sea creatures" (80) on the seabed eventually produced his beloved limestone. Daisy's life story is similarly an accumulation of layers. Sometimes viewing events close up and sometimes from a distance, hers is not the unitary, linear narrative privileged by writers and scholars of conventional autobiography. Rather, her story emerges from competing narratives, which accrete with little concern for reconciliation or coherence. Possessing as she does "the startling ability to draft alternate versions" of her life (190), she corroborates Hayden White's claim that "the historian does not bring with him a notion of the 'story' that lies embedded within the 'facts' given by the record. For in fact there are an infinite number of such stories contained therein, all different in their details, each unlike every other."[18]

In its use of accretion, and concomitant perspectival play, *The Stone Diaries* constitutes a sequel of sorts to Gertrude Stein's celebrated *The Autobiography of Alice B. Toklas*,[19] which applies to literary self-representation the insights of the Cubist visual artists so admired by its author. Stein's experimentation with multiple perspectives is most obviously accomplished through her displacement of the autobiographical voice onto her lesbian lover, a gesture loosely analogous to Shields's frequent oscillation between Daisy's first-person and third-person narration.[20] But this experimentation is accomplished too though Stein's use of fragmentation and repetition: tenuous narrative threads emerge from the incremental accumulation of isolated details.[21] In similar fashion does Daisy's life story evolve. For example, the description of her unexpected and violent birth that opens the novel is resumed 200-odd pages later, when we finally learn the significance of the foreign coin placed upon the newborn's forehead.

The accretion of narrative in *The Stone Diaries* issues to a large extent from the superimposition of other characters' perspectives as imagined by Daisy. Again, an allusion to *The Autobiography of Alice B. Toklas* offers an instructive analogy. Stein's decision to have Alice B. Toklas narrate her autobiography has been attributed not only to her aesthetic principles—a Cubist interest in perspective—but also to a more personal desire to limit her self-exposure.[22] The deployment of Toklas as narrator offered a valuable means of self-censorship. Toklas, after all, could not be expected to possess immediate knowledge of Stein's (painful) early adolescent years, warranting Stein's treatment of that period in a few brief sentences. Stein's privacy is further shielded by the rapid succession of sketches of writers and artists that propels the autobiography forward, papering over the many fissures in her portrait and obscuring the instability of the paradox-ridden autobiographical subject.[23] In *The Stone Diaries*, multiple voices similarly obscure the autobiographical subject, but here that obscuring is so acute as to seriously disable the subject. Just as Stein's autobiography is densely peopled, so does Shields's novel offer extensive description of "people whose lives have sometimes only fleetingly touched Daisy's."[24] Meanwhile, Daisy herself remains unrepresented in the clutter of photographs, letters, and journal entries. "Unseen, unheard, this woman occupies a cavern of vacancy at the centre of the text," Winnifred Mellor has noted only slightly hyperbolically.[25]

With the muffling of the autobiographical subject's voice, it is the other characters who provide essential contributions to the narrative script. An important example of this accretion of detail supplied by secondary characters appears in the narrative dealing with the death of Daisy's second husband, Barker Flett. We first learn of the death of this hitherto central figure through a letter from W.W. Kleinhardt, Solicitor, who writes pertaining Barker's will. From the next letter, one composed before his death by Barker himself, we discover that his death had been augured by painful headaches; subsequent correspondence proffers the condolences of Daisy's friends and, more importantly, the information that Daisy will replace her late husband as writer of a gardening column in the local newspaper. It is not until the subsequent chapter, in a section ostensibly written by her daughter Alice, that the cause of death is revealed as a malignant brain tumour. Another example of this use of accretion appears in the description of the sudden loss of Daisy's job, the only one she ever has and one from which she derives enormous satisfaction. While correspondence in the "Work, 1955–64" chapter suggests that she loses the position because it is coveted by a journalist with greater seniority, a section ostensibly composed by her editor in the following chapter implies that he engineered the loss to curtail his deepening romantic relationship with Daisy.

The sections by Alice and Jay, the editor, most vividly demonstrate the accretion of detail I have been discussing. Located in the chapter "Sorrow, 1965," the two segments form part of a longer sequence of passages theorizing the causes of the depression that gripped Daisy following the loss of her job. Thus, "Alice's Theory" is followed by "Fraidy Hoyt's Theory," "Cousin Beverly's Theory," "Warren's Theory," and so forth. (Substantiating Mellor's comment regarding Daisy's voicelessness, the final entry, Daisy's own, begins, "Surely no one would expect Mrs. Flett to come up with a theory about her own suffering" [261].) Each passage contributes new strokes to Daisy's portrait, but the veracity of that information, and thus of the resulting portrait, is thrown into question. First, each theory is obviously highly subjective, more a reflection of the speaker—or, more precisely, Daisy's construction of the speaker—than of its supposed object. Thus Alice, an ambitious academic and novelist, attributes her mother's depression to the loss of her employment, while Fraidy Hoyt's healthy sexual appetite obviously informs her assertion that her friend's illness stems from repressed libidinal urges. Second, the assorted theories are engaged in a complex game of subversion and revision. Fraidy's section begins, "You don't expect Alice Flett Downing to believe in her mother's real existence, do you?" (240). Her claim that another friend once described Alice as "Her Holy Miss Righteousness" (242) further colours our perception of Daisy's daughter and demands our re-evaluation of the theory she proposes. The dialogues in which the assorted strata engage are epistemologically unstable, rendering the life narrative dynamic and questionable, rather than fixed and referential.

Like the prairie limestone, then, Daisy's life narrative is constituted by accretion.[26] New layers appear indiscriminately, governed by chance and not by the dictates of the autobiographical script. The role chance plays here is analogous to its contribution to the formation of limestone, a contribution apotheosized by Cuyler in a typically prolix speech on the occasion of his daughter's wedding. It also reinforces Daisy's oft-repeated and well-substantiated claim that life is directed by accident.[27]

LIMESTONE: IRREGULARITIES

Because Daisy's life story develops from the chance accumulation of detail, rather than from the organic teleology associated with more conventional specimens of the genre, that life story is punctuated by distortions that image limestone's textural irregularities and "mottled" surfaces (64). As the preceding discussion suggests, *The Stone Diaries*, like *The Autobiography of Alice B. Toklas*, pays only lip service to the chronological map that typically structures self-representational literature. In Stein's text, the chapter headings attest to her revision of that map: the first four sections are entitled "Before I [Toklas] came to Paris," "My Arrival in Paris," "Gertrude Stein in Paris, 1903–1907," and "Gertrude Stein before she came to Paris." Shields's chapter titles do chart the conventional stages of autobiography, as we saw earlier. However, their implicit promise to function as reliable signposts along a linear life journey remains unfulfilled. All too often, the chapter demonstrates a blithe disregard for the dates it is supposed to be chronicling, so that, for example, much of "Ease, 1977" is devoted to detailing Cuyler's death twenty-two years earlier. As Simone Vauthier puts it, "a tension is created between the global frame, set up by the table of contents and disseminated in the chapter titles, on the one hand, and the local time-disruptions or the meanderings of the narrative parts, on the other."[28] Further, the discrepancy between chapter title and content is often one of substance as well as chronology. As Shields points out, section headings frequently speak ironically to content: that "the chapter on marriage is mostly the story of two men" dramatizes the fact that "we [women] construct our lives through men."[29] The effect of the temporal and substantial discordances between chapter title and content—both in turn a function of the text's randomly accretive structure—is to generate gaps in what are surely crucial sections of Daisy's life story. Missing are, among other things, details of her education, sexual initiation, and experience of childbirth, the latter described by Shields as "probably the most dramatic moment of any woman's life."[30] We are reminded again of the discrepancy between Daisy's actual life, marked by these milestones, and the meandering narrative that vainly aspires to represent it.

Returning to my geological metaphor, Daisy's narrative is, then, full "of holes that connect like a tangle of underground streams" (196). It is "an assemblage of dark voids and unbridgeable gaps" (76). Not only do details frequently appear with seeming disregard for the chronological map, but occasionally the introduction of a new layer of narrative yields information already possessed by the reader as though for the first time. For example, "Alice" informs us that her mother wrote her gardening column under the byline "Mrs. Green Thumb" (233) after we have already read numerous letters from readers that addressed Daisy by that pen name. This repetition suggests a discontinuity between narrative layers, a fissure slight but nonetheless indicative of an "unbridgeable gap."

If the effect is, as I have argued, analogous to the strata and fissures constitutive of the prairie limestone, it is also strikingly imaged in the description of the Orkney Islands. Like the prairie limestone a geological chronicle of time, they are palimpsestically inscribed with the stratified traces of successive, yet distinct, historical eras:

> Behind and beneath [its] pastoral scenery lie prehistoric ruins—villages, forts, cairns, burial chambers, and standing stones which might, or might not, be astronomical observatories. There are Iron Age remains, too, another layer. And the Norse monuments, ninth century. Also the medieval, the feudal, the monastic. And other more contemporary additions—for superimposed upon the ancient and bucolic are today's small humming Orcadian factories modestly producing such specialities as Orkney cakes (delicious) or Orkney cheeses; then there are the craft enterprises, knitting for the most part (but this sadly in decline), the tourist thrust (booming), and the ever-present background buzz of daily commerce and professional necessity—grocers, stationers, lawyers, clergymen, what have you. (289)

These stone diaries are characterized, like Daisy's narrative and like the tapestry limestone, by "ripples and echoes and variations" (124), as opposed to uniformity and coherence.

PRAIRIE LIMESTONE: EROSION

The irregularities that mark both limestone and Daisy's postmodern life narrative are the product of erosion as well as accretion. With the passage of years, the Tyndall stone from which Cuyler creates his monument to his wife becomes "sadly eroded" (114), victim of both the prairie elements and the touch of countless sightseers. Analogously, Daisy reflects that the "recounting of a life is a cheat" in part because that recounting erodes quotidian but essential detail, the "minor alterations of mood and varying tints of feeling" (28):

> It has never been easy for me to understand the obliteration of time, to accept, as others seem to do, the swelling and corresponding shrinkage of seasons or the conscious acceptance that one year has ended and another begun. There is something here that speaks of our essential helplessness and how the greater substance of our lives is bound up with waste and opacity. Even the sentence parts seize on the tongue, so that to say "Twelve years have passed" is to deny the fact of biological logic. How can so much time hold so little, how can it be taken from us? Months, weeks, days, hours misplaced— (27–28)

This gradual "obliteration of time" consumes the nine years of widowhood that follow her first, short-lived marriage. At a loss to account for the activities that filled those years, Daisy responds to suggestions from her new husband with only shakes of the head, until finally she concludes blankly and inadequately that she tended the garden (154). While this passage accentuates our sense of her debilitating insubstantiality, hollowing a gap in her story, the eroding forces of time elsewhere yield more empowering effects. When the middle-aged Daisy is in the grip of her paralyzing depression, a part of her remains oddly unmoved by its symptoms, for she "knows how memory gets smoothed down with time, everything flattened by the iron of acceptance and rejection" (262–263). (She is proven correct: in the subsequent chapter, chronicling her trip to the Orkneys, Daisy achieves the measure of happiness that had hitherto eluded her.) But whether it functions as a negative or a positive agent, this erosion problematizes the act of self-representation, reminding us yet again of the disjunction between historical fact and reconstructed narration. Like the celebrated Tyndall limestone, Daisy's life story is at once solid (in the persistence with which it demands, against all odds, to be narrated) and vulnerable (to the disintegration of essential detail).

LIVING STONE

Finally, life narrative shares the metaphorical exchange of the living and unliving, the organic and inorganic, that Shields has described as characteristic of limestone.[31] We saw earlier that the Tyndall tapestry stone owes its distinctive texture to the fossilized remains embedded within it. "As the flesh of these once-living creatures decayed," Daisy explains, "a limey mud filled the casings and hardened to rock" (25). Like the Orkney fossils avidly sought by Victoria and Lewis, its Canadian counterpart embodies "Life turned to stone" (301). The phrase echoes throughout the novel, representing as it does not only the geological narrative that is limestone but also literary autobiography, which paradoxically aspires to reify fluid identity within the fixity of the written word and of the genre's prescribed script. As Alice points out, and as post-structuralism has taught us, the human self is "not a thing carved on entablature" (231). Indeed, Daisy exemplifies the plasticity of the postmodern subject: she is "a dynamic subject that changes over time, is situated historically in the world and positioned in multiple discourses."[32] Her consciousness evolves as she progresses through life's stages, from motherless infant to self-conscious adolescent and through to old age. Though that consciousness often seems curiously, even disturbingly, detached from external realities, it is nonetheless subtly informed by the events of her historical age that periodically impinge upon the text: the birth of the Dionne quintuplets, Kennedy's assassination, the emergence of the Women's Lib movement, and so forth.[33] And she is defined in diverse ways by the sometimes contradictory discourses of daughter, wife, mother, homemaker, newspaper columnist, etc. Daisy herself recognizes that "her story marches ahead of her. Announces her. Declares and cancels her true self" (122).

Daisy, then, demonstrates all the protean instability of the post-structuralist, postmodern subject. In fact, the novel seriously queries the existence of an essentialist identity implicit in the phrase "true self."[34] However, like the once-animate creatures forever imprisoned in Tyndall stone, Daisy the autobiographical subject experiences ossification: as "powerless, anchorless, soft-tissued" (150) as they once were, she feels "caught in a version of her life, pinned there" (147). The analogy is underscored by several passages late in the novel that literalize the image of reification in stone. Visiting her during her hospitalization, Alice is momentarily appalled by the "[m]ineralized" appearance of her mother's hands (326), just as Daisy herself had earlier been dismayed by the fossilized condition of her 115-year-old father-in-law. And as she awaits her impending death, Daisy envisions herself as a statue, complete with stone scroll and pillow: "Stone is how she finally sees herself, her living cells replaced by the insentience of mineral deposition" (358).

Linda Hutcheon regards this exchange between what Shields calls the living and the unliving and what she herself discusses in terms of dynamism and stasis as an important and recurrent motif in Canadian postmodernism. She notes that the act of writing is "an act of reducing open, imaginative immediacy to framed form. Form in itself . . . is potentially sterile and dead."[35] Hutcheon sees the "paradox of concern for dynamic process (reading, writing) being unavoidably articulated in the form of a static product (the thing read and written)" exemplified in the frequent allusions to photography in Canadian postmodern literature.[36] *The Stone Diaries*, of course, engages with a double act of reification: not simply that inherent in any act of writing but also the unique hypostatization of lived identity demanded by the self-representational genre. Perhaps it is because of this double reification that Shields's novel treats photographic analogy more literally than does Timothy Findley's *The Wars* or Alice Munroe's *Lives of Girls and Women*. Unlike these and other recent Canadian novels, *The Stone Diaries* incorporates a generous selection of actual photographs into its "Motherhood, 1947" chapter, where they comprise a "family album" of sorts.[37] The photographs—labelled with names of the novel's fictional characters, many of whom are depicted in formal, stylized poses—remind us that "the camera records and justifies, yet [that] it also imprisons, arrests, and thus falsifies the fleeting moment."[38] (Of course, the reader's awareness that these photographs cannot, in fact, depict the fictional characters at all further accentuates that message of falsification, as does the dissonance between the photographic and verbal descriptions.[39]) Written descriptions of photographs elsewhere in the novel also highlight, albeit less dramatically, the act of reification inherent in both photography and autobiography. A photograph of the young Daisy depicts her "frozen in a camera's eye . . . solid, stiff, an unreadable smile playing on her lips" (61). Her smile is unreadable precisely because the camera has frozen her: has falsified her expression, imbued it with a quality unfamiliar, inscrutable. The photograph of Cuyler's tower is blurred for the same reason: the photojournalist's camera is unable to capture the transformations the stone undergoes in response to light and season, and the structure's essence is lost as a result.

Thus, life narrative is, even more than the novel, analogous to both photography and limestone in its distorting conversion of flux to stasis. That conversion highlights once again the problem of referentiality in the self-representational text. The question is whether the conversion is necessarily unidirectional. Hutcheon observes that Canadian postmodernists have foregrounded the ability of "a reactivating, a resurrecting process" to reverse writing's "reduction of dynamic process to static product."[40] Does Shields likewise affirm Daisy's potential to reverse or otherwise resist the reification associated with the creation of her life story? Metaphorically supporting this supposition is the disparity between the ostensible subject of the photographs (Barker, Warren, Fraidy, et al.) and the actual subject (Shields's daughters, other unknown but "real life" figures). The gap between signifier and signified here tentatively indicates a site of resistance to reification: the masquerade intimates that the stated subject's entrapment in the photograph is illusory. In fact, that subject has deftly eluded such fixity; it is another (always another) who is destined to gaze eternally from the photographic image.[41] More significant is Daisy's destabilization of her life story through the accretion of multiple versions and the reconstruction of others' perspectives. She might, as the quotation cited earlier attests, feel temporarily caught in *a* version of her life; however, we have seen that her engendering of multiple, unresolved versions undermines referentiality, rendering her ultimately unrepresentable. While that unrepresentability can be viewed as problematic, it does preclude reification. Further, autobiography does not threaten fluid identity with ossification when, as we have seen, that autobiography is itself rendered dynamic through the superimposition of irreconcilable narratives. In other words, to regard limestone as solely an emblem of the ossification of the self in narrative is to miss the alternate model for life narrative Shields offers. As a metaphor for accretive dynamism, limestone suggests a model that need not imperil fluid identity.

Hutcheon argues that Canadian postmodern texts figure the act of reading as one that can resurrect and reactivate the static text.[42] Implicit in my comments above is the idea that Daisy becomes not only the subject and author of her narrative but also its reader or, more accurately, its re-reader. That is, she continually rereads the fossil fragments of her life, reassembling them to devise alternate narratives. Hence Daisy's response to her encounter with Magnus Flett, whom she discovers to be still alive at 115, a national celebrity for not only his great longevity but also his (now diminished) ability to recite all of *Jane Eyre:* "Naturally it will take some time for her to absorb all she's discovered. A conscious revisioning

will be required of her: accommodation, adjustment. Certain stray elements which are anomalous in nature, even irrational, will have to be
tapped in with a jeweller's hammer. Reworked. Propped up with guesswork. Balanced. Defended. But she's willing, and isn't that what counts?"
(307). Daisy's multiple positioning—subject, author, and reader—iteral-
izes Hutcheon's observation that in Canadian postmodern metafiction,
"the object cannot be separated from the observer. 'You' [the reader]
become part of that which 'you' behold. 'You' become the source of the ...
life-giving power that transmutes the fixed illusion of print into the fluid
reality of literary experience."[43] The rereading of her life becomes for
Daisy a necessary act of self-resurrection.

Hutcheon's final comment raises another point relevant to Daisy's
capacity for escaping the reification of the self-representational genre. We
saw earlier that the narrative claims not, in fact, to be inscribed in "the
fixed illusion of print" but instead to be "written on air, written with imagination's invisible ink" (149). Daisy, paralleling a number of Canadian
postmodern authors, invokes the comparative fluidity of the oral mode
against the fixity of the written word.[44] On the other hand, of course, the
strategy is merely a provisional one, as the text is indisputably "printed in
visible ink."[45] Like Michael Ondaatje, Shields foregrounds, through
Daisy, "the impossible paradox of conserving the oral, in any sense, in
written form."[46] Hutcheon argues that postmodernism revels in the irony
of this paradox.[47] However, *The Stone Diaries*, published several years after
her seminal survey of Canadian literature, fails to conform to this model,
slyly reminding us of Hutcheon's own observation that postmodernism
resists the modernist urge for order. Unlike the novel's protagonist, the
autobiographical subject has too much at stake for revelling: Daisy is too
haunted by images of the ossified remains in the prairie limestone. For
the autobiographical subject Hutcheon's paradox becomes, figuratively
speaking, a matter of life and death. Just as Daisy's life narrative inhabits
an uneasy space between oral and written narration, so is she herself
poised between fluidity and stasis. Should she cease rereading her life's
fossils for the multiple narratives they contain, her autobiography would
lose its fluidity and she with it. Her father's words are a reminder of the
challenge she confronts in her struggle to resist reification—and of the
looming potential for failure: "'The miracle of stone,' [Cuyler] said a year
ago in his commencement address at Long College, 'is that a rigid, inert

mass can be lifted out of the ground and given wings'. Yes, but the miracle of the sculptor's imagination is required. And freshness of vision" (114). As the producer of increasingly banal, uninspired garden gnomes and miniature pyramids, the man whose carved surfaces once proffered a "shiver of yielded revelation" (65) has lost the imaginative power required to liberate stone. Daisy's efforts to avoid rigidity and inertness are provisionally more successful, but she is painfully and debilitatingly aware of the tenuousness of those efforts. Thus she cannot escape her sense while on a train travelling back to Canada that she is "a captive of her own drama" (145). And, with the disintegration of narrative into a heap of fragments in the novel's final pages, her autobiography undergoes a loss of fluidity that anticipates the stasis of her imminent death.

A HERITAGE IN STONE

"[W]hat is the story of a life?" Daisy asks from her hospital bed. "A chronicle of fact or a skilfully wrought impression?" (340). The answer, Shields demonstrates, rests somewhere in-between. Autobiography may be fashioned from the fossils of the past, but it can no more offer claims to a "truthful" representation of that past than can any other historical narrative. The story of a life rearranges those fossils, embellishing and reconfiguring them until they form a multi-hued, multi-textured tapestry. It is densely stratified, shot through with irregularities, and reshaped by erosion. The metaphorical associations between life narrative and the limestone shelf underlying the novel conjoin in the title of Cuyler's speech, "A Heritage in Stone" (86). But if those associations function to undermine the referentiality of Daisy's life narrative, they also remind us why we value the self-representational genre. We read life narrative not because it offers an unadulterated chronicle of fact, but rather for the skillfully wrought impressions it reveals, for its metamorphosis of life into story. Even Daisy's struggles to resist the ossification inherent in autobiography, painful as they may be, are beneficial in their engendering of a dynamic and richly layered narrative. *The Stone Diaries* repeatedly demonstrates Daisy's, and other characters', "gift for making a story out of things" (222). That gift may be compensation for a crippling sense of alienation, bewilderment, even paralysis. It may ultimately fail to yield insight or connection. But that it is a gift we are reminded anew each time we open the pages of Shields's novel.

ENDNOTES

1. Carol Shields, *The Stone Diaries* (Toronto: Vintage, 1993), 149. All further references are to this edition and page numbers are cited parenthetically in the text.

2. Leigh Gilmore, "The Mark of Autobiography: Postmodernism, Autobiography, and Genre," in *Autobiography and Postmodernism*, ed. Kathleen Ashley, Leigh Gilmore, and Gerald Peters (Boston: University of Massachusetts Press, 1994), 3–18. Gilmore describes that canon as the "Augustinian lineage drawn by traditional studies of autobiography [that] has naturalized the self-representation of (mainly) white, presumably heterosexual, elite men" such as Augustine, Rousseau, and Henry Adams (5).

3. Carol Shields, Lecture, Victoria College, University of Toronto, 24 February 1997.

4. Joan Thomas, "'The Golden Book': An Interview with Carol Shields," *Prairie Fire* 14, 4 (Winter 93–94): 56–62.

5. Shirley Neuman, "Autobiography: From Different Poetics to a Poetics of Difference," in *Essays on Life Writing: From Genre to Critical Practice*, ed. Marlene Kadar (Toronto: University of Toronto Press, 1992), 214.

6. Linda Hutcheon, *The Canadian Postmodern: A Study of Contemporary English-Canadian Fiction* (Toronto: Oxford University Press, 1988), 8.

7. While Shields's choice of the novel genre makes her project unique, the interrogation of autobiography's ostensible stability and referentiality is evident in much recent academic literature, which re-examines conventional assumptions about self-representational writing in light of post-structuralist views of identity and language. These studies, many by feminist scholars, include Ashley, Gilmore, and Peters, eds., *Autobiography and Postmodernism*; Shari Benstock, ed., *The Private Self: Theory and Practice of Women's Autobiographical Writing* (Chapel Hill: University of North Carolina Press, 1988); Leigh Gilmore's *Autobiographics: A Feminist Theory of Women's Self-Representation*; and Shirley Neuman, ed., *Autobiography and Questions of Gender* (London: Frank Cass, 1991).

8. Hutcheon, *Canadian Postmodern*, 4. Interestingly, Thomas observes that Shields's rural Manitoba setting is read as exotic by some foreign reviewers ("Golden Book," 61).

9. Hutcheon, *Canadian Postmodern*, 14.

10. Ibid., 22.

11. Hayden White, *Tropics of Discourse: Essays in Cultural Criticism* (Baltimore: Johns Hopkins University Press, 1978), 98.

12. Ibid.

13. Ibid., 125 (original emphasis).

14. Hutcheon, *Canadian Postmodern*, 16.

15. Winnifred Mellor, "'The Simple Container of Our Existence': Narrative Ambiguity in Carol Shields' *The Stone Diaries*," *Studies in Canadian Literature* 20, 2 (1995): 108.

16. While the scientists apparently fail in their search for the "buried life" they believe submerged in the Orkney stone (301), they do, significantly, uncover life of a different sort. Here the cynical Victoria and her Lewis uncover the "mystery" of genuine love: "Night after night," after Victoria has tiptoed past her sleeping aunt's door, "they go deeper and deeper into that mystery, sleeping and waking, and bringing to life those parts of themselves they had thought stunted, disentitled" (302). Their love affair and subsequently successful marriage cast an affirmative glow upon a novel otherwise littered with abandoned children, lonely wives, messy divorces, and messier infidelities. The myriad forms of alienation, imaged in the physical isolation of the stony prairie towns and the Orkney Islands, are an important force behind characters' various attempts to uncover affinities within apparent disorder. These attempts are evident not only in the crafting of historical narratives from isolated fragments but also in the fascination with genealogies Victoria remarks upon, in Barker's almost obsessive desire for taxonomies, in the doctor's wife's attempt to classify a butterfly she has found, in Fraidy's journal of sexual conquests, and in Daisy's making of lists under such headings as "The Things People Had to Say About the Flett/Goodwill Liaison" (155). These various efforts to "g[i]ve order to vast incomprehension" (142) are doomed to failure: as we shall see, *The Stone Diaries* evinces a typical postmodern urge to "trouble, to question, to make both problematic and provisional any [modernist] desire for order or truth through the powers of the human imagination" (Hutcheon, *Canadian Postmodern*, 2). Thus, Barker discovers that Linnaeus's system is not nearly as neat and logical as he had once believed, and even the uppermost branches of Daisy's family tree taper off into question marks.

17. See Philippe Lejeune, *Le Pacte Autobiographique* (Paris: Seuil, 1975).

18. White, *Tropics of Discourse*, 60. White's point is substantiated throughout the novel. Visitors to Cuyler's tower read in its carved images a narrative of love featuring different characterization—a "beautiful young wife" and "handsome young husband" (70, 71)—from that recounted by Daisy herself. Mrs. Hoad's "creative explanations" for the facts surrounding her husband's suicide and sons' inadequacies are profoundly disorienting for Harold, Daisy's first husband. The report of his tragicomic death (falling from a window on his honeymoon after Daisy sneezes) becomes the subject of avid speculation and multiple versions by her children.

19. Gertrude Stein, *The Autobiography of Alice B. Toklas* (New York: Vintage, 1933).

20. Occasionally, dissonances between the perspectives of author and displaced narrator of *The Autobiography of Alice B. Toklas* result in tensions. Such tension is particularly evident in the portrait of Hemingway, a man who provoked dislike in Toklas but ambivalence in Stein: hence "Toklas's" assertion that "whatever I say, Gertrude Stein always says, yes I know but I have a weakness for Hemingway" (238). Stein makes no attempt to reconcile the divergent voices, just as Shields does not impose coherence upon competing versions of events in *The Stone Diaries*.

21. For example, Stein's laughter at finding Toklas sitting beneath two paintings at a vernissage is not elucidated until much later in the autobiography. Only after

we have seen evidence of tensions between the 'Picassoites' and the 'Matis-seites' can we deduce that Stein's amusement derives from her awareness of rivalry between these two factions.

22. Elizabeth Winston, "The Autobiographer and Her Readers: From Apology to Affirmation," in *Women's Autobiography: Essays in Criticism*, ed. Estelle Jelinek (Bloomington: Indiana University Press, 1980), 109.

23. See Blanche Wiesen Cook, "'Women Alone Stir My Imagination': Lesbianism and the Cultural Tradition," *Signs: Journal of Women in Culture and Society* 4 (1979): 718–739. "She was Jewish and anti-Semitic, lesbian and contemptuous of women" (730).

24. Simone Vauthier, "Ruptures in Carol Shields's *The Stone Diaries*," *Anglophonia: French Journal of English Studies* 1 (1997).

25. Mellor, "Simple Container," 106. Mellor's comment overlooks the fact that Daisy's absence is only superficial. In fact, of course, her presence throughout is manifested in the fact that others' responses are filtered through her subjec-tivity. Daisy's decentred position in the text, her apparent invisibility and mute-ness, can also be considered in the context of feminist theories of life writing. That scholarship has remarked on the variety of strategies of self-erasure deployed by women autobiographers who recognize that authorship within the genre unmasks a "transgressive desire for cultural and literary authority" (Sidonie Smith, *A Poetics of Women's Autobiography* [Bloomington: Indiana Uni-versity Press, 1987], 50) at variance with patriarchal scripts equating femininity with self-effacement and passivity. As one critic notes, "The self that would reside at the centre of the text is decentered—and often is absent altogether—in women's autobiographical texts" (Benstock, ed., *The Private Self*, 20). In an interview Shields herself discusses Daisy in light of the invisibility of women in patriarchal culture: "I intend her to be evasive, although any woman in this century can understand what it feels like to be erased from the culture. I think of course of my mother's generation, who are more voiceless even than we are, but I think we remain fairly voiceless and powerless" (Thomas, "Golden Book," 60).

26. Shields explains her use of accretion differently, describing the novel as "a sort of postmodern box-within-a-box, within-the-box": "I'm writing the novel, and I'm writing her life, and I'm writing her knowledge of her life—so that's one. But it's also her looking at her life, so she has to be in first person sometimes to comment from outside" (Thomas, "Golden Book," 58).

27. The role chance plays in the novel is most clearly illustrated by Abram Skutari, the "Old Jew" (19) who is linked to many other characters in the novel by virtue of multiple instances of accident and coincidence. A wanderer like Magnus Flett, his work as a travelling peddler brings him to the scene of Daisy's birth, where he perceives in the newborn infant the same loneliness he himself experiences. Following the death of Mercy Goodwill in childbirth, Daisy is raised by Clarentine Flett, the estranged wife of Magnus, who had purchased *Jane Eyre* from the peddler. Clarentine's own death is the result of a collision with a bicycle purchased at Abe Skutari's by-now flourishing retail establishment. The founding of that establishment had been made possible by

a bank loan Abe had pursued while emboldened by the memory of Daisy's birth; his rags-to-riches story parallels that of Cuyler Goodwill. These "chance happenings, unexpected turns of events, [and] coincidences," evident throughout the novel, are explored by Simone Vauthier in the context of the scientific theory of chaotics ("Ruptures," 179).

28. Vauthier, "Ruptures," 179.

29. Thomas, "Golden Book," 59.

30. Ibid., 58.

31. Shields, Victoria College Lecture.

32. Betty Bergland, "Postmodernism and the Autobiographical Subject: Reconstructing the 'Other,'" in *Autobiography and Postmodernism*, ed. Ashley, Gilmore, and Peters, 134.

33. The extent to which the twentieth century constitutes the backdrop for her life is, of course, underscored by the fact that her date of birth (1905) roughly coincides with the arrival of the new century and that her date of death (not specified but sometime in the 1990s) anticipates that century's demise. Just the fact that each chapter title, with the exception of the final one, is anchored to a date or dates attests to the weight of the temporal context.

34. Winnifred Mellor offers a detailed analysis of Daisy, and the novel as a whole, in the context of post-structuralist theories of identity and language.

35. Hutcheon, *Canadian Postmodern*, 51.

36. Ibid., 139.

37. Vauthier, "Ruptures," 188.

38. Hutcheon, *Canadian Postmodern*, 47.

39. For example, Schnitzer observes that the photo of Mercy depicts a woman far less heavy than Daisy's extravagant language had led us to expect (Deborah Schnitzer, "Tricks: Artful Photographs and Letters in Carol Shields's *The Stone Diaries* and Anita Brookner's *Hotel du Lac*,' *Prairie Fire* 16, 1 [Spring 1995]: 30). Shields describes her intriguing decision to incorporate photographs in the novel: "I wanted them to be random photographs and not very good photographs, like the kind you find in the bottom of your drawer. . . . The editors found some of them in antique shops, and I found some in a postcard market in Paris. Some of them are from our family album . . ." (Thomas, "Golden Book," 59). For further discussion of Shields's use of photographs, see Vauthier and Schnitzer.

40. Hutcheon, *Canadian Postmodern*, 46.

41. Hutcheon's comments regarding *The Wars* suggest an alternate means of stating this. Drawing on the insights of Susan Sontag, Hutcheon observes with reference to Findley's written descriptions of photographs and tape transcripts that "their implication of instant access to the 'real' is what results in a distancing from the 'real'" (*Canadian Postmodern*, 49). These realistic trappings thus function as "mark[ers] of absence" (49–50). Unlike Findley, Shields does incorporate photographs in the text, suggesting a reduction in that distancing: in place of a double deferral—written description of a photograph of the 'real'—

we apparently have only a single displacement. However, our awareness that the images are not what they claim, and that certain photographs referred to in the text itself, such as the one of Daisy, are not represented in the collection, indefinitely magnifies the distance between the 'recorded' and the 'real.' The 'real' evades reification in the 'record.'

42. Hutcheon, *Canadian Postmodern*, 51.

43. Ibid., 50.

44. See Hutcheon, chapter 3, for analysis of this treatment of oral modes in recent Canadian literature.

45. Vauthier, "Ruptures," 184.

46. Hutcheon, *Canadian Postmodern*, 49.

47. Ibid., 58.

COYOTE AS CULPRIT

"Her-story" and the Feminist Fantastic in Gail Anderson-Dargatz's *The Cure for Death by Lightning*

by Heidi Slettedahl Macpherson

My story takes place in the midst of the Second World War, the year I turned fifteen, the year the world fell apart and began to come together again. Much of it will be hard to believe, I know. But the evidence for everything I'm about to tell you is there, in the pages of my mother's scrapbook, in the clippings describing the bear attacks and the Swede's barn fire and the children gone missing on the reserve, in the recipe for pound cake I made the night they took my father away, and in the funeral notices of my classmate Sarah Kemp and the others.[1]

Gail Anderson-Dargatz's first novel, *The Cure for Death by Lightning* (1997), depicts history as a (re)constructed narrative full of inevitable contradictions and competing discourses. Set in British Columbia, and thus outside the strict boundaries of a prairie narrative, the novel nonetheless engages with the land in a way that critical commonplaces suggest is uniquely associated with prairie literature. It specifically unsettles attempts to capture it, mimicking the prairie itself, which is both a geographical location and a cultural construction (which may or may not map directly onto a specific space). In *The Cure for Death by Lightning*, the reader is faced with a text that bespeaks alienation, unhousement, the overarching power of nature: elements that critics have (perhaps mistakenly?) specifically located within a prairie framework. The novel is both more and less than a prairie text. A postmodern and post-feminist text, it selectively draws on a variety of national and regional narratives in its exploration of "women's time" and magic realism, a genre more often associated with South America than with rural Canada.

The novel is a first-person narrative based on the memories of Beth Weeks, a fifteen-year-old girl who lives on a remote farm on the edge of Turtle Valley and near an untamed wilderness, or "bush" area—a space yet to be domesticated. The mixture of rural landscape and small town (linked metaphorically by "Blood Road"), Aboriginal reserve, open spaces and enclosed boundaries reveals its indebtedness to a variety of Canadian archetypal landscapes, and Anderson-Dargatz relies on concepts of women's relationship with the land to move her plot forward. It is also a text that relies on the knowledge of other texts—its multiple "post" categories (postmodern, post-feminist) suggest as much—as well as other genres.

Indeed, *The Cure for Death by Lightning* is both a traditional female *Bildungsroman*, in which an adolescent narrator comes to voice, and a text of magic realism that utilizes and indicts supernatural explanations for aberrant male behaviour. While the Second World War sets the time scale of events, as indeed the above extract notes, the war is merely a backdrop, a detail that clearly has an effect on, but does not structure, the rural community the protagonist inhabits. The narrative explores history more through Mrs. Weeks's recipe book, which also acts as a scrapbook, a site for forbidden knowledge, and a place for history and news to be located alongside myth and folklore. However, its contents are, for the most part, concealed from the protagonist and the reader alike. Snippets of recipes, the cure for death by lightning (with its "Ha! Ha!" gloss to indicate a self-consciously skeptical stance), newspaper clippings, and assorted curiosa combine to form an alternative history, which is localized, gendered, and incomplete. History thus becomes the story of the disenfranchised, and women's time and women's history are foregrounded. History is also examined through First Nations myths and recounted stories of abuse. The novel explores cycles and change, and focusses closely on the breakdown of the real through the imposition of the Coyote, that First Nations trickster figure who is a powerful source of fear and anxiety. The "truth" of Coyote's nature is never fully known in the text (given his trickster nature, perhaps this lack of clarity is formally appropriate); he shape-shifts through Beth's waking life and nightmarish dreams:

> The coyotes entered my dreams; they growled at me. Their weight made the floorboards groan. A darkness crossed the window and fell on my chest. When I cried out, the coyotes put their claws over my mouth. They lifted my nightgown. They rubbed their wet tails between my legs and over my belly. They told me to keep quiet. I hid my dream self in the darkest corner of my room and watched the shadows of the coyotes suck the breath from my body. (264)

In telling the story of Beth Weeks's encounter with the mythical and yet devastatingly real "Coyote," the novel blurs the lines of truth and fantasy. The result is a re-envisioning of the relationship between the two. As Rosemary Jackson asserts, by "[b]reaking single reductive 'truths', the fantastic traces a space within a society's cognitive frame. It introduces multiple, contrary truths. . . ."[2] In formulating the story as a recollection, the novel clearly indicates its constructed nature. Indeed, it deconstructs and reconstructs a gendered account of place and history, and raids earlier wilderness narratives while producing a startlingly original reading of the Canadian West.

The narrator Beth does not privilege a linear narrative that separates the real and the fantastical, nor does she assign more importance to "larger" events; bear attacks, barn fires, and missing children are discussed on par with recipes for pound cake. This is, after all, *her* account, and her adolescent, egocentric view ensures that the intensely personal rather than the broadly political forms the basis of her narrative. Indeed, the war itself is mentioned only in passing: as a site of escape for trapped, rural males; as the reason for the rationing of goods; as the cause of an elderly widow's fears. Hitler himself, that iconic figure who embodies fear and mania, and who remains the single most important figure of the war in cultural and critical terms, is invoked and dismissed in one small reference. Even then, he is acknowledged only in relation to the figure of Coyote, whom Bertha Moses describes as "'a clown, a scary little clown, like that Hitler, always getting into trouble'" (170). The marginalization of historically recorded events and people suggests the significance of "man-made" history in Beth

Weeks's life: war finds little place in this young woman's narrative of her rural surroundings.

In her essay "Women's Time," Julia Kristeva argues that "when evoking the name and destiny of women, one thinks more of the *space* generating and forming the human species than of *time*, becoming or history."[3] Kristeva's severing of the space-time continuum is important, for she indicates time as a "man-made" concept that obtains only after expulsion— the womb here is connected with Eden, too; thus the myth of the fall (and woman's responsibility for it) is also implied. One cannot forget that the fall also results in mortality, therefore time, yet it is only in leaving this "maternal" space that one becomes aware of linearity. Space thus becomes linked to the forbidden—to what is forbidden *to women* in particular. In *The Cure for Death by Lightning*, it is the space of exploration and the wilderness that are curtailed. When Beth wanders from the proverbial safety of the home, her mother links her behaviour to that of stray kittens. As a result, she suggests rubbing butter on Beth's "paws." Butter here signifies the family heart and maternal care, safety and concern, yet it is also a bribe, and there is the subtle suggestion that one would not return to the home willingly without this incentive. Indeed, as Beth's narrative progresses, the reader comes to understand that the home is no haven, but a place of terror and abuse.

The book sets up the opposition between the outside and home not to privilege the former, but to indicate connections that cannot be so easily polarized. Beth uses the bush as a hiding place, both for herself (she hides from "it" throughout the text, making clear her inability to name her experiences of abuse) and for products her father forbids her: the colour red, lipstick, perfume, nail polish. These accoutrements of femininity are all prohibited, and therefore treasured; despite their inferior quality and questionable appropriateness, they signify Beth's desire for female adulthood. They are significantly placed out of doors. The fact that Beth's knowledge of the human mating game is based on her own forced sexual encounters in the home and the perversion of family relations makes the use of the wilderness as a site of sexual expression all the more troubling. Moreover, the wilderness also houses the mythical and yet uncomfortably present Coyote.

Anderson-Dargatz's novel is a magic realist text, necessarily postmodern in its mixture of styles and genre, almost inevitably post-feminist in its quirky and apolitical use of motifs and ideas that have long been associated with the feminist movement. The blend of these forces is both unsettling and refreshing, as the novel strips bare some firmly held feminist principles (aberrant male behaviour, rather than being condemned, is assigned to Coyote possession) while maintaining an essential connection to the feminist *Bildungsroman*. The unequal relationship between male power (the facility to order and classify, including the right to name history through the lens of war and economic upheaval), and women's cyclical time, indicated through the (always violable) body, proceeds through a battle of the sexes, which appears at first to reinscribe the female in the position of the weak. As the novel progresses, however, it is clear that the magically powerful female has the facility to stand up to abuse, but she needs first to understand and harness her own authority, and recognize that her story forms an alternative history.

Kristeva writes that "female subjectivity would seem to provide a specific measure that essentially retains *repetition* and *eternity* from among the multiple modalities of time known through the history of civilizations."[4] Focussing on what she calls monumental time rather than linear time, Kristeva argues that women's awareness of time does not necessarily follow a sense of progression. In *The Cure for Death by Lightning*, time is linked to the female and is indeed cyclical—abuse is a constant, inexplicable deaths and disappearances are never resolved, and Coyote itself, the clearest indication of the fantastic and therefore non-linear, stands outside of time entirely. The linear history that defines "human" experience is thus set aside. Bertha Moses, matriarch of the Indian Reserve and potential guide for Beth, is the principal storyteller through whom Beth receives an awareness of Coyote and his tricks:

> "The thing is, Coyote keeps getting born, over and over," said Bertha Moses. "He rides on the spirit of a newborn into this world. It don't have to be a human newborn, it can be an animal, but once he's born into this world, he slips off and goes walking until he finds someone to have some fun with, eh? He takes that somebody over, see? Possesses him, like them demons in the Bible. Coyote has an awful thirst. Can't satisfy him nohow, that's what makes him so bad. You got to stay away from Coyote." (72)

What is inexplicable, non-linear, cyclical, and fantastic is either linked to woman or to a different "other"—Aboriginal, myth, the wilderness. When the narrator privileges fantastic explanations, she unsettles the cause-effect link that sorts and organizes the scientific world; when she focusses on the individual, she commits to the margins the historical events that "shape the world." Power, time, and history are thus all contested entities, and *The Cure for Death by Lightning* unsettles easy assumptions of truth or reality. As Diane Elam argues, "If realism can only deal with women by relegating her to romance, if real history belongs to men, and women's history is merely the fantasy of historical romance, postmodern cultural analysis of history and the 'real' offers a way of revaluing female discourse."[5]

Beth's discourse, and the discourses of her mother Maud, her potential mentor Bertha Moses, and her friend and lover Nora, follow different avenues of expression. Beth prefers silence, and finds it difficult even to supply the words necessary to purchase sanitary supplies. Beth's habits of silence and wishing away are products of her sexual abuse, an abuse that is so unspeakable that the family prefers to avert rather than confront this abuse. Beth herself refuses to believe fully in its existence, even as she believes in more fantastic occurrences.

> I removed myself into the forget-me-knots painted on the headboard of my bed, and watched from them, leaving all the fear and anger in my body. It was a moonless night. A few stars were winking just above the black trees. My room, though, was black, and my father was even blacker. He was a big black thing moving over my body, flattening me down to nothing, making me no more than a blanket on the bed. I felt nothing. I wasn't there. He didn't do that thing to me. That wisp of a black blanket under him wasn't me. The lightning arm moved, that was all. It pushed at the black shadow over it. My father took the lightning arm by the wrist and wrestled it down and made it part of the blanket he moved over, moved into. I watched him at it. (184)

Beth's "lightning arm," a product of her (disbelieved) encounter with a prairie storm, acts both as a measure of her power and of her powerlessness; it is alternatively deadened and electric. In some ways, it is a metaphor for the confusion in the novel as a whole. The confusion of inside and out, nature and the human-made, myth and history, self and other, is evident throughout. Later, when Beth is out walking, she reveals, "The dark tugged at my clothing, yanked on my hair, held my wrists with its long snaggy hand" (215). The wilderness here resembles her abusive father, in part perhaps because it is the wilderness, and not the home, which is supposed to be dangerous for the female. Indeed, underlying Beth's story only faintly is the prohibition against wandering in the woods that forms the basis of many a fairytale, "Little Red Riding Hood" included. (Indeed, it is not coincidental that the one colour forbidden to Beth is red.) All are complicit in this fiction, and even Mrs. Weeks, whose awareness of her husband's incestuous acts is coupled with the knowledge of her own sexual abuse as a young girl, reinforces this message: "I worry, you know, when you're out in the bush. You never know what's out there" (63).

Beth's mother Maud speaks more often to her own dead mother than to her living and vulnerable daughter, and prefers a discourse of the scrapbook—a text that is not a diary so much as a collection of footnotes and clippings. It thus represents less a narrative of history than an accumulation of disparate material, with no attempt made to sort and organize according to a universal principle of "great events." Moreover, this is a text that is forbidden to Beth; she can only sneak a glance occasionally, and it is entirely forbidden to any other woman. Indeed, when visitors arrive, the book is hidden because, as Beth notes, it "was a woman's pride, to have a recipe worth stealing" (64). The scrapbook represents a narrative of homemaking, of making do, but it is also a narrative of a suppressed and repressed femininity. Alongside sketchy baking instructions, Beth finds a newspaper clipping of a visit by Ginger Rogers: "All that glamour so close to home" (66). The glamour can be close to home, but not *in* the home, its presence a secret legacy for Beth. Both mother and daughter have been victims of familial sexual abuse; both were presented with silk stockings by the men who had raped them. That they desire this sign of femininity, neither can acknowledge, for to do so would be to acknowledge the history of abuse.

In contrast to the silence of the Weeks women, Bertha Moses prefers the discourse of First Nations myths, telling stories in which no final moral appears: "'It's just a story. You take what you want from it'" (170). Unlike historical narratives, told from the perspective of the victorious, Bertha's myths are told from the perspective of the disenfranchised, and are believed only by the disenfranchised—by her brood of magical and damaged daughters. Bertha herself represents a doubly displaced woman. She is the head of an entirely female household, having lost two husbands and a son. Her first marriage to a white man ensured that she lost her status as a Treaty Indian, yet the old man is buried on the Turtle Creek Reserve. Her second marriage was to an Indian man who had adopted a white man's name, but they lived outside the strict confines of the reserve. Thus she is both inside and outside the community of the First Nations people, but, at the same time, not fully accepted by the townsfolk, either, and the townsfolk vociferously reject her explanations of Coyote possession.

Recognizing her myths' inability to explain and contain fully, Bertha acknowledges the *partial* nature of her storytelling, a factor only implicit in recorded history, and often denied. Bertha's belief in the supernatural, and in the power of telling, is contrasted firmly to the silence of the Weeks family. Bertha's granddaughter Nora is the most common audience for her tales, and she acts as the go-between who reveals many of the stories to Beth. However, Nora also retreats into the non-verbal; her discourse is one of magic presence, explicit sexuality, and unnerving bodily harm. Her position is ambiguous: she represents First Nations folklore and lives (unhappily) on the reserve, yet her putative father is white; she introduces Beth to consensual sexual encounters, physical and emotional connections, yet she uses sexuality as a weapon; she implicitly protects Beth from Coyote, yet injures herself by deliberately marking and cutting her arms.

Whatever discourse is envisioned here—silence, folklore, magic presence—it is a discourse of an alternative history that is related to the unspeakable or the inexplicable. At one point, Beth claims to fill "a white ceramic bowl with the sweet green peas I'd imagined into existence..." (20). This claim of power is not questioned, but assumed. Later, when Beth is struck by lightning, the image combines the real and the fantastic: "the lightning rolled towards me in a series of loops, pinkish and sparked bluish white, like a snake all knotted up, evolving and transforming as I watched straightening itself out and coming right for me, as if meant for me" (79). The fact that lightning is an inexplicable power, which can be neither tamed or nor fully understood by science, contributes to its mystical designation here. Less fantastically, perhaps, Beth connects the swooping purple bird with visits from Bertha Moses and her entourage of female descendants who, with their multicoloured eyes and webbed fingers, bear the mark, perhaps, of Coyote.

Coyote is both a shape-shifting spirit who controls damaged men's behaviour, *and* a real animal who kills the helpless and the vulnerable, animal and human alike. Coyote is thus both inside and out of the home and the wilderness, explicitly male and focussed on female destruction. Chapter One begins, "When it came looking for me I was in the hollow stump by Turtle Creek at the spot where the deep pool was hidden by low hanging bushes ..." (3). This "it" is never described, defined, or contained, and the wilderness itself invades the space that Beth occupies:

> A cobweb stretched over my face, an ant roamed over the valleys in my skirt, spiders invaded my hair ... but I stayed still. I closed my eyes and willed it away, and after a while the sound of crashing did move off. It became nothing but wind playing tricks on me, a deer I scared up with my own fear. (3)

Throughout the novel, this magical "it" takes on various forms, and its animal, human, and imaginary natures are intertwined. Beth recognizes that it is sometimes no more than her "fear at play" (7); while this is a comfortable conclusion, it can not be supported unproblematically. "It" is out there. Later in the novel, the "thing that followed" her reveals its human nature: "I saw its footprints, a man's footprints picking up the wet dirt on Blood Road and leaving dry red tracks that quickly disappeared in the rain" (90). Later still, Beth is chased by a "path through the grass" and is confronted with "[a] pair of hands [which] clutched the boards of the fence, as if someone were leaning on it, but nobody was there" (96).

"It"—which is linked to fear, sexuality, abuse, and her father—is also inextricably linked to Coyote, who takes a variety of forms in the novel. It is a real animal that disfigures and kills other animals, but it also has its human form. Coyote is connected to Bertha's menacing stories of cyclical power and destruction, and therefore provides an explanation for aberrant behaviour. Indeed, when Beth is nearly raped by her classmate, Coyote is invoked as an explanation. Beth's rescuer, Filthy Billy, argues that Beth's attacker Parker "'doesn't know what he's doing.'" Beth disagrees, but Filthy Billy, who also believes himself to be possessed by Coyote, argues, "'He won't remember. Or if he does, he won't know why he did it. You'll see'" (146). While this sounds suspiciously like a poor excuse that rids the male of any responsibility, the reader must remember that Anderson-Dargatz never provides a definitive answer as to the question of Coyote possession. Certainly there appear to be inexplicable events attached to him. Filthy Billy, whose name obtains from his (undiagnosed) Tourette's Syndrome, is himself not immune: "Billy looked suddenly confused, moved back from me, and began swatting some invisible thing away, as if he were being attacked by a swarm of wasps. Then he was at it again, swearing under his breath and scratching. The muscles under his eyes twitched" (147).

Coyote is also invoked in an outsider "bushed" character whose mental state is at best unstable and whose habit of "sliding in and out of shadows" leads the Aboriginal people to call him Coyote Jack (11). His own position as part myth, part monster overrides his humanity throughout the novel, and his very presence is enough to cause unease: "It was Coyote Jack skulking towards the door in the hillside that was our root cellar. He looked up at the window and then he was gone. Just gone. For no reason at all, a panic came over me" (70). Later, in the most graphic example of magic realism, Beth actually sees Jack turn into a coyote:

> He twisted, batted the air, and screamed, and the scream became a howl. His body flitted back and forth between man and coyote, then the coyote dropped on all fours and cowered away from me. He bristled and growled. I stood slowly and clapped my hands, as I would to scare off any wild animal. The coyote turned and trotted off and disappeared into the bush. I slumped back into the snow, exhausted by fear, staring at Coyote Jack's clothes sitting in a heap in front of me. (272)

Beth's ability to stand up to the coyote signals a change in the narrative, and, not long after, Coyote Jack commits suicide, Filthy Billy is "cured" of his uncontrollable swearing, and Beth's father loses his power over Beth, too. This is in stark contrast to her earlier acceptance of powerlessness, as well as the opening pages of the book, which catalogue female destruction. Indeed, the beginning of the novel recalls the violent death of Beth's classmate, blamed initially on a bear, though even this "explanation" is doubted, given the facts of the case: "'They said she was pulled apart from the crotch up,' said my brother. 'And the tops of her legs were just gone. Nothing.... They say her breasts were eaten off'" (24). Only a man who is an "animal" can possibly be to blame, so it makes sense that first a bear, and then, only later, a coyote, are seen as possible culprits. That Coyote possession is the only viable explanation for female destruction and male violence indicates an unwillingness to confront the reality of women's experiences; if such destruction happens in the woods, then blame can be laid at the feet of the victims, who transgressed their proper spaces. Yet because Coyote is a myth the townspeople do not accept, they are left with the increasingly unlikely prospect of a crazed bear as culprit, and they hang on to this theory despite its blatant improbability.

Beth's father is also linked to the bear, for his bizarre and violent behaviour is blamed on his encounter with the animal the summer before. Here, the novel asserts connections that actually mask the more "realistic" explanations for John Weeks's incest and abuse of his daughter. The summer of the bear attack, Beth reached adolescence and developed her sexual body. Her father's abuse of her begins roughly at the same time, but it is easier for the narrator to assert her father's unspeakable behaviour is the result of his equally unnarratable encounter with a crazed animal.

John's repeated raping of Beth is so unspeakable that the novel only hints at it obliquely for the first third of the book: she fears his presence, and she is forced to adjust her clothing after encountering him. More subtly, perhaps, but equally telling is her habit of wearing additional layers of clothing, which only one other character ever comments upon: "'You wear so many clothes you'd think you were a suitcase,'" her lover Nora contends (187). Beth refuses to acknowledge her own tactics here, for to do so would be to acknowledge her father's behaviour. Beth's layering of clothes also has another meaning: by wearing jeans (male clothing) under her dresses (female clothing), she wishes to blur the lines between the genders in this heavily regulated, gendered community. It is only when she takes on male roles—shooting a bear, fishing, protecting livestock—that she is powerful; when she is most closely associated with her femininity, she is most at risk.

Indeed, throughout the book, what is female is damaged, sometimes irreparably, and even animals are not immune. One of Beth's secure places is the barn, and a family argument sends her out to the "solace of the cows" early in the text (63). But this very area of refuge is also defiled. Awaking one night to the sound of bellowing, Beth goes to the barn and discovers her cherished brother having sex with the lead cow. Like much of the unspeakable that exists in this text, it is never directly discussed; Beth simply rebrands her brother like all the others, "filth and shame" (206). More violently, her father performs an operation on one of the cows and forces Beth to help him. The cow had never become pregnant and is thus useless; her infertility acts as a metaphor for the sterility of the farm as a whole. Beth's father, however, attempts to interfere with nature. Since she was worthless as a milking cow, she was to be sold as beef, and he decides to remove her ovaries in an attempt to make her gain weight faster. The farmhands refuse to help, so Beth's father bullies her into joining him. He performs the botched operation in a sexual frenzy: "His face shone and he sweated in excitement" (84). Moreover, once the operation is complete, he brandishes the ovaries like prizes: "'You have these,' he said. 'This is what makes you female'" (85). In addition to these larger passages, animals are damaged and controlled by men and Coyote throughout the text. A sheep has her "cunt eaten by coyotes" (182) and one character even takes prurient pleasure in the idea that Nazis are training dogs to rape women; however, male defilement of female bodies is generally more direct than that. It is this direct and unabsolvable violence that holds the key to Beth's fantastic experiences.

If, following Jackson, we see fantasy as a way of simultaneously suggesting two contradictory modes of perceiving the real, then Beth's fantastic experiences can be better understood. A clear example is the way in which blood takes on a fantastic presence in the text, most specifically in Beth's supernatural visions. Blood is clearly female in this text, linked as it is to Nora and her ritual bloodletting, but also to menstruation and the loss of virginity. Blood is therefore part of the unspeakable, part of the taboo, yet it figures highly in Beth's imagination. A second example is the way in which hands feature in her fantastical experience, often reaching out to her. As we have already seen, she suffers abuse at the hands of men: not only from her father, but also from her male classmates and even a stranger at a dance. Perhaps it is not coincidental that Beth's fantastic experiences remain confined to the year in which she endures repeated physical and mental trauma.

Anderson-Dargatz's novel is a post-feminist text that reads like a feminist *Bildungsroman* (after all, Beth eventually finds both a voice and power), yet it allows for, indeed encourages, a reading of male violence that excuses men from culpability. *The Cure for Death by Lightning* is sited in the Canadian rural landscape, bounded by wilderness, a symbolic space that has long intrigued Canadian women writers. Kathleen Kirby argues that space connects with identity through the metaphors of geography and nation, a particularly apt connection, given the idea of the prairie that is played with and distorted in the text. According to Kirby, space

> seems to offer a medium for articulating—speaking and intertwining—the many facets, or phases, of subjectivity that have

interested different kinds of theory: national origin, geographic and territorial mobility (determined by class, gender, and race), bodily presence and limits, structures of consciousness, and ideological formations of belonging and exclusion.[6]

All these elements coexist in Anderson-Dargatz's narrative, and all speak to the *when* of the prairie as well as to the politics of the narrator's location. Space, as Kristeva argues, is more important than time, and this is graphically illustrated by the novel's use of cycles and repetition rather than linearity, and by the narrator's exploration of "unsafe" sites. Coral Ann Howells writes, "the wilderness has provided a textual space for women writers' exploration of female difference and a site of resistance to traditional structures of patriarchy and imperialism."[7] Beth forcefully resists patriarchy in the closing pages of the book when she says to her father, "'You never touch me again.... Keep your goddamned hands off me. You're my father, for Christ's sake'" (290).

For thirty years, second-wave Canadian feminists have been invoking the wilderness, rewriting a male script where the unknowable or the sexual are feared and rebuffed, only occasionally incorporated. In feminist novels of the 1970s, for instance, it is the space of the wilderness that allows—or provokes—a new sense of female identity. From the vantage point of the *fin de siècle* and all the concerns that such an era provokes, including a skepticism of any notion of certainty, as well as the dawn of a new century, it may seem that the almost essentialized nature of this retreat to the wilderness is a facile solution, and, indeed, it appears that Anderson-Dargatz takes issue with this refuge even as she graphically utilizes the retreat motif. If in paradigmatical wilderness texts, such as *Bear* by Marian Engel, *Surfacing* by Margaret Atwood, and *Abra* by Joan Barfoot, the wilderness is an essentially "real" if somewhat utopian location, in *The Cure for Death by Lightning*, the wilderness is a problematic space. It is the site of consensual sexual relations, but it also houses the ambiguous Coyote and maintains its status as a site of the inexplicable.

The final pages of the novel are devoted to an index of recipes and remedies, and a photograph of a handwritten recipe for coyote scent. Thus these pages reinforce women's history, send the reader back to the middle of the text, and invoke, yet again, Coyote. Moreover, this blend of media, and incorporation of "real" handwriting and visual evidence, reinforces the message that *The Cure for Death by Lightning* merges "fact" and "fiction"—and the reader cannot quite be sure which is which. In Margaret Atwood's *Alias Grace*, one character notes, "What he wants is certainty, one way or the other; and that is precisely what she's withholding from him."[8] These words could just as easily be applied to Anderson-Dargatz's novel. Moving away from any kind of certainty, the novel instead defers answers, questions "reality" and "history" (inserting a fantastical "her-story" instead), and unsettles both the *where* and the *when* of the prairie.

ENDNOTES

1. Gail Anderson-Dargatz, *The Cure for Death by Lightning* (London: Virago, 1997), 2. All further references are to this edition and page numbers are given parenthetically in the text.

2. Rosemary Jackson, *Fantasy: The Literature of Subversion* (London: Methuen, 1981), 23.

3. Julia Kristeva, "Women's Time," in *The Kristeva Reader* (Oxford: Blackwell, 1986), 190. Italics in original.

4. Ibid., 191. Italics in original.

5. Diane Elam, *Romancing the Postmodern* (London: Routledge, 1992), 3.

6. Kathleen M. Kirby, "Thinking through the Boundary: The Politics of Location, Subjects, and Space," *boundary 2: A Journal of Postmodern Literature* 20, 2 (1993): 174.

7. Coral Ann Howells, *Private and Fictional Words: Canadian Women Novelists of the 1970s and 1980s* (London: Methuen, 1987), 106.

8. Margaret Atwood, *Alias Grace* (London: Bloomsbury, 1996), 322.

ROBERT KROETSCH, MARSHALL McLUHAN, AND CANADA'S PRAIRIE POSTMODERNISM

The Aberhart Effect

by Russell Morton Brown

What a Godsend the radio is.

William Aberhart

POSTMODERN

[I]n every country, postmodernism has emerged at a different time and often for different reasons....

Janet Paterson, *Postmodernism and the Quebec Novel*[1]

Canadian literature evolved directly from Victorian into Postmodern. Morley Callaghan went to Paris and met the Modern writers; he, for Canada, experienced the real and symbolic encounter; he, heroically and successfully, resisted. The country that invented Marshall McLuhan and Northrop Frye did so by not ever being Modern.

Robert Kroetsch, "A Canadian Issue"[2]

One long-standing view of the evolution of Canadian culture and literature assumes that because of Canada's (post)colonial history of existence on the periphery of empire, or as a result of a deeply conservative national psyche, we have been fated not to originate new trends but to respond, usually belatedly, to developments from abroad. In this way of seeing things, postmodernism has been one of the many literary and cultural movements that has come to us from elsewhere (in this case, chiefly from the United States[3]), one that, as with other innovations and as with other American influences, was at first resisted and then, eventually, assimilated.[4]

Certainly, the Canadian novels that have been identified as important early instances of postmodern fiction—such as Leonard Cohen's *Beautiful Losers* (1966), Robert Kroetsch's *The Studhorse Man* (1969), and Michael Ondaatje's *The Collected Works of Billy the Kid* (1970), along with later examples like George Bowering's *Burning Water* (1980)—have been seen as inhabiting a tradition created by American writers such as John Barth (in *The Sotweed Factor*, 1960, and *Giles Goat-boy*, 1966); Thomas Pynchon (in *V.*, 1963, and *The Crying of Lot 49*, 1966); Donald Barthelme (especially in *Snow White*, 1967); and Robert Coover (whose short stories collected in *Pricksongs and Descants*, 1969, had been appearing in literary journals since the early 1960s); and by the Russian émigré to America, Vladimir Nabokov (especially in *Pale Fire*, 1963, but anticipated by the stories collected in *Nabokov's Dozen*, 1958). When postmodernism began to be regarded, in the 1970s and '80s, as a distinct literary movement, these American writers were grouped together as having initiated, in their fiction, a new kind of writing.[5] Barth, in his essays, voiced what was understood as the new aesthetics of these writers, especially in "The Literature of Exhaustion" (1967),[6] which became a postmodern manifesto: writers after 1960 were described as existing in a world in which there had been a "contamination of reality by dream" (71) and for which they had inherited only "exhausted" and outworn resources. The writers' task, therefore, was to complete the exhaustion of that inheritance by foregrounding—and thereby calling their readers' attention to—these exhausted forms, techniques, and conventions, creating a self-reflexivity that would also encourage self-consciousness on the part of their readers. Thus a greater break with realism and, especially, the introduction of a pervasive self-reflexivity came to be regarded as the identifying features of the new mode of fiction that emerged. Such writing came to be designated *metafiction*—and for a time postmodernism and metafiction were nearly synonymous.

An additional feature (more evident from our later perspective) of fiction of this period was its self-conscious use of historical material: Linda Hutcheon identified this as the one distinguishingly new form of postmodern fiction, which she dubbed "historiographic metafiction."[7] With these features as the identifying signs of postmodern fiction, it is not surprising that Hutcheon saw the publication of Leonard Cohen's *Beautiful Losers* in 1966 as marking the advent of postmodern fiction in English Canada.[8]

I would like to offer another way of reading the coming of Canadian postmodernism, one that calls attention to the impact of one of Canada's most controversial theorists, Marshall McLuhan, especially in the context of the two books that made his reputation—*The Gutenberg Galaxy* and *Understanding Media*—and that singles out a different novel, one published in the same year as *Beautiful Losers*, as marking the advent of a particularly *Canadian* postmodernism. That novel is Robert Kroetsch's tale of prairie politics, *The Words of My Roaring*,[9] and it introduced a kind of postmodern fiction different from that being celebrated in the US. It began a Canadian strain of postmodernism that was not a response to or continuation of American literary influences, but a way of telling the story that grew directly out of Kroetsch's experiences of his prairie milieu. It also reflected Kroetsch's need to negotiate between Modernist ways of shaping the tales of those experiences and what McLuhan was telling him about a new way of telling the tale.

One thing that particularly intrigues me about identifying both McLuhan and Kroetsch as founders of postmodernism in Canada is the fact that both come from prairie backgrounds. (Both were born in Alberta: Kroetsch stayed there through university; McLuhan grew up in Manitoba.) Thus, while American postmodernism is identified with the urban east, Canadian postmodernism seems to have a prairie flavour about it. It is a prairie postmodernism that arose from a specific set of historical circumstances. Despite this difference in their ages—McLuhan was born in 1911, and Kroetsch in 1927—both men came to maturity in a region that was experiencing, to an extreme degree, severe disruptions of drought and economic depression along with the powerful rhetoric of apocalyptic evangelism and populist politics. These experiences served as a kind of inoculation against the "international" Modernism that had recently come to dominate the cosmopolitan centres in North America and Europe.

Arguments about the influence of the landscape on prairie writing and prairie culture have been made for a long time now. In his 1973 novel *Gone Indian*, Kroetsch playfully gives these a contemporary turn by having the overweening Professor Mark Madham (a comic portrait of the author) suggest that the prairies engenders a postmodern view of the self when he observes that "the consequence of the northern prairies" on "human definition" is "the diffusion of personality into a complex of possibilities rather than a concluded self."[10] This suggestion that the Canadian prairie landscape might inevitably be productive of postmodernism seems largely self-mocking, but the idea has been seriously advanced by Frances Kaye and Robert Thacker. In their 1994 essay, "'Gone Back to Alberta': Robert Kroetsch Rewriting the Great Plains," they postulate that Kroetsch's postmodernism found a congenial home on the Canadian prairies (which they treat as part of the larger geographical area of the North American Great Plains) because it was "an intellectual movement that defines itself by what it is not . . . its primary characteristics *dis*continuity and indeterminacy," which "aligns it with the region of the Great Plains, habitually defined in terms of what it lacks—*lack* of rainfall, *lack* of trees, *lack* of hills."[11] While I would not want to deny the remarkable power of the prairie landscape, in the rest of this essay I do want, after suggesting what was distinctive about Kroetsch's postmodernism, to direct our attention to other factors.

Kroetsch has long been recognized as having taken the lead in establishing the postmodern movement in Canada.[12] But it has usually been assumed, as it is by Stanley Fogel in *A Tale of Two Countries: Contemporary Fiction in Canada and the United States*, that Kroetsch's commitment to postmodernism came as a result of his experiences after he left the Canadian prairies, and was shaped by his time on the faculty of an American university.[13] In this view, Kroetsch's years from the early 1960s to the mid-1970s at the State University of New York at Binghamton (where he helped to found *boundary 2: A Journal of Postmodern Literature*) were crucial in shaping his fiction, his criticism, and his poetry. In this construction of the narrative, Kroetsch's role in Canada becomes that of a conduit for American postmodernism, increasingly so after his return to the Canadian prairies in the mid-1970s.

Such a critical history can make Kroetsch either a villain or a hero. It made him an agent of infection for the hyper-nationalist Robin Mathews, who (in *Canadian Literature: Surrender or Revolution*, 1978) strenuously objected to the success of Kroetsch's fiction in Canada on the grounds that he had given us only "the novels of an expatriate ... moving the US anarchist individualist onto the Canadian landscape as a part of imperial myth replacement."[14] In contrast, in a prefatory note to *A Tale of Two Cities*, Fogel celebrated Kroetsch as a "figure of rapprochement," valuing his ability to bring together the otherwise "unassimilable modes" of American and Canadian criticism and aesthetics that divided the two nations, importing an American dynamism into the too-staid, too-conservative Canadian literary establishment.

I want to avoid such evaluations entirely by offering another way of seeing things. While Kroetsch undoubtedly did encounter, as a result of his years in the US, much that stimulated him artistically, his developmental years on the prairie preconditioned his aesthetics and made him receptive to the postmodern ideas he encountered there—because he had already begun to find his way towards the creation of a fiction that permitted him a distinctive way of inserting himself into that emerging movement.

MYTH AFTER MODERNISM

> life is a peculiar medley
> Robert Kroetsch, *The Words of My Roaring*

The novel that brought Kroetsch to the attention of the Canadian literary and critical community was *The Studhorse Man*, which won the Governor General's Award in 1969. Published three years after *The Words of My Roaring*, that novel may have been successful because, unlike the novel that had preceded it, its overt use of metafiction made it recognizably "contemporary" and (to later readers) recognizably postmodern. In contrast, when *The Words of My Roaring* appeared in 1966, what first struck most readers' attention was its depiction of small-town prairie life, in conjunction with a use of myth that looked Modernist.

The way myth provides the subtext for that 1966 novel's retelling of prairie history, along with the degree to which the novel still operates within a realist tradition—though tilted towards the tall tale and handled with more comic verve than in most previous fiction in Canada—made the novel look more like Modernist rather than postmodernist fiction, particularly like the kind of fiction influenced by that late Modernism arising out of Northrop Frye's influence. Regarded in this way, *The Words of My Roaring* seems consonant with the work that had grown out of James Reaney's contact with Frye and was being made visible in Reaney's magazine *Alphabet* from 1960 forward. Reaney's goal was to find a way to join transcendental mythic forms with representations of the local. Reaney's idea (expressed in his first editorial for *Alphabet*) of balancing "Documentary on one side and myth on the other" looked like a description of the way Kroetsch's novel blended "local" concerns and history—small-town Alberta undergoing the political crisis and the drought-stricken climate of the 1930s—with a mythic understructure.[15] For example, in one of the most striking scenes in the novel, the protagonist, J.J. Backstrom, an undertaker-turned-prairie-politician who has described himself as "a heller with women" (4), seduces the daughter of his opponent—her middle name is Persephone—in a garden. Readers who recognized this scene as a contemporary retelling of the Greek myth of Hades abducting the goddess of spring may have felt they had found the novel's presiding myth.

This response does provide a way of reading the novel, and it would especially have done so for readers who, in 1966, were still accustomed to Modernist conventions,[16] but it is, in fact, responsive to only a small part of the way myth is used in *The Words of My Roaring*. Kroetsch's handling of myth is not, as it at first seemed, simply a continuation of a Modernist aesthetic: it is also a reconsideration of Modernist presumptions. Looking back from the vantage of *Labyrinths of Voice* (*LV*) in 1982, Kroetsch does not see himself as having used myth to produce the sense of underlying importance and universality that Modernists like T.S. Eliot thought it created, nor does he want to move towards the transcendent vision of human possibility that Frye thought myth could bring.[17] Though he says he was obsessed with myth when he began writing, he also felt—in contrast to earlier Modernists *and* to the writers inspired by Frye—that myth could be dangerous, potentially an "entrapment."[18] He therefore wished to avoid the example of "the Modernist [who] was tempted by the cohesive dimensions of mythology" (*LV*, 112). Instead, for Kroetsch, one of the tasks for the *post*modern writer would be to guard against myth's taking control of the narrative. His way of doing so, according to his retrospective account, was to seek "the decentering rather than the centering function of myth," trying "to avoid both meaning and conclusiveness" by continually "retelling, . . . transforming the story" (*LV*, 131). Such constant retellings of myth would, by decentring it, allow it to "become generative again" (*LV*, 131).

There are several important differences between Modernist handlings of myth and Kroetsch's that arise from this desire to decentre. In *The Words of My Roaring* and the fiction that followed it, because the protagonists are simultaneously bumbling *and* mythic-heroic, Kroetsch's myths are both important structural elements *and* ironized and parodied.[19] But treating myths farcically is not the only way Kroetsch decentres them. A second strategy, one shared with many postmodernists, is his move away from depth. Rather than exploiting the Modernist model of encouraging readers to feel that by peeling an onion, they can struggle to reach a work's hidden "depths," Kroetsch brings "depths" to the surface by being over-explicit in the way he calls attention to at least some of the myths and mythic elements within his novels. Thus, when that woman named Persephone meets an undertaker in a garden of asphodels—just as in *The Studhorse Man* when a horse named Poseidon delays the protagonist's journey home in a tale told by a narrator named Demeter; or when, at the end of *Gone Indian*, the hero rides off on a snowmobile called Sleipnir with a woman named Beatrice—we are confronted with mythic allusions more overt than any found in those precursor works, such as *Heart of Darkness* or *Ulysses*, that defined mythic Modernism.

There is a third feature of Kroetsch's treatment of myth that marks him as postmodernist rather than Modernist, one that runs counter to my last point and is especially important to my argument here: once we really begin to look, we find that these novels have *many* mythic levels—levels upon levels, we might say; vertiginously layered one upon another—and produce so many allusions to precursor and archetypal narratives, and suggest so many other texts to be investigated or thought about, that there is no resting point for the reader. In contrast to *Heart of Darkness* or *Ulysses*, no presiding subtext can be identified. In mythic Modernism, the readers' interpretive powers are challenged; in novels like *The Words of My Roaring*, *The Studhorse Man*, and *Gone Indian*, they are rather acknowledged and engaged while at the same time overloaded and overwhelmed.

Consider again that figure of Persephone in the garden. She may seem like a call to us to read Kroetsch's novel in terms of a single, overarching, mythic narrative until we recall that the full name of that woman in the garden is Helen Persephone Murdoch. Thus, even while her middle name evokes mythic stories about the Greek Queen of the Underworld and the renewing power of spring, her first name (though it may reinforce that mythic narrative with its punning reference to "Hell") links her to another, quite different, Greek story, one that is no less useful as a frame (the political contest in the novel's foreground is heightened by the implied comparison to the Trojan War, and our understanding of the central characters may be influenced by connections we may make with the abduction of Helen). This second allusion makes us hesitant about resting our final understanding of the novel on the Persephone narrative, yet we also hesitate to abandon that reading. The existence of different mythic parallels that will not readily cohere led Peter Thomas, in the first full-length critical treatment of Kroetsch's work, to observe:

> This continual sense of metamorphosis, as one mythic context gives way to another, related but distinguishable, is entirely characteristic of Kroetsch's method. Any attempt to insist upon a single referential narrator, such as the Pluto-Demeter-Persephone archetype, must be forced. It is more instructive to see his writings as inhabiting a symbolic field dominated by the paradoxical union of Eros and Thanatos and drawing upon the immensely rich material this contains....[20]

In his own analysis of *The Words of My Roaring*, Thomas nevertheless emphasizes the "Orphic and narcissistic motifs, which reconcile erotic and thanaturgical elements."[21]

For other critics, other myths. Robert Lecker, in his later discussion of Kroetsch's body of work, saw Backstrom as "clearly a Dionysian, Priapic figure."[22] Kenneth Graham evocatively linked Backstrom to both Christ and "Hermes Psychopompos, the only Olympian god who can pass between the upper world and the realm of Hades where Persephone dwells when the land is waste."[23] I would suggest that Kroetsch's use of myth in the novel includes all these but, by intertwining its classical allusions with those drawn from a range of other cultures, it goes well beyond this already dazzling multiplication of classical traditions, interlayering its classical background with numerous and sometimes self-contradictory biblical allusions, and with large invocations of Babylonian mythic fields of reference.

Let me begin with the biblical field. The protagonist's full name, *John Judas* Backstrom, might seem biblical load enough to carry, but his nickname, J.B., associates him with a biblical character from the Hebrew scriptures by linking him (via Archibald MacLeish's 1958 play, *J.B.*) to Job. In addition, the allusion in the novel's title is to Psalm 22, and thus connects Backstrom to both the Psalmist and Christ (whose last words come from this Psalm). The name of Backstrom's best friend is Jonah Bledd (another J.B.), which not only connects the novel to another Old Testament narrative, but, as a small sentence in itself, invites allegorical readings of the whole. But the text sets up other possible mythic parallels for Backstrom's friend, making it impossible to say how exactly this allegory would work.

These observations do not nearly begin to suggest the superabundance of intertextuality and mythic layering and overlaying in *The Words of My Roaring*. Helen Persephone Murdoch's *surname* moves the novel's multiplications of allusion into quite a different area: it allows the reader to make a connection between that name—specifically in the case of Helen's father, Doc Murdoch, against whom Backstrom is campaigning—and the Babylonian deity Marduk, a lawgiver "who cares for human beings and their sufferings"[24] and whose overthrow is sought by the oppositional underworld figure of Erra—who controlled floods and influenced the fertility of the land.[25] That Kroetsch wants us to make this connection becomes clear when Doc Murdoch's garden, in which Backstrom makes love to Helen, is said to resemble "the Hanging Gardens of Babylon" (156). And Helen Persephone, in this context, becomes linked to Ereskegal, another goddess queen ruling over another underworld.[26]

In Backstrom's predictions of rain for the drought-stricken prairies, Kroetsch not only interweaves echoes of the biblical story of Noah[27] but also invites further connections with Babylonian myth. The Bible's story of the flood, scholars now suggest, is derived from *The Epic of Gilgamesh*, and if one comes to this novel from a reading of that ancient epic, its presence is felt everywhere. *Gilgamesh* may be the last major intertext we notice in the novel, but once we do observe it, we can see that it has been extensively used as a structuring device and subtext. Thus, where the canonical Modernists investigated relatively few mythic sources, and those almost exclusively in the Western tradition, Kroetsch draws not only on Greek myth and on biblical sources but on the major narratives of Near Eastern mythology—entirely leaving behind the Modernists' mappings of myth. And, in addition to all this mythic free play, *The Words of My Roaring* is further interlayered with folklore motifs and echoes of other texts.[28]

The effect of this superabundance of myth, intertextuality, and allusion is to create a work of fiction that, even while making use of the resources of the Modernist tradition, resembles what Michel Foucault had in mind when he wrote that, in contrast with the unexamined historicism of previous eras—which had supplied "romanticism with the knight's armor, and the Wagnerian era [with] the sword of a German hero":

> [T]he new historian, the genealogist, will know what to make of this masquerade. He will not be too serious to enjoy it; on the contrary, he will push the masquerade to its limit and prepare the great carnival of time where masks are constantly reappearing. No longer the identification of our faint individuality with the solid identities of the past, but our 'unrealization' through the excessive choice of identities.[29]

Vincent B. Leitch's characterization of Foucault's position as described here could also serve as a description of a Kroetsch novel: "Extending traditional monumental history, we practice parodic and farcical exaggeration, pushing everything 'sacred' to the carnivalesque limit of the heroic."[30]

Thus, giving his protagonist a name that invites the reader to look for parallels with Judas and also with John (and not only with the John whose gospel began with the Word, but also, in a novel about the need for renewal by water and about the conjunction of beginnings and endings, with John the Baptist and with John the author of the Apocalypse), while also associating this protagonist with both Christ and Satan, with both the mischievous Erra and with the heroic Gilgamesh, Kroetsch has created a deliberately unstable text, using what we now recognize as the *postmodern* logic of surplus, supplement, and excess. His is the technique of a writer who will later have one of his characters tell us "There are no truths, only correspondences,"[31] an aphorism that could be taken as the credo of this kind of postmodernism. These texts have about them a mythic supersaturation that might be described in terms like those Kroetsch will later use to introduce a selection of poems by another prairie westerner, Eli Mandel: "a collage in which the pictures are placed, not beside each other, but on top of each other; [so that] each picture evokes, announces, its own violation; every violation evokes its own parodic inversion."[32]

Indeed, while Kroetsch's narratives may be overtly comic and his retelling of myths already parodic, this act of overloading the text with a multiplicity of myths adds a further dimension to the comedy *because* of the interpretive instability it introduces. *The Words of My Roaring* dramatizes that comic instability when Backstrom uncovers a calendar with a picture that he ambiguously identifies as "the Wise Men or the Three Shepherds or the Three Kings," adding: "I can never quite tell those Arabs apart" (170).

Kroetsch thus created, through a deliberately bewildering overlay, a *mythic postmodernism* that seems to have been his own way of finding a suitable form. If he had any literary precursors who guided him to this way of writing fiction, it may not have been among the famous American postmodernists so much as two mid-century writers, each with a kind of Canadian pedigree and neither usually associated with postmodernism: Malcolm Lowry, especially in *Under the Volcano*, and Saul Bellow, in *Henderson the Rain King*—novels that were unusual for their time in their use of an overload of myth and intertextual material.[33] In responding to, and in further developing, what were experiments for these earlier writers, in turning them into a recognizable *mode* of fiction, Kroetsch created a new opening in the Canadian tradition. Through it have emerged some of our most engaging and important works of fiction. This kind of multilayered mythic overload can be seen not only in Kroetsch's novels (most particularly—in addition to the prairie triptych formed by *The Words of My Roaring*, *The Studhorse Man*, and *Gone Indian*—in *Badlands* [1975] and in *What the Crow Said* [1978]), but also, in various shades and handlings, in novels such as Mordecai Richler's *St. Urbain's Horseman* (1971) and *Solomon Gursky Was Here* (1989);[34] Jack Hodgins's *The Invention of the World* (1978); Adele Wiseman's *Crackpot* (1989); Margaret Atwood's *Surfacing* (1972) and (especially) *The Robber Bride* (1995); Timothy Findley's *Not Wanted on the Voyage* (1984) and *Headhunter* (1993); and Michael Ondaatje's *The English Patient* (1992).

This kind of mythic postmodernism is, I would point out, quite different from what (at least initially) typified the way myth and narrative would be handled in the American postmodern fiction. There, when myth was employed, the realist surface narratives that Modernists had used to play off against their mythic subtexts tended to be displaced entirely by fabulous, surreal, and quasi-mythic narratives—as in Barth's *Giles Goat-boy*, Coover's *The Public Burning*, and Ishmael Reed's *Flight to Canada*—or even by narratives that directly (if humorously) portrayed mythic events—as in

Barth's *Chimera*, with its tales of Scheherazade, Perseus, and Bellerophon. Indeed, Barth might be said, in that collection of novellas and in some of the stories in *Lost in the Funhouse*, to make use of myth to *stabilize* his exhausted and deconstructed narratives and techniques, while in Kroetsch's fiction of this period it is the myth that destabilizes the narrative and the myth itself that is deconstructed.

MYTH MEETS PRAIRIE HISTORY

> I have also been concerned with what we might call deconstructing the myth. . . . One can try to move the other way, back to the specifics, the occasions of narrative.
>
> Robert Kroetsch, *Labyrinths of Voice*

When Fogel complained, in *A Tale of Two Countries* in 1984, that Canadian writers had not yet made use of the innovations that came with the rise of postmodernism, much of his regret about this fact arose from the lack of what he found so attractive in contemporary American fiction: its counter-discursive nature, the way it set itself in opposition to the authoritarian discourse of the American political and corporate establishments by serving "to denaturalize the facts, forms, or disciplines by which Americans authenticate and understand experience" (71). Fogel felt that this oppositional fiction could flourish in the US rather than in Canada because intellectuals and artists in America had a well-established national narrative to contest. Acknowledging that because Canadians were still in the process of constructing their national narratives, they had less need to deconstruct a threatening national order, Fogel nevertheless regretted the lack, in Canadian fiction, of the "feisty, obstreperous quality" of American postmodern experimentation (72). And though he may have been Canada's most successful postmodernist, Kroetsch was not, in Fogel's reading of his work, a counterdiscursive writer. In contrast to Coover and William Gass, who had had to "confront a solidly constructed and ensconced edifice that has for some time gloried in its sense of self, making greedy, deadly history along the way," Fogel thought that Kroetsch, as a Canadian, had never found himself in the situation of being confronted by a hostile "monolith or reified set of values" (81).

Although other critics, many of whom were attacking American postmodernism for its *lack* of a political stance, might not have read the politics of the situation quite as Fogel did, counterdiscursivity was a shaping force on American postmodernism. Indeed, it seems to have long been the fate of the American artist to feel she or he is in resistance to whatever establishments there be. But I think Fogel overlooked the counterdiscursivity that was also present in Kroetsch's work, a pervasive counterdiscourse that is aimed not at dominant national discourses but at the power of myth—a power to which Kroetsch was also attracted.

Why did Kroetsch respond in this way to myth? What simultaneously drew him to myth yet led him to feel threatened by it? The answer lies, I believe, in the subject matter of *The Words of My Roaring*, the novel that also announced Kroetsch's new way of handling myth. Readers familiar with prairie history will recognize in the background to this story of Backstrom, impoverished and restive in his job as undertaker, campaigning for elected office in 1935, the Alberta provincial general election, which brought into power the world's first Social Credit government—and one of the few Social Credit governments ever elected anywhere.[35] Such readers would also recognize the leader of Backstrom's party, a radio evangelist called John George Applecart, as a lightly fictionalized version of the founder and leader of Alberta's Social Credit Party: William ("Bible Bill") Aberhart. Readers who recognized that historical background would know from the outset of Kroetsch's tale what the likely outcome of Backstrom's campaign would be: in the 1935 election nearly every SoCred candidate was swept into office on Aberhart's coattails.

One of the prairie's most colourful politicians, Aberhart is an important figure in Kroetsch's *personal* mythology. Kroetsch has mentioned him in more than one interview, and in his travel book *Alberta*, where a detailed portrait of this charismatic figure is Kroetsch's only digression away from landscape and into history. Drawing on John A. Irving's extensive (and largely hostile) portrayal of Aberhart in *The Social Credit Movement in Alberta*,[36] Kroetsch observes that

> in his size and energy, in his hyperbolic humour, in his delight in talk and argument, in his longing for, and suspicion of, respectability, in his Christian humility and his will to excel and dominate, in his distrust of the Ontario from which he came, in his anticipation of damnation for the wicked and rewards (both spiritual and material) for the good—he was the embodiment of a people's dreams and nightmares.[37]

In a rare personal moment in that travel book, Kroetsch also recalls how, in 1935, he himself "was eight years old" and he tells us that what has remained in his memory from "that frenzied summer" is "not Aberhart's words, but his voice" (25).

That last phrase is significant. Though Kroetsch characterizes Aberhart as a figure of epic proportions, Applecart is present, in *The Words of My Roaring*, only as a voice heard over the radio.

> Inside of two seconds he was Who-ering this and Who-ering that. . . . Sometimes we couldn't exactly follow. But we could understand. Applecart had got it into his head that things can be changed. He pointed out how everything was absolutely wrong: the price of goods brought and sold, the nature of dividends. The cultural heritage itself was threatened. He just ripped loose about everything. It made us all feel a lot better, even me.
>
> . . .
>
> "Who?" he said. He let his voice drop. "I ask you, who?" And he stopped, he left us hanging. "Who is that red beast of a Who'er?" . . . Applecart let out a roar. "The fifty Big Shots," he roared, his voice crushing the silence. "That's who!" he said. "That, I mean to tell you, my dear tormented friends, is who!"
>
> . . .
>
> Applecart was onto the dirty Easterners who were gouging the West. He had built up to that and now he was onto them. He was talking about the Second Coming and the Last Judgment, the final reckoning of the Fifty Big Shots. Just wait, he said. And he gave them a blanket condemnation. "Just wait, and in short order the wicked will be punished and the suffering good will be rewarded." It was a great formula. (32–36)[38]

I think Applecart/Aberhart is reduced to a voice on the radio for reasons other than those of narrative economy. In telling us that what remained in his memory was "not Aberhart's words, but his voice," Kroetsch becomes one more witness to the power of that famous voice. Irving records being told: "He had a voice that made the pilot lights on your radio jump. You simply had to believe him";[39] one of the respondents in Barry Broadfoot's oral history of the prairies describes hearing Aberhart at a political rally this way: "He had a marvellous voice, a beautiful voice, and his speech just rolled out, and everything he said made sense. That was Mr. Aberhart.

Nobody there except a few, I guess, knew that what he was saying was not going to work."[40]

But what made Aberhart's voice special and gave it such an important place in history was the fact that Aberhart was among the first anywhere to utilize the new *technology* of voice—broadcast radio—as a way of influencing a large population. One of the very first evangelists to see the advantage of the new medium, Aberhart took his religious ministry onto the airwaves in 1925, just six years after the advent of general broadcasting, attracting mass audiences never before available to a single speaker. (Irving estimates that Aberhart reached a radio audience of perhaps half a million listeners.[41]) When, in response to the Great Depression, Aberhart converted to Clifford Douglas's Social Credit doctrines in 1932 and began to mix politics with religious ministry, the world was still in the process of understanding just what the potential impact of this new technology might be. His use of radio created a potent and intoxicating combination, one that enabled him to bring into existence a new Canadian political party and to launch his political career.

Looking back, we can see that Aberhart's impact was the result of an unusually fortuitous combination of person, time, and place. His rhetorical talents and the power of a message perfectly pitched to the beliefs and contemporary experiences of his prairie listeners and their circumstances were unexpectedly amplified by the new technology that had suddenly become available. Radio evangelists became among the most successful of early exploiters of broadcast technology. Perhaps this was because, as Jeffrey Sconce suggests in his fascinating study, *Haunted Media: Electronic Presence from Telegraphy to Television*, the experience of early radio produced a combination of utopian and spiritual fantasies in its listeners—as well as provoking anxieties.[42]

The immense power of this newly emerging technology of broadcast radio was heightened on the prairies. Observing that Aberhart's "greatest attraction" may have been "his capacity to project his personality over the air," Irving wrote: "Whoever has observed in Alberta the far-flung loneliness of the country-side ... can appreciate the psychological significance of the penetration of Aberhart's radio voice into thousands of isolated farm homes. He thundered his exposition of Social Credit in a voice which had many tones and ranged up and down the octaves."[43] As the protagonist of Max Braithwaite's 1965 novel about the prairie thirties,

Why Shoot the Teacher, similarly remarks: "The overworked phrase, 'magic of radio,' had real meaning on the prairies in the thirties. It was the beginning of the end of the soul-killing isolation."[44] And as one of the locals tells the young teacher in Braithwaite's semi-autobiographical novel, what many were listening to in rural Saskatchewan was

> "Aberhart over in Alberta. He's trying to do something about it. Ever listen to him on the radio?" ... "Too bad. Why that man's talking sense. Give people the money, he says. Twenty-five dollars a month to every man, woman, and child.... Don't you see? He earns it by being a consumer. You pay a man for consuming. So he buys things. Buys things to keep the wheels of industry turning.... Brought you a couple of books. One by Major C.H. Douglas. He's the British economist Aberhart keeps talking about. Another by G.D.H. Cole, *A Guide Through World Chaos.* We've got chaos right enough...." (76–77)

Aberhart's radio broadcasts were the key to the 1935 election. "It may be doubted if there could have been a Social Credit movement without Aberhart's use of the radio," Irving says.[45] Social Credit may have originally seemed an economic program and a political movement, but Aberhart transformed it, through his intuitive genius for media and his populist and charismatic religious leadership, into something else, something mythic. Irving is only one of many observers to describe the campaign of 1935 as resembling a "crusade":

> Old-line politicians and partisan newspapers had tried desperately to make a political issue out of Social Credit. They had failed hopelessly. They must fail hopelessly because the Social Credit movement was not a political party. What, then, was it? As the spring of 1935 passed into summer, Aberhart's mass following became aware of the answer. The Social Credit movement was, under God, a crusade beyond politics.[46]

Aberhart's spiritual crusade was contextualized by a large mythic drama, one that, at the end of the nineteenth century, was being newly promulgated by the rise of Christian evangelism, the tale of a final combat between good and evil in the earth's final days. While these doctrines were preached by many, Aberhart was an important early agent in shaping this powerful—and still enduring—narrative.

It has become something of a commonplace among apocalypse scholars to suggest that, to succeed, apocalyptic movements need a body of believers who feel threatened, overwhelmed, or oppressed. In *Disaster and the Millennium*, Michael Barkun suggests that though "disasters serve to predispose individuals" to millenarian and apocalyptic belief systems, disaster by itself is "a necessary but hardly a sufficient condition." Other contingencies Barkun points to are an area that is "relatively homogeneous and insulated," in which there need to be "multiple rather than single disasters." In such a setting, apocalyptic movements emerge only if "a body of ideas or doctrines of a millenarian cast [is] readily available; [and] a charismatic figure ... present to shape those doctrines in response to disaster."[47] All these conditions were present in 1935 Alberta. World War I, together with the less clearly defined cataclysms of religious modernism and cultural modernity, set the stage for Aberhart's 1920s articulation of his end-time doctrines, and the visible ecological and economic disasters of the 1930s then made the prairies ripe for Aberhart's translation of these religious beliefs into utopian political doctrines.

To prairie farmers listening to his radio broadcasts as agricultural markets collapsed and terrifying droughts burned up their crops, Aberhart's apocalyptic narratives must have had the immediacy of local weather forecasts. As Kroetsch observed in *Alberta*, about the 1930s:

> The Canadian prairies were hit as hard as, or harder than, any region in the world.... In the experience of starvation and suffering and poverty, a whole society found a new common denominator, the ambition to be fulfilled was replaced by the need simply to survive. Out of this recognition, or resignation, came a religious fundamentalism and a political upheaval that were fused in the Alberta election of 1935. The soil and the wind and the absence of rain had made an agricultural society aware of new dimensions of daily despair and ultimate hope: in that fateful year, in that year of decision for contemporary Alberta, it was significantly to the Book of Revelation that political leader William Aberhart turned for deliverance. (5–6)

When Backstrom brings his constituents into his home to hear a radio broadcast, and we are given a sample of Applecart's Revelation-laden rhetoric ("'The first angel sounded,' he said, 'and there followed hail and fire mingled with blood, and they were cast upon the earth; and the third part of trees was burnt up, and all green grass was burnt up'"), he connects this mythic account with his own experience of the external world:

> He was speaking my language. Everything was gone to the dogs, gone haywire and kaput.... I couldn't tear myself away.
>
> Applecart was laying it on—without exaggerating by so much as an ell. Our trees and grass were the living proof; you could see which third of the world we lived in. (33)

Aberhart's odd combination of apocalypticism, new technology, and progressive (if utopian) economic programs created one of the most effective blends of visionary and political rhetoric in the history of North American politics. Joining his constantly evolving religious vision to an eccentric reinterpretation of Major Douglas's already eccentric economic salvationism, while leaning heavily on the Book of Revelation for his controlling mythology, he turned the 1935 Alberta general election into an event of immense symbolic import and gave his followers a sense that they were taking part in a drama of cosmic proportions.

Kroetsch later said he was harder on Aberhart in his novel than in *Alberta* "because in that imaginative construct he becomes a more dangerous, and I think more interesting figure."[48] What makes Applecart/ Aberhart both dangerous *and* interesting in *The Words of My Roaring* is his role there as religious demagogue. The liquor that Backstrom keeps hidden inside his radio is clearly meant to suggest that its broadcasts were a potent intoxicant. Kroetsch shows Applecart's sermons both identified with and displacing that whisky: Backstrom, listening to that radio evangelist "laying it on," is reminded that his "micky of rye was concealed in the back of that radio," and thinks: "I was dying for one small swig. But all that hard-hitting truth was enough to make a man swear off for life" (34).

Irving records the range of intoxicating effects—the excitement, the deep divisions, the fear, the hostility, and even the paranoia—that resulted from Aberhart's politics. "To Social Crediters the provincial election of 1935 was a glorious episode in a glorious movement.... To Liberals and Conservatives it was an exhibition of mass hysteria unparalleled in the history of democracy";[49] "there was always the tendency under the stimulation of great mass meetings, for more or less normal people to behave like the most fanatical of Aberhart's followers. Even when seemingly dormant, religious feelings contained explosive possibilities, especially after the developments of bitter opposition to the Social Credit movement."[50] One anti-Aberhart farmer who had previously been a well-liked member of his community found the shunning and the "silent hostility of his neighbours so unbearable, that he decided to leave Alberta."[51]

While Kroetsch found Irving's account useful in writing *The Words of My Roaring*, he didn't need Irving to tell him about the divisive nature of Aberhart's doctrines. In *Alberta*, Kroetsch recalls how his "father, a die-hard Liberal, was under constant attack" during Aberhart's campaign because "the Liberals were associated ... with the bankers and the financial 'barons'" (25). In *Labyrinths of Voice*, he alludes to the effect this experience had on him when he was "a child during that period of the thirties": "my father was anti-Social Credit, vehemently so in a community that was going Social Credit. I had a doubly bad experience of the whole movement, not only on ideological grounds but on personal grounds as well. It *was* a bad experience" (122).

Kroetsch does not mention what must have been the most disturbing aspect of that childhood experience—something that emphasizes more than anything else the real dangers of Aberhart as mythmaker and as pro-claimer of myth—which is that because they were Roman Catholics, Kroetsch and his family were members of the religion demonized in Aberhart's radio sermons as followers of the Antichrist, and as the agents of evil who were implicated in the apocalypse of which Aberhart spoke, responsible for bringing visible ruin upon the earth and its faithful.

Given this background, it makes a special kind of sense to find Kroetsch attracted to what we now think of as postmodernism—and especially to those theoretical approaches related to the postmodern movement, such as deconstruction, with its anti-totalizing poetics of resistance. Think about how usefully such a deconstructive postmodernism opposes what made Aberhart so dangerous. As a Christian fundamentalist, Aberhart maintained that biblical narratives were all part of one inspired and unified whole, and that that unified text lacked any prior antecedents—any inter-textuality, any competing myths—that might inform or destabilize its unity. In one of his early pamphlets, Aberhart explained his way of reading:

> [T]he Bible is plain enough for the individual to read for himself, and ... it is infallible, and inerrant from cover to cover.... While in my university courses I had listened to the vaporing of modern theology. I heard them say that the first twelve chapters of Genesis was an allegory; that the story of the Flood was an Eastern Exaggeration, for the water had not covered the whole earth; that the crossing of the Red Sea was Eastern Imagery, and that it was the natural result of an East wind; that the yarn of Joshua and the Sun standing still was merely National legend, and not by any

means scientifically accurate; that the story of Jonah and the whale was picturesque and figurative, and not meant to be taken in any literal fashion; that the first chapter of Matthew, which describes the virgin birth, was unscientific and fanciful. I heard them say these things, and for a time I hardly knew where I was at.[52]

For Aberhart, however, as for most biblical literalists, some interpretation *is* necessary. For example, he explains that there has been a change in religious "dispensations" that make it unnecessary for us to burn "incense as in Leviticus" or "keep the Sabbath Day as the Jews were told to do in Exodus." Thus, to the faithful in his congregation and in his massive radio audience, Aberhart not only preached that the unified voice of a single, unified, and coherent text was the ultimate authority over individuals, he also assumed the role of authority as interpreter of that text that was absolute, and that resided in his insistence on and understanding of the authority of that book.

Thus, in *The Words of My Roaring* and elsewhere, Kroetsch is creating a counterdiscourse after all. He *is* writing back to his experience of an established and authoritarian discourse, though it seems cosmic rather than national. It is therefore no surprise that Kroetsch came to fiction wanting to decentre mythology. And it is certainly no surprise to find him embracing a movement associated with indeterminacy and a skepticism towards metanarratives. Aberhart's particular monomyth provided a frightening example of how dangerous a metanarrative could be. Yet it also served to make Kroetsch acutely aware, from an early age, of the attractiveness in the terrifying power of mythology.

Kroetsch's much-cited 1975 essay, "Unhiding the Hidden: Recent Canadian Fiction," which served him as a critical manifesto—and which begins "Survival itself is the Canadian apocalypse"—blends deconstructive postmodernism with an emerging post-colonial sensibility, suggesting that the Canadian writer needs to struggle against being unwittingly shaped by inherited discourses. Celebrating novels such as *Surfacing*, *The Manticore*, and *The Temptations of Big Bear*, Kroetsch described them as works engaged in "the radical process of demythologising the systems that threaten to define them" and saw them as responding to threatening external discourses that were "sometimes British, sometimes American."[53] As we can now see, for Kroetsch himself, the prior myth that had threatened to "define" him had not come from without but had been encountered at home, on the Canadian prairies, in Aberhart's compelling fusion of biblical prophecy and utopian politics.

Curiously enough, one of the fascinating things that becomes apparent when we view Aberhart and the new version of Christianity with which he was associated[54] is that this prairie evangelist was involved in an act strikingly like that of his contemporaries among literary Modernists—the reinvigoration of an old myth to make it suitable to the contemporary situation in order to restore a lost synthesis. In an often-cited passage in "'Ulysses,' Order, and Myth" (1923), Eliot wrote:

> In using the myth, in manipulating a continuous parallel between contemporaneity and antiquity, Mr. Joyce is pursuing a method which others must pursue after him.... It is simply a way of controlling, of ordering, of giving a shape and a significance to the immense panorama of futility and anarchy which is contemporary history. It is a method already adumbrated by Mr. Yeats, and of the need for which I believe Mr. Yeats to have been the first contemporary to be conscious. It is a method for which the horoscope is auspicious.... Instead of narrative method, we may now use the mythical method. It is, I seriously believe, a step toward making the modern world possible for art, toward that order and form which Mr. Aldington so earnestly desires.[55]

When it was thus formulated, this literary-Modernist view of how myth allowed the artist to cope with an increasingly confusing world seemed empowering. But when the context is no longer literary, then it has alarming resonances with less benign ways of ordering. Compare Stephen O'Leary's valuable discussion, in *Arguing the Apocalypse: A Theory of Millennial Rhetoric* (1994), of the attractions of apocalyptic narrative as a controlling myth:

> apocalyptic myth functions in our culture as a well of metaphor, a subterranean spring of symbolic resources drawn upon by those who seek to define and construct their own historic epoch.... [T]his well of metaphor is capable of sustaining attitudes toward history that range from political passivity to triumphalist nationalism.... [T]he recurring fallacy of apocalyptic eschatology seems to rest in human tendency to identify the particular with the ultimate; to identify this or that nation or ruler as an embodiment of ultimate evil or divine righteousness, this or that moment in time as the inception of ultimate catastrophe or millennial bliss.[56]

Indeed, we can hear an echo of Eliot's anxieties about anarchy when

O'Leary further observes that what "Eliade identifies [as] the 'terror of history'" has driven "humanity's ongoing attempt to negate time through ritual and historical action," and that "the epochal myths of a culture represent its attempts to overcome this terror by ordering the life of humanity into a sequence that is intelligible through, and enacted in, its rituals and its history" (220).

But where Eliade, like Eliot, regarded myth as redemptive, O'Leary and Kroetsch and their postmodern contemporaries have come to see it as what Kroetsch called an "entrapment." They, like Iris Murdoch, have come to feel that "The desire for total myth ... is part of ... the totalitarian mind."[57] The young Kroetsch inherited a world in which Conrad, Yeats, Joyce, Eliot, and Lawrence could teach him the power of myth as a means of organizing and heightening experience, but he also found himself dwelling in a world where a mythic system could threaten one's very being. Perhaps that's one reason why Kroetsch's Backstrom does not long for order, but instead cries out: "I needed chaos, the old chaos" (101).

In *The Words of My Roaring* Kroetsch foregrounds the apocalyptic myth that was central to both Aberhart's religion and politics. But at the same time he also subverts it by surrounding it with so many other, competing, mythic narratives that the Aberhartian vision cannot remain single or whole. Nor does he permit Aberhart's mythic vision to escape from its genealogy: one of the subtler pieces of mischief in the novel is Kroetsch's introduction of Babylonian myth, because it returns the monologic narratives, on which Aberhart's power was so dependent, to a dialogic context. *The Epic of Gilgamesh* and other Babylonian narratives *were* the "Eastern" myths that Aberhart was at such pains to deny when, in the passage quoted earlier, he opposed what the nineteenth-century Higher Criticism, with its recently deployed tools of textual scholarship, had uncovered: previously unrecognized or invisible sources for the Bible's chief narratives. The fact that *The Epic of Gilgamesh* is the very text Aberhart was surely reacting to when he uneasily referred to the idea that "the story of the Flood was an Eastern Exaggeration" gives further meaning to Kroetsch's decision to make that the most important intertext for *The Words of My Roaring*.

Kroetsch's use of *Gilgamesh* thus becomes a political act as well as a literary one, especially so since it was the recovery of that text, in the middle of the nineteenth century, that played a crucial role in challenging the received view of the Bible as a text without earlier sources. The new ways of looking at the Bible that resulted from the recovery of *Gilgamesh* and from the other Bible scholarship of the period—the treatment of biblical texts as like other texts of its time, that is, as having historical contexts, and sources, variants, and a history of transmission—was an important part of religious "modernism."[58] It was the rise of this "Higher Criticism" and of the closely associated religious modernism that galvanized "anti-modernists" like Aberhart and the other early Christian fundamentalists who staked their claims for a Bible that was "infallible, and inerrant."

By building his narrative around that apocalyptic myth so successfully promulgated by Aberhart, while at the same time introducing countermyths that compete with and oppose that apocalyptic monomyth, Kroetsch created a counterdiscourse *within* his novel. Yet the novel does not so much counter Aberhart's apocalyptic vision as contain it. "I suppose I write against systems," Kroetsch later remarked, "even if I, ironically, end up incorporating a system."[59] In *The Words of My Roaring*, locating the apocalypse among a larger body of myths, reminding us that it is but one of the Near Eastern combat myths, is part of the pluralizing act (continued in the novels that conclude the triptych) that, as Kroetsch was later to suggest, decentres the individual myth.

We might say that this is Kroetsch's *Canadian* way of creating a counterdiscourse, in that it does not strive to negate and thereby be rid of a threatening hegemonic narrative, which is what Coover does in a novel like *The Burning of America*, but instead seeks to counter Aberhart's exclusiveness with a literary form of mythic inclusiveness that is simultaneously generous *and* disruptive.

But we still may want to ask what led Kroetsch to choose this way of using myth against myth, of making mythic overload his particular way of holding out against the dominance of myth. Why this specific direction into postmodernism?

McLUHAN MEETS MYTH

> We all feel that the electronic mass media are transforming the conditions of education, religion, politics, and even science and philosophy. But few can articulate clearly what is really happening to our culture.
>
> John Irving, *Mass Media in Canada*[60]

> In Canada, for physical and cultural reasons (that is, because of our geography and bi-cultural or rather multi-cultural situation) problems in communication have taken on a peculiar urgency. It may be that the CPR, CNR, CRTC, CBC, Air Canada, and Marshall McLuhan really do express our fate.
>
> Eli Mandel, *Eight More Canadian Poets*[61]

I noted earlier that, even while operating from opposed perspectives, both Mathews and Fogel thought of postmodernism as something foreign that was at first resisted in Canada. A different account of the coming of post-modernism, one that sees Canada as already predisposed to acceptance of the postmodern paradigm, has been suggested by Linda Hutcheon and by Kroetsch. Hutcheon argues that Canadians were not only "primed for the paradoxes of the postmodern by their history"[62] but were generally pre-pared for a postmodern way of viewing the world because a native emphasis on difference and a willingness to accept contradiction provided a meaning-ful context for postmodernism's themes.[63] However, in *Labyrinths of Voice*, Kroetsch articulated a different version (a prairie-inflected version) of why Canada had been ripe for postmodernism:

> I think that Modernism was more present as a force for the Amer-ican writer.... Modernism was the product of a high urban civi-lization and we just didn't have any.... McLuhan seems to emerge suddenly as a postmodernist figure, with little or nothing to pre-pare his way. He illustrates what I mean by saying that we [in Canada] came into contemporary writing easily. I think that has been because we had little contact with Modernism but also because we have a different sense of communication here. We have basically an open, discontinuous sense of communication. A great deal of what happens in Canada, including our literature, has to do with our having always to deal with gaps and spaces. Our national discontinuities made us ripe for Postmodernism. McLuhan was just a symbolic figure in that sense. (112)

In the last part of this essay, I want to expand on this suggestion that McLuhan was our gateway into postmodernism.

For Kroetsch, who encountered McLuhan's work early,[64] this cultural theorist must have been an interesting figure indeed. Where Frye had already confirmed Kroetsch's intuition that myth was a powerful force, McLuhan had something different to tell him about myth. In a 1970 lec-ture on the prairie novelist as mythmaker (given at Lakehead University and never published), Kroetsch spoke about his sense of Northrop Frye and McLuhan as two powerful influences on and makers of contemporary Canadian culture. Though both were by then at University of Toronto, Kroetsch emphasized McLuhan's western background, and pointed to what he saw as a regionally derived creative opposition between the two. On one side of the opposition he set Frye, who, as eastern Canadian, longed for synthesis and therefore began his analysis with the largest unit of communication, the controlling myth, and worked from there to individual texts. Against that impulse, he set McLuhan as prairie westerner, who focussed on parts rather than on totality, and who had, in *The Gutenberg Galaxy*, stressed the smallest units of communication, the letters of the phonetic alphabet, and the unexpected effects that arose when using them to construct larger wholes. In such an opposition, Frye becomes a late spokesman for Modernism, reconstructing the Modernist project of containing and synthesizing through myth, while McLuhan provides an alternative direction—one that leads into what, from our current vantage point, looks like a deconstructive postmodernism, in which coherence gives way to a multiplicity, and synthesis and meaning become elusive.

What Kroetsch didn't mention in that lecture is that what may have made McLuhan especially attractive is that he also had important things to say about myth, and that he even offered a connection between myth and radio. In his 1962 magnum opus, *The Gutenberg Galaxy*, McLuhan suggested it was the new electronic media of the telegraph and the radio that first brought about a new shift to an "inner landscape"—this same shift that today focusses attention on myth in all its modes.[65] Furthermore, though McLuhan saw myth as playing a new and important role in the twentieth century, he did not view it, as so many of his contemporaries did, as a positive move towards a synthesizing and totalizing experience of an otherwise chaotic reality. Instead, he associated the revival of myth with the new *pluralism* that he thought was generally being brought about by the arrival of electronic media: "We can now live ... pluralistically in many worlds and cultures simultaneously" (*Gutenberg*, 31). In an early and important essay, published in *Daedalus* in 1959, McLuhan provided a statement that could serve as a guide to a writer thinking about how to make use of myth in the second half of the century:

> myth is always a montage or transparency comprising several external spaces and times in a single image or situation. Such

compression or multilayering is [also] an inescapable mode of the electronic and simultaneous movement of information.... [W]e now have to possess many cultural languages for even the most ordinary daily purposes.[66]

That statement of McLuhan's neatly anticipates the passage from Claude Lévi-Strauss's *The Raw and the Cooked* inserted by Kroetsch and his interviewers into *Labyrinths of Voice* as representative of the postmodern way of understanding myth: "The layered structure of myth ... allows us to look upon myth as a matrix of meaning which are arranged in lines or columns, but in which each level always refers to some other level, which way the myth is read. Similarly, each matrix of meanings refers to another matrix, each myth to other myths."[67]

While it was Aberhart's use of the radio that led Kroetsch to dramatize Applecart's broadcasts in *The Words of My Roaring* ("He had a magnificent voice, Applecart. He just about tore the top off my old Atwater-Kent. He talked so loud I was afraid his voice might crack the mickey of whisky concealed under the speaker. The people loved it. Some of the women cried" [36]), encountering McLuhan would have given Kroetsch a theoretical framework within which to reconsider his experience of Aberhart and myth and radio, and would have provided him with an opportunity to think more deeply about the conjunction of myth and radio—and the fuller implications of Aberhart's electronically mediated rites.

This is especially true because in the book that established McLuhan's popular reputation, *Understanding Media* (which was published two years before *The Words of My Roaring*), radio is the electronic technology McLuhan most often turns his attention to:

> Even more than the telephone or telegraph, radio is that extension of the central nervous system that is matched only by human speech itself. Is it not worthy of our meditation that radio should be specially attuned to that primitive extension of our central nervous system, that aboriginal mass medium, the vernacular tongue? The crossing of these two most intimate and potent of human technologies could not possibly have failed to provide some extraordinary new shapes for human experience.[68]

Although in the second half of the sixties McLuhan was widely regarded as an enthusiastic apostle of electronic communication, he had often registered warnings as well. When he was later accused of overenthusiasm for the newer media, McLuhan liked to strike an attitude of scientific detachment—characterizing himself as one who simply described what could not be changed. But in fact, his early work is filled with dystopian cautions about the changes coming into being. And in *Understanding Media* the medium about which he expresses the gravest concerns is radio. Characterizing it as a "tribal drum," he describes radio as having introduced a new "discontinuity" into society (36) and as having served as "a mighty awakener of archaic memories, forces, and animosities" (306). By displacing literacy with a new orality, radio "turns man over to universal panic" (156) and becomes a "medium for frenzy" (310). It is anti-rational because it "plays the disk or film of Western man backward, into the heart of tribal darkness" (111). Being anti-rational, radio moves communication back into a pre-rational, tribal, and *terrifyingly* mythic mode providing both Spengler and Hitler with "a subconscious mandate to announce the end of all 'rational' ... values" (112).

Phrases like "tribal darkness" speak to McLuhan's general view, throughout *Understanding Media*, that the mythic dimension electronic communication has returned to human consciousness is dangerous. In contrast to most of his contemporaries, McLuhan generally distrusted rather than idealized the effects of myth. This is most evident in *The Gutenberg Galaxy*, where, despite his use of phrases like "preliterate vitality," we can see what McLuhan felt was really at stake in an electronic era of mythic thinking when he stages a debate with Mircea Eliade—at that time the best-known and most passionate advocate for a return to mythic consciousness. Warm in his appreciation of earlier scholars everywhere else in *The Gutenberg Galaxy*, McLuhan is surprisingly hostile to Eliade and his ideas ("Eliade is under a gross illusion ..."; "Eliade's own work is an extreme popularization ..."; "I question the quality of insight ..." [69]). The nature of his objections to this renowned scholar of myth and religion is made clear when he writes:

> The later section of this book will accept the role declined by Eliade when he says: "It does not devolve upon us to show by what historical processes ... man has desacralized his world and assumed a profane existence." To show by exactly what historical process this was done is the theme of *The Gutenberg Galaxy*. And having shown the process, we can at least make a conscious and responsible choice concerning whether we elect once more the tribal mode which has such attraction for Eliade. (69)

This question of choice was important because McLuhan was

disturbed by a larger issue that he saw Eliade as representing: a romanti-cization of irrationalism that was one troubling aspect of the emerging "tribal mode":

> That Eliade chooses to call the oral man "religious" is, of course, as fanciful and arbitrary as calling blondes bestial. But it is not in the least confusing to those who understand that the "religious" for Eliade is, as he insists from the start, the irrational. He is in that very large company of literacy victims who have acquiesced in supposing that the "rational" is the explicitly lineal, sequential, visual. That is, he prefers to appear as an eighteenth-century mind in rebellion against the dominant visual mode which then was new. Such was Blake and a host of others. Today Blake would be violently anti-Blake, because the Blake reaction against the abstract visual is now the dominant *cliché* and claque of the big battalions, as they move in regimented grooves of sensibility. (70–71)

Eliade's return to a preliterate tribal mode holds no attractions for McLuhan in *The Gutenberg Galaxy* and *Understanding Media*; he wrote in the latter book: "The ear turns man over to universal panic" (156), a panic that arises when the new "village" life of electronic interconnectedness displaces print culture.[69] Believing that education could be our "civil defense against media fallout," McLuhan sought to wake up his readers[70] so that they would become aware of these forces shaping our destinies— and of their inherent dangers—and exercise "responsible choice" over them (*Understanding*, 305).

McLuhan may have been concerned about the imposition of the "lin-eal, sequential, visual" dominance imposed by the Phonetic alphabet and then, with more authority, by the spread of printing, but he declined to identify mythic thinking as a corrective to such linearity. When he sug-gests that a perceptive forward thinker such as Blake would, in today's context, become "violently anti-Blake" (and readers will suspect that this passage is a repudiation of Frye as much as of Eliade), it is clear that McLuhan identifies himself with this anti-Blakeian position and that he connects the re-emergence of myth in the contemporary world with a corresponding and perilous anti-rationalism.

Reading McLuhan's statements about how "Radio restores tribal sensi-tivity and exclusive involvement in the web of kinship" (*Understanding*, 215), Kroetsch would have been particularly responsive to these warnings about radio, because he would have found in them a further source of insight into the phenomenon of Aberhart.[71]

One very good reason why McLuhan's analysis of radio and myth may have provided Kroetsch with such a useful perspective from which to analyze Aberhart's dangerous radio presence—a reason that may not have gone unnoticed by Kroetsch—is that McLuhan's theories themselves could have been provoked by his own encounter with Aberhart. After all, although he was about sixteen years older than Kroetsch and although he and his family were never threatened in the way that Kroetsch and his family were, McLuhan would certainly have been aware of Aberhart's rise to power and of the crucial role of radio as a factor. People all across the prairies and into British Columbia were acutely aware of Aberhart—first in his role as preacher and then, more intensely, as politician. There were lively discussions throughout western Canada about whether Aberhart's Social Credit doctrines were desirable or workable. His political ideologies were the subject of regular examination and tough criticism by newspaper journalists in virtually every prairie paper, and the Winnipeg *Free Press* was especially hostile to his visionary politics, rhetoric, and methods. Aberhart's vitriolic and frequent counterattacks against the print media, along with his very disturbing attempts to muzzle the press in his own province once he was in power, made his career an embodiment of what McLuhan saw emerging in the twentieth century: an attack of a new oral/aural culture on the older one of print.

After finishing his studies at the University of Winnipeg, McLuhan left the Canadian west for Cambridge University, departing the year before election brought Aberhart into political office. Nonetheless, by 1934 he had had ample opportunity to have gained an extensive awareness of Aberhart as a radio presence. Aberhart's radio broadcasts were heard in all three prairie provinces and they were being listened to in the Winnipeg of McLuhan's youth.[72] McLuhan had grown up in a household that was sympathetic to Aberhart's kind of religious belief and in a city that was always intensely engaged in political activity and interested in all manner of political ideas. (And economic theories were an especially popular topic of conversation during the Depression.) Even once he was in Cambridge, he would have continued to hear reports of Aberhart's progress and would surely have taken great interest in the fact that this Canadian prairie figure now began to attract worldwide attention. (McLuhan would certainly have been aware of Aberhart's victory. In London, Social Credit "green-shirts" marched around the Bank of England to celebrate, and Dr. Hewlett Johnson, the Dean of Canterbury, marked the occasion by saying: "The Douglas scheme is the fulfilment of Christ's teaching. Here are the hungry. Let us feed them. Alberta will kindle a world-wide torch.") Leaving his home far behind did, however, give McLuhan the opportunity to make an important religious decision—which was to abandon his family's pietistic Protestantism, converting (in 1937) to the religion that Aberhart was regularly attacking in his broadcasts—the Roman Catholicism that had become important to McLuhan during his undergraduate years at the University of Manitoba.

Although he seems never to have mentioned Aberhart in his writing, it is noteworthy that, when he joined the University of Toronto in 1946, McLuhan became a colleague of John Irving, the man whose definitive book on Aberhartian Social Credit would later serve as Kroetsch's source for history in *The Words of My Roaring*. McLuhan contributed one of his important early essays, "The Electronic Age—The Age of Implosion," to *Mass Media in Canada*, a volume that Irving edited. (It appeared in 1962, the same year that *The Gutenberg Galaxy* was published, and some three years after Irving published *The Social Credit Movement in Alberta*.)

Irving, McLuhan, and Kroetsch: three men interested in the effects on the subject of mass media and all responding at some personal level to Aberhart's career and its after-effects.[73] Although Aberhart is not mentioned in the essays collected in Irving's book on the media—which Irving characterized as "the first book written by Canadians and published in Canada that attempts to deal systematically with the nature and function of mass media in this country"—that book's very first words not only provide Irving's version of McLuhanesque concerns but could also serve as a comment on Aberhart's moment in prairie history: "Two technologies of communication coexist in Western civilization today—the typographic and electronic. The conflicting claims of these diverse technologies bring trauma and tension to many people...."[74]

Thus, in his extraordinarily successful use of a new technology that was both electronic and oral, and in his remarkable union of charismatic religious leadership with political ends that remains unequalled in North American history, Aberhart created an historical moment that was so striking and, for these three intellectuals, so alarming that it gave them a problem to puzzle over, a conundrum to respond to, each in his own way. For Irving, it became a subject to be probed by a social historian: his examination of Aberhart's rise to power gave him the content of his most important book. For McLuhan, the theorist of communication, Aberhart's impact may have stimulated some of his most crucial insights into the power and the danger of the new media. And for Kroetsch, the experience of Aberhart during his childhood not only provided the subject matter of his first important novel, it also profoundly shaped the way he would come to view and respond to the world in which he found himself.

McLuhan's subsequent experience of the rise of Fascism provided him with plenty of examples of the dangerous power of the new electronic media, and in *Understanding Media* it is Fascism to which he points, arguing that the fact that "Hitler came into political existence at all is directly owing to radio and public-address systems" (300). But McLuhan didn't need a Hitler to tell him what happens when charismatic demagoguery meets the electronic revolution in communication. Aberhart had provided him with a first and sufficient demonstration of the relationship between mass media and mass power, and had already given him all the experience he needed for those later warnings in *Understanding Media*—about how, "As the printing press cried out for nationalism, so did the radio cry out for tribalism" (49); and about how the "action of radio on the world of resonant speech and memory was hysterical" (315); and about how radio could thereby bring about an "almost instant reversal of individualism into collectivism, Fascist or Marxist" (304). And McLuhan's experience of Aberhart's powerful narrative of a coming apocalypse, of the last days, and of a war between good and evil—still powerful and still electronically promulgated today—would also have demonstrated the dangerously attractive and irrationally persuasive powers of myth.

One way to understand McLuhan's famous and provocative maxim that the medium is the message is as a warning about the power of such mythic communication. (Indeed, in "Myth and Mass Media" McLuhan defined myth as a mass medium that renders historical records in compressed and articulate form.) It is illuminating to place McLuhan's famous aphorism next to that remark Kroetsch makes in *Alberta* about Aberhart as orator: "I can recall ... not Aberhart's words, but his voice" (25). Similarly, Backstrom says, of the fictional Applecart's ability to use apocalyptic rhetoric drawn from the book of Revelation to bypass the rational mind of *his* listeners, "Sometimes we couldn't exactly follow. But we could understand" (33).

It is this irrational appeal of a medium that Irving is also most at pains to describe. Mixing religious belief with ill-thought-out economic reform, Aberhart's politics were entirely based on an appeal to unreasoned faith. To reassure listeners that they need not understand the complexities of Social Credit (of which he himself had, at best, a shaky grasp), Aberhart frequently invoked a metaphor of electricity powering a light bulb (a habit that may have served as inspiration for McLuhan's recurrent use of the light bulb as a metaphor for the way electricity conveyed pure information). Albertans recalling the 1935 election repeatedly spoke of their "lack of understanding of the technical mechanisms or procedures that would be involved,"[75] but Aberhart repeatedly reminded his followers that they didn't have to understand the technology of the electric light in order to turn on the switch. One of the individuals interviewed by Irving even sounds a bit like Backstrom: "I don't claim to understand the fine points of the system, but if Mr. Aberhart says it is so, then I am sure everything will be all right."[76]

Perhaps the final paradox then is this: Aberhart, as an anti-modernist, disturbed the Modernism that would have formed both McLuhan and Kroetsch, and thereby became a factor in bringing *post*modernism into existence. McLuhan seemed to enthusiastically embrace Modernism in his student days in Cambridge, but he ultimately came to see it as his rear-view mirror and—in constructing a new, McLuhanesque, version of it—he became a significant force in ushering in both American and Canadian postmodernism.[77] During the 1960s, McLuhan became one of the most attended-to theorists in the world and his impact on postmodern ideas has yet to be fully assessed. In particular, little has been said about his having had an influence on postmodern fiction, yet in "The Literature of Exhaustion," John Barth emphasizes McLuhan's impact, speaking of how he felt challenged, early in his career, by the uneasy sense that he was still just "a 'print oriented bastard,' as the McLuhanites call us."[78] When, in a later essay, Barth reflected on why certain concerns had become so central to him in "The Literature of Exhaustion," he returned to his early experience of McLuhan, pointing to the way he was then teaching at the University of Buffalo, where "from across the Peace Bridge in Canada came Professor Marshall McLuhan's siren song that we 'print-oriented bastards' were obsolete."[79] Indeed, McLuhan's—and Canada's—impact runs through Barth's essays in *The Friday Book*. In the preface that he there appends to "The Literature of Exhaustion," he reiterates his sense of the impact, while teaching at SUNY, Buffalo, of living on the border of "endless Canada, to which hosts of our young men fled as their counterparts had done in other of our national convulsions, and from which Professor McLuhan expounded the limitations, indeed the obsolescence, of the printed word in our culture" (63). And in Barth's autobiographical sketch in that volume, he says he moved to Buffalo "to savor (especially in the noisy late 1960s) another sort of border state: the visible boundary of our troubled republic and the comforting sight of great Canada across the river, . . . haven for dispossessed Americans in every upheaval since the States united. . . . [A]s a writer I'm glad to have sniffed tear gas and to have heard—if only like Odysseus tied to the mast—the siren songs of Marshall McLuhan" (12).

Like McLuhan, Kroetsch was initially drawn to the Modernist aesthetic. And he was especially drawn to, but ultimately uneasy with, the Modernist preoccupation with myth as a source of textual power. With the lessons of Aberhart in his past, lessons that were refreshed by the publication of Irving's fine narrative history, and with the lessons of McLuhan in his present, Kroetsch transformed his own Modernist aesthetic into a prairie-based postmodernism, one that responded to his early confrontation with a transcendental political vision by undermining it with a destabilizing humour, by answering *voice* with voices, and by turning *myth* back into myths. Although Aberhart is now being forgotten by most Canadians (or remembered only as having something to do with "funny money"), the lessons of Aberhart's Alberta—which were lessons about the conflicts between centre and margin, and about the tensions between myth and history, and about the contests among narratives and between narrative and that which cannot be subsumed into narrative—and the way Aberhart's career ultimately demonstrated some of the unexamined consequences of the modern age continue to reach far beyond their place and time.[80]

ENDNOTES

1. Janet Paterson, "Introduction," *Postmodernism and the Quebec Novel*, trans. David Homel and Charles Phillips (Toronto: University of Toronto Press, 1994).

2. Robert Kroetsch, "A Canadian Issue," *boundary 2: A Journal of Postmodern Literature* 3, 1 (Fall, 1974): 1–2.

3. The view that postmodernism arose in the US is generally accepted today; see, e.g., Hans Bertens's history of the term, in which he observes that "postmodernism as it has been variously defined since the 1960s has its origins in American literary and cultural criticism" (*The Idea of the Postmodern: A History* [London: Routledge, 1995], 17).

4. Writer-critics such as George Bowering would argue that there was a resistance to postmodernism in Canada not simply as part of this general tendency to resist change, and not so much as a result of a resistance to all things American, but because of the predisposition in the Canadian artistic community towards old-fashioned realism in representation. (The idea that twentieth-century Canadian literature remained conservatively grounded in realism after its conventions were successfully challenged in the US and UK is another version of Kroetsch's suggestion that Canadian literature never entirely entered modernism.)

5. Compare Bertens: "[F]or many of the American literary critics that bring the term postmodernism into circulation in the 1960s and early 1970s, postmodernism is the move *away* from narrative, from representation. For them, postmodernism is the turn towards self-reflexiveness in the so-called metafiction of the period, as practised, for instance, by Samuel Beckett, Vladimir Nabokov, John Barth, Donald Barthelme, the Surfictionalists, the *nouveau romanciers*, and a host of other writers. For them this particular form of postmodernism rediscovers and radicalizes the self-reflexive moment in an otherwise representational modernism (the self-reflexivity of the late Joyce, especially of *Finnegan's Wake*, of the experiments of Raymond Roussel and others). Seen from this perspective, postmodernism is a move towards radical aesthetic autonomy, towards pure formalism" (*Idea of the Postmodern*, 4). In her introduction to the English translation of *Postmodernism and the Quebec Novel*, Paterson cites Coover, Pynchon, Barth, and the British writer John Fowles as the standard names in the postmodern canon of fiction prior to the reassessments of the late 1980s (among these, she emphasizes Hutcheon's *The Canadian Postmodern: A Study of Contemporary English-Canadian Fiction* [Toronto: Oxford University Press, 1988]) that enabled critics to decentre this reading of the tradition.

6. John Barth, *The Friday Book* (New York: Putnam/Perigee: 1984).

7. In *A Poetics of Postmodernism: History, Theory, Fiction* (New York: Routledge, 1988), Hutcheon identifies historiographic metafiction as standing at the intersection of the chief concerns of postmodernist fiction (5) and argues that, despite the earlier identification of postmodern fiction with metafiction, "the term postmodernism in fiction be reserved to describe the more paradoxical and historically complex form I have been calling 'historiographic metafiction'" (40).

8. See her chapter in *The Canadian Postmodern*, "Caveat Lector: The Early Postmodernism of Leonard Cohen," 26–44.

9. Robert Kroetsch, *The Words of My Roaring* (Toronto: Macmillan, 1966).

10. Robert Kroetsch, *Gone Indian* (Toronto: new press, 1973), 152.

11. Frances W. Kaye and Robert Thacker, "'Gone Back to Alberta': Robert Kroetsch Rewriting the Great Plains," *Great Plains Quarterly* 14 (1994): 167.

12. See, in particular, *The Canadian Postmodern*, in which Hutcheon assigns him the central role in postmodernism's development in Canada, light-heartedly dubbing him "Mr. Canadian Postmodern" (160).

13. Stanley Fogel, *A Tale of Two Countries: Contemporary Fiction in Canada and the United States* (Toronto: ECW, 1984).

14. Robin Mathews, *Canadian Literature: Surrender or Revolution* (Toronto: Steel Rail Educational Publishing, 1978), 132.

15. James Reaney, "Editorial," *Alphabet* 1 (1960).

16. I number myself among such readers, having first come to the novel in 1969.

17. In stressing the problems Kroetsch saw in myth, I am in danger of simplifying his position on Frye, to whom he has several times paid homage. However, even when Kroetsch writes, quite positively, of the importance for him of Frye and of his great precursor James Frazer, it is hard not to feel that his responses to *Anatomy of Criticism* and *The Golden Bough* are examples of that kind of creative misreading that Harold Bloom would characterize as a strong rereading of the fathers.

18. Robert Kroetsch, *Labyrinths of Voice: Conversations with Robert Kroetsch*, ed. Shirley Neuman and Robert Wilson (Edmonton: NeWest, 1982), 131.

19. On the way Kroetsch has used comic farce as a "mode of demystification," see Ann Mandel's seminal 1978 essay, "Uninventing Structures: Cultural Criticism and the Novels of Robert Kroetsch," *Open Letter* 5, 8 (Spring 1978): 52–71, as well as Hutcheon's description of Kroetsch's "parodies of the familial and seemingly 'universal' [myths]"; this particular use of parody, Hutcheon suggests, does "not so much destroy myth as de-myth-ify and demystify it into stories, fictions" (*Canadian Postmodern*, 165).

20. Peter Thomas, *Robert Kroetsch* (Vancouver: Douglas & McIntyre, 1980), 42.

21. Ibid.

22. Robert Lecker, *Robert Kroetsch* (Boston: Twayne, 1986), 40.

23. Kenneth Graham, "Picaro as Messiah: Backstrom's Election in *The Words of My Roaring*," *Mosaic* 14, 2 (Spring 1981): 184.

24. Gwendolyn Leick, *A Dictionary of Ancient Near Eastern Mythology* (London: Routledge, 1991), 115.

25. Since Erra's rule, when he takes over from Marduk, is disastrous, the presence of this mythic subtext suggests that the outcome of Backstrom's victory over Murdoch—and Social Credit's over their political opponents—will not be a very happy one.

26. Erra is often identified, in Mesopotamian myth, with the good Nergal, who descends into the underworld, where Ereskegal reveals her body to him after bathing, luring him into seven passionate days and nights of lovemaking

(Leick): all these details have explicit parallels in the Backstrom and Helen union in the garden. Ereskegal is, in turn, linked to Ishtar in Mesopotamian myth, especially through the story of the latter's descent into the underworld—and Kroetsch has elsewhere shown himself fascinated by Ishtar as a figure of the goddess. On the parallels between Persephone and Ishtar, see, e.g., Stephanie Dalley, who observes: "There is an obvious similarity in basic theme" between the story of the descent of Ishtar into the underworld and "the Greek myth of Persephone, who was abducted by Hades," in *Myths from Mesopotamia: Creation, The Flood, Gilgamesh, and Others* (Oxford: Oxford University Press, 1989), 133. Ishtar is Marduk's sister in many accounts.

27. There are other allusions to rainmaking myths and folktales. See my discussion of Kroetsch's use of rainmaking narratives from earlier Canadian drama and folklore, from popular American culture, and (especially) from *The Golden Bough*, where Frazer treats the rainmaker as the reigning figure in mythology, in "'The Same Old Story Once Again': Making Rain and Making Myth in *The Words of My Roaring*," *Open Letter* 9th Ser., Nos. 5–6 (1996): 129–146.

28. *The Rainmaker*, by the Canadian prairie playwright Gwen Pharis Ringwood, based on an oral account collected in Robert Gard's *Johnny Chinook* (1945), as well as the later American movie also called *The Rainmaker*, are among Kroetsch's many intertexts.

29. Michel Foucault, "Nietzsche, Genealogy, History," in *Language, Countermemory, Practice: Selected Essays and Interviews*, ed. Donald F. Bouchard (Ithaca: Cornell University Press, 1977), 160–161.

30. Vincent B. Leitch, *Deconstructive Criticism: An Advanced Introduction* (New York: Columbia University Press, 1983), 159.

31. Robert Kroetsch, *Badlands* (Toronto: General, 1982), 45.

32. Robert Kroetsch, *The Lovely Treachery of Words* (Toronto: Oxford University Press: 1989), 12.

33. Kroetsch signals his interest in Lowry in his essay in *The Lovely Treachery of Words*, "Hear Us, Oh Lord and the Orpheus Occasion," 163–178. Bellow was receiving considerable attention in the US at the time Kroetsch was writing *The Words of My Roaring* and *Henderson, the Rain King* was taught at Binghamton in Sheldon Grebstein's Modern American Fiction course, which was a companion course to Kroetsch's Modern Fiction course (they were given in alternate terms). As is suggested in my quotation from Bertens (see fn. 5), behind these writers looms the figure of the late Joyce, whose *Finnegan's Wake* exemplified an extreme version of a text with mythic overload.

34. Indeed, Richler's late novel *Solomon Gursky* seems to nod to Kroetsch's influence in several places. For example, as well as taking a situation that has parallels to the basic conceit of *The Studhorse Man* (Moses struggling to complete his biography of Solomon Gursky), Richler quotes the portion of Psalm 22 from which Kroetsch took the title of *The Words of My Roaring* (49) and later mentions one Reverend Shipley who could be gone with the Indians (354).

35. This is especially true if one distinguishes between Social Credit as a movement and "Social Credit" as merely a convenient name for a political party—which is what it later became in western Canada.

36. John A. Irving, *The Social Credit Movement in Alberta* (Toronto: University of Toronto Press, 1959).

37. Robert Kroetsch, *Alberta* (Toronto: Macmillan, 1968), 26.

38. Applecart's attacks on "the fifty big shots" (and therefore on the party of Doc Murdoch) recalls, within Kroetsch's allusive play, the fact that Marduk was known by his fifty sacred names and functions and attributes—the result of his assimilation of previous deities.

    The title of *The Words of My Roaring* is taken from the King James Version of Psalm 22 ("Why art thou so far from helping me, and from the words of my roaring?"). While critics like Kenneth Graham have taken the title and that allusion to be a reference to Backstrom's own use of language (Graham, "Picaro," 183), Applecart, as this passage reminds us, is also said to "roar." Compare the description (quoted in Irving) given by one of his former teachers of Aberhart when he was a school principal: "He would roar at us with his tremendous voice, and the walls of his office would seem to shake" (Irving, *Social Credit Movement*, 18).

39. Irving, *Social Credit Movement*, 265.

40. Barry Broadfoot, *Next-Year Country: Voices of Prairie People* (Toronto: McClelland and Stewart, 1988), 92–93.

41. Irving, *Social Credit Movement*, 110.

42. Jeffrey Sconce, *Haunted Media: Electronic Presence from Telegraphy to Television* (Durham: Duke University Press, 2000).

43. Irving, *Social Credit Movement*, 343.

44. Max Braithwaite, *Why Shoot the Teacher* (Toronto: McClelland and Stewart, 1968), 30.

45. Irving, *Social Credit Movement*, 43.

46. Ibid., 180.

47. Michael Barkun, *Disaster and the Millennium* (New Haven: Yale University Press, 1974), 128 and 6.

48. Russell Brown, "An Interview with Robert Kroetsch," *University of Windsor Review* 7, 2 (1972): 5.

49. Irving, *Social Credit Movement*, 290.

50. Ibid., 260.

51. Ibid., 288.

52. William Aberhart, "God's Great Divisions of the World's History," Lecture 2, in *God's Great Prophecies* (Calgary: Calgary Prophetic Bible Conference, ca 1922), 27–28. Reprinted in *Aberhart Outpourings and Replies*, ed. David R. Elliott (Calgary: Historical Society of Alberta, 1991), 13.

53. Robert Kroetsch, "Unhiding the Hidden: Recent Canadian Fiction," in *The Lovely Treachery*, 58.

54. As several recent commentators suggest, though apocalyptic Christianity flourished early, it was generally repudiated by the dominant modes of Christianity after post-Augustinian Catholicism. The reappearance, in twentieth-century America, of a powerful new version of apocalyptic vision, associated with various evangelical sects, had its roots in nineteenth-century movements such as the Plymouth Brethren and the Millerites, and it was given great impetus by the late nineteenth-century dispensationalist doctrines of C.I. Scofield, and by the emergence at the end of the nineteenth and the beginning of the twentieth centuries of Pentecostalism, Fundamentalism, and related movements. The importance of the cultural context in which a new religious synthesis has emerged, emphasizing Bible literalism and inerrancy and the nearness of an apocalyptic moment, has led some commentators to view it as a distinctively American religion. However, its sources are Canadian as well: not only was Aberhart an important agent in developing, promulgating, and further disseminating these ideas, but so was the Canadian woman now usually characterized as one of the first "American" evangelists, Aimee Semple McPherson. Another significant groundbreaker in pioneering the use of religious broadcasting, McPherson began her career in her home province of Ontario before travelling widely, chiefly in the US, and eventually basing herself in California. The thirty revivals she conducted from 1919 to 1922 "had a mass appeal unequalled by any touring phenomenon of theatre or politics in American history" (Daniel Mark Epstein, *Sister Aimee: The Life of Aimee Semple McPherson* [New York: Harcourt Brace, 1993], 156). Her tours took her several times back to Canada, most often into the prairies: preaching in Calgary in 1935, she praised Aberhart for his blending of religion with politics (David R. Elliott, "Knowing No Borders," in *Amazing Grace: Evangelicism in Australia, Britain, Canada, and the United States*, ed. George A. Rawlyk and Mark A. Noll [Montreal: McGill-Queen's University Press, 1994], 363).

55. T.S. Eliot, "'Ulysses,' Order, and Myth," in *Selected Prose of T.S. Eliot*, ed. Frank Kermode (London: Faber, 1975), 177–178.

56. Stephen D. O'Leary, *Arguing the Apocalypse: A Theory of Millennial Rhetoric* (New York: Oxford University Press, 1994), 218.

57. Quoted in Richard Wasson, "Marshall McLuhan and the Politics of Modernism," *Massachusetts Review* 13 (1972): 569.

58. The use of the word "modernism" in a religious sense emerged in the early twentieth century. In one of its manifestations (especially in the first decades of the century) it was associated with the liberalizing trends in the Roman Catholic Church, and it also became a central feature of mainstream Protestantism. In North America the term became useful shorthand (especially for its opponents, who used it only in a deprecatory sense) for referring to those who wanted religion to respond positively to the changing face of the modern world and especially those who accepted the Higher Criticism and the "documents hypothesis" (i.e., the idea that, in books such as Genesis, several texts have been drawn together by a later redactor) and who therefore rejected biblical literalism and inerrancy and the doctrine of divine inspiration. This use of the term "modernism" in this context significantly antedates and may precondition its

use in English to refer to a movement in the arts that leaves behind traditional materials, aesthetics, and forms in response to the pressure of twentieth-century changes.

59. Kroetsch, *Labyrinths*, 160.

60. John A. Irving, "Preface," in *Mass Media in Canada* (Toronto: Ryerson, 1962).

61. Eli Mandel, "Introduction," in *Eight More Canadian Poets* (Toronto: Holt, Rinehart and Winston, 1972).

62. Hutcheon, *Canadian Postmodern*, 4.

63. Ibid., ix. In 1993, the British Association of Canadian Studies, perhaps responding to suggestions such as these, dubbed Canada (in the title they gave to their annual conference) "The First Postmodern Country."

64. "About McLuhan—somehow or other I got hold of McLuhan's *The Gutenberg Galaxy* very soon after it was published—the early sixties I would guess. I was probably drawn to Gutenberg's name rather than McLuhan's at the time. Except that I have a vague recollection of being aware of the McLuhan-Frye rivalry by then.... In the late '50s I took a course in myth at Breadloaf College one summer, and the instructor may have mentioned McLuhan even way back then" (Kroetsch, personal correspondence, 2 Sept. 1994).

65. Marshall McLuhan, *The Gutenberg Galaxy* (Toronto: University of Toronto Press, 1962), 31.

66. Marshall McLuhan, "Myth and Mass Media," *Daedalus* 88, 2 (Spring 1959): 339–348. Reprinted in *Media Research: Technology, Art, Communication*, ed. Michel A. Moos (Amsterdam: G+B Arts, 1997), 14.

67. Kroetch, *Labyrinths*, 125. As Garry Genosko points out in *McLuhan and Baudrillard: The Masters of Implosion* (New York: Routledge, 1999), Lévi-Strauss's relationship to and even possible debts to McLuhan have been frequently noted (18). (While Genosko's book focusses particularly on McLuhan's impact on Baudrillard, it also provides a valuable general discussion of McLuhan's reception in and assimilation into French theory.)

68. Marshall McLuhan, *Understanding Media: The Extensions of Man* (New York: McGraw-Hill, 1964), 302.

69. McLuhan later sought to correct the utopian understanding of his famous phrase "the global village": "The more you create village conditions, the more discontinuity and division and diversity.... It never occurred to me that uniformity and tranquility were the properties of the global village. It has more spite and envy.... The tribal-global village is far more divisive—full of fighting—than any nationalism ever was" (Marshall McLuhan with Gerald Emanuel Stearn, "The Hot and Cold Interview," in *McLuhan: Hot and Cool: A Critical Symposium*, ed. Gerald Stearn [New York: Dial, 1967]). Reprinted as "Interview," in *Media Research: Technology, Art, Communication*, ed. Michel A. Moos (Amsterdam: G+B Arts, 1997), 57–58.

70. The figure of the "somnambulist" is one of his frequent metaphors.

71. Although McLuhan's influence on *The Words of My Roaring* has not previously been noted, Hutcheon has pointed out Kroetsch's extended comic response to

McLuhan's theories in *What the Crow Said:* "In that novel Kroetsch creates a wonderfully absurd allegory of McLuhan's prophecies for the fate of 'typographical man'" (*Canadian Postmodern*, 54).

72. I was able to confirm this fact by interviewing several elderly Winnipeggers on my visit to the city in September 2001.

73. Unlike McLuhan and Kroetsch, Irving did not grow up in the west. However, he did have some direct experience of western Social Credit, having joined the University of British Columbia's Department of Philosophy in 1938, around the time Alberta-style Social Credit was attempting its first inroads in BC. It was not, however, until 1953, eight years after Irving left UBC for the University of Toronto, that the Social Credit Party, as reconceived by W.A.C. Bennett, began its long tenure in British Columbia. (I am indebted to Chris Hives at the University of British Columbia archives for the dates of Irving's tenure there.)

74. Irving, ed., *Mass Media*, vii.

75. Irving, *Social Credit Movement*, 256.

76. Ibid., 106. It should, of course, be acknowledged that Aberhart's failure to grasp the workings of Social Credit lay partly with the inherent silliness of Douglas's doctrines, which were already quasi-religious and irrationalist before their Canadian transformation into something even less well-though-through. Douglas himself sometimes fell back on such statements as this one from 1937: "My experience of life . . . is that explanations are fatal" (18). S.D. Clark's remark about the muddle at the centre of Social Credit philosophy suggests something of what someone like Kroetsch would have felt in reconsidering the campaign in Alberta from the vantage point of the mid-1960s: "For someone who believed that political action was the outcome of a rational process of discussion and deliberation, the . . . political developments in Alberta in the years 1932–35 would have been a disillusioning experience" (in Irving, *Social Credit Movement*, vii).

77. The importance of McLuhan's role as one of the major influences on postmodernism is increasingly recognized. See, e.g., the discussions in Hutcheon, *Canadian Postmodern*; Francesco Guardiani, "'The Postmodernity of Marshall McLuhan," *McLuhan Studies* 1 (1991): 141–162; Genosko; Paul Grosswiler, *Method Is the Message: Rethinking McLuhan through Critical Theory* (Toronto: Black Rose Books, 1998); and Glenn Willmott, *McLuhan, or Modernism in Reverse* (Toronto: University of Toronto Press, 1996).

78. Barth, *Friday*, 71.

79. Ibid., 205.

80. Among the very many colleagues who have kindly commented on this as a work in progress, I would especially like to acknowledge the suggestions made by Allan Bewell, Brian Greenspan, and Donna Bennett. I am also grateful for the research support furnished me by the Social Science and Humanities Research Council and by University of Toronto at Scarborough.

THE "PRECARIOUS PERCH" OF THE "DECENT WOMAN"

Spatial (De)Constructions of Gender in Women's Prairie Memoirs

by S. Leigh Matthews

In the wild west, where men were men and life was hard, women were supposed to be one of two things—commodities or prizes....
We are not here counting the wives of homesteaders, of course. They were neither commodities nor prizes. They were, like anything that was likely to produce, used as devices to prepare the dream of a future.

George Bowering, Caprice (1987)

Dad straddled one wall, I straddled the other, then Dad fitted the log....The blows of the axe sent shivers up and down my thin arms, and often I almost fell off my precarious perch. . . . Mother couldn't straddle the walls the way I could. Her long skirts got in her way, and since no decent woman exposed her ankles in those days she couldn't do a thing about them. She tried sitting sideways on the walls, but that didn't work very well. She couldn't balance both the log and herself, so the log slipped, the notch was wrong, and the whole thing had to be done over again, which irritated everybody.

Mary Hiemstra, *Gully Farm* (1955)

Space is abstract. It lacks content; it is broad, open, and empty, inviting the imagination. . . .

Yi-Fu Tuan, "Place: An Experiential Perspective" (1975)

The issue of "space" has long dominated studies of prairie settlement in Canada; indeed, whether seeking to determine the evolutionary history of a western "landscape of the mind shaped by the myths, stories, and attitudes"[1] of a culture, or to delineate the "remarkable unity" of fictional representations of "prairie man's" reaction to the "surrounding emptiness,"[2] what stands prominent in scholarly treatments of western settlement is the dialogic engagement between the physical vastness—the seeming unboundedness—of the area and the limited and culturally specific language used by contemporaries to represent that area. Examination of both historical and literary images of the Canadian prairies further suggests that the language settled on to describe this space is often gendered as female, so that western expansion becomes figured as a physical projection of Anglo-Saxon culture into the (supposedly) fertile landscape as a means to conceive a new national identity, one that is sustained on an individual level by the (male) farmer's battle to control the productions of the land through cultivation. Accordingly, contemporaries averred that the type of "healthy society" being imagined in the Canadian prairies could only be "successfully erected" by "men of British tradition."[3] Most of these gendered descriptions of "Man" on the prairies stem from the imaginations of male writers, which begs the following question: given that women's implied role in prairie settlement was to be "used as devices to prepare the dream of a future," is there any difference in the way that female writers have represented this geographic space, which has attained mythological status as being "blessedly free of most conventional restrictions"?[4]

More explicitly, my concern in this paper is to examine how gender is (de)constructed within specifically located spaces, including the geographic space of the Canadian prairies, the physical space of the female body, and the textual space in which memoir writers represent their lived experience of prairie settlement. Mary Hiemstra's *Gully Farm: A Story of*

Homesteading on the Canadian Prairies (1955) and Kathleen Strange's *With the West in Her Eyes: The Story of a Modern Pioneer* (1937) are two texts chosen for this essay because they have garnered at least some measure of public and academic attention, and together they provide an historical overview of the most intense period of western settlement. Hiemstra's family homesteaded as part of the Barr Colony near what was eventually to become Lloydminster, Saskatchewan, in 1903, and Strange's family took over an existing farm located in a well-settled district near Fenn, Alberta, in 1920. These three spaces—geographic space, the physical space of the female body, and textual space—are interrelated, so that the memoirists themselves have to perform sometimes complex negotiations of spatial boundaries; that is, the authors often simultaneously represent conformity to cultural constructions of the female body in geographic space at the moment of settlement, while at the same time using the textual space of the memoir to map new embodiments of prairie women, to document female transgressions of geographic and corporeal space, both as they occurred within the cultural moment of settlement and as new and empowering constructions at the moment of writing. As in the case of the epigraph above from Hiemstra's *Gully Farm*, the image of living precariously, of moving into a new geographic territory that challenges conventional constructions of the female body and the work the female body is able to perform, erupts again and again within women's prairie memoirs.

Through implication, the phrase "precariously perched" suggests spatial location, both the space upon which one is perched as well as the space of downfall below that perch. For many women settlers, even those who emigrated in the first two decades of the twentieth century, "precarious perch" adequately describes the Victorian values that dominated cultural expectations about the type of society being created in the Canadian prairies, as well as women's reproductive role within that society. To be precarious, however, is to be uncertain, without solid foundation, and certainly many of the earliest women settlers discovered that "civilization" in the prairie west was "the dream of a future," and that the isolated conditions of prairie life demanded behaviour that threatened to topple them into the perilous depths lurking below social/cultural convention. Liberation from convention was thus not simply a matter of historical progression, for sometimes it was precisely the isolated conditions of prairie life that allowed women to perform the "incoherence"[5] of lived experience with cultural image. Ironically, as time and "civilization" marched on, women settlers who had experienced a feminist revolution of behavioural codes in the wider world emigrated to the prairies only to discover that rather Victorian attitudes and values had solidified and become the norm, meaning that women often had to consciously choose between ascending or rejecting the prevailing cultural perch. The immediate experiences/choices of women settlers remain largely silent within historical narratives; however, women's written representations of those experiences/choices provide us with a means to revisit contemporary codes of female behaviour as well as to discover the "traces of the past that are less than exemplary"[6] in terms of those codes.

If we view women's memoirs of prairie life as participating solely in the heritage discourses that abound in recent decades, then we are in danger of reading them as being uncritically nostalgic, as "necessarily static and unchanging in [their] attempt to retrieve a lost utopian space,"[7] both corporeal and geographic. However, if we view the memoirs as examples of folklife narrative, as representative of "the *total* lifeways of any human community,"[8] including the ways that settler women negotiated their bodily behaviour between the demands of culture and geography, then we will be able to read these texts as spaces of "tactical dis/identification"[9] with scripts of the "decent woman." If we accept Tuan's definition of space in the epigraph above, then the palimpsest structure of the prairie memoir as geographic/corporeal/textual possibility allows for considerable and imaginative play with the settler woman image, and becomes an "interface between individual and communal identities."[10] The space of the text becomes a public performance that "puts the female body on display in ways that contradict many of the constructions of femininity" and "these contradictions enable some transgressive feminist performances."[11]

Time thus becomes a primary concern in the study of such texts, for there is a distinction between the cultural moment of experience within the geographic space of the prairies and the cultural moment (in some cases several decades later) in which that experience is re-presented within textual space. The link between these two cultural moments is at the site of the female body, which is both inscribed upon (by being prescribed to the performance of what was deemed appropriately feminine behaviour at the time of settlement) and inscribing (through the narrative representation of resistance to such prescriptions in the act of writing). My examination of the two texts chosen as the focus of this essay provides a glimpse into the unique facility of memoir—as distinct from other autobiographical forms of writing—as a tool with which the individual "creates a space in the margins" of *his*tory and demands "inclusion in the discourses of one's community."[12]

The two texts have been chosen from a "virtually untilled field"[13] of settler women's prairie memoirs. At least one of the reasons for the current lack of academic attention to this body of texts is that the memoir form itself has been uneasily categorized by critics; indeed, memoir as genre is transgressive of traditional textual expectations. Speaking to the exclusion of memoir from serious critical attention in recent years, despite the resurgence of academic interest in this form, Marcus Billson, one of the first critics to provide some "New Perspectives on a Forgotten Genre," suggests it is the form's generic instability that produces critical distrust: "literary critics have faulted memoirs for being incomplete, superficial autobiographies; and, historiographers have criticized them for being inaccurate, overly personal histories."[14] For many readers, memoir texts appear to suffer from a lack of critical depth; they contain neither the central consciousness traditionally desired in autobiographical texts nor the objective distance traditionally assumed to be the priority of the professional historian, with the inevitable result that neither discipline wants to lay claim to such a field of works.

In fact, the truth of memoir lies somewhere at the intersection of history and autobiography; somewhere between disciplinary misunderstandings of the form as being either too personal or not personal enough. In autobiographical terms, the "I" of memoirs is less self-centred: it represents a self *"being*-in-the-world rather than *becoming*-in-the-world"[15]; it is a self "concerned with the human subject always historicized by the 'times' rather than a construction of subjectivity that is a self-actualizing, discrete entity."[16] Thus does critical recognition of the memoir form's generic peculiarities participate in a deconstruction of the notion that "individualism figures as the very stuff of autobiography" in favour of the idea of the individual as "grounded in ties of community—ties of class and race, of kinship and culture."[17]

In historical terms, the inevitable result of the memoirist's acknowledgement of social context, says Francis Russell Hart, is that "memoirs are *of* a person, but they are 'really' of an event, an era, an institution, a class identity,"[18] etc.; indeed, as Billson suggests, "historicity is the mode

of the memoir" and such a text "recounts a story of the author's witness-
ing a real past which [she] considers to be of extraordinary interest and
importance."[19] In the representation of this "real past," says Billson, the
author implicitly acknowledges the impossibility of an absolutely objective perspective and, accordingly, adopts a tripartite "rhetorical stance" as
"the eyewitness, the participant, and the *histor*."[20] The first two position-
ings are "often combined simultaneously," and together they provide the
basis from which "the author derives [her] authority to narrate" on any
given event. Despite the implicitly subjective nature of these stances, however, the author also undertakes to make her account "empirically recognizable" by adopting the stance of "*histor*," "whenever [she] narrates events
[she] has not seen with [her] own eyes, whenever [she] tells what [she] has
overheard, read about, or accumulated by research through historical
records, or whenever [she] provides background material to elucidate the
narration or to set the stage for [her] story."[21] Thus, despite the fact that
"the current critical tendency is to put the issue of genre aside,"[22] recognition of memoir's position at the intersection of autobiography and history—of self and social context—becomes especially important as a means
to preserve such texts from pronouncements of failure according to the
traditional prescriptives of either category.

In the considerable time since Billson and Hart wrote their articles,
there have been only two other critics who have undertaken to establish
the importance of generic definitions of the memoir form in order to
allow for more productive readings of such texts, and both these writers
help us to move from a consideration of memoir as being merely the
social/historical contextualization of the individual towards a more
dynamic treatment of the form as being "something like a borderline or
an interface between the demands of social and subjective existence."[23]
For example, in her 1992 consideration of "The Subject of Memoirs," Lee
Quinby provides a rereading of Maxine Hong Kingston's *The Woman
Warrior* (1975), which, despite the fact that its subtitle "specifies its genre"
as *Memoirs of a Girlhood among Ghosts*, has been consistently misread as an
autobiographical text. Such misreadings, suggests Quinby, have resulted
from memoir's "marginalized status" in the "post-Enlightenment West,"
a culture that persists in "establishing autobiography as a privileged aesthetic and ethical discourse of the modern era." Asserting that the systematic application of "the label 'autobiographical' to all types of life writings

... tends to reduce and narrow our reading" of any given text, Quinby goes on to posit the "overtly dialogical" nature of the memoir form, which is used by writers such as Kingston to "negotiat[e] a confrontation with disciplinary power relations."[24] In a similar vein, in her 1997 article titled "Memoir with an Attitude," which, like Quinby's article, provides a feminist rereading of Kingston's frequently misread *Woman Warrior*—Helen M. Buss theorizes that it is precisely the memoir's generic instability that results in the form's "usefulness as a women's writing genre."[25] Indeed, it is the imprecise nature of the self being constructed in memoir texts that highlights the form's essentially radical nature: as Buss suggests, the "'inner self' construction in memoir, unlike in some other autobiographical practices, always has the potential—because of the memoirist's preoccupation with historicity—of 'confrontation' with accepted versions of subjectivity."[26] When dealing with texts written by Englishwomen who emigrated to a region of Canada that, as I will shortly illustrate, was explicitly intended to be an imperial stronghold, the "accepted versions of subjectivity" might naturally tend to predominate. Therefore, the importance of the reader's awareness of the distinctive features of memoir is paramount in establishing the existence of "confrontations," for she must listen carefully to catch the "undercurrent of forbidden discourse, a discourse of rebellious accusation," which sometimes lies hidden just below the surface narratives of "obedient conformity"[27] to cultural prescriptions of female behaviour.

My own repetition of these critics' theorizations about the individual's ability to confront—to reject or refuse—externalized constructions of selfhood thus represents my acceptance of intersecting notions about subject formation; that is, I rely exclusively on *neither* the humanist belief in the individual as a transcendent and self-determining subject who reproduces himself in the life writing text, *nor* on post-structuralist assertions that the individual (for lack of a better word) is subject*ed* to social forces of self-construction and is constituted at the moment of language use, so that the life writing text cannot be said to refer to a reality outside its pages. Rather, I prefer to take a more mediated view of the individual as both *subject to* certain social forces demanding general adherence to behavioural prescriptives related to gender, class, race, etc., yet also the *subject of* her own particularized needs in daily life, and always capable of inscribing a different reality of lived experience within her text. To achieve this inscription of difference, the memoir text must be viewed as a performative space in which the individual actor achieves a certain level of agency in terms of adherence to social scripts.[28] For example, Sidonie Smith notes the constant tension felt by the performative subject between the processes of "identification and disidentification," between conscious adherence to "those calls to take up normative subject positions" and an unconscious "repository of surplus, of excess, of unbidden and forbidden performativity" that rests below the surface of "imposed systems of identification."[29] Bridging the gap between these two forces is the life writing text, in which the authorial subject performs "tactical dis/identifications" and thereby "adjusts, redeploys, resists, transforms discourses of autobiographical identity."[30] This is not necessarily to suggest, however, that the performing subject consciously constructs the narrative tension noted by Smith; rather, once again we must consider the importance of the reader/audience in recognizing this tension. As suggested by Smith, the notion of "an audience implies a community of people for whom certain discourses of identity and truth make sense"; however, "audiences are never simple homogeneous communities. They are themselves heterogeneous collectives that can solicit conflicted effects in the autobiographical subject."[31] Consequently, the performing subject is read according to the prescriptives of any one audience member at any given time, so that recovery of the "tactical dis/identifications" within the text becomes an effect of the dialectical engagement between the author and the reader, the latter of whom performs an enabling act of agency by the simple act of reading the space of the memoir text deconstructively.

In order to read the two chosen memoirs deconstructively, however, we must first consider the "imposed systems of identification" that dominated women's experiences of early western settlement. As R. Douglas Francis suggests, western expansion was seen in the second half of the nineteenth century as the "fount" of both "national and imperial greatness": indeed, harnessing this vast region meant the establishment of "sufficient natural resources and population potential to make Canada one of the most powerful nations of the world," while also providing "the means to ensure the future greatness of the British Empire."[32] Of paramount importance to the achievement of this dual agenda was immigration and settlement, the domestication of the West as a means to ensure the region's new status as the "promised land, a garden of abundance in which all material wants would be provided and where moral and civic virtues would be perfected."[33] In taking up this "imperial burden," eastern Canada's "hopes lay with the pioneer farmer," and the federal government under John A. Macdonald quickly established immigration and land policies that provided "the basic structure of settlement and remained significant determinants of western history throughout the period 1870–1930."[34] A determined program advertising the advantages of western Canadian settlement was begun, and was directed at potential emigrants from a variety of cultural backgrounds. Nevertheless, while the reality of western settlement established a visible mosaic of cultural diversity on the Canadian prairies, the desire for the creation of a distinctly national identity (based on imperial norms of human behaviour) was always evident.[35] Ideally, whatever the actual cultural backgrounds of immigrants to the Canadian prairies, the project of prairie settlement was ideologically based on the reconstitution of Anglo-Saxon norms of civilization in a radically different geographic space; it was based on the belief that "the Anglo-Saxon peoples and British principles of government were the apex of both biological evolution and human achievement" and that "Canada's greatness was due in large part to its Anglo-Saxon heritage."[36]

That the Canadian prairie was intended to inspire a rebirth of the British Empire, together with all its perceived superior and "civilized" values, inevitably meant that both historical and literary narratives of western expansion and settlement became inscribed by a spatial politics of gender: "in constructing and reconstructing the West—from wilderness wasteland to economic hinterland to agrarian paradise—expansionist discourse perpetuated the myth of the West as a 'manly' space, assigning to it a moral and political force that underwrote elite Anglo-Canadian men's hegemony in the territories."[37] The national project of bringing the prairie landscape under cultivation was seen as necessarily masculine in nature, as reflected in the vocabulary chosen by contemporary writers on the subject: for example, as J. Ewing Ritchie phrased it in 1885, "there is a good deal of hardship to be encountered by any who would *penetrate* to the dim and mysterious region we denominate the North-West."[38] Into that "dim and mysterious region," that geographic void, spilled millions of immigrants. Accordingly, "in the language of western expansionists, the land had to be 'opened' to commercial agriculture and 'filled' with white settlers—as if it had been 'closed' and 'empty' before."[39]

Significantly, in terms of the relationship between western immigration policies and the creation of the Canadian nation, Daniel Coleman uses the phrase "the 'allegory of manly maturation' to emphasize the metonymic and masculinist modalities deployed in this oft-repeated story of national legitimation"[40] in contemporary literature.

Meanwhile, the landscape itself—the "garden of abundance"—was often represented in feminine terms. Indeed, as Jean Pickering and Suzanne Kehde suggest, "the object of colonial encounters is typically feminized, held to be in want of masculine (imperial) authority. This feminization can be applied both to geography ... and to the colonial population."[41] The need for "masculine (imperial) authority" is seen in an 1875 essay titled "The New Canada" by Charles Mair, one of the founders of the Canada First movement, who configured the nationalist enterprise of western settlement in the following way:

> This new Dominion should be the wedding of pure tastes, simple life, respect for age and authority, and the true principles of free government on this Continent. It [the new Dominion] stands, like a youth upon the threshold of his life, clear-eyed, clear-headed, muscular, and strong. Its course is westward. It has traditions and a history of which it may well be proud; but it has a history to make, a national sentiment to embody, and a national idea to carry out.[42]

Mair's insistence on the masculine nature of the "new Dominion" and its need to, as he goes on to suggest, "project into the fertile immensity of the west"[43] as a means to "embody" forth "national sentiment," delineates the contemporary narrative of western settlement as a sort of "gendered romance,"[44] a "wedding" of Anglo-Saxon cultural values and the feminized prairie landscape as a means to achieve a legitimate national identity.[45] As one early twentieth-century author described the advent of spring on the prairies, "the land is clothing herself with verdure as a bride adorning for her husband."[46] Sixteen years after Mair's essay, in 1891, Nicholas Flood Davin was able to assure "the farmers and farm labourers of Europe" of the "bracing influence" of western settlement, for, while "the Ontario farmer is a fine specimen of the yeoman, but three years in the North West raises him higher on the scale of manhood."[47] To climb the "scale of manhood," the individual farmer as representative of the new nation needed only to become master of his own section of land by bringing it under cultivation and establishing a family home; he needed only to harness the riches that, in George Livingstone Dodds's popular description of 1906, "the fair Canadian West" would inevitably "pour from her fertile breast."[48] He must, through hard work and perseverance, unlock "the wonderful, mysterious promise" which "hang[s] over" the "abundant broad bosom of earth!"[49]

Given these sensual directives to the male farmer regarding his possession and use of prairie lands, one might well ask if there was room for the presence of real women in such abstract narratives of western settlement. Were the Canadian prairies really only a place "where strong men gathered"[50] and where the ideal prairie woman, like Martha Perkins in Nellie L. McClung's *Sowing Seeds in Danny* (1908), could be described as "a nice, quiet, unappearing girl"?[51] In many representations of the immigrant family, the main focus was on the male head of the family—the individual who would undertake the actual process of land cultivation and who, in a marketplace-driven economy, represented a real monetary value to the process of western settlement. The woman settler, on the other hand, often appeared as merely an appendage to her husband; indeed, Immigration Minister Clifford Sifton's famous "description of the immigrant most likely to succeed in western Canada" highlights this gender differential: "'I think a stalwart peasant in a sheepskin coat, born on the soil, whose forefathers have been farmers for generations, with a stout wife and a half-dozen children, is good quality.'"[52] The "stout wife" and her children thus become merely a part of the implements necessary to a farmer's success on the Canadian prairies, as seen in a Department of the Interior promotional pamphlet titled *Western Canada: How to Get There; How to Select Lands; How to Make a Home* (1902), in which settler W.E. Cooley testifies to the origins of his success as a farmer: as he states it, "My earthly possessions at the time I reached this place were $1.75, a wife and seven children," all of which, by dint of "work[ing] hard and faithfully," he translated into "520 [of 800] acres under cultivation, . . . 12 horses, 81 head of cattle, 15 hogs and all the equipment necessary for a farm," and "as fine a residence as there is."[53] Women and children were literally accorded a lesser monetary value than men, as seen in the fact that "the Canadian government paid American railway booking agents a bonus of $3 for every male agricultural immigrant over 18 [the necessary age for obtaining a "free" homestead in Canada], $2 for every female and $1 for each dependent child."[54] Ralph Allen increases the value of the male immigrant when he notes that "Sifton sold huge tracts of Canadian government land at give-away prices to private colonization companies, then paid them a bounty out of the Dominion treasury for every settler they could produce—five dollars for the head of a family, two dollars each for women and children."[55]

However, as Sarah A. Carter suggests in *Capturing Women: The Manipulation of Cultural Imagery in Canada's Prairie West*, within the explicitly British-Canadian imperative of western settlement, women occupied a position of paramount importance: in the late nineteenth and early twentieth centuries, the image of the (ideally white) prairie woman was represented as the central vessel through which the Anglo-Saxon ideology of "civilization" would be replicated in the West. Despite the fact that a Department of the Interior immigration pamphlet titled *Twentieth Century Canada* (1906) suggested that "Canada is a man's country, from the fact that all new countries first attract men, because the labour required for early settlement calls for that of man rather than that of woman,"[56] in fact women's labour was also needed in the making of a nation—after all, the prairie woman "was to be the civilizer and the reproducer of the race"[57] in the Canadian West. On the local level, "both the bachelors and the immigration officials agreed that a person couldn't establish a family farm without a farm family to help with the work. And families meant women."[58] The woman settler's function was thus both metaphorical (as image, in her role as disembodied reproductive vessel of a culture—a particularly fitting role for the gender who would not be formally declared "Persons" until 1929) and literal (as lived experience, in her real-life role as a mother). This dual function is clearly articulated in contemporary literature on the subject of western settlement: in Marion Dudley Cran's *A Woman in Canada* (1910), for example, the author suggests that, "In the North-West, where wives are scarce, a work of Empire awaits the woman of breed and endurance who will settle on the prairie homesteads and rear their children in the best traditions of Britain."[59] In a similar vein, in her travel narrative *An English-woman in the Canadian West* (1913), Elizabeth Keith Morris suggests that women settlers could fulfill "their highest and noblest mission in life" simply by becoming "the mothers of Canada," "our true empire builders."[60] Thus does the master narrative of western settlement appear to rely upon the population of the prairies as a reproductive act—that is, reproductive of the "best traditions of Britain"—with actual women being represented as the cultural vessels through which the failing greatness of the British Empire would be given new life.

The inevitable result of this ideological conception of woman's role as "moral and cultural custodian"—as the one "charged with disseminating morality and purity"[61]—within the geographic space of the Canadian prairies, notes Carter, was a rather "limited repertoire of behaviour available to white women":

> The wise women from the East would exemplify all the qualities of the ideal Victorian woman, which included purity and piety. At times it proved useful also to emphasize the frailty and delicacy of the white woman, as well as her dependence on males, though these were scarcely the qualities that would ensure stability or success in the Prairie West.[62]

What is clear from the prescriptions on female behaviour here articulated by Carter is that "the prairies were not, after all, culturally isolated from the rest of the world."[63] Carter's listed ideals are commensurate with the ideals perpetuated throughout the British Empire and North America, as in the Victorian "Angel in the House"[64] and what Barbara Welter identified in nineteenth-century American society as the "Cult of True Womanhood."[65] These images demanded that the prairie woman participate in "the government's purpose of recreating the middle-class domestic ideal on the prairies,"[66] that she adhere to an ideology that, when transplanted westward, demanded that women not only fulfill their maternal "role of moral guardian and spiritual centre of the home," but also become "economically productive,"[67] although only within the confines of the family farm. But therein lies the paradox: on the one hand, prairie women were meant to adopt the accepted female role as domestic icon; on the other hand, the practical nature of their participation in the settlement of the Canadian prairies would, in many ways, be profoundly unsettling of this role. Indeed, the demand on women for "purity and piety," "frailty and delicacy," and a "dependency on males," as Carter notes about prairie women, had far less to do with the reality of women's lives than cultural ideologies. There has been scholarly debate about the extent to which these prescriptions actually influenced the behaviour of women who migrated to western lands.[68] However, as Deborah Gorham suggests of "those women who came to North America as pioneer wives," they accepted and brought with them as cultural baggage the Victorian "image of themselves as moral guardians and protectors of the hearth."[69] Similarly, although speaking specifically of women settlers who emigrated to Saskatoon in the late nineteenth century, Jacqueline Bliss suggests that "the ideal of the Victorian lady was, therefore, part of the baggage brought by the settlers—men and women."[70] And it was certainly not only the earliest "pioneer wives" who felt the weight of Victorianism upon them, for, as Gerald Friesen suggests of "the settled society of the post-1900 prairie west," it was "imbued with the atmosphere of Victorian England and Ontario."[71] This conventional atmosphere is evident in contemporary literature: as ironically suggested by Elizabeth Lewthwaite in a 1901 article in *The Fortnightly Review*, "robust health in England is not a necessary qualification, though of course desirable, for the prairie atmosphere is so pure and invigorating that many delicate folk on their arrival become new creatures; and I have often been amazed at what fragile, delicate-looking women are able to accomplish."[72] The civilizing presence of "fragile, delicate-looking women" was acknowledged in 1913 by Morris, who noted regarding the "shaggy appearance of some of the [male] settlers" that "these men had become rough through the lack of a woman's refining influence, but it was a roughness that could be very quickly rubbed off by a dainty, gentle hand."[73]

It is in the subjection of women's bodies to cultural ideologies of behaviour appropriate to the reproduction of "civilization" in the prairie West that I would suggest we see the conflation of geographic space with the space of the female body: indeed, the "gendered romance" of territorial expansion is a process in which "person as well as territory constitutes property."[74] In fact, I would argue that in the master-narrative of western settlement, the female body functions as "a space of mimetic representation"[75] of the larger cultural project. I would further suggest that the universalizing demands for purity and piety, frailty and delicacy, and a dependence on males ensured that the female body as culturally inscribed space would be veiled in an "illusion of transparency."[76] As suggested by Henri Lefebvre, "the illusion of transparency goes hand in hand with a view of space as innocent, as free of traps or secret places. Anything hidden or dissimulated—and hence dangerous—is antagonistic to transparency, under whose reign everything can be taken in by a single glance from that mental eye which illuminates whatever it contemplates."[77]

In their Introduction to *Writing Women and Space: Colonial and Postcolonial Geographies*, Alison Blunt and Gillian Rose suggest that "essentialist or universalist accounts of femininity produce and depend upon" Lefebvre's notion of "transparent space," which tends towards "homogeneity, toward a denial of difference."[78] Thus, if we apply such a notion to the behavioural performances of the female body, insofar as they are subject to the moral and cultural criteria implicit to the imperialist project of western settlement, these corporeal spaces are considered to be unproblematically judged as either pure and pious, frail and delicate, etc., or not. Historian Julie Roy Jeffrey suggests that the ability to judge people on the basis of, among other things, physical behaviour was essential to "civilizing" efforts in the American west in the mid-nineteenth century, and "because middle-class white woman and men relied on their own cultural standards to judge others, they found many groups deficient and unworthy of social inclusion when they did not adopt white values and standards of behavior."[79] Thus do we see corporeality as "performance," or the "offering up [of] the body/the self to public consumption, and of being assessed on the adequacy of the performance."[80] The female body thus enters into the "rituals of gender etiquette" as an "institutionalized social performance" and becomes a "vehicle for the transmission of socially normative meanings of gender,"[81] which then, in turn, assure the achievement of the nationalist agenda. Most importantly, at all times the female body, as a space reproductive of imperial civilization, must perform its denial of a "space of the 'impure' beyond [its] own utopian boundaries."[82]

The question inevitably becomes, is the cultural pressure for conformity to ideals of behaviour so overwhelming that the female bodies performed in memoir texts remain complicit in the imperialist project, even though they were written sometimes many years after the cultural moment of settlement life? Or do the published texts of these women display, in the words of Buss, "an undercurrent of forbidden discourse, a discourse of rebellious accusation" running below and serving as narrative "interruptions" of what is so often revealed to be only a surface of "obedient conformity"[83] to the social performance of gender scripts? After all, as Blunt and Rose acknowledge, "there is always a space of some kind for resistance"[84] to the cultural imposition of universalizing notions of transparency, and I would suggest that a memoir text functions as just such a (temporally safe) space of resistance. Indeed, we might say that memoir functions as "a space of the 'impure'"; as a textual frontier in which the woman writer stakes her claim in his-story and embodies forth her resistance to the "totalizing metanarrative"[85] of western imperialism's construction of female behaviour. It is thus important to consider that an individual's reconstruction of the "rituals of gender etiquette" of an earlier state of society within a memoir text may be an attempt to render such "institutionalized" symbols as "vehicles of social change" by "reject[ing] [them] as sexist and as dissonant with [her] cognitions."[86] By reading women's memoirs with the possibility of such "dissonance" in mind, we can see that the "social system *does not act uniformly* on individuals with different experiential histories."[87] Although a surface reading of these texts often does suggest identification with past gender scripts, nevertheless it will be seen that the "Prairie Angel"[88] was sometimes required to step down from her pedestal and participate in the realities of settlement life, thus necessitating a rather less delimited repertoire of behaviour from the female body. Indeed, as Silverman has discovered in her many examinations of cultural prescription versus the lived experience of prairie women, "the myth of the lady crumbled, inappropriate to the demands of a west which must be transformed from merely a geography to a society. Women seized chances, or responded out of necessity, to act, to do more than adorn the hearth or their men's status."[89]

One of the ways in which women's bodies were subjected to cultural ideologies of female behaviour is through the dictates of fashion, including such adornments as clothing and hairstyles. If, as I have argued, the female body exists as a "transparent" space subject to an imperialist agenda of appropriate behaviour, then certainly clothing can be said to function as "an encroachment of social norms upon the body's surface."[90] Indeed, "social identity expressed in dress becomes not only an answer to the question of *who* one is, but *how* one is, and concerns the definition of the self in relation to a moral and religious value system."[91] If the "female costume" was one form of "cultural power employed specifically to regulate the [behavioural] options for women," it is no wonder that women found it "difficult to deviate from fashion"; in fact, "women's self-regulation in costume was encouraged by the sense that society expected, even demanded, conformity to a rigid feminine standard."[92] For many of the earliest female settlers to the sparsely settled Canadian prairies, regulation of their behaviour was non-existent, except at the level of the individual; that is, for well-socialized women of Anglo-Saxon background, Lefebvre's "mental eye which illuminates whatever it contemplates" exists as a sort of self-monitor used by women to negotiate their own behaviour, even when living at the very margins of "civilization." Significantly borrowing from the language of land ownership, John Berger suggests that "a woman must continually watch herself. She is almost continually accompanied by her own image of herself . . . she comes to consider the *surveyor* and the *surveyed* within her as the two constituent yet always distinct elements of her identity as a woman. . . . The surveyor of woman in herself is male: the surveyed, female."[93]

Thus was it difficult for early women settlers to relinquish the "ways of seeing" themselves learned as part of their inherited cultural knowledge. For example, Hiemstra's *Gully Farm*, the story of the Pinder family's 1903 emigration to Canada from England with the ill-fated Barr Colony enterprise, provides a glimpse into the practical difficulties of maintaining Victorian standards of "purity" as related to clothing and the expression/repression of female behaviour. Prior to her family's arrival on their homestead, while still on the train ride from St. John to Saskatoon, Mrs. Pinder unproblematically adheres to the orderly physical symbols of her position as a "decent woman": as Hiemstra writes, "Her long, lovely hair was never unkept and frowzy. She always combed it first thing in the morning and twisted it into a neat, thick roll on top of her small head. Her dress was as tidy as her hair. There was never a gap between her trim skirt and bodice, and she never walked about with her shoes unlaced as some of the women did."[94] It is especially in Hiemstra's insistence on the symbolic lack of "a gap between her trim skirt and bodice" that Mrs. Pinder's body denies the possibility of, as Blunt and Rose suggest regarding transparency, a "space of the 'impure' beyond [its] own utopian boundaries." From her meticulously maintained hairdo, right down to her shoelaces, Mrs. Pinder has evidently not yet been "undone" as a result of her journey to the margins of civilization. However, once she has arrived in a virtually unpopulated— and hence uncivilized—portion of the region, Mrs. Pinder finds herself living in a tent and facing the advent of a prairie winter. Despite her fear of the great outdoors, she is forced by necessity to emerge from the family tent and aid her husband in the construction of their first home on the prairies. As suggested in the scene used as epigraph to this essay, Mrs.

Pinder and the then six-year-old author are placed in what Hiemstra calls a "precarious perch" (162) as they find themselves sitting atop the ever-growing walls of the new structure, helping to pull up logs. For Mrs. Pinder, especially, such work places the female body in a position that threatens the maintenance of Victorian values in terms of female behaviour and, as Hiemstra takes care to note, it is only the log that slips and not her mother's strict adherence to ideals of the "decent woman." As this scene illustrates, in the early period of western settlement when "women were called upon to both substitute for and supplement the work of men," the "women who were so compelled by necessity had to watch that they were not tarred with the brush of unwomanliness."[95]

In counterpoint to Mrs. Pinder's position as "decent woman" are the images Hiemstra draws of the formidable (and unnamed) "Dukhobor women," who, described as being built like *percherons:* large, thick-chested animals, accustomed to hauling huge loads without any fuss or bother," "toil in the fields from daylight to dark" (90) and accomplish the work normally reserved for animals and men. In direct contrast to Mrs. Pinder's petiteness—she is, after all, described as being "only a little woman with soft round arms and small hands, not the axe-swinging type at all"—the Doukhobor women are described as being "more like oaks than willows," for they are "wide and strong looking, deep of bust and thick of thigh" with "bare feet and ankles" as "big as the feet and ankles of most men" (156, 90).[96] In *God Bless Our Home: Domestic Life in Nineteenth-Century Canada*, Una Abrahamson provides an anonymous quote that identifies the prevailing concept of the ideal female body in this period, a concept quite foreign to the descriptions provided by Hiemstra of the Doukhobor women: "Small feet and small ankles are very attractive, because they are in harmony with a perfect female form, and men admire perfection. Small feet and ankles indicate modesty and reserve, while large feet and ankles indicate coarseness, physical power, authority and pre-dominance."[97] In Hiemstra's text we are able to see the female body rep-resented as a transparent space subject to cultural scrutiny for signs of "impurity," or non-adherence to the demands for "purity and piety," "frailty and delicacy," and a "dependence on men." Although the descrip-tions of the Doukhobor women come prior to the scene of Mrs. Pinder straddling the log wall of her home, Hiemstra's statement in that later scene, that "no decent woman exposed her ankles in those days," must necessarily recall to the reader the ankles of the Doukhobor women as they are presented in all their stark unfemininity.[98]

As Mrs. Pinder's stay on the prairies lengthens and necessity demands an increasingly "indecent," or "impure," repertoire of behaviour, we begin to see Hiemstra construct a textual space of liberation for her mother, a growing freedom from cultural constraints that is reflected in fashion. Keeping in mind her orderly image while on the train ride to Saskatoon, we must compare that to a scene in which Mrs. Pinder participates with her husband and another immigrant couple in chasing a bear. Having sighted a bear, Mrs. Pinder leaves her children—themselves "startled at being left alone" by their mother—and makes an instinctive decision, ostensibly in concern for her husband's safety, to "dash" after him (her husband, or the bear?) into "a little grove" (166). When Mrs. Pinder returns, she is described by Hiemstra as follows: "She didn't look at all like the quiet mother I was used to. She was young and excited, a Diana enjoying the chase. Her cheeks glowed pink, her blue eyes sparkled, her lips smiled, even her knot of hair that had slipped a little looked adventurous. A long bramble clung to her skirt, but she didn't seem to notice" (167). Hiemstra's description—written half a century after the moment of settlement, although long before second-wave feminism's recovery of alternative female archetypes—is particularly interesting, given what I have found to be the most common female memoirist's characterization of the displaced settler woman as a modern-day Ruth, the always loyal servant to and follower of her husband and family, an image Hiemstra herself utilizes in her text.[99] As a Ruth, we might well assume that Mrs. Pinder is indeed following her husband into the grove as an act of self-effacement, of concern for his safety; however, by very deliberately invoking an earlier cultural script for female behaviour—and especially by invoking the image of Diana (Artemis, in Greek mythology), "the huntress, with her golden bow and moaning arrows, who leaves in her trail howling animals and a shuddering earth, is goddess of the wild, virgin nature, all the inviolate places of the earth where humans dare not enter,"[100] Hiemstra deliberately represents her mother in a more self-interested chase after the bear and away from Victorian concerns of female "decency" and "purity." In details such as the "knot of hair that had slipped a little" and the "long bramble [which] clung to her skirt," Mrs. Pinder's perch seems ever more precarious as her reflective memoirist-daughter begins to redefine the spatial politics of western settlement.

Hiemstra clearly constructs her mother's final plunge into the depths of behavioural transgression in another fiery scene. Although Mrs. Pinder has stated that in the event of a prairie fire she would be able to do nothing more than "run away" (183), at the first signs of a fire, perhaps as a result of the disobedient pleasures of bear-hunting, she unhesitatingly plunges into the burning bush. Admonishing her obviously panicked husband not to "'stand there looking gormless,'" Mrs. Pinder rejects the notion that she should stay safely "'in the house with the bairns'" and heads off, wet sacks in hand, to do battle with one of the many enemies of the prairie farmer. When she finally emerges again from the smoke and ash-filled air, Hiemstra shows her mother ironically cleansed of her complicity with acts of "decency" and now carrying the bodily symbols of her conversion to acts of "impurity": the daughter-author writes, "Mother came out of the smoke, but she looked so unlike the pretty mother we were used to we were almost afraid of her. Her face was black, and her eyes were red. Her hair was singed, and so were her eyelashes and brows" (185). After her second plunging "into the smoke," Mrs. Pinder emerges once again, this time represented by Hiemstra in a symbolic tableau of Victorian woman resisting the physical restrictions of her clothing: "Mother was driving the team and doing very well at it. She was running and her long, wide skirts streamed out behind her, and so did the little shawl tied around her neck" (186). While Mrs. Pinder arrives from the Old World initially complicit with the "totalizing metanarrative" of female behaviour, the opportunities provided by early conditions of social isolation in the West for bodily transgressions of the "rituals of gender etiquette," as noted above, are various. Indeed, despite the fact that she has been socialized to follow an "Angel in the House" script, New World conditions lacked any consistent audience, outside herself and her family, to monitor her performance of that script. Thus we see that "an expanding frontier sometimes provided women with the chance to contravene sex-role expectations and expand the scope of female culture."[101] In the end, the cumulative effect of Mrs. Pinder's adventures beyond the confines of appropriate female behaviour is significant for, as Hiemstra tells us, at least for a while after these experiences, "Mother never mentioned going back to England" (189).

Almost twenty years after Mrs. Pinder's immigration to Canada, Kathleen Strange arrived from England at a CNR station in central Alberta in 1920 to discover that an increase in prairie population often meant a loss of liberation from social/cultural constraints on the female body. As described in a memoir titled *With the West in Her Eyes* (1937), Strange arrived from the Old World with a new behavioural script in hand and herself fully marked with evidence of her "impurity," only to discover that the establishment of close-knit prairie communities seems to have consolidated the "rituals of gender etiquette" of an earlier period. Despite the burgeoning emancipation of women in the post–World War I outside world, women living in prairie communities, which were now less isolated than when Hiemstra's mother arrived, seemed to be clinging to older ideals of female behaviour: indeed, as Bliss notes of women in a Saskatchewan context, "as the need for survival skills in Saskatoon women diminished with the growth of the community, women began to revert more closely to the Victorian ideal."[102] Strange's first impression of the small prairie community is that years of settlement have, as Mair had suggested they would, succeeded in "binding the scattered communities of British America together in the bonds of a common cause, a common language, and a common destiny,"[103] and she immediately stresses her sense of exclusion:

> Not only did they *expect* us to fail, but I rather fancy they unconsciously *wanted* us to fail. We were so obviously city products, and we were, also, by way of being interlopers, since we had come into a community that consisted mainly of one large family from a certain part of Ontario, related, if not by ties of blood, then by ties of marriage and long association. (12)

Strange here marks her family's difference as being based on their status as "city products," as members of a class of people whose values differ radically from rural populations, as well as their being imperial "interlopers" in a colonial community that, especially after World War I, was beginning to feel its independence from the mother country.

While all her family members are subject to disapproval, however, Strange appears to merit special attention in being judged for settlement life. As she steps off the CN train, she finds herself immediately confronted with cultural prescriptions for the performance of the female body as she becomes the object of public scrutiny: "word had evidently gone forth that the newcomers would arrive on the noon train, and so our future neighbours had turned out in full force to look us over, and to pass judgment on us" (11). Once again the female body functions as a public symbol, a transparent space subject to judgement according to "socially normative meanings of gender." As Strange admits, she does not fair well in her first social performance:

> I realize now that we must have appeared to them to be rather queer-looking people. I myself, for instance, did not look the part of a farmer's wife in any particular. I was small and none too robust-looking. I was dressed, city fashion, in a tailored suit, and wore a little hat that had its inception in Paris. I also wore high-heeled shoes and the filmiest of silk stockings. To make matters worse, I had my hair cut short, and wore it in a straight Dutch bob with heavy 'bangs.' Short hair had been a fairly general custom in England since early in the war.... (11)

Leaving aside the issue of Strange's apparent physical inappropriateness for "the part of a farmer's wife," we see here that her clothing problem stems specifically from the fact that she is dressed "city fashion," a style apparently too frivolous for the practical necessities of rural life. Like many settler women before her, Strange is perched precariously (on high-heeled shoes); she is on the verge of exceeding rural notions of female decency and purity as they relate to corporeal construction through clothing. In addition to inappropriate shoeware, Strange's hairstyle—despite its obvious practicality for women's work anywhere—marks her as "strange," as not feminine enough, to play "the part of a farmer's wife." Although, as Aileen Ribeiro notes in her study of *Dress and Morality* in Britain, in the first decade of the twentieth century the fashion ideal had become "a young, slim girl with short hair fitting close to the head, ... a curious mixture of sophistication and boyishness,"[104] this style trend had obviously not become the norm in western Canadian society, probably due to the existence of a colonial mentality whereby gendered customs from the Old World were preserved as a mark of communal stability and identity. Indeed, the "bob" style had caused considerable controversy in this period, as evident in a contemporary Canadian novel, Douglas Durkin's *The Magpie* (1923), in which Marion Nason, whose hair was "'bobbed' in the latest mode," finds herself subject to prescriptions of female decency, for, "although her mother had once hinted that longer hair might be more becoming in the wife of Craig Forrester, she had refused to forsake the 'bobbed' hair mode that she had affected before her marriage."[105]

Thus, from her fashions to her hair, Strange is feminine in a style that, as she ironically—yet aptly for the historical context of this chapter—phrases it, "appeared not to have penetrated this particular part of Western Canada at all" (11). Strange, who first published her memoir in 1937, with a reissue in 1945—which marks its participation in the vast change in cultural attitudes about the spatial politics of female "decency" and "purity" as a result of women's work during World War II—does not wait long to challenge both geographic and corporeal space in relation to gender prescriptions on clothing. She very boldly enters the "space of the 'impure'" when she and her mother-in-law undertake "something that greatly shock[s] the community":

> We had decided that we would both like to do some horseback riding ... I had brought with me ... some new riding breeches, in which I felt I looked quite smart. Naturally I put them on. Grandma was induced to wear a pair of Harry's army slacks. They were rather a tight fit, I confess, but we trusted they would stand the strain. (39)

Together the women ride forth, intending to pay a visit to a female neighbour. Initially stunned by the subsequent and "decidedly frigid reception" they receive from the woman, they soon become aware of the cause of the "charged atmosphere" of their visit. As Strange narrates,

> A few days later a deputation of ladies called at the shack and asked to see my husband alone.
> They told him they had called to protest against my wearing breeches. They said that no women had ever appeared in such an immodest garb in that community before, and they wished to inform my husband that I must be stopped from ever appearing in such an outfit again. (40)

As Angela E. Davis has noted elsewhere—and as Strange here discovers—prairie women "seemed unable to break free of traditional values. Women were 'doomed to the skirt,' said one writer, 'any attempt to get away from it has raised a hue and cry of immodesty and ridicule.'"[106]

Strange's response to the charge of "immodesty" is one of angry "defiance" (40), an emotional response that she uses as what Marilyn Frye would call "an instrument of cartography"[107]; Strange admits, "I went on wearing the offending garments, and in time apparently wore the resistance down" (40). Thus, in this one small but ultimately effective way, Strange's determination to resist cultural prescriptions results in the remapping of certain "rituals of gender etiquette"; in the simple act of riding out over the vast space of the prairies "indecently" clad, she destabilizes the boundaries erected on the female body as a culturally defined space and ultimately frees other women in the community to dress in a way that makes their work more comfortable.

For women settlers who had experienced extra-domestic, paid, wartime employment prior to their arrival in a prairie community, it quickly became apparent that "World War I had not had the broad effect on the reality of women's lives for which it has sometimes been given credit,"[108] at least not immediately. As a result, women settlers such as Strange, who emigrated to Alberta in 1920, and who openly confesses in *With the West* that "domestic life had never had any great attraction" for her (31), found it necessary to push the boundaries of decency and purity as related to the subject of women's work. Back home in England, Strange had worked in the Ministry of Munitions, where, as she states it, "at a comparatively early age, I had learned to stand on my own feet and to fight my own battles. I had encountered men and competed with them on an equal footing, and had gained an experience of life that has undoubtedly stood me in good stead during the years that have passed" (5).

Despite the general assertion that "women's attitudes about their own proper role, and in turn prevailing attitudes about women, were changed dramatically by the Great War,"[109] Strange's commencement of prairie life is marred when, the local community of women demands that the "stranger," as she labels herself, adapt her behaviour to reflect more traditional "rituals of gender etiquette." Initially, Strange does appear to be generally complicit with "the virtues of domestic femininity," at least with regards to the work she performs. The Strange family emigrated to Alberta and took over an existing farm from another couple, the Aungers, who stay on a while to help the newcomers settle in to rural life and work. Within the domestic space of the farmhouse, it is Mrs. Aunger who becomes the prototype of the ideal prairie wife, an ideal against which Strange quickly determines to attain equal measure. Joining Mrs. Aunger in the shack's kitchen, Strange makes the following confession to her reader: "I knew nothing about cooking. The fact was that I'd never even boiled an egg or prepared a meal in my life"; however, Strange quickly resolves to learn to perform the "natural dut[ies] of the farm housewife" alone, and she goes on to document her gradual struggle to "adapt herself" to her new lifestyle (44). Indeed, she soon appears to become champion to the cause of appropriate gender etiquette, and is eventually able to assert that she is adequately "running [her] own affairs—the domestic end of the farm—with a greater smoothness than [she] had ever dreamed possible" (218).

Nevertheless, as with her decision to continue wearing breeches while riding, Strange seizes more than one occasion to be disobedient to social/cultural codes, and, as Hiemstra would twenty years later, in 1937 Strange also uses the textual image of the settler woman positioned on a "precarious perch." For example, feeling anxious about progress on the building of their new home, she offers one day to step outside her domestic duties and "haul a load of lumber" from the nearby town (54). Laughed at by the men, she nonetheless sets out, has the wagon loaded, and begins her return trip. Once out on the prairie landscape, Strange is quickly forced to acknowledge that she has perhaps exceeded her capabilities as a farm wife: losing control of her horses while going down a hill, she admits she "had neither the skill nor the strength to manage [the] team" (55). The geography beyond the homestead continues to threaten her with defeat for, while the upward trend of the next hill slows down the uncontrolled progress of the horses, "another problem confront[s her]": "looking downward I discovered that I was slowly but surely moving backward on the load of lumber! There was an increasingly widening space between the front end of the wagon and the ends of the boards up on which I was perched." Unlike Mrs. Pinder, who determines to maintain both her perch and her sense of decency by letting the logs slip instead of herself, Strange rejects the helplessness of her situation by "jump[ing] down into the half-empty wagon box, lean[ing] over the front end, and concentrat[ing] all [her] attention on keeping the horses in hand" (55–56).

Although she does lose the load of lumber and becomes the subject of a "good laugh at [her] expense," the more important narrative focus is that she does control the situation, she eventually makes it home safely, and the family home gets built. At a later time, braced by the "confidence" gained in that first experience driving the wagon, Strange decides to "take a wagon into Big Valley and bring back a load of coal for the farm herself" (92–93). Once again, near disaster strikes as the trap in the coal chute fails to close; she admits, "in the excitement of the moment I did not have the sense to pull ahead, but just sat there, watching the coal pour down on to my already over-full wagon." As a result, "the horses jumped forward, broke the wagon pole, and almost threw me from my perch" (93–94). Once again, however, Strange manages to complete her self-appointed task, even despite having to listen "to some of the most expressive and colourful language [she had] ever heard in [her] life" coming from the mouths of the attendant miners. In both cases, Strange willfully undertakes her geographic and corporeal confrontations with domestic scripts, and neither the threat of falling from her precarious perch, nor the less than supportive judgements of men, deter her from inscribing her bodily resistance across the prairie landscape, across the memoir page.

In their representations of women's bodies chasing bears, fighting fires, straddling horses while clothed in pants, and driving wagons, the memoirists examined here provide us with a narrative space in which to get beyond the rhetoric that constructed women as (re)productive of both the larger social/cultural as well as the individual "dreams of a future." In their texts we see that lived experience of prairie life often resulted in the settler woman's needing and/or wanting to perform her disobedience to, her transgression of, spatial constructions of gender. Within the temporally safe textual space of the memoir, then, these authors demonstrate the precarious nature, the constantly shifting boundaries, of what it meant to be a "decent woman" in prairie society. For early women settlers such as Mrs. Pinder, the pressure to conform to domestic ideals came largely from within, but that internal monitor of "decent" behaviour often had to be ignored when prairie isolation demanded the settler woman's participation in activities beyond the pale of female "purity." Extra-domestic activities thus became a necessity, and sometimes even a guilty pleasure. For women like Strange, the pressure to conform to domestic ideals came largely from without, from a female community for whom domesticity provided security and identity in a time of social change. In both cases, looking back across the gulf of time, the vast geography of the prairies becomes a narrative vehicle allowing for a more dynamic construction of the settler woman, whose corporeality "disidentifies" with the supposed "transparency" of conventional categories of femininity and "transfers to a form of female subjectivity that exceeds the phallic definition."[110]

ENDNOTES

1. R. Douglas Francis, *Images of the West: Changing Perceptions of the Prairies, 1690–1960* (Saskatoon: Western Producer Prairie Books, 1989), xvi.

2. Laurie Ricou, *Vertical Man/Horizontal World: Man and Landscape in Canadian Prairie Fiction* (Vancouver: University of British Columbia Press, 1973), 1, ix.

3. Elizabeth B. Mitchell, *In Western Canada before the War: Impressions of Early Twentieth Century Prairie Communities* (1915; Saskatoon: Western Producer Prairie Books, 1981), 108–109.

4. Wallace Stegner, *Wolf Willow: a history, a story, and a memory of the last plains frontier* (1955; Toronto: The Macmillan Company of Canada Limited, 1967), 29.

5. Allison Weir, *Sacrificial Logics: Feminist Theory and the Critique of Identity* (New York: Routledge, 1996), 127.

6. Katarzyna Rukszto, "Representing Canada: Heritage, History and the Politics of Belonging," Nationalism, Citizenship and National Identity Conference, Mount Allison University, Sackville, New Brunswick, 11–13 November 1999, p. 17. While the concern of this paper is to respond to several calls for the reconciliation of women's first-hand accounts of prairie settlement to the historical record, and to read the written reminiscences of women who actually experienced settlement over and against contemporary constructions of gender, it is important to note the considerable scholarship that has already been done on the subject of prairie women's lives. For a good overview of this work, see Ann Leger Anderson's "Canadian Prairie Women's History: An Uncertain Enterprise," *Journal of the West* 37, 1 (January 1998): 47–59, in which the author refers to the following regional collections: Mary Kinnear, ed., *First Days, Fighting Days: Women in Manitoba History* (Regina: Canadian Plains Research Center, 1987); David De Brou and Aileen Moffatt, eds., *"Other" Voices: Historical Essays on Saskatchewan Women* (Regina: Canadian Plains Research Center, 1995); and Catherine A. Cavanaugh and Randi R. Warne, eds., *Standing on New Ground: Women in Alberta* (Edmonton: University of Alberta Press, 1993). More recently, Cavanaugh and Warne are the editors of a new anthology, *Telling Tales: Essays in Western Women's History* (Vancouver: University of British Columbia Press, 2000), in which it is asserted that academic attention to "new or unused sources," including "memoirs," is necessary as a means to "reimagine the past in ways that reflect women's perspectives—what women thought, felt, and did, and how their experience was mediated by culture and society" (11–12).

7. Lynne Huffer, *Maternal Pasts, Feminist Futures: Nostalgia, Ethics, and the Question of Difference* (Stanford, CA: Stanford University Press, 1998), 19.

8. "folklife," in *Folklore: An Encyclopedia of Beliefs, Customs, Tales, Music, and Art*, ed. Thomas A. Green, 2 vols. (Santa Barbara: ABC-CLIO, 1997), 322; emphasis added.

9. Sidonie Smith, "Performativity, Autobiographical Practice, Resistance," *a/b: Auto/Biography Studies* 10, 1 (Spring 1995): 21.

10. Margaret R. Higonnet, "New Cartographies, an Introduction," in *Reconfigured*

Spheres: Feminist Explorations of Literary Space, ed. Margaret R. Higonnet and Joan Templeton (Amherst: University of Massachusetts Press, 1994), 2.

11. Barbara Brook, *Feminist Perspectives on the Body* (London: Longman, 1999), 111.

12. Andrea L. Bell, "Creating Space in the Margins: Power and Identity in the cuentos breves of Pía Barros and Cristina Peri Rossi," *Studies in Short Fiction* 33 (1996): 345.

13. Martin Fowler, "Pioneer Memoirs," in *The Oxford Companion to Canadian Literature*, ed. Eugene Benson and William Toye, 2nd ed. (Toronto: Oxford University Press, 1997), 923.

14. Marcus Billson, "The Memoir: New Perspectives on a Forgotten Genre," *Genre* 10, 2 (Summer 1977): 259.

15. Ibid., 261; emphasis added.

16. Helen M. Buss, "Memoir with an Attitude: One Reader Reads *The Woman Warrior: Memoirs of a Girlhood among Ghosts*," *a/b: Auto/Biography Studies* 12, 2 (Fall 1997): 204.

17. Elizabeth Fox-Genovese, "Between Individualism and Community: Autobiographies of Southern Women," in *Located Lives: Place and Idea in Southern Autobiography*, ed. J. Bill Berry (Athens, GA: University of Georgia Press, 1990), 20, 26.

18. Francis Russell Hart, "History Talking to Itself: Public Personality in Recent Memoir," *New Literary History* 11, 1 (Autumn 1979): 195.

19. Billson, "The Memoir," 268, 261.

20. Ibid., 271.

21. Ibid., 278.

22. Buss, "Memoir with an Attitude," 203.

23. Paul Smith, *Discerning the Subject* (Minneapolis: Minnesota University Press, 1988), 120.

24. Lee Quinby, "The Subject of Memoirs: *The Woman Warrior*'s Technology of Ideographic Selfhood," in *De/Colonizing the Subject: The Politics of Gender in Women's Autobiography*, ed. Sidonie Smith and Julia Watson (Minneapolis: Minnesota University Press, 1992), 299.

25. Buss, "Memoir with an Attitude," 203.

26. Ibid., 206.

27. Helen M. Buss, "Settling the Score with Myths of Settlement: Two Women Who Roughed It and Wrote It," in *Great Dames*, ed. Elspeth Cameron and Janice Dickin (Toronto: University of Toronto Press, 1997), 167.

28. I borrow the term "scripts" here from Sidonie Smith's delineation of the "four predominant life scripts available to women of the late medieval and Renaissance periods," scripts that served to ensure that "woman's subjectivity and her public voice remain[ed] silenced." Sidonie Smith, *A Poetics of Women's Autobiography: Marginality and the Fictions of Self-Representation* (Bloomington: Indiana University Press, 1987), 31. I am thus suggesting that, although the nature of

such scripts evolves over time and across cultures, nevertheless the notion of social scripts that seek to control women's behaviour remains historically constant.

29. Smith, "Performativity," 20–21.

30. Ibid., 21.

31. Ibid., 19–20.

32. Francis, *Images of the West*, 73–74.

33. Ibid., 107.

34. Gerald Friesen, *The Canadian Prairies: A History* (Toronto: University of Toronto Press, 1987), 162, 181.

35. For example, although Clifford Sifton, who held the position of Minister of the Interior from 1897 to 1905, sought to appeal to farmers of various national backgrounds, he also clearly "believed in assimilation of the immigrants to a British-Canadian norm." Likewise, Frank Oliver, who succeeded Sifton in 1905, was "staunchly British" in his thinking, and thus "he was more inclined to reduce the recruiting activity in central and eastern Europe and to increase it in Great Britain, including its cities, in order to preserve the 'national fabric' of Canada." See Friesen, *Canadian Prairies*, 246.

Nowhere is the assimilationist nature of western expansion better expressed than in Ralph Connor's *The Foreigner: A Tale of Saskatchewan* (New York: George H. Doran Company, 1909), in which the author provides the following prefatory note: "In Western Canada there is to be seen to-day that most fascinating of all human phenomena, the making of a nation. Out of breeds diverse in traditions, in ideals, in speech, and in manner of life, Saxon and Slav, Teuton, Celt and Gaul, one people is being made. The blood strains of great races will mingle in the blood of a race greater than the greatest of them all."

This same philosophy is less romantically stated within the text itself, as one of Connor's characters remarks about the presence of a colony of "Galicians" that they "'exist as an undigested foreign mass. They must be digested and absorbed into the body politic. They must be taught our ways of thinking and living, or it will be a mighty bad thing for us in Western Canada'" (255).

36. Howard Palmer, "Strangers and Stereotypes: The Rise of Nativism, 1880–1920," in *The Prairie West: Historical Readings*, ed. R. Douglas Francis and Howard Palmer, 2nd ed. (Edmonton: Pica Pica Press, 1992), 311.

37. Catherine A. Cavanaugh, "'No Place for a Woman': Engendering Western Canadian Settlement," *Western Historical Quarterly* 28, 4 (Winter 1997): 494.

38. J. Ewing Ritchie, *To Canada with Emigrants: A Record of Actual Experiences* (London: T. Fisher Unwin, 1885), 160; emphasis added.

39. John Herd Thompson, *Forging the Prairie West* (Toronto: Oxford University Press, 1998), 51.

40. Daniel Coleman, "Immigration, Nation, and the Canadian Allegory of Manly Maturation," *Essays on Canadian Writing* 61 (Spring 1997): 85.

41. Jean Pickering and Suzanne Kehde, "Introduction," *Narratives of Nostalgia, Gender, and Nationalism*, ed. Jean Pickering and Suzanne Kehde (Washington

Square: New York University Press, 1997), 6. The feminization of the landscape in terms of American settlement patterns was noted by Annette Kolodny in *The Lay of the Land: Metaphor as Experience and History in American Life and Letters* (Chapel Hill: University of North Carolina Press, 1975), in which the author examines "what is probably America's oldest and most cherished fantasy: a daily reality of harmony between man and nature based on an experience of the land as essentially feminine—that is, not simply the land as mother, but the land as woman, the total female principle of gratification—enclosing the individual in an environment of receptivity, repose, and painless and integral satisfaction" (4). Although Kolodny notes that "other civilizations have undoubtedly gone through a similar history," she suggests that they did so "at a pace too slow or in a time too ancient to be remembered" and that "only in America has the entire process remained within historical memory" (8). For the purposes of Kolodny's study, "America" means the United States of America, although many of her conclusions are applicable to the Canadian case of land settlement. Indeed, in *Unnamed Country: The Struggle for a Canadian Prairie Fiction* (Edmonton: University of Alberta Press, 1977), Dick Harrison notes that "the identification of woman with the land [in Canadian prairie fiction] is not uncommon," citing Arthur Stringer's *The Mud Lark* (Indianapolis: Bobbs-Merrill, 1931), and Ralph Connor's *Gwen, an Idyll of the Canyon* (Toronto: Fleming H. Revell, 1899) as prime examples (97).

42. Charles Mair, "The New Canada," *The Search for English-Canadian Literature: An Anthology of Critical Articles from the Nineteenth and Early Twentieth Centuries*, ed. Carl Ballstadt (Toronto: University of Toronto Press, 1975), 151.

43. Ibid., 153.

44. W.H. New, *Land Sliding: Imagining Space, Presence, and Power in Canadian Writing* (Toronto: University of Toronto Press, 1997), 107.

45. The image of national expansion into the West as a process of legitimation gains significance when contrasted with the words chosen by Canadian imperialist George R. Parkin to describe the proposed effect on Canadian identity of continentalism: "In a Great Britain reorganized as a federation, or union, or alliance, Canada would hold an honorable place, gained on lines of true national development; in annexation to the United States she could have nothing but a *bastard nationality*, the offspring of either meanness, selfishness, or fear." Quoted in Paul W. Bennett, et al., *Emerging Identities: Selected Problems and Interpretations in Canadian History* (Scarborough: Prentice-Hall, 1986) 303; emphasis added.

    Mair's narrative relies heavily on a rhetoric of constriction: as he suggests, the new nation's "power and cohesiveness are being felt at last, and already it is binding the scattered communities of British America together in the bonds of a common cause, a common language, and a common destiny" (152). In this way, then, did narrative constructions of the Canadian west as both geographic and ideological space seem to preclude individual resistance to the common bonds of nation and empire building.

46. Emily Ferguson [Janey Canuck], *Open Trails* (London: Cassell and Company, Ltd., 1912), 72.

47. Quoted in Francis, *Images of the West*, 124.

48. Quoted in ibid., 127.

49. Arthur Stringer, *The Prairie Wife* (New York: A.L. Burt Company, 1915), 220.

50. I am referring here to Douglas Hill's *The Opening of the Canadian West: Where Strong Men Gathered* (New York: The John Day Company, 1967). In contemporary "masculinist definitions of the ideal settler," says Catherine Cavanaugh, "women's exclusion continue[d] to be so taken for granted that it seem[ed] to be less an idea than the natural order of things" ("No Place," 504).

51. Nellie L. McClung, *Sowing Seeds in Danny* (1908; Toronto: The Ryerson Press, 1922), 199.

52. Quoted in Jean Bruce, *The Last Best West* (Toronto: Fitzhenry and Whiteside, 1976), 7.

53. Quoted in Francis, *Images of the West*, 131.

54. Bruce, *Last Best West*, 19.

55. Ralph Allen, "Clifford Sifton's Medicine Show," in *Canadian Content*, ed. Nell Waldman and Sarah Norton, 3rd ed. (Toronto: Harcourt Brace, 1996), 262.

56. Quoted in Bruce, *Last Best West*, 22.

57. Sarah A. Carter, *Capturing Women: The Manipulation of Cultural Imagery in Canada's Prairie West* (Montreal & Kingston: McGill-Queen's University Press, 1997), 8. Cavanaugh also suggests that women settlers' role within expansionist discourse was to ensure a gender hierarchy of power ("No Place," 497–498).

    In her discussion of early female immigration to rural Manitoba, Mary Kinnear states the function of women thus: "Women were needed to help produce crops and goods, and they were needed to swell the population. Women were in the spotlight both as producers and reproducers." Mary Kinnear, *A Female Economy: Women's Work in a Prairie Province, 1870–1970* (Montreal & Kingston: McGill-Queen's University Press, 1998), 22.

58. Linda Rasmussen, et al., *A Harvest Yet to Reap: A History of Prairie Women* (Toronto: The Women's Press, 1976), 13.

59. The implicit connection between the fertility of the western landscape and the fertility of the ideal prairie woman can be seen in Cran's poetic description of one of the women she met on her travels: "Here, where they found virgin prairie, she stands; the heavy ears [of corn] lap against her splendid hips, and here and there they tip her breast; round her skirts the children cling, she moves in this beautiful, fruitful land like Ceres among plenty." Mrs. George [Marion Dudley] Cran, *A Woman in Canada* (London: John Milne, 1910), 14–15, 137.

60. Elizabeth Keith Morris, *An Englishwoman in the Canadian West* (Bristol: Arrowsmith; London: Simpkin, Marshall, 1913), 26.

61. Eliane Leslau Silverman, "Writing Canadian Women's History, 1970–82: An Historiographical Analysis," *Canadian Historical Review* LXIII, 4 (1982): 522.

62. Carter, *Capturing Women*, xv and 8.

63. Rasmussen, et al., *A Harvest*, 88.

64. Joan Perkin, *Women and Marriage in Nineteenth-Century England* (Chicago: Lyceum Books, 1989), 233.

65. See Barbara Welter, "The Cult of True Womanhood: 1820–1860," *American Quarterly* 18 (1966): 151–174.

66. Cavanaugh, "No Place," 505.

67. Deborah Gorham, "Singing up the Hill," *Canadian Dimension* 10 (June 1975): 36.

68. For example, although in *Women and Men on the Overland Trail* (New Haven: Yale University Press, 1979) John Mack Faragher suggests that "feminine farm roles had little to do with the fetishized domesticity that was a part of the womanly cult flowering in the East, for in most ways these pioneer wives and mothers were the very antithesis of that antiseptic and anesthetized version of femininity" (171); in *Frontier Women: "Civilizing" the West? 1840–1880* (rev. ed., New York: Hill and Wang, 1998). Julie Roy Jeffrey asserts that "frontier images of women were closely tied to images of middle-class women current in the East. The concept of woman as lady, the heart of domestic ideology, survived" (129).

69. Gorham, "Singing," 36.

70. Jacqueline Bliss, "Seamless Lives: Pioneer Women of Saskatoon, 1883–1903," *Saskatchewan History* XLIII, 3 (Autumn 1991): 84.

71. Friesen, *Canadian Prairies*, 315–316.

72. Elizabeth Lewthwaite, "Women's Work in Western Canada," *The Fortnightly Review* LXX (1901): 717.

73. Morris, *An Englishwoman*, 25.

74. New, *Land Sliding*, 107.

75. Alison Blunt and Gillian Rose, "Introduction," *Writing Women and Space: Colonial and Postcolonial Geographies*, ed. Alison Blunt and Gillian Rose (New York: The Guilford Press, 1994), 5.

76. Henri Lefebvre, *The Production of Space*, trans. Donald Nicholson-Smith (Oxford: Basil Blackwell, 1991), 27.

77. Ibid., 28.

78. Blunt and Rose, *Writing Women*, 5.

79. Jeffrey, *Frontier Women*, 7.

80. Brook, *Feminist Perspectives*, 113.

81. Seymour Parker, "Rituals of Gender: A Study of Etiquette, Public Symbols, and Cognition," *American Anthropologist* 90, 2 (1988): 374.

82. Blunt and Rose, *Writing Women*, 6.

83. Buss, "Settling the Score," 167–168.

84. Blunt and Rose, *Writing Women*, 15.

85. Ibid., 14.

86. Parker, "Rituals of Gender," 374, 382.

87. Ibid., 382.

88. Carol Fairbanks, *Prairie Women: Images in American and Canadian Fiction* (New Haven: Yale University Press, 1986), 76.

89. Eliane Leslau Silverman, *The Last Best West: Women on the Alberta Frontier, 1880–1930* (Montreal: Eden Press, 1984), xii.

90. Eva Maria Stadler, "Addressing Social Boundaries: Dressing the Female Body in Early Realist Fiction," in *Reconfigured Spheres: Feminist Explorations of Literary Space*, ed. Margaret R. Higonnet and Joan Templeton (Amherst: University of Massachusetts Press, 1994), 20.

91. Ruth Barnes and Joanne B. Eicher, "Introduction," in *Dress and Gender: Making and Meaning in Cultural Contexts*, ed. Ruth Barnes and Joanne B. Eicher (New York: Berg, 1992), 2.

92. Faragher, *Women and Men*, 105–107.

93. John Berger, *Ways of Seeing* (London: Penguin Books, 1972), 46–47.

94. Mary Hiemstra, *Gully Farm* (1955; Calgary: Fifth House, 1997), 46. Further references are cited parenthetically in the text.

95. Faragher, *Women and Men*, 108.

96. In fact, Hiemstra's Doukhobor women fulfill Clifford Sifton's by-now famous characterization of the ideal female immigrant as being the "stout wife" of a "stalwart peasant in a sheep-skin coat." The inefficiency of being "fragile" and "delicate" is eventually even admitted by Mrs. Pinder, who "often said she wished she was a bigger and stronger woman" (162).

97. Una Abrahamson, *God Bless Our Home: Domestic Life in Nineteenth-Century Canada* (Toronto: Burns and MacEachern Limited, 1966), 6.

98. Although Hiemstra wrote her descriptions of these women in 1955, half a century after her family's emigration to the prairies, contemporary images of Doukhobor women reinforce the idea that all women settlers' bodies were subjected to Anglo-Saxon ideals of form and behaviour. For example, in his 1911 book titled *Canada's West and Farther West*, journalist Frank Carrel includes an article (originally published in *Collier's Weekly*) written by Jean Blewett and titled "The Doukhobor Woman." Similar to Hiemstra, Blewett focusses on the physical details of these women, noting that "the Doukhobor woman is no Venus. A long while ago she acquired the habit of working, and, theorists to the contrary, hard, incessant work does not tend toward beauty of face or form." Blewett asserts that "doing the whole year round a man's work, has given her the figure of a man. She has muscles instead of curves; there is no roundness or softness visible.... Her hands and arms are the hands and arms of a working man." Blewett concludes, supposedly in direct contrast to the ideal life of a British-Canadian woman settler, that "there is no romance in the life of a Doukhobor woman." Quoted in Frank Carrel, *Canada's West and Farther West* (Toronto: The Musson Book Company Limited, 1911), 227.

99. Hiemstra writes about a time when her father has left Mrs. Pinder alone with the children and details some of the ways that her mother passed the time, including the following emotionally resonant moment:

> One afternoon she read to us from the Book of Ruth. Her voice
> flowed evenly until she came to the place where Ruth elected to go
> with Naomi. . . .
>
> Mother's low voice faltered as she read, and when she came to the
> end of the verse she stopped reading altogether and looked at the lit-
> tle window for a long time, then softly and as if speaking to herself
> she said: "It ought to have been written about marriage." (261)

The other memoirist considered in this paper, Kathleen Strange, also provides biblical context for her decision to emigrate with her husband, saying, "a
woman has to follow her mate. With Ruth I had said: 'Whither thou goest, I
will go . . . and where thou lodgest, I will lodge.'" Kathleen Strange, *With the
West in Her Eyes: The Story of a Modern Pioneer* (1937; Toronto: Macmillan,
1945), 273. Further references are cited parenthetically in the text.

100. Anne Baring and Jules Cashford, *The Myth of the Goddess: Evolution of an Image*
(New York: Arkana, 1993), 321.

101. Silverman, "Writing," 521.

102. Bliss, "Seamless Lives," 97. The stifling effect a small prairie community can
have on female behaviour is most clearly illustrated by Sinclair Ross in his
novel, *As For Me and My House* (1941; Toronto: McClelland and Stewart, 1957).

103. Mair, "New Canada," 152.

104. Aileen Ribeiro, *Dress and Morality* (London: B.T. Batsford, 1986), 149–150.

105. Criticism of short hairstyles for women could even take on political connota-
tions, as seen in Durkin's mention of another female character, Rose, the "com-
munist," who is "'a disciple of the Thing-that-is-not'," as evidenced by the fact
that "'[she] bobbed her hair before anyone else in her crowd.'" Douglas
Durkin, *The Magpie* (1923; Toronto: University of Toronto Press, 1974), 25,
127, 162.

106. Angela E. Davis, "'Country Homemakers': The Daily Lives of Prairie
Women as Seen through the Woman's Page of the Grain Growers' Guide
1908-1928," *Canadian Papers in Rural History*, ed. Donald H. Akenson, vol.
VIII (Gananoque, ON: Langdale Press, 1992), 169.

107. Marilyn Frye, *The Politics of Reality: Essays in Feminist Theory* (Trumansburg,
NY: Crossing Press, 1983), 93–94.

108. Mary Vipond, "The Image of Women in Canadian Mass Circulation Magazines in the 1920s," *Modernist Studies* 1, 3 (1974–75): 5.

109. Bennett, et al., *Emerging Identities*, 381.

110. Teresa de Lauretis, "Eccentric Subjects: Feminist Theory and Historical
Consciousness," *Feminist Studies* 16, 1 (Spring 1990): 126.

DOCUMENTS IN THE
POSTMODERN LONG PRAIRIE POEM

by Dennis Cooley

It is one thing to question the fictionality of a document's presumed objectivity and another to suggest that a document ceases
to have a referential function in the long poem.
                    Smaro Kamboureli, *On the Edge of Genre*

It is common knowledge that Canadians have been fervent in their long
affair with documentary, a romance probably best known through the
work of John Grierson[1] and others at the National Film Board. It is
becoming known that Canadians show a hankering for the long poem too,
and have done so almost from the beginnings of a national literature. In
his book *The Family Romance* Eli Mandel, perhaps forgetful of those earlier accomplishments, or perhaps thinking of a special development in
Canadian literary history, has called the long poem "perhaps the proudest
invention . . . of contemporary writing in Canada" (215). Earlier, earlier
that is than the period to which Mandel addresses himself, E.J. Pratt was
renowned as a specialist in the form, visiting the long narrative poem,
which is to say Pratt's kind of long poem, with a zeal that at the time the

rest of the English-speaking world seemed to have left behind.[2] And, for some time before Pratt, we had a plethora of long poems, many of them texts on settlement. Six of them—Oliver Goldsmith's *The Rising Village*, Joseph Howe's *Acadia*, Charles Sangster's *The St. Lawrence and the Saguenay*, William Kirby's *The U.E.: A Tale of Upper Canada*, Alexander McLachlan's *The Emigrant*, and Isabella Valancy Crawford's *Malcolm's Katie*—were gathered in an anthology edited by David Sinclair in 1972.

The fever would seem never to have left us. At the moment there are in print at least three large and recent anthologies that gather long poems: Sharon Thesen's *The Long Poem Anthology* (1991) (which supersedes Michael Ondaatje's 1979 version of the book with a different set of texts, predominantly from Ontario and British Columbia), D.M.R. Bentley's *Early Long Poems on Canada* (1993), and Daniel Lenoski's edition of prairie long poems, *a/long prairie lines* (1989). (I would note here, too, since I will have little chance later to do so, Bentley's formidable book on early long poems in Canada, *Mimic Fires*, published in 1994.) And, most recently, we have a second edition of Thesen's collection (2001).

Over the years there have been a proliferation of essays and the holding of two conferences—in 1984 a major York conference whose papers were later collected in a special issue of *Open Letter;* and a later conference at the University of Ottawa, directed at reading and theorizing the genre in Canada, whose papers have appeared as a book, *Bolder Flights*, in 1998. Perhaps the best-known and most-cited of the statements—certainly one of the earliest of them—has been Dorothy Livesay's "The Documentary Poem: A Canadian Genre," in which, influenced by Grierson,[3] she argues that the long poem creates "a dialectic between the objective facts and the subjective feelings of the poet." These texts, which are not unusual in Canadian poetry, are "more than" narrative, she tells us: they constitute "a new genre, neither epic nor narrative, but documentary" (267). In them we find "Documentation combined with raw experience; direct, plain, accurate language; sudden leaps into metaphor" (279). The strategy, Livesay argues, allows Canadian poets to engage history in productive ways:

> Such poems record immediate or past history in terms of the human story, in a poetic language that is vigorous, direct, and rendered emotionally powerful by the intensity of its imagery. Thus we

have built up a body of literature in a genre which is valid as lyrical expression but whose impact is topical-historical, theoretical
and moral. (281)

More particularly, the documentary poem, though "based on topical
data," is "held together by descriptive, lyrical, and didactic elements"
(269). In stressing theme and precept (269) and in promoting "argument"
(280), Livesay makes the didactic and the representational crucial to her
theory.[4]

Livesay's essay, based on a talk she gave in 1969, echoes in some ways
the terms Northrop Frye laid down in a paper almost a quarter of a century earlier. In "The Narrative Tradition in English-Canadian Poetry"
(published in *The Bush Garden*, 1946), Frye muses on the provenance of
place—what he calls "nature"—in Canadian long poems. Frye's poet, confronted by a nature of "primeval lawlessness and moral nihilism" (146),
yet informed by "sophisticated witticisms and emotional refinements"
(147) acquired from contemporary writing and the long tradition leading
into it (145), seeks in the earliest English-Canadian poetry forms adequate
to Canadian experience (146). Drawn to a "primitive" sense of place, the
poet has turned often to "the narrative poem" and the possibilities its tradition makes available. It would, Frye proposes, "give the flat prose statement
a poetic value" (150) and it would take the writer presumably into stories of
great national importance.[5] Frye shares with Livesay, then, a perception of
large and guiding representation in these texts, though he gestures toward
tribal and discursive qualities that approach the epic, perhaps something
very much resembling what Pratt, Frye's favourite poet, was doing.[6]

Confidence in such strategies more or less collapses in a second phase
of criticism, when, informed by new texts, writers find that clear themes
lose their allure and large stories shed their credibility. Robert Kroetsch's
madly punning, laconically broken "For Play and Entrance: The Contemporary Canadian Long Poem" (1981)[7]—it, too, derived from a talk
given at an academic gathering—throws story into such disrepute it virtually sloughs all glamour. The long poem, in Kroetsch's libidinal deconstruction, approaches something like a scattered seizure. Kroetsch, we might say,
is playing a hunch. In his model the poem offers "distrust of system, of grid,
of monisms, of cosmologies perhaps, certainly of inherited story" (62).
Kroetsch rejoices in setting "against the grammar of inherited story, the
foregrounding of language" (65), which figures for him as 'bad' grammar

or disruptive speech. That foregrounding becomes a "grammar of delay" (69), a series of spasms perhaps, in which the writer, the reader too, moves "towards" ends and "towards" narrative that "cannot be located" or that, "possibly, we do not wish to locate" (77).[8]

Spurning metanarratives, Kroetsh would have us become "archaeologists"—not historians, but archaeologists—who proceed by "clues, fragments, shards, leading or misleading details, chipped tablets written over in a forgotten language" (78). The poet moves in surmise and conjecture, turns up things, surrenders to guesswork, flaunts her suppositions. "We threaten to write . . . fragments, pieces, journals, 'takes'" (74). In the archaeology that supplants history, there can be "only abrupt guesswork, juxtaposition, flashes of insight" and a discovery that is always "forthcoming" (64). The long poem, Kroetsch adds, addendingly, often configures as travel poem: "Separation and delay and fulfillment are elements in the grammar. Surprise and temptation take the traveller away from and towards" (79). In that Freudian delay, refusing "the consolation of an accepted grammar," comes "the sweet taste of madness" (78), the daring "to be carried away, transported" (81).[9] Even as document emerges for Kroetsch as "temptation" akin to "history," it proves susceptible to its own "kind of madness" (64). He says this though he also writes that document (in the form of photograph and collage) represents a "resort beyond language" and a "flight from language" into apparent "artlessness" and "the reality of reality." The long Canadian poem in which such icons are embedded plays "obsessively (madly?)"—these are Kroetsch's words—in divine malady, with "photos and illustrations that do and do not fit."

Frank Davey was quick to respond. In 1981 he gave a talk at a conference and by 1983 he had brought it out in a separate chapbook[10] and then, titled "The Language of the Contemporary Canadian Long Poem," as part of a book. Objecting to what he reads in Kroetsch as a metaphor of sexual energy threatened with orgasmic closure, he situates the Canadian long poem in a phenomenal world of constantly renewing sequence. For Davey the poem "requires recurring orgasm, movement from surprise to surprise" and "is prolonged not only to delay but to continue." It accedes to "the joy of continuing and varied culmination" rather than any "fear of ending." Davey's theoretical version of the long poem proceeds not in fear but in rejoicing. As a result, immersed in time, in hope of libidinal utopia, it anticipates even as it prolongs (185).

It also, Davey argues, enters "life-experience" and the "drawing of the daily breath"—give us this day our daily breath—without resorting to "the enhancement of rhetoric." Quite how it could do so (step outside rhetoric, that is), or why Davey would believe it could do so, I cannot say. It may be revealing that here he, too, draws close to the representational, calling for voices we hear in "the language of the street" (189). He elaborates the argument in a full and rich way, stressing writing as a "collaborative" act and as a "cooperation with language and event" (193). He further identifies generic strategies writers have used in their attempts "to replace narrative"—the promotion of place, foregrounding "language itself," using "the recurrent image," and release into "game, jest, and play" (184)—and draws out the power of subtext in the poems he reads (baseball, the ledger, the seed catalogue, journals, sagas, other long poems), elevating these items of 'low' culture into unexpected source and poetic standing.

It is precisely the provenance of subtexts, when they figure as 'quoted' text, that I want to address in a moment. But there are other critics to consider, those who get in on the conversation that swirls around what we know as the long poem in Canada. Eli Mandel gave a talk—if there is one thing constant in these entries, it is the talk—at the 'long-liners' conference in 1984. Provocatively titled "The Death of the Long Poem,"[11] it addresses not so much the end of the poem as the inadequacy of theory. In Mandel's view the contemporary long poem in Canada is misleadingly read when it appears, as it does, say, in another essay by Davey, as a "contention between a humanist and projectivist account of poetry" (217); or when it is read, as it is by George Bowering, as a preferring of the long poem to the lyric (221, 228). Locating the long poem as the latest in a centuries-old tradition that began in the classical European epic, Mandel finds that its "hierarchy" and "origins" continue to preside over the form (218).[12] His position leads him to name unity and structure as troubling issues in recent texts.

Mandel's preparedness to situate the form within a genre, and within historical reshapings of the genre, brings him to virtual agreement with Louis Dudek's version of the long poem in Canada, and to a lesser extent Frye's and Livesay's modernist accounts of it. Mandel wobbles in his allegiances, seeming to opt for a relatively static sense of genre: "the long poem cannot be a form—its endless process resists the very definition of structure, centre, foundation we want to put upon it" (228). As narrative, he says, the form could simply "amble on, from story to story, until its author ran out of plots." Mandel here seems to lament such an outcome, deciding that as "encyclopedic poem [in the history of the form] it lacked a structural principle and bloated itself on mere detail, accumulations of erudition" (220). More bluntly and, one might say, more conservatively, he supposes that when the long poem "resists definitions, as it resists system, grid, cosmology, belief" (227), "the poem as we know it is no longer there" (229). As a result, a prospect that Kroetsch and Davey find exhilarating, Mandel finds "bleak" (225). And yet, half-persuaded though Mandel is by Louis Dudek's linking of the contemporary long poem to the image and to the lyric (223), and to the modernist long poem (224),[13] he remains suspicious of given authority (229).

At that same York conference Frank Davey re-entered the discussion. His talk, "Countertextuality in the Long Poem," appeared along with Mandel's and several others in the special issue of *Open Letter* dedicated to the proceedings and later, in 1988 in his collection of essays, *Reading Canadian Reading*, as "Recontextualization in the Long Poem." In a wide-ranging survey of the long poem, Davey reviews versions of the documentary, Livesay's chief among them. Conceiving of document in the widest possible sort, to include source, quotation, parody, subtext, and intertext, Davey concludes that the contemporary long poem in Canada seeks to bring "old material" "to the possibility of further meaning" in "implicit interaction of past with present, of earlier writer with later writer, a rejoining of then and now" (131). Various documents, selected and revised, enter new contexts into which they are appropriated, co-opted, or recast "for one's own needs and times" (133). In effect we get a give-and-take between the original texts and the new texts into which they are introduced (133). Newly situated, the document serves as "a ground out of which the new text grows, as a countertext, a pretext, as rhythm and syllable" for the emerging host text (134).[14]

There are several other important statements, among them Stephen Scobie's view (1984) of the form as a site of liberation through possession and the encountering of the 'other.' Scobie summarizes what he finds in "the documentary poem as it has evolved in Canada in the fifteen years since Livesay's essay":

> It is a long poem, or sequence of poems, usually of book length,

and narrative in structure. The events which make up this narrative are documented, historical happenings, although the poet will frequently modify or shuffle these events, or add to them purely fictional incidents. The poem often focuses on a single character who took part in these events, and this character's biography . . . provides the structure of the book. Many of the poems adopt the person or speaking voice of this central character. The idea of the 'document' remains within the poems, as a source of historical fact, and as an element of intertextuality: the central characters are frequently artists . . . or else keep journals, draw maps, or in some other way produce 'collected works' which the poem may either quote directly or else refer to. The relationship of poet to persona is one of dramatic irony . . . the major form assumed by the 'dialectic between the objective facts and the subjective feelings of the poet.'[15]

Other important statements include Laurie Ricou's poetic survey in 1990, "The Long Poem,"[16] in which he distinguishes several versions of the contemporary long poem in Canada: the "serial long poem" (27), the "process-poem" (29), the "documentary long poem" with its "compulsion to authenticate" (35), and, a catch-all category, what he calls "fringe forms" (39).

More fully, there are two books that appeared in the early 1990s. One was Smaro Kamboureli's *On the Edge of Genre* in 1991, an impressive attempt, contrary to Mandel's formulation, to define the contemporary long poem in Canada as a mobile, mixed, and radical form:

> The long poem's aesthetic and ideological complicity is meant to engage the reader in its politicized and therefore political poetics. Its function is diacritical. . . . Moving away from the givenness of facticity through its self-reflexive gestures, disclosing the problematics of mastery hidden behind any sovereign genre, the long poem avoids reconciliation, shuns synthesis. . . . Its contradictions and paradoxes do not swerve away from one master narrative in order to create another. Rather, it is produced within . . . the very generic and cultural fissures it observes between the epic and the lyric, between its colonial predecessors and postcolonial instances, *between referentiality and self-reflexivity*." (emphasis added)[17]

The other book, less concerned with the long poem, but deeply engaged in revisiting issues of document, was Manina Jones's series of essays, culminating in a superb book, *That Art of Difference* (1993), to which I will return. More recently, in 1999, we have had another collection of papers from the University of Ottawa symposium on the long poem in Canada. None of these essays, none until the Ottawa conference at least, has addressed the long poem as it exists on the prairie, and, until that point, few essays had lingered over prairie texts other than Kroetsch's. And yet, what we find in the arguments about the long poem elsewhere in Canada would apply, I think, to many examples from the prairies.

What we do have, however, is another set of statements on prairie literature, most of them based on the longer tradition of prose fiction from the prairies. Those critical texts—virtually all of them—appeal to representation at some point or other. Whatever their differences, to some degree they all somewhere appeal to authenticity, to the local, to the mirror. They make the case for a world that had not been allowed full admission into literature. We find statement after statement about the overrun or unacknowledged; come across passages that lament the unwritten, the unspoken, the unheard, unseen culture that is, or could be, the prairies.

In those readings, the prairie is a space of silence,[18] an empty page under whose layer of snow the mute Canadian lies. "Nivation," writes Jon Whyte, himself a writer of long prairie poems, robber of texts, shopper of documents. Nivation refers to a state of living that is just beneath the snow, barely breathing, under the sheets we long to write on, across the snow on which we wish to leave our tracks.[19]

The dilemma facing the writer of the long poem on the prairies is obvious. Alongside the desire for representation sits the realization that the world is already scripted. The poet, wanting to accord legitimacy to place, and yet knowing the world finally is beyond any final reach of language, beyond any fixing in words at least, bounces between reference and reflex. As a result the poems turn hybrid and flirt with the evidential and the fictive. They learn to entertain both the given and the made.

The ambition may seem trivial or naïve to some. Those who are *au courant* might wonder: is this a sign of simple facticity, a hick preference for the quotidian? proof of a cautious and practical imagination at work? a Puritan retraction from imagination? Is it yet another version of prairie realism, governed by the weight of those precedents? Is it, as some would argue, signs of nostalgia for the past, mistaken attempts to recuperate what perhaps never was, and never could be known in any case?

Certainly the surveys of prairie literature, overwhelmingly based on earlier prose fiction, especially realist novels, stress the importance of reference. Those statements, in the felt pressure of literary mode and literary history, continue to inform our thoughts about writing from the prairies.

The use of document is crucial too as poets seek to enter a literary world in ways that respect their place and seek to speak of it in the face of a world that would ignore or demean it.[20] Theirs is a felt need for a place to start. I'm thinking about a desire to articulate prairie experience by finding adequate representation, what Kroetsch has called in "Disunity as Unity: A Canadian Strategy" a "compulsion to speak its own validity."[21] Many of the writers I am about to turn to seek signs of being located in and of the place we call, problematically, the prairies. In some versions, the poems may risk the romanticism that Frank Davey charges them, unfairly I think, with holding.[22] For the most part the writers see "prairie" as what has been unsaid and what in many ways remains unheard as a culture. They think of themselves, sometimes, as culture builders (if the expression is not, now, intolerably sententious). They see the prairies, in all its multifariousness and unspokenness, as a place that needs to be brought into expression, in ways that inevitably will be partial and tentative. How could the writing be otherwise when it is done on the margins of empires? And so the authors seek for legitimacy and for recognition in writing out of the prairies 'as it is' (the words are put into uncertainty) and not as it exists on the stem end of Europe. Or the United States. Or central Canada. Arguably post-colonial, the writers seek not so much ultimate meaning as local meanings.

Such a claim raises questions about sufficiency in language. In asking for something appropriate to a place and a time, it risks disappointing critics and offending readers. We can easily rehearse the objections.

A strange muse, forgetfulness, Kroetsch writes, musing over the bombing of the Old World. For his is a post-colonial world—one in which representation matters crucially. In it you get into naming, hearing, citing, listing, reciting, you think of bringing things into the text. You do this in a big way. You are tired of being written out. You resent being written off, written out of existence, dismissed as mistaken or ill-informed.

For what is the 'real' in a post-colonial situation?

The "authentic" appears for the postmodern prairie poet as representations of "here" and "now." It means writing out of a world, writing a world, that has seldom been written and scarcely even spoken. It is a world that can seem unspeakably provincial. How embarrassing, how painfully mistaken, it must sound to those who know we ought to be writing in other ways. This is the condition of being in a "new" world—where writers experience both the exhilaration and the uncertainty of writing on what looks a lot like a clear slate, or a full slate (for it may already be written upon, as in versions that would recognize Aboriginal life, say, it certainly has been already inscribed). In any case, the poet is trying to make a new start, a fresh beginning unencumbered by ways of writing that don't "belong."

The poets oscillate among erasing old inscriptions, retaining versions of old subscriptions, and authoring new inscriptions; between wiping out the great-given words or writing out the new and 'fitting.' Ambivalently, they do both. They have no choice, nor would they want, finally, to unload all their cultural baggage even if they could.

And yet, they might think, there may be no page at all, no surface upon which they could write or words anyone could ever read, knowing they are 'ours.' In that state, wanting to write prairie texts, writers seek what is distinctive. They seek to attend to what is 'really' there, what might mark the writing as somehow related to the place. As Robert Kroetsch says, flourishing the contradiction, "We contrive authentic origins."[23] In "On Being an Alberta Writer" Kroetsch more directly sounds an old prairie grievance, one that goes largely unheard, and so unheeded, within the kinds of understanding critics such as Davey have brought to prairie poetry. Kroetsch speaks there, in that essay (and it is a text more quoted by prairie readers than by critics from elsewhere, who tend to prefer the "postmodern" Kroetsch to the "prairie" Kroetsch), of naming the prairie out from under the official language and literature that tells us we don't matter. Don't even exist. Here in formal voice is Kroetsch's complaint: "Our genealogies are the narratives of a discontent with history that lied to us, violated us, erased us even."[24] And here is Kroetsch as he speaks that removal in folksy anecdote:

> There was an older boy a mile from our farm who, as we kids liked to put it, knew everything. He was so smart a lot of people thought he'd become a priest. I remember that he could recite the names and dates of kings and prime ministers from whomever was thought to be first to the latest. I asked him about buffalo wallows. He'd never even heard of buffalo wallows. But more: he

made considerable show of not caring that he hadn't heard. He
was educated. . . .
  History as I knew it did not account for the world I lived in.[25]

The claim is there in the perfect paradox, the bravado of its reach—the
double act the writing seeks to perform.

Even Eli Mandel—persistent in his belief in invention, thorough in his
arguments on behalf of literature as self-engendering and self-regarding—
even he writes, longingly, of Andy Suknaski's realist *Wood Mountain Poems:*
"that's the book I should have written, its terrible authenticity, its powerful directness, its voices and places echoing in its time and truth."[26] It is
this same Mandel who takes himself to Regina as writer-in-residence in
the winter of 1978–79. When he arrives he speaks admiringly of the new
Saskatchewan writing and of his wish to be part of it: "you want to get an
authentic speech, you want to get an authentic set of images, you want to get
an authentic locality." "When I was a young writer here [in the prairies],"
he explains, "one never tried to identify oneself" with the place, but now
"You want to say that you belong to this particular world."[27]

We find in such writers an acute awareness of contemporary theory,
including a wariness of reference, knowing that the world will never stand
still for names, that it can never be brought into presence, and that it can
never coincide with its signs. In that understanding, they realize, there
can be no final truth and in staggering ways texts can be answerable only
to other texts. In this reckoning we live in a scripted universe, local realities no more than scraps scraped from the plate. In the already written,
words do not bring the "real" to us, but form the world in dialogue with
other words. In other words, ours, in the teasing phrase of Roland
Barthes, is a world of the "déja lu." How derivative our lives are, then,
how 'inauthentic.' Already written, subject to revision, they suffer contradiction, jurisdiction, prediction, somebody else's predilection. They can
never be our own. Writing is scarcely able then to deliver satisfactorily
'true' accounts or 'accurate' perceptions of the place, and we are forever
held in a position of duplicate culture.

You can see how many authors find themselves oddly positioned: wanting, out of sense of cultural aspiration, and, I would think, personal impul-
sion, that too, to speak adequately about, out of, for, their place on the
prairies; and believing too, under ordinance of contemporary theory, that
those wishes can never be realized.

Shit we're up against it, K. writes, finding everywhere an absence—an unhappy and a fortunate lack of high European culture. But he believes, too, somewhere between regret and rejoicing, that the prairie muse must be found in an anti-muse that is forgetfulness. It must be the form of a radical not remembering. He comes quickly to celebrate that lack. Fuck the past, he says. But he doesn't mean it, not really (though he does think, I think—certainly *says*—we should "F the ineffable").[28] He's not thinking of all pasts, not a local past, certainly, when he denounces history, and, finally, not even a literary past. He has in mind only the fixed past, the honoured past, the imposed past, inasmuch as it legitimizes narratives that slight prairie experience. That is what he would consign to a kind of forgetting, that is not a full or final forgetting. And so he seeks not a governing culture but an informing one.

That's where document comes in—not as facsimile, but as fact-simile. As if it were 'true.' "It is one thing to question the fictionality of a document's presumed objectivity," writes Smaro Kamboureli, "and another to suggest that a document ceases to have a referential function in the long poem."[29] Documents serve in such long poems, she proposes, a "desire to redraw cultural geography, to shift the designated centre off centre" (95). As a result, the document occupies with enormous purpose a place we might think of as somewhere between the worldly and the self-regarding. It exists where fidelity to the local collides with a suspicion that such a loyalty is untenable. Things come, we might say, to a terrible impasse.

One solution, option at least, has been to write the metalingual—to see the land as language. It has been perhaps the most defensible strategy available to those who care about the 'realities' of the place—resenting the savage misreadings of it, the glib not knowing of those who, foot to the floorboard, cross the land in a state somewhere between contempt and stupor. Such disregard deeply offends prairie people, but the writers of the discontinuous and polyphonic long poems know irrevocably too that language finally can never simply represent the place, not because the world is too complex, but because it is in all ways and in all places mediated.

So we get the writer as doubly informed. We get writer as double agent who cites and recites the world. Who sights and so sites it, who hears it and so heres it.

This is a position Eli Mandel, probably more than any other prairie poet, has occupied. When he turns in the aptly titled *Out of Place* (1977) to the narrative of his homecoming to Estevan, we get not a restoration to roots but a "reading" of a world already written in native and Jewish script. This from "lost place":

> in the book of years
> berner told me could be found
> your own name exactly spelled
> his own his sons the russian
> names of villages and jews
>
> twelve strangled ducklings
> laughter in bed
>
> you were written
>
> I read the land for records now (23)

The "documents" Mandel finds, and incorporates, include passages from earlier texts on Estevan and letters about Jewish settlements, but there are photographs too, pictures of a desolate and abandoned landscape, a calligraphy of human wreckage left behind. Everywhere the land is already signed. There is also, embedded in Mandel's book, another narrative about a man who has returned to the place, a manuscript Eli and his wife Ann find in a littered vault. It is this document that presides over the subsequent long poem, *Out of Place*, and that in a structural way inaugurates it. Here are the words of Ann Mandel, author of the "preface:" that describes the finding:

> Our work proceeded over days. Some papers were clearly accounts, farm machinery bills, shipping invoices, feed allotments, egg sales' receipts, storage charges from elevators. Others concerned religious matters, the finances of the congregation, salary of the rabbi, attempts to finance a visiting cantor. We assembled all these as chronologically as we could. . . . Some pages did not seem to fit anywhere, seemed to be a diary or fiction of a kind. . . . Not numbered. And containing, we came to see, local place names, references to this colony, this farm, even to this vault. Using sentence structure from bottom and top lines, we put the sheets together in what we conceived was the right order, then began to read. (7–8)[30]

Whatever Eli Mandel may profess elsewhere, the Mandels here find what we might call a documentary muse in the repository of texts. The creative set of pre-texts, the "preface:" implies and seems to provoke at least part of what follows.

Using document as list leads Mandel to discovery and to self-affirmation, in the most basic poetry of our lives, the names that inhabit and inform us. In one reading, such entries are obdurately there. But they speak perhaps a basic making too, a recitation in which we might hear the sounds of the most ancient writing, a naming that constitutes things and calls them into force.[31] Here, for example, from *Out of Place*, is Mandel's recitation of toponyms, introduced by the claim that "we drive through names":

> Coronach Canopus Constance
> Big Beaver Hart Ceylon Glasnevin
> Ogema Horizon Assiniboia
> La Fleche McCord Mankota
> Stonehenge Montagu
> Readlyn Willow Bunch
> Dahindel Wheatstone Crystal Hill
> Galilee Truax Amulet
> Pangman Khedive (35)

This is a striking compendium of European and First Nations names, a strange and wonderful music in their sounding. In such simple and reso-nant litanies we hear, for a moment perhaps, an impetus we might know as epic, in its building and affirming of culture. The act serves in less grandiose forms too. "Naming," Smaro Kamboureli tells us—and she is thinking of Mandel in *Out of Place* as she does so—naming "is a performa-tive act, invents the past as memories and creates poetry as 'recitation'" (139). It is a point that Lenoski, too, makes in his introduction to *a/long prairie lines*: "Such naming [throughout long prairie poems] confers exis-tence on the west as a cultural entity of value and dignity" (xvii).

But what about the play between "document" and the fictive field into which it is transferred and released? As "document" moves into literary texts, it apparently sheds whatever gestures it might innocently, or not so innocently, once have made toward the "real" world, and it takes on sec-ondary and literary meanings within self-referring acts we know as liter-ary. When that happens, what once was 'certain,' or for most purposes reliable, is rendered shaky. That shift is crucial to all postmodern long prairie poems: the representational made reflexive and literary, the "true" made ludic, the dependable made doubtful, the innocent brought into doubt, the accidental now motivated, the naïve rendered artful.

But, so situated—and this point is crucial to what I am trying to develop here—document still retains a residue of the world it has left. Recent arrival to a new world, it never loses its accent. It never completely drops the tongue of first speaking. It shows signs of having come from elsewhere and of having been introduced into the long poem. The field within which we hear documents turns us back to origins too, to hear passages not simply as newly activated for literary purposes, but to hear, to really hear, properties of language as they can be discerned in the original text.

Manina Jones, in *That Art of Difference*, her very fine book on document in Canadian writing, has made the point about as well as anyone can. Drawing on a variety of scholars, she speaks of the discontinuous long poem that appropriates much of its material as being "both historical and historically subversive, serious and playful, representational and antirepresentational." The documentary impulse "situates the text in terms of its literal dimensions involving reference to empirical reality" by *"relativizing without completely discrediting the 'documentary'* dimension." As Bahktin has so compellingly shown us about the power of the cited text, any writer who uses document within a larger frame inevitably "gives new meaning to another's word, *while maintaining its 'old' meaning too"* (emphasis added).[33]

How alive, how 'charming,' how 'mannered,' we might then say, how volatile. How rhetorical. How poetic. Who would have thought? In the acknowledgement of what we may have overlooked, the discovered language, once so unpromising, turns out to be more promoted than demoted, and as a result often granted as much esteem as ridicule.[34] We may realize, seeing now, for the first time, how 'made' the text was in the first place, how skilful was its composition, whatever its primary use or its undistinguished lineage. We do not then take the document for granted, nor do we confine it to its original 'purpose.' Once we induce within it a literary hearing, we free its words from the limits of their initial value.

John Robert Colombo has written perceptively in *New Direction in Canadian Poetry* of what is involved in such transmigrations. "Many reviewers maintain that contemporary poetry is simply prose rearranged to look like poetry," he has noted years ago (in 1971), using words that have appeared in arguments made many times since. Colombo recognizes that the objection rests on assumptions about defining or inherent qualities in poetry, which some texts purportedly simply lack. Against those kinds of claims, which are essentialist and ahistorical, Colombo opens another line of argument, which would accord with later statements from figures such as Jonathan Culler (see fn 14). The use of found material, Colombo says, acts by "giving a new, poetic lease on life. By 'quoting' another's lines in a poetic context," the poet "is able to claim they are poems because they look and feel like poems, and they act like poems when they are read." In Colombo's view there are no intrinsic qualities that would enable us to distinguish prose from poetry, but "as readers, we are conditioned to respond differently to them" or to what we take to be "them."[35]

What happens in that emigration from 'prose' to 'poetry,' which deploys its own kind of imagination, is laid out by Jean Mallinson with exemplary grace and perception in "John Robert Colombo."[36] The 'found,' she says, in honouring Colombo, is "subversive and inclusive" (subversive perhaps because it is inclusive) (18). It is also "the most democratic of poetic kinds" and Colombo himself is priest of the ordinary because he "has eschewed the hieratic and redeemed the demotic, the banal, the everyday, the ignored" (13). That kind of poet "celebrates the poetry which is all around us but which we often fail to notice" (14). In moving to "rehabilitate the commonplace" and in taking various measures to redeem, rescue, and rearrange things, the poet shows a "humble and tender respect for what is already there." Such a poet serves not as ingenious inventor, but as patient and loving noticer. A "safekeeper" (16), the poet records and piously compiles (17), apparently in agreement with Samuel Johnson when he regrets "how in our snobbery or thoughtlessness we have ignored the possibilities of beauty in what we take to be ordinary things" (17).

So there is that initial act of recognition—one that sees merit or meaning in places where ordinarily it goes unnoticed. But there is a second move. If the first approaches the religious, or the ludic, in its recognition of near innocence and clarity, the second is more literary, more knowing—more semiotic, we might say. For an artist of the found, Mallinson says, is alert always to the constraints of "genre, convention, expectation and the forms it generates, on every action which is expressed in language" (17). The passage the poet effects in filling out the proper papers, in bringing imports across the border, or, illictly, in running contraband, is effected by means of "framing" and "arranging" the newly arrived in such a way as to release or to make manifest what is latent in them. It is to turn them into citizens of a new country where, even as they clear the customs officers and learn a new language, they speak still, always, in an old tongue, shocked perhaps to learn they've been had, they've been framed.

But they are given latitude too, permission to new associations and unexpected redefinitions. "When the subject is not given priority, the intentionality pervading inherited documents is rendered obsolete," Kamboureli notes in *Edge of Genre* (96). The poet's role, then, is one of freeing into new prospects, on the other side of the law. Poet as smuggler, a dealer in contraband. When the writer inserts such language ("failed utterances") into the respectable system of literature, writes Gerald Bruns, s/he speaks in refreshing originality, in an obstinate "failure to preserve what everyone had thought valuable." Like what, for instance? Well, "such gestures as Duchamp's":

> the decision to compose a pickax (or whatever) by picking one up at the nearest hardware store was an authorizing decision, as much an act of interpretation as of creation, and an individual appropriation of the cultural procedures by which many brute and transient things get institutionalized as things worth preserving.[37]

In such a verbal world you openly draw on a series of the 'already made' and the 'non-artistic.' Documents inevitably will bear signs of being previously shaped, whether spoken or written. They will show the marks of having been composed for other ends and located in other situations. The traces of a previous existence, or of an apparently previous existence (for a document can be, and sometimes is, fabricated),[38] accompany its transfer into the host text and register its prior life, which is to say its status outside the text that receives and reactivates it. When printed inside the new frame and brought within the attention it both permits and requires, the material can be seen often as possessing hitherto unrecognized merit and (this is a point often overlooked) as itself having been artfully made, to a point of being shaped by what elsewhere we would recognize as literary skills and artistic purposes. There it stands—shivering in its peculiar grammar, blushing perhaps in its odd conventions of print. What are we to make of its punctuation, paragraphing, orthography, typography, as well as more specialized instances of its graphic formations? The newly placed text will bear, too, indications of its original genre: headlines, dates, salutations, numerical entries (for dates, weights, references, etc.), columns, testimonials, legal forms, personal signatures, formulaic constructions such as oaths, a propensity for passive voice, question-and-answer format, and so on. It will often bristle with deictics, which, read within the literary frame the author provides, will lose their original gestures and come to point to the surrounding text(s) within which they are embedded, newly responsive to *that* give and take.

The poetic seizure is (usually) done without the knowledge or consent of those whose words have been thieved. The open confiscation is a wrenching away from previous control and the breaking of original purpose. In the transposing it passes into and enters within another textual formation that the 'original' author(s) would likely have neither anticipated, nor perhaps even wished, and might well have opposed or resented were they in a position to do so.[39]

Take for example Robert Kroetsch's *Seed Catalogue*, published in 1977.[40]

Buy my seeds, the original seed catalogue, the 'real' seed catalogue—the one Robert Kroetsch finds and quotes so colourfully—exhorts. In full volume it cries its hucksterism. How wonderful are these words, we are tempted to say, how inventive, now that we hear them, in a sense for the first time really hear them. Now, accorded the special reception that the larger text in swallowing accords them, the text we also know as *Seed Catalogue*, we can find novelty in their second-hand existence.

Within such hearing we become aware of how stylized the extracts are, the realization throwing us back upon the 'found' texts to reconsider them in a new light. The excision invites us to read the passages with new care and with increased appreciation. It would not be claiming too much if we were to say that it activates them as cultural expressions, as acts of writing that in their own right are accomplished.

Here, in the noise of bold letters, the clamour of hyperbole, is the first part of the poem we know as *Seed Catalogue* (for the sake of convenience, I will be quoting from the later, and available, Turnstone edition of 1979):

No. 176—**Copenhagen Market Cabbage**: "This **new introduction, strictly speaking**, is in every respect a **thoroughbred,** a cabbage of **highest pedigree,** and is **creating considerable flurry among professional gardeners all over the world.**"

The capitalized and enlarged letters (their topography well may have been even more dramatic in the catalogues Kroetsch is using) mark the material as an instance of advertising display. That mode of lettering, Johanna Drucker tells us in *The Alphabetic Labyrinth*, serves the ends of "overblown commercial persuasion succeeding through tactics of rhetorical inflation."[41] In Kroetsch's act of recuperating—when the words enter the polyphony of the long poem, susceptible to its noise, its airing and sharing of voices—we begin to forget the flagrant rhetoric of the sales talk as it attempts to induce purchases, and we begin to notice the 'literary' properties of the passage. The old 'meaning' recedes as a new significance surfaces to our attention, the first and intended use of its language as an affective act acceding to an unveiling of its formal properties. Drucker proposes that when we turn to advertising that has run amuck with typographical vertigo, we can find "an eclectic vernacular vocabulary the end result of which were sheets which resonate across the space of more than a century with particular poetic and cultural suggestivity" (243). The sheer size and elasticity of the long poem open it to a writing that the lyric can hardly sustain or carry and, as a result, texts such as Kroetsch's are able to house for literary ends all kinds of oddities, documents lifted from commercial catalogues among them.

Throughout *Seed Catalogue* we observe in the quoted material a flamboyance that leads to a steady stream of superlatives. Here, in this particular extract about cabbages, we observe the promotion of plants into animals, the protests of outlandish exactness ("strictly speaking"), the trope of aristocratic lineage attached to the most mundane of vegetables ("thoroughbred," "pedigree"), the extravagance of unrestrained hyperbole ("in every respect," "all over the world"), the appeal to myths of origin ("this new introduction"—Edenic? Inaugural?), the release of metapoetry in the inclusion of the passage within a poem and in the leading position of a poem ("this new introduction," we realize, announcing, with bravado and comical ingenuity, Kroetsch's poem itself). The move that brings such awareness to the fore, allows us (requires us?) to notice signs of outrageous invention in the extracts themselves.

What we have, once we have brought the words into literary regard, is not "raw" material, nor even innocent writing, but texts in their own right, formed, to be sure, within the conventions of advertising and commercial practices that inform their own purposes and determine their occasions.

But in a way the passages surpass those needs. In the extracts we are able to notice that the anonymous and perhaps collective act of authorship has produced its own kind of poetry. I suspect it is as much in wonder, as mockery, that Kroetsch brings these entries forward for our inspection. Inasmuch as that is the case, we hear the document not simply in an ironic or comic register;[42] we begin to find in it a working toward lyrical and possibly even epic expression. We start to find a poetry, and acts of special merit, in documents we well might never have appreciated in such a way.

We may even begin to hear the poetry as something more than accident. If we do, we then are in a position to think of the anonymous authors of these catalogue entries as something more than shameless hucksters. If we were to acknowledge them in such a way, they would become available to us as closet authors who have thrown their words—playfully, parodically—into motion, even as they observed the mercantile constraints of their publication.[43]

Margaret Atwood, in *Second Words*, has similarly identified the role: "The documentarist's . . . stance towards such raw material, and thus towards everyday life, is that it is intrinsically meaningful but the meaning is hidden; it will only manifest itself if the observer makes the effort to connect."[44] The act, motivated by curiosity and, perhaps, a kind of modesty that is willing to find value in what is 'there,' shows a sense of worth in the hitherto disregarded, or unregarded, and of the necessity to be receptive to its promise. We are asked to hold odd bits of writing in a new and higher regard by entering into an act of recognition, or invited recognition: oh yeah, now that you mention it . . . would you look at *that?*

We might think of that move as seeking an act of authenticity, then, however much it might disappoint or embarrass those who prefer their postmodernism pure of reference, though I myself agree with Linda Hutcheon when she argues that in postmodernism (as opposed to a residual modernism) the representational is not configured as impossible or deluded, but as problematic and provisional. There is, I think, in this penchant for digging up old documents, an investment in culture making.

Hence too the obsession with names and naming in Canadian writing. Readers, precipitant (head-long), already knowing (head-strong), who dive head-first into the self-reflexive, may be failing the texts in some very basic ways, being too impatient with their authors' cultural aspirations and the forms that perhaps best accord with the authors' avowed aims. There can be a disallowing—we are not impressed—which can be damaging, if not imperious.

The nature of these extracts, eminent in their apparent lack of accomplishment, their unwillingness to seek literary status, makes them of special interest to the author of the postmodern long prairie poem. Many of those poets have turned to what ordinarily we would think of as unliterary texts, or subliterary texts, without merit. But in found art that material serves as a basis for literary writing, not simply as source, but as worthy accomplishment in its own right. We are asked to appreciate the value of language that for reasons of apparent lack—its literalness, its awkwardness, its commercial designs, its infelicities, its naïveté, its unassumingness, its untutoredness—we have not heard very well. In turn the appropriations of that very writing show a blithe disregard for the high and literary, the learned and allusive, the dense and the difficult, the elegant and the imaginative.

Hence the love affair with document: language that is brought into textual play when it is found and repositioned, but—it's here that my argument locates itself—language that, whatever significance we accord it as part of literary text, still carries with it a residue of truth and credibility. In Manina Jones's words, the annexed document acts by "relativizing without completing discrediting" its referential force and, once activated within its new domain, it "gives new meaning to another's word, while maintaining its 'old' meaning too."[45] It carries, I am supposing, marks of its place and time and offers, therefore, some representation of it.

There are many other examples of what I have described, and it is to a few more I will now, briefly, turn. Monty Reid has published a long poem, *Karst Means Stone* (1979), which plays off the poet's grandfather's memoirs: "I have used that memoir as a basis for these poems. Many of the details I have invented or taken from other sources but each poem is initiated by an incident in the memoir. I do not believe that I have created a consistent character. . . . But that would also have meant that I could not write about some of the things I wanted to include."[46] Memoir functions here as amphora.

Reid plumbs the memoirs, circles them, recirculates them in his own text. He uses them most conspicuously to lead a poem, opening with a quotation, then following each quotation with a poem that varies, evidently, from being highly indebted to a document, to playing off and away from it. Even as the book becomes increasingly self-aware in its metalingual and lyrical moments, it is remarkably documentary in spots: the spillage of proper names, the verbal elisions, the syntax of explanation, the deictics of number and place, the prominence of toponyms. These are the common conventions of documentary. The extracts serve to occasion or to permit the individual poems, responsive to the poet's personal lineage—some of them more apparently under the jurisdiction of the journal than are others. We have the quantified language of wheat production over a period of several years, for example (47). In others (on page 52, say) image, trope, lineation, rhyme, cataphora emerge more emphatically and declare the texts to be original expression. In those poems the language intensifies and seeks to push the material into other and larger hearings.

In another long poem, Birk Sproxton's *Headframe:* (1984), we find at its end this tongue-in-cheek entry: "Quotations have been borrowed, and sometimes modified."[47] Here the document is put into uncertainty in the very moment when it is invoked. Nevertheless this text throws itself with a passion into a full-time courting of document. It draws in sources from newspapers, mining journals, the book of Flin Flon (yes, there is such a book), the book that is behind and, by dint of quotation, inside the new book of Flin Flon. Sproxton goes so far as to visually reproduce the inside title page of that book, *The Sunless City* (99). He draws, too, on Alexander Henry's journal of his early explorations in the Canadian West, quaint in its style to modern ears (its extended titles, use of columns, profusions of dates, strewings of passive voice).

The sub-literary (seed catalogue, settlers' letters, explorers' journals, newspaper reports, ledgers, mining registers) is thus brought into the literary. In a sense the move is part of the deflating of literature and of extending it into domains of subject and voice that once would have been prohibited—at least in poetry.

Jon Whyte, another worker with document, does not merely draw upon the ambience of source in Henry Kelsey or other anonymous explorers, his poem *Homage, Henry Kelsey*[48] actually includes Kelsey's, absorbing and surrounding it, even as it leaves it presumably unaltered and intact. In doing so it shows respect for the material brought forward or brought across. It is a transposing—a structural equivalent to metaphor, one that brings many domains into contiguity and a new cohesion, largely of the reader's making since it provides an instance of metonymy (which occasions, permits, provokes connections), not metaphor (which asserts connections). Whyte practises housing, taking in, hosting the words. A postmodern capacity to allow the "other"? A capacity to give over, to let the tribe 'speak for itself'? This act goes beyond radical modernists such as Pound or Eliot, say, for Pound sought to purify language and Eliot longed for purity of source.

David Arnason, better known as a writer of prose fiction, wrote as his first major, and I think to this day his most daring, text a long poem called *Marsh Burning* (1980).[49] In it we find as we get further into the text an increasing turn to document, including a series of letters that mark the Icelandic experience of settlement during the ravages of tuberculosis. *Marsh Burning* begins in its first section with Norse mythology, then in subsequent sections, radically marked off from one another, it moves to scientific mythology, from there to personal memory, and then finally to historical document. (It includes, too, a series of photographs brought with some kind of documentary force into the poem.) I want to read to you what Arnason has said about where the later pieces came from:

> The voices that started to speak were a whole series of different voices—my imagination of the voices of some of the earliest settlers, the people that first came here. So that the narrator's voice had lost its integrity, had lost its way by moving back into the community. Some of the voices in there are not made out of me at all. *They're found, I found them in archives. But they worked and it seemed to me: why should I try and invent a letter when I've got one that's perfect? The image is there, the language is there, that's perfectly good, it works. Exactly as I would have done or I would have tried to do it. But it's perfectly authentic and so I just included that.*
>
> *And so that's the way the poem moves, it's a movement backwards in some kind of search for authenticity.* (my emphasis)[50]

So Arnason decides, as aware as anyone that representation is in no way available as simple strategy to him, to go for the power of the understated texts he has found, the nearly naked authenticity of what they declare. Here's one letter, so poignant in simplicity and the unaltered oddities of its orthography, paragraphing, and punctuation (most conspicuous in a splattering of dashes that splice the text—nervously, hastily: authentically?—together), that I quote it in full, wondering what it would have been to have reproduced it in the original hand:

> For three months I did nothing but treat for smallpox so you can imagine that I have seen enough of it - When I went to some of the houses, I would find perhaps some six or eight sick, some that had only a few hours to live - You would see Old Men and woman, Young men and girls, and poor little infants that would make the hardest heart ache for them and to see them at their Mothers breast and perhaps the next time I came around their little bodies would be put out side till they had time to make a rough box to bury them in. On my second trip I heard that there was a family on Big Black Island. So I went to see them. And such a sight. The Mother had just got over the small pox and her infant at her breast, dieing and they had not a thing to cover the poor thing - The house was so small that I could not stand up in it. I was compeled to sit down. I brought my tea and pamican, and me and my Indian guide had to have our dinner on that a lone - after a whole days travel - They had no flour in fact, had nothing but fish - I left what medicine and nourishment I had - which I brought for the sick - and to see their eyes brighten up, to hopes that it came in time to save their little one can never be forgotten - But alas, the little thing only nine months old, died next day. And then they had to put the little thing on top of the house till they could get some boards to make box for the little one— (74)

The narrator goes on—there is no break in the text—to speak of his own difficulties and relief:

> I had a pretty hard time myself, but when I looked at the poor Icelanders I faired like a King - Though I had to sleep on a bed made of hay - No body, but one that has a strong stomach could have eaten what I did this winter, unless they were the Icelanders themselves - In one house a woman asked me if I would have a cup of coffee. I said yes, as the day was cold, so while I was making up some medicine for a poor sick boy, What do you think I saw the woman do - She no doubt thought that the cup was not clean enough for me, so she licked the cap all around and with her tongue and then took a towel and black as it could be - without it

being a bit of black cloth and dried with it, and then gave it to me
to drink. A nice sight to see for a man that wanted a drink to warm
him. I could tell you worse than this. (74)

And then—in addition? amendment? the 'invention' of document? the
alteration of 'fact'?—we get a shift in the prose. It moves to a more educated and more considered punctuation, a more involved sentence structure, to obsessive repetitions and parallel structures, and to a more fluid
syntax. It is more personal and lyrical in its qualities, more intimate in
mode, and given to the conditional and the prepositional—to constant
signs of its lesser 'immediacy':

> I could tell you worse. I could tell you of the first swelling on the
> child you love. I could tell you of a trip across the ocean, across
> miles of land by train, a trip down a river, and through a lake
> larger than a sea, a dream journey to a land of pestilence. I could
> tell you of nights so cold that nothing could make you warm, of
> insects and lice and illness. I could tell you all this and more. (75)

Sometimes the found documents are intriguing, humorous in a
macabre way—"fascinating" may be the word, if we think of it in its root
sense—as in this entry about a drowning in Lake Winnipeg:

> Description of a body found by Edward Smith in Lake Winnipeg
> south of Willow Harbour on the 1th of July, 1878.
>
> The body is of a man about 5 feet 6 inches. It was very much
> disfigured and swollen; the hair and beard, which seem to have
> been light or red was almost entirely fallen off. The body was
> dressed in a suit of fine black cloth, cotton undershirt & drawers
> and striped flannel overshirt; white woolen socks and moccasins:
> black silk necktie and striped linen collar. In the breast pocket of
> his coat was found a passbook with some writing in, a Map of the
> Northwest Territory and a letter, showing that the name of the
> deceased had been Charles Funck. In the inside vestpocket were
> $56.00 in four dollar bills: in the pantspocket a purse containing
> $1.75 in Canadian silver and a ring with stone in.
>
> The body was examined by twelve persons and the verdict
> given by them was: Found dead in Lake Winnipeg.
>
> E. Fridricksson
>
> foreman of the examiners
>
> Gimli July 3th 1878 (78)

What could be more 'obvious' than the jury's verdict, less explanatory, less illuminating, less adequate within literary terms of significance? Arnason's text brings into play our sense of the laughably tautological. How woefully inadequate, we would say.

We get yet another kind of "hearing" for document in Walter Hildebrandt's *Sightings* (1991),[51] a book with eighty-nine pages of text, counting the credits page, a page of no small significance to Hildebrandt's ends, which are to demote document and to ironize it. The move would be in keeping with what Manina Jones has said about other, related texts. For her, the use of quotation marks (the term covers all instances of designated quotation) serves "both as an indication of a borrowing and as a sign of the refusal to accept the borrowed passage at face value." An act of signing or co-signing "does not necessarily qualify as endorsement."[52] In short, the confiscation of words can act to promote or demote their value.

Most of Hildebrandt's text is "found" and comes from various historical sources (Hildebrandt is himself a trained historian), some of them not identified immediately in the text. I count fifty-two pages of quoted material (that makes sixty per cent of all pages) that consist of "documents" as I am naming them here. That makes this text, among all the texts I've mentioned, by far the most reliant on given texts. By my count we get the following distribution:

10 pages of Big Bear's speeches (25, 35, 47, 49, 56, 58, 60, 62, 70, 75)
3 pages for Kehistakaw (44-6)
1/2 page for Imasses (82)
1/2 page for Four Souls
3 pages for Louis O'Soup (53, 54, 56)
1/2 page for Middleton (8)
1 page for an unidentified scholar's page, reproduced as facsimile (48)
1 page for a Who's Who entry (40-1)
2 pages for an Imperial Song (38-9)
1 page for a judge's pronouncement (36)
1 page for a modern historian (27)
1/2 page for Stanley (82)
1 page for Sir Wilfred Laurier in a newspaper (86)
1 page for a quotation from *Pilgrim's Progress* (19)
1 page for a Methodist minister (76)

1 page for Water Benjamin (8)

1 page for a treaty (57)

3 pages for an historical (a journalist's?) entry (92-4)

1 page for the Indian Act (43)

9 pages of watercolours by Bill Lobchuk (9, 17, 23, 29, 33, 51, 65,
    73, 89)[53]

9 blank pages to back the watercolours (10, 18, 24, 30, 34, 52, 66,
    74, 90)

1 page for credits (95)

By my reckoning, that makes fifty-two pages of pure document, and that's not even counting many pages that evidently consist of close paraphrase from various sources or are heavily committed to summation. Given the near omnipresence of such passages, there are many stretches over which we would be hard pressed to think of Hildebrandt as a poet in any conventional sense.

In short, most of the book is not even 'written' by Hildebrandt, if by "written" we mean composed or invented from 'nothing.' It may be pertinent to note that Hildebrandt has been trained as an historian, and at the time of writing was employed as an historian, a background that might go some way to explaining the text's inordinate faith in replication. In my view *Sightings* incorporates that enormity of documents partly out of a respect for them, a sense that they might enter the context Hildebrandt provides by 'speaking for themselves'—in an apparently unmediated way, or—and it is this reception I seek particularly to promote—in a special way as they are induced into highly politicized meaning. Clearly the book is impelled by an ethical and an ideological desire to bring those texts into play, and to find in them both a certain 'reality' and a significant power.

Perhaps one indication of what Hildebrandt is up to comes in the way he sets two of the documents in his book. In altering normal topography he draws attention to the documents—what's this then?—and marks them off as serving an aesthetic purpose. He then puts the documents into play in ironic ways. He re-signs them and in doing so he makes them his 'own,' by way of design. In a creative way he reauthorizes them. He pulls off the masks that have hidden them, lifts their supposed neutrality, and shows that what in them might have seemed to be simply reportorial is, inevitably, and, in his resetting at least, damagingly rhetorical.

One of the texts, which reproduces the words of a treaty, is squeezed by means of nearly indecipherable small print onto one page (57). Even if we were to suppose the lettering were in part occasioned by practical consid-erations (space requirements, costs), one of the aesthetic consequences is that we begin to hear the language of negotiation as what is found in the 'small print,' words pinched nearly into oblivion, scarcely to be read and scarcely then to be honoured or to believed. Who would read 'the fine print' with its cynical dodges and exemptions, its acts of subterfuge and denial? We are invited to suppose that the Aboriginals have in no way been accorded a generous understanding, but rather that they have been sold a bill of goods, underwritten by a suspect agent.

In *That Art of Difference* Manina Jones has written astutely, and for my purposes pointedly, on the force of irony that is commonly released by the repositioning of documents as they are allowed to 'say' something quite other than what their first authors might have intended or wished us to hear (for example, pp. 45, 129). The transposition removes the words from a condition in which "the production of meaning is regulated by unacknowledged and unexamined sources of authority, to the deficit of oppressed 'others.'. . . Citation, in other words, can operate as a challenge to the ideological assumptions of the received text" (37). This certainly would seem to hold for Hildebrandt's text.

In another entry, "after/word," he breaks a description, a proper and official-sounding account, of Aboriginal men dressed in a white-man's regalia into very small words and parts of words in a thin column stretch-ing down the left side of the page and covering three pages (92–94). The effect is largely one of comic mockery in bringing the language into disrepute. The broken syllables allow new and other words to emerge from among the found material, and to create an effect of new meanings and spastic rhythms that undermine the solemn intent and presumed harmlessness of the original passage. In effect, the document, or more precisely its author's, or speaker's, stance, is called into question and ridiculed.

The
go
vern
or
in
vest
ed

ea
ch
ch
ief
with
h
is
uni
form
flag
and
me
dal
. (92)

Elsewhere in the poem the device frees words within words with real force: "scarlet" becomes "scar" and "let," the word "decorate' falls apart into "decor" and "ate"—the terms of the colourful and the glamorous broken open to reveal the violence that lies behind or within them. The poem ends, appropriately, in similar manner, but releases only two words into normal recognition. They stand out with mock respect, then, in the only line that is 'correct' and allowed its nearly original weight. Though surrounded by lines whose newly sprung words are brought into ridicule and instability, the two 'recognizable' words—"the Queen'" and "head"— we surely hear in multiple irony:

The
me
dal
b
or
e
an
etch
ing
of
the Queen'
s
head
and
an
ap
pro

pri
ate
in
scrip
tion. (94)

It is striking to find the words of D.G. Jones, who, in *Butterfly on Rock*, has written years earlier words that would apply to Hildebrant: "Isolated from its formal context and a whole set of conventional assumptions, the text of an Indian treaty may discover new meanings: governmental eloquence may become pompous hypocrisy; native simplicity may become honest eloquence."[54]

If many quotations (Mandel's, Reid's, Sproxton's) enable us to find hitherto unnoticed worth, Hildebrandt's citations put under ironic scrutiny the legal and political documents of imperialism, and Arnason's use of document frees up macabre moments of stunning disparity and releases another kind of irony.

Either way—in elevation or discredit—the document is read as it is put to other purposes and subjected to a new kind of reading. That attention brings out certain properties that would in its original framing quite probably have gone unnoted. But it does, finally, honour those documents as material for literature, and as rich and informing resource for the writing of the prairie long poem.

We could go on to consider any number of other texts, including Bruce Rice's long poem *Daniel*. An archaeology of its own kind, it traces four generations of one family, and lays out its musings to include seven photographs (all but one of them annotated or captioned) and reproductions of two certificates—one certifying a minister, the other a nurse and midwife. We could include, should in any adequate accounting include, Barry McKinnon's *I Wanted to Say Something* (1975), republished in 1990 by Red Deer College Press, a remarkable mix of word and photograph, one of the first, one of the best, and one of the least-known of the postmodern long prairie poems. We could turn, too, to Roberta Rees's *Eyes Like Pigeons* (1992), which deftly and fluidly incorporates speaking voices (in their own way 'documents'). Or Patrick Friesen's *The Shunning* (1980).

Or Robert Budde's *Catch as Catch* (1994). Or Marvin Francis's *City Treaty* (2002). And more.

But that will have to wait for another time. Another place.

ENDNOTES

1. There is a collection of Grierson's writings, *Grierson on Documentary* (London: Faber, 1966), that tells us what document meant to him. Mainly it involved a production—especially in the face of Nazi threat and Nazi propaganda—heavily directed toward effects, but it had something to do with a kind of poetry as well. Apparently Grierson was thinking of something more than neutral recording: "Speaking intimately and quietly about real things and real people will be more spectacular in the end than spectacle itself" (100). What that amounted to, according to Grierson, was an abandoning of the "spectacular" art favoured by totalitarian regimes, if only "the writers and the poets and the picture men among us would seize upon the more intimate and human terms of our society." It required reappraising canonical texts, and preferring "the common or garden expression" to be found in other varieties of poetry: "I find myself less interested at the moment in Milton and Shakespeare than in Crabbe and Burns. To use Gogarty's word, the graffiti of the people were never more important than now" (95). The quiet intimacy that Grierson was coming to recommend would seem to require a certain strategy in pacing and proximity that would inform a composition.

2. So prominent was Pratt that A.J.M. Smith once observed (this was as recent as 1969) that "Pratt is the only Canadian poet who has mastered the long poem" (*Towards a View of Canadian Letters: Selected Critical Essays 1928–1971* [Vancouver: University of British Columbia Press, 1973], 114). My own words are meant to distinguish between Pratt's long poems, or rather the common perception of them as conservative and antiquated, and the spate of long discontinuous poems—Pound's, Williams's, Eliot's, Olson's, Stein's, Bunting's—that in the same period filled our century. Though the distinction is neither easy nor adequate, Pratt's poems (especially *The Titanic*) being far more polyphonic and discontinuous than we sometimes suppose, it is useful when we set his work alongside the more flagrantly mixed discourses that inform the other and later texts I've mentioned.

3. Dorothy Livesay, "The Documentory Poem: A Canadian Genre," in *Contexts of Canadian Criticism: A Collection of Critical Essays*, ed. Eli Mandel (Chicago: Universityof Chicago Press, 1971). See entries such as the following in *Grierson on Documentary:* "realist documentary, with its streets and cities and slums and markets and exchanges and factories, has given itself the job of making poetry where no poet has gone before it" (41).

4. D.G. Jones has argued (*Butterfly on Rock: A Study of Themes and Images in Canadian Writing* [Toronto: University of Toronto Press, 1970]) that, opposed to the French tradition in Canada, which prefers "fable, allegory, fantasy and myth," English writing "is horizontal in vision and realistic in mode: it favours the representative and representational descriptive, discursive and narrative

forms such as the catalogue and travelogue—as Dorothy Livesay has stressed, the documentary. It moves toward prose" (42). Jones is not happy with the trend he perceives, and complains that "In English, reality is reduced to an inventory of what exists, to things in space" (49).

5. I say "presumably" because Frye at no point uses these terms. He more gently invokes "those aspects of our literature that a poet would naturally be most interested in," then itemizes hinge moments of historical import: the "martyr-dom of the Jesuit missionaries, the holding of the Long Sault against the Iro-quois, the victories over incredible odds in the War of 1812, the desperate courage of the Indians who died with Tecumseh and Riel, the 1837 outbreak, the spear-heading of the plunge into Amiens, the forlorn hope at Dieppe" (*The Bush Garden: Essays on the Canadian Imagination* [Toronto: Anansi, 1971], 149).

6. D.M.R. Bentley, in the "Bibliographical Afterword" to his edition *Early Long Poems on Canada* (London, ON: Canadian Poetry Press, 1993), conflates Frye and Livesay, seeing them as sharing much the same view of the long poem.

7. The original essay was presented at the Modern Languages Association in Houston, 29 December 1980. I am quoting from the version printed in *Dande-lion* 8, 1 (1981): 61–85.

8. I am struck by how Freudian is Kroetsch's sense of narrative and how much it resembles Peter Brooks's understanding in his essay "Freud's Masterplot: A Model for Narrative." Here is part of what Brooks writes:

> We emerge from reading *Beyond the Pleasure Principle* with a dynamic model which effectively structures ends (death, quiescence, nonnar-ratability) against beginnings (Eros, stimulation into tension, the desire of narrative) in a manner that necessitates the middle as detour, as struggle toward the end under the compulsion of imposed delay, as arabesque in the dilatory space of the text. We detect some illumina-tion of the necessary distance between beginning and end, the drives which connect them but which prevent the one collapsing back into the other: the way in which metonymy and metaphor serve one another, the necessary temporality of the same-but-different which to Todorov constitutes the narrative transformation. The model sug-gests further that along the way of the path from beginning to end—in the middle—we have repetitions serving to bind the energy of the text in order to make its final discharge more effective. In fictional plots, these bindings are a system of repetitions which are returns to and returns of, confounding the movement forward to the end with a movement back to origins, reversing meaning within forward-mov-ing time, serving to formalize the system of textual energies, offering the possibility (or the illusion) of "meaning" wrested from "life."

This extract comes from David H. Richter, ed., *The Critical Tradition: Classic Texts and Contemporary Trends* (Boston: Bedford, 1998), 1041–1042, and it dif-fers from the corresponding passage in Brooks's *Reading for the Plot: Design and Intention in Narrative* (New York: Vintage, 1985), 107–108.

9. Kroetsch's own poems, wild though they get, observe a semiosis so knowing that it is hard to think of their narrators as falling into delirium.

10. The essay appeared in the interim as a chapbook with the kind of long and deictic title Davey at the time was given to—*Notes on the Contemporary Canadian Long Poem as presented to the Simon Fraser University weekend conference festival / The Coast Is Only a Line June 25, 1981* (Lantzville, BC: Island Writing Series, 1983). The cover page bears a shortened version of the title: *The Contemporary Canadian Long Poem.*

11. In a wonderful moment of accident, I had earlier typed these words: "The Death of the Long Poe." I was tempted to keep the mistake, loving the irony—renaming the man who had announced that the long poem was a contradiction in terms and that, for want of density or brevity, it could not be satisfactorily written.

12. Milton Wilson made much the same point years earlier, when he was discussing poets such as James Reaney, Isabella Valency Crawford, Archibald Lampman, Earle Birney, Philip Child, Jay Macpherson, Daryl Hine, Louis Dudek, E.J. Pratt, and Eli Mandel, himself. Wilson finds that "the discontinuous long poem, the cyclical short poem and the cycle of lyrics *have always been the most fruitful cluster* of genres in our poetic history" (from *Recent Canadian Verse* [Kingston: Jackson Press, n.d.], 2, my emphasis).

13. "Dudek connects the contemporary Canadian long poem with the moderns from 1920 on, moving it back from where its interpreters want to begin it, somewhere in the 70s," Mandel writes (*Out of Place* [Erin, ON: Porcépic, 1977], 224), though Mandel himself later decides that the form came into its own in the early '70s (227).

14. Frank Davey, *Reading Canadian Reading* (Winnipeg: Turnstone Press, 1988). Franz K. Stanzel supposes in such cases that the "newly acquired poeticalness must . . . reside in those *elements which are added to the original text* when it is printed as a found poem" ("Texts Recycled: 'Found' Poems Found in Canada," in *Gaining Ground: European Critics on Canadian Literature*, ed. Robert Kroetsch and Reingard M. Nischik [Edmonton: NeWest, 1985], 95, my emphasis), those elements being for him the enabling of new contexts. Stanzel comes close to Jonathan Culler, who in "Poetics of the Lyric" (in *Structuralist Poetics: Structuralism, Linguistics and the Study of Literature* [Ithaca: Cornell, 1975], supposes that what matters in reading literature, or more precisely in reading any text as literature, is to bring to it a literary attention that reactivates the words within a literary set of expectations, subject to new organization, and so renders them poetical.

15. Stephen Scobie, "Amelia Or: Who Do You Think You Are? Documentary and Identity in Canadian Literature," *Canadian Literature* 100 (1984): 269.

16. Laurie Ricou, "The Long Poem," in *Literary History of Canada: Canadian Literature in English*, 2nd ed., vol. 4, ed. W.H. New (Toronto: University of Toronto Press, 1990).

17. Smaro Kamboureli, *On the Edge of Genre: The Contemporary Canadian Long Poem* (Toronto: University of Toronto Press, 1991), 204.

18. The prairie is often a place of silence for Kroetsch too, though his sense of silence is more of an enforced muteness and a lack of voicing, which it was his passion to counter. Here is one of his many statements on prairie silence (he is speaking of himself and Margaret Laurence): "Both she and I begin from geography. . . . we really felt life was a literal place in the world, on the Prairies. We'd work out of that place, and I think we would both feel that silence in our generation, as writers on the Prairies, a kind of wrestling with that silence, which I think went on until the end of life. . . . To resist the silence, in resisting it through story" (from *A Very Large Soul: Selected Letters from Margaret Laurence to Canadian Writers*, ed. J.A. Wainwright [Dunvegan: Cormorant, 1995], x).

19. To occupy, supposedly, a blank or empty space, then, is not necessarily to exist outside of cultural definition; it is to be named in such a way that your world can be appropriated and written within somebody else's narrative.

20. Laurie Ricou, "The Long Poem," adapts Bakhtin's work to propose that in recent Canadian literature "As the novel abandons the convention of realism, we detect the increasing novelization of poetry; the developing long poem absorbs the realistic convention" (*Literary History of Canada*, 26).

21. Robert Kroetsch, "Disunity as Unity: A Canadian Strategy," in *Canadian Story and History 1885–1985*, ed. Colin Nicholson and Peter Easingwood (Edinburgh University Centre of Canadian Studies, n.d.), 3.

22. See "A Young Boy's Eden: Notes on Recent Prairie Poetry" (*Reading Canadian Reading*) in which Davey hears claims for localism in prairie poetry, based often in appeals to voices or voicings, as naïve or narrow. Davey supposes that those who have made, or advocated, such moves have assumed there can be unproblematical references to a past, or even the present, world. He sees in much prairie poetry a nostalgia for a naturalized and pastoral world (the words appear across his essay) that does not acknowledge, perhaps is not even aware of, its own constructedness and intertextuality.

   One could mount a counter-argument that would see in the texts Davey finds so unknowing and simple, more complexity than he has allowed. My essay here, on document, is meant in part to make that point; as does Smaro Kamboureli in her book on the long poem in Canada. She finds, sympathetically, that "nostos" "informs the protean movements" of many long poems in Canada, George Bowering's among them (*On the Edge of Genre*, 99). Kamboureli is implicitly distinguishing a productive nostos from a "regressive" nostalgia that once tied Canadian poets of the nineteenth century to "the *symbolism* ingrained in the mother country while ignoring the *semiosis* of the new country" [what is part of a more recent and positive nostos] (21). Where Davey sees confusion or error, Kamboureli sees acts of cultural intervention. She honours the poet's attempt to "retrieve an individual from historical misinterpretation or anonymity" against a vast indifference or wilful unknowing (90). Kroetsch, too, speaks to the liberating power of orality in Canadian and, especially, prairie writing: "The local pride speaks. The oral tradition speaks its tentative nature, its freedom from the authorized text" ("Disunity as Unity," 11). In my view the postmodern prairie poet is not interested in rescuing a fixed and shining past but she is actively seeking ways of producing meaning and pushing language into new and adequate expression.

23. Robert Kroetsch, "The Fear of Women in Prairie Fiction," *Open Letter* 5th series, no. 4 (1983): 55. The essay first appeared in 1979 and was originally read at the Crossing Frontiers conference in Edmonton in 1978.

24. Robert Kroetsch, "Beyond Nationalism: A Prologue," *Mosaic* 14, 2 (1981): vi.

25. Robert Kroetsch, "On Being an Alberta Writer," *Open Letter* 5, 4 (1983): 70.

26. Eli Mandel, *Another Time* (Eric, ON: Press Porcépic, 1977), 69.

27. Eli Mandel, "authentic speech," *Freelance* (1979), n.p.

28. One record of this rude refusal can be found in the title to a gnomic Kroetschean entry in an obscure publication in the mid-1970s: "voice / in prose effing the ineffable" (*Freelance* 8, 2 [1976]: 35–36). The article is reprinted as "Effing the Ineffable" in a special issue of *Open Letter*.

29. Kamboureli, *Edge of Genre*, 88, 95.

30. The scene startlingly parallels a passage in Mary Shelley. Here, at some length, is what Sandra M. Gilbert and Susan Gubar have to say about such an occasion as it involved Shelley:

> In a fictionalized "Author's Introduction" to *The Last Man* (1826) Mary Shelley tells another story about a cave, a story which . . . constitutes yet a third parable of the cave. In 1818, she begins, she and "a friend" visited what was said to be "the gloomy cavern of the Cumaean Sibyl." Entering a mysterious, almost inaccessible chamber, they found "piles of leaves, fragments of bark, and a white filmy substance resembling the inner part of the green hood which shelters the grain of the unripe Indian corn." At first, Shelley confesses, she and her male companion (Percy Shelley) were baffled by this discovery, but "At length, my friend . . . exclaimed This is the Sibyl's cave; these are sibylline leaves!" Her account continues as follows.
>
> On examination, we found that all the leaves, bark, and other substances were traced with written characters. What appeared to us more astonishing, was that these writings were expressed in various languages: some unknown to my companion . . . some . . . in modern dialects. . . . We could make out little by the dim light, but they seemed to contain prophecies, detailed relations of events but lately passed; names . . . and often exclamations of exultation or woe . . . were traced on their thin scant pages. . . . We made a hasty selection of such of the leaves, whose writing one, at least of us could understand, and then . . . bade adieu to the dim hypaethric cavern. . . . Since that period . . . I have been employed in deciphering these sacred remains. . . . I present the public with my latest discoveries in the slight Sibylline pages. Scattered and unconnected as they were, I have been obliged to . . . model the work into a consistent form. But the main substance rests on the divine intuitions which the Cumaean damsel obtained from heaven.

(From Sandra M. Gilbert and Susan Gubar, *The Madwoman in the Attic: The Woman Writer and the Nineteeth-Century Literary Imagination* [New Haven: Yale University Press, 1979], 95–96; all elisions are those of the authors.)

31. Here is what Atwood has to say on the matter: "in a cultural colony a lot of effort must go into simply naming and describing observed realities, into making the visible real even for those who actually live there" (*Second Words: Selected Critical Prose* [Toronto: Anansi, 1982], 253).

32. Daniel Lenoski, *a/long prairie lines* (Winnipeg: Turnstone Press, 1989), xvii.

33. Mariana Jones, *That Art of Difference: Documentary-Collage and English-Canadian Writing* (Toronto: University of Toronto Press, 1993), 61. Scobie raises the point when he writes that "The document is the point of intersection, for the documentary poem, between its equivocal realms of history and imagination" ("Amelia," 273). He elaborates: "The poem works both ways: it directs both poet and reader towards a fuller understanding of an historical character, event, or epoch, but it also directs them back to their own subjectivity, to their definitions of themselves" (275).

34. Diminished though it is in the kind of misgivings that Davey raises.

35. John Robert Colombo, *New Direction in Canadian Poetry* (Toronto: Holt, Reinhart and Winston, 1971), 16.

36. Jean Mallinson, "John Robert Colombo: Documentary Poet as Visionary," in *Brave New Wave*, ed. Jack David (Windsor: Black Moss, 1978).

37. Gerald Bruns, *Inventions: Writing, Textuality, and Understanding in Literary History* (New Haven: Yale University Press, 1982), 158.

38. As these days even photographs can be altered, changed so skillfully by means of digital technology that it is virtually impossible to discern the forgery. See, for instance, Brian Winston, "The Documentary Film as Scientific Inscription" (*Theorizing Documentary* [London: Routledge, 1993], 55–56). What then of verity? As for that, what of Robert Colombo's report on the "pseudo-found or found manqué"? The "found," he claims (and I am myself entirely persuaded), is a style, not a content (in Mallinson, "Colombo," 15).

39. Franz K. Stanzel has written an elegant essay, "Texts Recycled: 'Found' Poems Found in Canada" (in *Gaining Ground*) on found material in Canadian poetry. In it he quotes Louis Dudek to the effect that "the found poem is really a piece of realistic literature, in which *significance appears inherent in the object*—either as extravagant absurdity or as unexpected worth" (91, my emphasis). Stanzel himself adds, pointing to other sources of new meaning, specifically the creative act of the reader, that "aesthetic significance will be attributed to the text, where originally no such significance was intended" (96).

40. Robert Kroetsch, *Seed Catalogue* (Winnipeg: Turnstone Press), 1977.

41. Johanna Drucker, *The Alphabetic Labyrinth: The Letters in History and Imagination* (London: Thames and Hudson, 1995), 243.

42. Mikhail Bakhtin, who has had a strong influence on Kroetsch, and who has tuned his ear to the creative sounds of the low and common, says that popular advertising "is always ironic, always makes fun of itself to a certain extent"

(*Rabelais and His World*, trans. Hélène Iswolsky [Bloomington: Indiana University Press, 1984], 160).

43. The rhetorical (the urging to action: buy these seeds) and the literary (look at what else these words say and do) meet in a reinvention of the garden myth whose terms are so profuse, so fulsome, so thick with the shapes and textures of love, it is hard to imagine what the words might have meant for recipients of the actual catalogue. We might wonder at a supposed obliviousness of first readers to the import of the passages. Would the original language, which is to say the language in its commercial capacity, ever have been read innocently? Would no one have noticed all those figures of speech and suggestive terms, allowing even for the bombast of advertising? Could anyone have written such words unknowingly? I am supposing, still, that whatever suspicions readers of the actual McKenzie's *Seed Catalogue* might have harboured, they would not likely have read the passages, full bore, for signs of their rhetorical or literary flourish.

44. Margaret Atwood, *Second Words*, 95. Atwood also mentions the documentary in *Conversations* (Willowdale, ON: Firefly, 1990), as crucial to the journal (59) and the long poem (61).

45. Jones, *That Art*, 61.

46. Monty Reid, *Karst Means Stone* (Edmonton: North West Press, 1979), 6.

47. Birk Sproxton, *Headframe:* (Winnipeg: Turnstone Press, 1985), 133.

48. Jon Whyte, *Homage, Henry Kelsey* (Winnipeg: Turnstone Press, 1981).

49. David Arnason, *Marsh Burning* (Winnipeg: Turnstone Press, 1980).

50. Dennis Cooley, "David Arnason Interview," *Fostudagur* 20 (19 March 1981): 3.

51. Walter Hildebrandt, *Sightings* (Dunvegan, ON: Cormorant, 1991).

52. Jones, *That Art*, 38.

53. The pages on which the reproductions appear are not actually numbered on the page, though their pages count, silently, in the pagination of the book. I have put the numbers into brackets, as I have for the following example as well—the blank pages behind the illustrations—for convenience sake.

54. Jones, *Butterfly on Rock*, 175.

RECONSTRUCTIONS OF LITERARY SETTINGS IN NORTH AMERICA'S PRAIRIE REGIONS

A Cross-Cultural Comparison of Red Cloud, Nebraska, and Neepawa, Manitoba

by Sarah Payne

Literary tourism merges imaginative literature and the geographical reconstruction of cultural heritage. Writings both by and about particular authors contribute to the creation of 'valuable' landscape, which is valued for its associational qualities and not, in the first instance, for its physical features. The harnessing of these associational qualities has resulted in certain localities or literary landscapes being popularized by visiting tourists approaching these places with a heightened sense of expectation.[1]

Academic studies of literary tourism have typically, though not exclusively, focussed on the ways in which the literary movement known as Romanticism has influenced the idea of a tourist landscape. The geographical implications of English literature in shaping and constructing a tourist's 'sense of place' have been well researched by Nicholson, Newby, Butler, Squire, Pocock, and Luftig.[2] William Wordsworth's Lake District, Samuel Taylor Coleridge's Quantock Hills, the Brontë sisters' Haworth, Thomas Hardy's Wessex, and David Herbert Lawrence's Eastwood have long evoked images, in place as well as time, that have fascinated the public. These literary figures and their personal associations with particular landscape views have come to connote much of what is understood experientially and artistically by the terms 'England' and 'English Landscape.' In this sense, such tourist sites of consumption have become representations of cultural heritage and national identity.

In this paper, the lives, works, and literary heritage sites of two North American prairie writers, Willa Cather (1873–1947) and Margaret Laurence (1926–1987), are examined as they pertain to broader and more controversial issues of heritage and nationalism in Canada and the United States. The cross-cultural aspect of this research reveals important differences in national identity and heritage. The practical implications of such a project for the small rural towns of Red Cloud, Nebraska (population 1200), and Neepawa, Manitoba (population 3500), and the many other small rural towns in similar states of economic decline, is the other important reason behind this comparative cross-cultural research. This type of heritage tourism represents one definite response to the decline experienced by many frontier towns throughout North America.

While many small towns across North America's prairie region are becoming shadows of what they once were, the prairie towns of Red Cloud and Neepawa are the focus of this essay. These two towns have been chosen for several reasons. First, both Willa Cather and Margaret Laurence found much of their literary inspiration there. They have portrayed their personal visions of these small towns in many of their works of prairie fiction. As a result, both writers and their particular fictional narratives have transformed these two towns into literary shrines where tours of the childhood home and other important literary landmarks have become sites of consumption for visitors. The region of Webster County has been officially named *Catherland*, which is indicated by many signs along the roadside in the region. The town of Neepawa is no less forthcoming about its literary associations, indicating itself as *The birthplace of Margaret Laurence*.

Second, using both a Canadian and an American literary shrine enables a more comprehensive study of prairie fiction's particularly unique relationship with the literary tourism industry. Both these small towns possess a long history by prairie standards, beginning decades before the turn of the nineteenth century. Their similar early function as pioneer farming communities for immigrant populations and their contemporary function as literary shrines also made them compatible for comparison purposes. Willa Cather's Red Cloud and Margaret Laurence's Neepawa are poignant examples of places and, indeed, regions benefitting from particular literary associations: each town receives thousands of visitors annually. While conducting my research on tourist expectations and experiences of prairie landscape, I developed a questionnaire to administer to the many visitors in both areas. In the summer of 1997, I travelled to both Red Cloud and Neepawa to carry out this fieldwork.

The questionnaire itself was influenced by D.C. Pocock's chapter "Haworth: The Experience of Literary Place" and Shelagh Squire's article "The Cultural Values of Literary Tourism."[3] These studies provided the foundation for the questionnaire, which examined tourists' anticipation of and encounter with the experience of Red Cloud and Neepawa. The questionnaire can be broken down into three main sections, those that deal with tourists' 'anticipation' of place, those that focus on tourists' 'encounter' with place, and a final section that deals with demographic information. The structure of the questionnaire consists of fourteen open-ended questions, three yes/no questions, five Likert Scale questions, and nine questions that focus entirely on socio-demographic information concerning the respondent. Each questionnaire takes about fifteen minutes to complete. Red Cloud generated 153 completed surveys; Neepawa, 103. The literary tourism survey approach raised some interesting issues about the historical reality of these prairie towns versus the influences of heritage and literature in their reconstruction.

As part of the expanding heritage industry, this kind of specialized tourism activity highlights the wider links among tourism, culture, and society. An investigation of social, economic, and ideological underpinnings provides information about the context from which a writer's personal heritage is reconstructed. Tourists' interpretations, together with an appropriate theoretical framework, reveal the successful presentation and commodification of certain myths regarding North America's frontier heritage. Before illustrating these particular prairie myths and how they are interpreted by tourists, it is crucial to understand the term 'heritage' as it pertains to tourism.

HERITAGE: WHAT DOES IT MEAN FOR TOURISM IN THE PRAIRIES?

Heritage is known in ways utterly unlike history. It is sanctioned, not by proof, but by present-day exploits. As D. Lowenthal points out, "no one in the fourteenth century would have thought to test the date of the Turin Shroud. What mattered was the shroud's current miraculous efficacy."[4] The value of heritage is similarly gauged, not by critical tests, but by current potency. History is for all; heritage is for ourselves alone. It is presented as the secret, sometimes personal, history, created to generate, protect, and/or enhance group interest. Heritage is sometimes equated with reliving the past. More often, it improves the past to suit present needs. In literary tourism, for example, heritage is reconstructed, exclusive, and biased in favour of the author. The period within which he/she wrote is usually glossed over. Exclusion and bias consolidate into a generalized version of the writer's past. Often, this revamped legacy of the writer reflects what people think of the present, or what they want it to be. Heritage departs from history in what it sees, what it stresses, and what it changes. To be a living force, the past must be ever remade. Heritage is not to be stored away in archives and vaults; the story seeks to be transmitted, and refurbished into a resonating legacy.[5] Heritage tourism must feel durable, yet be pliable and open to interpretation. It is more vital to reshape than just to preserve. It is a partisan perversion, the past manipulated for some present aim. Substituting an image of the past for its reality, heritage replaces history's intricate coherence with piecemeal and mendacious celebration to present tourists with a version of the past.[6]

In remaking these images of the past, meticulous regard for minutiae is an 'authentic' heritage hallmark. For example, when television showed the polar explorer Scott as a bungling knave, rather than a tragic hero, visual fidelity was felt to verify the calumny. Reconstruction of the ship, the costumes, and the landscape was right, but the history was all wrong.

Today, people use this type of tourism experience to negotiate and redefine other social and cultural values. How is this so? The empirical material discussed here in an attempt to answer this question has been gathered from the 253 tourist responses to my literary tourism survey of Red Cloud, Nebraska, and Neepawa, Manitoba. The significance of the information gained by tourists, and the links that can be made between this information and its broader meanings, become very interesting in the context of literary tourism. The two survey questions acted as a catalyst for including a whole range of social and cultural heritage issues in the written responses. These include ideas of national/regional identity, exclusion of minority heritage, authenticity and the preservation of 'history,' and the contemporary significance of fictional prairie writers. How, therefore, does this definition of 'heritage' relate to the responses to these questions? In the case of Red Cloud, they showed that the town's heritage is represented as a legacy of Willa Cather's literary associations with this prairie town. In the case of Neepawa, the reconstructed heritage that resulted from Margaret Laurence's literary legacy is confined to her childhood home. Neepawa, outside this home, contains no 'signs' to indicate Laurence's literary associations with this place.

Modern preoccupation with heritage dates from the 1980s, a time of strong conservatism characterized politically by Reagan's America, Thatcher's Britain, and Mulroney's Canada. It manifested differently in different places. According to Lowenthal,

> each country or region treats its newly inflated heritage concerns to be unique, reflecting some trait of character or circumstance, some spirit of veneration or revenge that is peculiarly its own. Some impute these concerns to patriotic ardor, some to nostalgia, others to mourning or celebrating.[7]

Vaunting its own legacy, each place seems unaware of how strikingly concurrent it often is with those of its neighbours. For example, a typical list of unique heritage sites listed in brochures from 1997 from the Canadian Identity Cultural Development and Heritage ministry includes: chestnut canoes, cowboys, O Canada!, the Rockies, totem poles, fields of the prairies, Peggy's Cove, moose, autumn leaves, mounted police, fishing villages, loons, northern lights, strong and free, maple syrup, Jack pine wilderness, Group of Seven, hockey, Inuit, toboggans, Anne of Green Gables, the Great Lakes....

These items are Canadian, but the resonant words and stress on wilderness, national pride, ethnicity, and childhood typify heritage anywhere. American self-praise is equally sweeping, but punctuated by stronger ideological undertones than those found in Canadian heritage. This is reflected in the use of expressions such as: 'freedom-loving,' 'hard-working,' 'egalitarian,' 'generous,' 'civil liberty,' and 'manifest destiny'; all qualities and attitudes that typify the American legacy in heritage tourism literature. The various ways in which these inflated national legacies are interpreted by visitors to the numerous tourist sites in Canada and the United States remain unknown, as heritage, a source of national identity and the 'past,' continues to increase across North America.

Those who express a desire to experience this type of tourism are a relatively new legion. Heritage expands because more and more people now have a share in it. Another partial explanation for the growth in heritage, put forward by Weiss, illustrates that, in fact, until recently, "tradition was always valued, and that it is not until modernism that the past and its offerings were considered impractical."[8]

REPRESENTATIONS OF CULTURAL HERITAGE ON THE PRAIRIES

The issues of heritage, prairies, and the literary sites of Cather and Laurence are inextricably linked. History in the case of literary tourism is not simply remnants of the past, but a past coloured by a writer's personal vision. In the case of Red Cloud, Nebraska, it is Willa Cather's version of the past as reflected in her fiction that dominates the town of Red Cloud's heritage, just as it is Margaret Laurence's childhood home and details from the settings of her fiction that are offered as integral parts of Neepawa's heritage.

Red Cloud, Nebraska

In the town of Red Cloud 153 completed surveys were gathered. The actual community of this town has approximately 1200 permanent residents, and lies nestled in the Republican Valley, as part of Webster. Red Cloud is the largest precinct in Webster County, with two main creeks, the Republican River and the Crooked Creek, surrounding the town. The town is centrally located in southern Nebraska, approximately thirty kilometres north of the Kansas state border.

The origins, function, and structure of this small prairie town are typical of the many similar small towns established during the 1870s in Nebraska. The location of the town was determined by the development of the railroad; the main economic activity was farming; and its early population was comprised largely of immigrants. The distribution of Red Cloud and the similar towns of Bladen, Cowles, Inavale, Amboy Mill, and Guide Rock along a line of tracks indicates their intended purpose to serve as marketing centres for the agricultural land of the surrounding region.

Each of these towns is situated approximately twelve kilometres apart. This distance, the railroad believed, best served the railroad's interests.[9]

On Wednesday, 1 March 1867, Nebraska was admitted into the Union as the thirty-seventh state. President Andrew Johnson signed the State-hood Proclamation. Under the Homestead Act, which went into effect 1 January 1863, Governor David R. Butler invited new home-seekers to the Republican Valley region by placing paid advertisements in the major newspapers of many eastern cities such as Chicago and New York. These advertisements told of "Vast Areas of Virgin Farmlands Available in the New State of Nebraska. . . . Be among the first to claim for yourself a choice tract of land."[10]

The first homestead claims were filed 17 July 1870 by Silas Garber, Dr. Peter Head, W.H. Price, August Roats, and David Heffelbower, who, in the fall, along with later arrivals, built a stockade on the Garber claim. This defense, incidentally, was never needed as protection against the Aboriginal communities of the area. In 1871, the first businesses were built on the Red Cloud townsite that was part of the Garber homestead.

The town's design was commissioned by the railroad's own surveyors. The surveyors usually platted towns with a beehive of forty streets and alleys, with the aim to project notions of activity, population density, and prosperity. Surveyors platted all prairie towns on one of three basic plans: the symmetric, the orthogonal, and the T-town. The T-town was the most popular and was used for Red Cloud. Red Cloud's main street began at the Burlington and Missouri River Railroad depot, and the whole town stretched back on one side of the tracks. Surveyors used a standardized system of naming the streets, in which they labelled the north-south-running streets with the names of trees and the east-west-running streets numerically.

Design and housing architecture of Red Cloud strongly resemble most small prairie towns. By the late nineteenth century, the notion of stan-dardized products had seized the immigrant community and had extended to architectural structures. Popular magazines and trade journals made standardized blueprints widely available, and settlers avidly read them. Consequently, the houses, banks, and business buildings of Red Cloud were constructed from virtually identical plans all across the prairies. Between 1885 and 1891, Webster County's countryside also underwent a speedy transformation as settlers moved out of their soddies and into pre-fabricated A-frame houses usually constructed adjacent to the soddies.

The ethnic composition of the original inhabitants of Red Cloud reflected a microcosm of Nebraska's population. In 1910, second- and third-generation Americans comprised over 50 per cent of the total population. Germans comprised 16.9 per cent, Great Britain and Canadian immigrants 8.5 per cent, Scandinavians 8.2 per cent, Austria-Hungarians (Bohemians) 5.4 per cent, Russians 2.1 per cent, and Swiss 1.6 per cent of Red Cloud's immigrant population.[11]

During the twentieth century, the viability of Red Cloud as a community has faltered. First, Rural Free Delivery farm families bypassed local merchants to order goods from mail-order catalogues. Then, in the 1930s, the Great Depression and the Dust Bowl decimated the population in and around Red Cloud. In the 1940s, the New Deal WPA road-building projects paved the way for stores and banks in the bigger economic communities of Grand Island, Kearney, and Lincoln to recover. World War II, while pulling the United States out of the Depression, also set the stage for tremendous economic expansion, including that of agribusiness. Both the war and the prosperity of the 1950s placed an ever-increasing drain on the population of Red Cloud.

Today, many small prairie towns exist as the faintest shadows of their former selves. Trains no longer run through Red Cloud to stop at the Burlington depot, and much of the grain and livestock is hauled by truck. The neighbouring towns of Inavale and Cowles are virtually ghost towns as the businesses and populations continue to dwindle. Red Cloud's population, however, remains stable. While agricultural activity continues to decrease, the town's tourism industry is thriving.

The impact of Willa Cather on the sustained development of Red Cloud cannot be overlooked. Today, the town and its surrounding region have become a thoughtfully reconstructed tribute to the life and writings of this American author. The development of Red Cloud as a literary shrine began decades ago, largely through the efforts of Mildred R. Bennett, whose book *The World of Willa Cather* (1951)[12] first indicated the importance of Red Cloud, Nebraska, as a literary landscape. In 1955, the Willa Cather Pioneer Memorial (WCPM) was incorporated with the following original cultural, economic, and political agendas regarding tourism development in Red Cloud:

Provide and Perpetuate an interest throughout the world in the works of Willa Cather. Identify and restore to their original condition, places made famous by the writings of Willa Cather. For Willa Cather a living Memorial in the form of Art and Literary and Historical collection, relating to the life time and work of Willa Cather.

The WCPM later added: "Secure the bonding, insurance and housing of a permanent art, literary and historical collection relating to the life, time and work of Willa Cather." The first memorial was established right after the organization incorporated itself. In 1959, the old Silas Garber Bank building was sold to the WCPM to be restored and used as a museum.

Today, along the town's main streetscape and beyond, evidence of Willa Cather's literary influence is represented by dozens of buildings that have been carefully and accurately restored and then converted into literary sites. The sites have been combined, through tourist brochures, leaflets, and maps, to create a choice of several different literary and historical tours of Willa Cather's Red Cloud. While visitors are encouraged to explore the town of Red Cloud on their own, there are also hourly driving tours conducted by the staff of the WCPM Foundation.

Essential to the continued development of Red Cloud as a literary shrine has been the determined attention to authenticity that the WCPM Foundation has demonstrated in the reconstruction and conservation of many of the historically literary-significant buildings: Farmers' and Merchants' Bank Building; Burlington depot; St. Juliana Falconieri Church; Episcopal Church; Memorial Prairie (244 hectares of native grasslands); and currently the 'authentic' reconstruction of the Opera House. All these efforts have contributed to the continued reflection of Red Cloud as preserver of Willa Cather's numerous literary images. Consequently, homes and buildings not acknowledged in Cather's literature are left out of this reconstruction strategy. Those proponents who work actively on this redevelopment of Red Cloud and its surrounding area into *Catherland* raise important questions about what this type of preservation and reconstruction teaches visitors about the prairies then and now. This issue is further illustrated by the fact that the WCPM Foundation serves unofficially as the headquarters for all visiting tourists to Red Cloud and its surrounding region. The office, gift, and bookshop, with an art gallery displaying paintings that illustrate scenes from Willa Cather's writings, opened its doors on Webster Street, on 9 December 1979, and has been growing in popularity ever since. In May 1999, through the continued efforts of the WCPM Foundation, the stretch of a highway leading into Red Cloud was renamed Catherland Highway by Nebraska Senator Kearney.

Today, the Foundation's records indicate that on average, approximately 12,000 tourists, scholars, and students visit the town of Red Cloud annually. Since the WCPM is the building most visited by these tourists, it is here that the identity of Red Cloud and its prairie landscape begins for many people: an identity synonymous with Willa Cather's life and literature.

The Willa Cather Pioneer Memorial has sought to solidify and commodify its interpretation of Cather's version of the past, not for disinterested reasons, but to access political and economic capital in order to devise and sustain a particular strategy of redevelopment for this small prairie town through an infusion of resources from the American tourism industry. This type of political and economic strategizing represents important lynchpins in Red Cloud's reconstructions of the town's heritage. It also explains why the historical realities of the local Aboriginal community, those of the many and varied immigrant settlers, and other architectural influences in and around the town are visibly absent from the tourist's visit and, at present, not part of the redevelopment plans for Red Cloud. The production of a sense of realism and authenticity provided through the meticulous reconstruction of Willa Cather's literary images of Red Cloud has created a town that represents for tourists an appearance of a very specific "pastness" regarding America's cultural heritage: that of Willa Cather, her imagination, friends, and family. The town's promotion of Cather culture has, in a broader context, become a nostalgic symbol of the romantic western pioneer and frontier. This harkening back to the myth of "simpler times" or the "good old days" approach to the prairies represent an important part of American nationalism and ideology, which America's heritage tourism industry has been strongly promoting through access to particular types of national and state funding sources, public appearances from local politicians, and numerous tourist brochures and pamphlets throughout the region.

Valuing Cather's personal visions as the dominant version of Red Cloud's past can create interesting facets of heritage pride and national vainglory associated with this particular place and even the entire prairie region. Lauding triumphs and lamenting tragedies, literary tourists from Red Cloud, for example, claimed unique qualities for Americans, such as 'wholesome,' 'tenacious,' 'friendly and proud,' 'realized American dream,' 'hard-working,' 'frontier spirit,' 'love of the land,' 'homesteaders love of prairie,' 'folks dedicated to the prairie,' 'farming,' 'rural life and people,' 'communities dedicated to preserving their past,' 'strength,' 'no-nonsense,' 'welcoming,' 'development of the nation, expansion, growth and struggle,' 'reflection of quaint pioneers and their town,' 'the heart of the USA,' 'an appreciation of our ancestors,' and 'American imperialism at work.' Such traits typify a political legacy of self-sufficiency—the independent and free-dom-searching pioneer carving a democratic utopia out of the Wild West. These frontier heritage ideals also reflect, at least in part, the values held by Cather herself and are found in much of her literature. She was indeed a strong traditionalist whose writings revere those immigrant farmers and their families as they struggled and made their lives from the land. Through the promotion of particular sites in Red Cloud and its surround-ing prairie region, which were made possible by infusions of capital from numerous political and private donations, both Cather's heritage and its links to a wider, more nationalist, heritage have been achieved, according to the various tourist responses.

Neepawa, Manitoba

In the town of Neepawa, 103 completed surveys were collected. The town is comprised of approximately 3500 permanent residents and is located in the southern region of the province of Manitoba, approximately 150 kilo-metres west of Winnipeg near the start of the Yellowhead Highway.

The history of the establishment of the town of Neepawa is a familiar one. The area is a fertile park-like district, drained principally by the White Mud River and its many tributaries. Free land grants or home-steads were made available to settling farmers. Provision was also made for the purchase of additional land or pre-emption, at one dollar per acre. Homesteaders moved into the surrounding area in 1872 and settled in the Arden district around Burnside on Rat Creek. The first Neepawa settlers were a group of thirty colonists from Listowel, Ontario, in 1877. Fourteen of the people in this group were members of the Graham clan, who set-tled on a section, now the Riverside Cemetery, within the Neepawa town limits. In 1880, two former Palestine (now renamed Gladstone) business-men, John A. Davidson and Jonathon J. Hamilton, arrived at the settlement, purchased land, and surveyed town lots. They established a general store just south of the Graham family homestead. In 1882, the Manitoba and Northwestern Railway (later leased by the CPR) was planning to extend the rail line further west. Davidson and Hamilton owned land near the Graham homestead where the proposed M & NW line was to be built. The community was incorporated on 3 November 1883, and given the name Neepawa. A railway track and depot were built just within the northern limits of the town, almost a kilometre away from the Davidson and Hamilton General store. The result was the development of two rival commercial districts—the North End or Old Town, centred on Railway Street, and the South End, situated near Hamilton Street and Mountain Avenue. The rivalry was short-lived, however, as the South End began to surpass the commercial activity along Railway Street. Neepawa's first business centre was located along Hamilton Street. The construction of the Davidson Block in 1889, on the northwest corner of Hamilton Street and Mountain Avenue, however, precipitated a westward shift in the establishment of business enterprises. With the construction in 1902 of a second rail line by the Canadian Northern Railway, on Hamilton Street West, the South End emerged as the commercial heart of Neepawa, and remains so today.

The town's grid pattern reflects a standardized town design and structure used at the time, with numbered streets north-south, and east-west streets named after townspeople. Railway tracks mark the town's western border and northern perimeters. The residential architecture in Neepawa is diverse, representing the large Ukrainian and British ethnic groups. Within the town, there is a small population of French-Canadians, who have a long and rich history in Neepawa.

The development of Neepawa reflects the town's progress from a rough, mud-spattered prairie village to a community of tree-lined streets. Early buildings were typically utilitarian in design and constructed mainly from wood. Brick—a material that brought a sense of permanence and stability to prairie communities—was a scarce commodity in Neepawa until 1889, when William Currie & Co. established a brickyard north of the town. This brickyard has had a lasting impact on the town's streetscape along Mountain Avenue and Hamilton Street. The Davidson Block (1889), the B.R. Hamilton Hardware Store (1891), Knox Presbyterian Church (1892), and the Hamilton Hotel are all built from Currie bricks. In 1905, a second brickyard was established, providing bricks for the construction of the Neepawa Post Office (1908–1909) and the Bank of Commerce (1907).

Neepawa's church architecture reflects a clear expression of the town's ethnic diversity. Buildings like the First Baptist, Knox Presbyterian, Neepawa Methodist, and St. James Anglican reflect the English, Scottish, and Irish origins of the town's earliest settlers. Spires, stained-glass windows, and decorative interior woodwork are traditional British church characteristics. St. Dominica's Roman Catholic Church and, later, St. John the Baptist Ukrainian Catholic Church reflect a different wave of immigrant populations arriving in the early twentieth century.

In 1896, the town's population was 1500 residents and today the population is stable at approximately 3500 people. Farming remains one of the main economic activities around the town of Neepawa, but with almost one-third of the town's residents being senior citizens (over the age of sixty), convalescent homes, retirement villages, and apartment buildings form a growing industry in this community.

The town of Neepawa sees approximately 3500 tourists annually. Although these visitors participate in the town's Lily Week, the town also hosts a number of special events and historical walking tours. Overwhelmingly, however, the relationship between Canadian writer Margaret Laurence and the prairie town of Neepawa draws most of these visitors to the Margaret Laurence Home, now a provincial heritage site and Level II museum.

In 1985, the Margaret Laurence Home, then a boarding house for mentally handicapped girls, was purchased by the newly formed Margaret Laurence Home Committee Inc. The committee's original mandate was to pay off the mortgage, and restore and renovate the structure. This mandate was expedited by two unexpected windfalls. Afraid of losing a potential tourist draw, the Neepawa Area Development Corporation offered to share some of the costs. Consequently, the old brick Simpson house was renovated and the mortgage burned on 24 June 1992.

The home contains a memorial to the author, a restoration of her living room, and the Manawaka Souvenir and Gift Shop. Tours of the home and brochures illustrating the Margaret Laurence walking tour are available on request. While the ML Home is Neepawa's only building pertaining to Laurence restored for tourists, the numbers of visitors who include this literary shrine in their itinerary indicates the powerful influence of

Laurence on Neepawa's tourist industry. Compared with Red Cloud, however, the preserved or reconstructed cultural heritage depicted through the literary images of Laurence's Manawaka is incipient. This fact probably explains the differences in questionnaire response rate from the tourists visiting this town.

Literary tourists from Neepawa claimed unique endowments, which, however, differed only slightly from those of Red Cloud. Patriotism and national pride were again very much in evidence. Comments described the representations of such a town as: 'quaint,' 'strong and enduring,' 'how settlers rooted themselves,' 'beautiful,' 'culturally representative of Canadian prairies,' 'prosperous and clean,' 'full of Canadian heritage of the west,' 'a place of high culture because of Margaret Laurence,' 'wheat bowl,' 'typical close-knit prairie communities,' and 'a Canadian landmark.' These comments reflect not only images of Neepawa's heritage, but also of a heritage of the Canadian West and its inhabitants. Characteristics such as clean, upstanding, ordered, conservative, and prosperous resonate to punctuate the ideological undertones that have created an image of Canadian small-town heritage. Words that stress qualities like unassuming, hard working, and wheat-bowl prairie inhabitants typify the heritage of this region. The similarities continued, but to a lesser extent, in the numerous references visitors made to the importance of Neepawa's literary associations. This presence of 'high culture' in a small prairie town with 'low culture' positioning made this town special, since, because of its literary and historical associations with Laurence, it represented for tourists the roots of a Canadian icon. The town's own history was irrelevant to the visiting tourists. Its associations with Laurence's heritage, and its contemporary importance as a place of beginnings for a literary artist, gave it a much more distinct, if recent, heritage, which distinguished it from all other small prairie towns.

CULTURAL THEORY AND PRACTICE

Contemporary cultural studies offer other meaningful ways of conceptualizing the various interpretations of the meaning of Red Cloud's/Neepawa's heritage. Studies such as Squire's and Corner's, in particular,[13] examine how interpretations of meaning made by literary tourists are part of wider processes of cultural production and consumption. Literary tourism is not simply a function of literary influences. On the contrary, how meanings may be forged through tourism requires an examination of the links between tourism activities and wider social structures. Such an examination should develop understandings of the social and cultural meanings of tourist experiences, and the relationship between cultural production and consumption.

The social and cultural significance of tourism is built on two premises: one, understanding its role and function in everyday life; and two, developing an appreciation of how specific meanings of cultural heritage are created, communicated, and interpreted. As Duncan and Duncan have stated, "This production of landscapes, how they are constructed, how they are read, and how they act as a mediating influence, shaping the reader's ideas and images of what the landscape represents speaks directly to the question of nationalism, ideology and identity."[14] In order to conceptualize this process of cultural heritage creation and landscape interpretation, it is important to recognize that the creation of such literary sites as Red Cloud and Neepawa is not the result of a single creative subject—i.e., Willa Cather or Margaret Laurence—but is embedded within complex and collective patterns of social interaction. As Cosgrove and Daniels have shown:

> Culture is seen as more substantial these days. It is not uniquely because of its morphologies—the physicality of the cultural landscape—but because landscape is itself now recognized as 'a concept of high tension': one which contains multiple and competing claims about the constitution of social order. Geography enters these discussions by recognizing that culture's geographies are extraordinarily complicated texts of social, political and economic interplay.[15]

The social interaction of those who develop and promote these literary sites is comprised of a multitude of political, cultural, and economic agendas communicated through the sites themselves.

According to R. Johnson's "circuit of culture," these communications may be theorized as a circuit of culture forms through which meanings are encoded by specialist groups of producers and decoded (or interpreted) in many different ways over time and in diverse contexts.[16] Differentiation has also been made between public representations and private lives. Johnson states that cultural consumption is always a process rendering the public private again. The application of this contention to literary tourism provides Johnson with strong practical evidence. For example, a published novel becomes public property, but when people read the novel and interpret its literary meanings, they assimilate these meanings into their own thoughts and feelings, and the novel becomes private again. In literary tourism, heritage and setting are constructed, the private childhood home and various personal belongings of the author become public domain, but as visitors interpret these settings and cultural artefacts for themselves, private meanings are created. The relationship between production and consumption is a fundamental component of literary tourism. The writer's text becomes part of a wider symbolic system read by different tourists in different ways. Influenced by factors such as gender, class, ethnicity, nationality, religious beliefs, age, place of residence, and views on the writer, meanings are incorporated from our everyday lives into a particular heritage experience.

PRAIRIE, HERITAGE TOURISM, AND THE CONSTRUCTION OF NATIONAL IDENTITY

More and more, heritage tourism denotes what we hold jointly with others—the good and bad—that belongs to and defines a group. Collective legacies have long lent pride and purpose to locale, creed, and trade. But their customary arena is now larger: ethnic group, nation-state.[17] This type of tourism, in particular, reveals sites and signifiers that represent the typical English village, the typical midwest frontier town, the typical German beer garden. These sites in a sense help to encapsulate, for many, all that is English, North American, or German. According to James Urry, this type of heritage tourism illustrates how tourists "are in a way semioticians reading the landscape for signifiers of certain constructed indicators derived to represent particular aspects of national identity."[18] Even a past negatively portrayed can be turned on its head to convey the opposite message. Frederick Jackson Turner's portrayal of the American frontier as the seedbed of democracy is an important heritage contribution. This same landscape, however, was once termed 'a stagnant putrid pool' and a 'dunghill.'[19] The heritage industry's relationship to nationalism represents an important interpretation that is communicated to tourists, and serves as a visible guarantor of national identity. Since the doctrine of nationalism requires people to believe their nation has existed for many centuries, even when its existence was not socially and politically notice-able, according to Herbison:

> The proof for its existence depended on the continuity of its lin-guistics and cultural coherence. Not even that coherence was obvious to the naked eye, historians had ... to demonstrate that the ruins and documents of the past ... were part of the cultural heritage of each nation, monuments to the existence of cultural continuity.[20]

In Red Cloud, a tourist's experience with elements of Willa Cather's literary heritage also drew out associations with the prairie landscape and American regional and national identity. In particular, the literary sites were subsumed within a larger framework, as people negotiated literary associations and made many powerful connections among Cather, Ameri-can nationalism, and the frontier history of the prairie. Again, these con-nections raise questions about what the proponents of literary tourism and their particular representations of local and regional heritage narrate to visitors and what they exclude and why.

The associations and connections were evident in tourists' responses to questions from the survey. The first question asked what people had learned from their visit to Red Cloud/Neepawa and the next question inquired about what they thought Red Cloud/Neepawa represented about America/Canada. The responses to these questions, when analyzed for structure, produced findings for Red Cloud quite different from those for Neepawa.

Red Cloud's Heritage Linkages

In Red Cloud, interesting interpretations were derived from tourists' strong views about the value of the rural American landscape, a frequent setting for Cather's novels. Comments declared a pride and appreciation for the 'rural past.' These comments led to broader associations regarding issues of heritage and preservation. Comments on the issue of heritage were either quite complimentary or equally critical. The complimentary responses stated strong pride in the 'development of a nation built on struggle and desire,' 'realized American dreams,' 'history of those who settled this part of America,' and the 'small American town proud of its history.' Those more critical of the reconstructed heritage of Red Cloud stated that its 'images of a time and a place allow for only one history of America,' and remarked on 'the tenacity of Anglophones to settle and make a living, not the Native American history of the region,' and 'the displacement of Native American populations on the prairie.' While most comments concerning representation reflected nationalist views, some respondents also acknowledged that the particular heritage presented in Red Cloud has silenced the heritage of others whose history has also taken place on the American prairies.

The issue of preservation is associated with an ideology of conservation that unequivocally fuses that 'past' with the 'rural.' In America, the rural small-town past has recently become an important feature for the heritage industry as a way of responding to the economic decline facing many communities (Red Cloud being no exception). The past is also an important component in experiencing and valuing tangible living history as it is perceived by many visiting tourists. (Again, Red Cloud is no exception.) The preservation of these places maintains the hallmark of authentic Middle American heritage for many tourists. Preservation and conservation of the rural allows visitors a link with their past.

Neepawa's Heritage Linkages

Margaret Laurence's Neepawa, on the other hand, has yet to be reconstructed into a town that represents, for tourists, an assembly of literary sites that together create images of her Manawaka culture and society. Instead, only her childhood home provides an interpretation of Laurence's own personal heritage, and even here, most of the artefacts are not associated with Neepawa directly. Tourist interpretations of what Neepawa broadly represents for Canadians were ambivalent, with 'small prairie town ideals and history' being the most frequently stated response after remarks about the town's connection with Laurence.

Visitors did, however, couple the Neepawa they encountered through Laurence's literary connection with the many Canadian ancestors who had settled the prairie. For example, one visitor wrote that "this is the town of my people who gave it its rich cultural heritage and strong religious values." Many others commented on the importance of perpetuating Canadian heritage through sites like these. Neepawa is 'a part of Canadian culture and an important ingredient to Canadian heritage.

Neepawa is Margaret Laurence as she brings it alive in her literary works,' and 'the home of a Canadian writer who helped to put the prairies on the map.' The importance of Neepawa in relation to Canada's broader national identity and heritage is prevalent throughout the responses. Laurence has become part of a wider symbolic system and, correspondingly, these interpretations occurred cross-culturally. In Germany and Japan in particular, fascination with Margaret Laurence and her town of Neepawa continues to grow, to some extent because of widespread fascination for rural Canada and the possibility of experiencing Laurence's Manawaka first-hand.

Respondents also expressed different notions of country. In a larger sense, the tourist experience also helped people to fulfill certain understandings about the prairies in general and Canada in particular. Here again, both Laurence and the tourist's exposure to the town itself were subsumed within a larger symbolic framework, as people negotiated literary associations to make some powerful statements about other social and cultural values. For example, Neepawa represented for some visitors 'any town in prairie Canada,' 'a friendly Canadian small town,' 'our Canadian cultural heritage of the west,' and a 'typical Canadian landscape.'

These ideas of Canada have their origins in other cultural traditions, which reflect an intricate combination of historical fact and myth, perpetuated and promoted, among other sources, through contemporary tourism literature. Because cultural approaches are about meanings and communication, the way that Laurence has been incorporated into such defined ways of seeing the Canadian prairie provides graphic illustration of the various producers, consumers, and interactions that underlie interpretations of literary tourism sites. As these meanings and values of "Margaret Laurence" intersect with wider cultural influences and sources, certain interpretations of what is Canadian prairie become accepted.

A wider cultural studies perspective to analyze questions of representation in literary tourism reveals how tourists visiting Red Cloud and Neepawa interpret the cultural heritage of these places by linking meanings to a variety of political, social, and cultural values. While these meanings and interpretations of literary tourism sites are never static, they should be understood as beginnings from which values about national pride, biases of heritage, Canadian identity, and issues associated with preservation are experienced, contested, and constituted.

Cather's and Laurence's heritage sites on the prairies highlight how the meanings of this kind of tourism are a significant medium through which values about broader social, political, and cultural issues are negotiated for visitors. These understandings, consumed within wider social contexts, reflect the importance of realizing the value of contemporary tourism. The findings from this research respond to questions concerning the process of conception, development, and maintenance of two literary heritage sites, which now stand as successful prototypes for future growth in this type of tourism activity.

ENDNOTES

1. D.C. Pocock, "Haworth: The Experience of Literary Place," in *Geography and Literature: A Meeting of the Disciplines*, ed. W. Mallory and P. Simpson-Housley (Syracuse: Syracuse University Press, 1987), 135–142.

2. See N. Nicholson, *The Lakers: The First Tourists* (London: Robert Hale, 1972); P.T. Newby, "Literature and the Fashioning of Tourist Taste," in *Humanistic Geography and Literature: Essays on the Experience of Place*, ed. D.C. Pocock (London: Croom Helm, 1981), 130–141; R. Butler, "Literature as an Influence in Shaping the Image of Tourist Destinations: A Review and Case Study," in *Canadian Studies of Parks, Recreation and Tourism in Foreign Lands*, ed. J.S. Marsh (Peterborough: Trent University Press, 1986), 122–128; S. Squire, "Wordsworth and Lake District Tourism: Romantic Reshaping of the Landscape," *The Canadian Geographer* 32: 237–247, and "Wordsworth and Lake District Tourism: A Reply," *The Canadian Geographer* 34: 164–170; Pocock, "Haworth"; and V. Luftig, "Literary Tourism and Dublin's Joyce," in *Joyce and the Subject of History*, ed. M. Wollenger (Ann Arbor: University of Michigan Press, 1996), 141–194.

3. See Pocock, *Humanistic Geography*; and S. Squire, "The Cultural Values of Literary Tourism," *Annals of Tourism Research* 21: 103–120.

4. D. Lowenthal, *Possessed by the Past* (New York: Free Press, 1995), 102.

5. B. Bailyn, *On the Teaching and Writing of History* (New Hampshire: Hanover, 1994).

6. P. Burke, "History and Social Memory," in *Memory, History, Culture and Mind*, ed. T. Butler (Oxford: Oxford University Press, 1989).

7. Lowenthal, *Possessed*, 102.

8. R. Weiss, *The Renaissance Discovery of Classical America* (Oxford: Oxford University Press, 1959), 65.

9. "Creating the Plains Community: A Visual Essay" in the Webster County's Museum Exhibition, 1997.

10. Ibid.

11. "Red Cloud," *US Census*, 1910. Nebraska Reference Bureau Archives.

12. Mildred R. Bennett, *The World of Willa Cather* (1951; Lincoln: University of Nebraska Press, 1961).

13. S. Squire," Cultural Values." J. Corner, "Codes and Cultural Analysis," in *Media, Culture, and Society: A Critical Reader*, ed. R. Collins, J. Curran, N. Garnham, et al. (London: Sage, 1986), 49–62.

14. J. Duncan, and N. Duncan, "(Re)reading the Landscape," *Environment and Planning D: Society and Space* 6 (1988): 120.

15. D. Cosgrove, and S. Daniels, eds., *The Iconography of Landscape: Essays on the Symbolic Representation, Design, and Use of Past Environments* (New Jersey: Prentice Hall, 1988), 4.

16. R. Johnson, "The Story So Far and Further Transformations," in *Introduction to Contemporary Cultural Studies*, ed. D. Punter (London: Longman, 1986), 277–313.

17. R. Hewison, *The Heritage Industry* (London: Methuen, 1987).

18. J. Urry, *The Tourist Gaze* (London: Sage, 1993), 112.

19. R.S. Taylor, "How New Salem Became an Outdoor Museum," *Historic Illinois* 2 (1979): 256–268.

20. R. Herbison, *Deliberate Regression* (New York: Knopf, 1980), 233.

A TIMELESS IMAGINED PRAIRIE

Return and Regeneration in Margaret Laurence's Manawaka Novels

by Debra Dudek

The objectives of this essay are threefold: first, to describe a feminist Canadian literary modernism in order to draw attention to revisions that need to take place in the conception of a misleadingly unqualified modernism; second, to locate this strain of modernism historically, geographically, and aesthetically; and third, to analyze time-space compression as a crucial aspect of feminist Canadian literary modernism. This essay argues that Margaret Laurence's Manawaka novels—*The Stone Angel* (1964), *A Jest of God* (1966), *The Fire-Dwellers* (1969), and *The Diviners* (1974)—are representative of a modernist strain of literature closely associated with nationalist and feminist movements that took place in Canada in the 1960s and 1970s. More specifically, it responds to the question "When is the Prairie?" by suggesting that the prairie is timeless because it is an imagined construct that resists occupying a single time. Instead, it is a fluid coordinate on a space-time continuum that challenges homogeneous models of nationalism and modernism.

9:00 p.m. 11 May 1992. Blue Note Café. Main Street across from the forks of the Red and Assiniboine rivers, a site just behind the train station in Winnipeg, Manitoba, Canada.

I sit in the Blue Note, an after-hours coffee house that is famous in Winnipeg as the centre of the city's music scene. The Crash Test Dummies played here at least once a month before they were *The* Crash Test Dummies. Neil Young has come here to sing after more than one of his concerts. If the owner knows you are a regular, then you can get wine after 2:00 a.m, even though liquor cannot legally be sold after this time. Ask for red or white tea, and your wine comes in a teacup. It is closed by the liquor inspectors on a regular basis. Before the Blue Note left Main Street, I went there for a poetry reading one night during my first year as a graduate student studying Canadian literature. I sat with my teacher Robert Kroetsch, and classmate and poet Nicole Markotic. Patrick Friesen read from the small stage on the other side of the red vinyl booths. I could barely see Friesen through a smoky haze, but his voice was clear—an intimate whisper and a raspy touch: "Is the dream loud enough? Can you feel it on your skin?"

I sit across from Kroetsch and Markotic, alone on my side of the booth. My back is to the window. I watch Kroetsch gaze out the window, eyes lost, fingers clenched. He leans over to Nicole, unfurls his fingers, and points out the window behind me: "Look. A train—the vision of an urban landscape." A symbol of the prairies. Like Friesen's whisper, Kroetsch's observation was simple and profound. It still lives in my skin.

Kroetsch will likely tell you a different story.

Markotic will tell it in another way.

Friesen may not even have known we were there.

I cannot look at a train without thinking of Kroetsch, Markotic, Friesen, and the prairie. When I read about a train, I understand the hold it has on prairie people. The train in Margaret Laurence's Manawaka novels haunts the people of Manawaka, at times a spectre of hope, at other times a shadow of destruction. Always a sound leading away from and towards home. Always a contradiction.

Before the invention of the train, rivers and their banks—and other bodies of water—were utilized as transportation routes, trade posts, and dwelling areas, and, later, were used to order and settle the land. Gerald Friesen in his history text *The Canadian Prairies* discusses how Cree peoples travelled interior river systems; Anishinaabe peoples inhabited land from the Manitoba Interlake to Hudson and James bays and Lake Superior; Assiniboines lived in the Rainy River corridor from Lake Superior to Lake Winnipeg; and Chipewyans lived along the Churchill watershed.[1] In Manitoba after European contact, fur trade posts were established on Hudson Bay, on lakes Winnipeg and Manitoba, and on the Churchill, Assiniboine, and Qu'Appelle rivers.

I call attention to the river and train because I argue that each is a symbol of modernist transformation, with the train being a more common modernist image. Two concerns that I believe are central to literary modernism are representations of time-space compression and the contradiction between the eternal and the ephemeral. David Harvey in *The Condition of Postmodernity* discusses the concept of time-space compression as a signal of the

> processes that so revolutionize the objective qualities of space and time that we are forced to alter, sometimes in quite radical ways, how we represent the world to ourselves. [I use] the word 'compression' because a strong case can be made that the history of capitalism has been characterized by speed-up in the pace of life, while so overcoming spatial barriers that the world sometimes seems to collapse inwards upon us.[2]

The image of the train represents, not exclusively but among other things, time-space compression in Canada. Canada compressed with the building of the railroads. Railways allowed people and products to move more quickly from one end of the nation to another. The landscape was demarcated according to where the railway was built, and time was ordered according to the arrival and departure of the trains. Towns were created along the railway lines, which replaced the waterways as places of settlement. The Manawaka novels revise this time-space compression and return to the river as a paradigmatic place that is a middle ground, a neutral territory that is neither the town nor the farm. With this revision, time is no longer configured linearly or chronologically and space is expanded instead of compressed. Water, and the river in particular, is a metaphor for transformation and possibility.[3]

This essay had one of its beginnings as an observation by "Mr. Canadian Postmodern" about the train as a vision of the urban landscape. What Robert Kroetsch gave no indication of seeing was the river flowing behind the train. In this essay, I revise Kroetsch's observation, putting his words to work in order to bring attention to the river, which has a history reaching even farther back than the train. Those waters contain the paddles of the Cree peoples, the reflections of Anishinaabe and Assiniboine dwellings, the hopes of the fur traders, the tears of the settlers, the generosity of the Métis, the determination of Riel, and the progress of the trains. If part of the task of revising modernism is to seek out and counterpose alternatives to dominant traditions, then this paper posits a feminist Canadian modernism that acknowledges the linearity of the train track without losing sight of the winding river.

An oft-quoted statement made by Robert Kroetsch about the formation of a Canadian literary tradition claims that "Canadian literature evolved directly from Victorian into Postmodern."[4] This essay writes into that gap and claims that there is a modernist movement in Canada closely associated with women's fiction writing.[5] Modernism has been constructed as a male-centred phenomenon, and while much work has been done to call attention to women's modernist work, at this point a silently male-gendered, masculinist, modernism is the norm. Therefore, it is important to foreground the ways in which revised modernisms displace, or correctively supplement, mainstream male—or, to use a playful term with a nevertheless serious intent, malestream—modernism.

When I use the terms *modernism*, *nationalism*, and *feminism*, I understand they are contested terms that imply multiple meanings. However, I also find myself unwilling to let go of these terms simply because they are problematic and immense. Instead, I hope to open them as I seek to include a feminist Canadian modernism into a fairly closed Canadian literary history, which is based primarily on a patriarchal, white, middle-class model. I will attempt to show that Margaret Laurence's Manawaka novels serve as a model that represents a Canadian nationalism based on Canada's heterogeneity, but I also acknowledge that she is writing from an arguably privileged position of a white, middle-class woman born in the geographic, if not the power, centre of Canada. However, she does expand Canadian borders in her writing: her settings are not limited to Canada; her heroines sometimes see beyond whiteness and often belong to the working class; and the protagonist of her final novel loves a Métis man and gives birth to a Métis child. Laurence's novels primarily articulate a middle-class, Canadian prairie, Scottish immigrant sensibility, but the

novels also engage in meaningful ways with hegemonic and nonhege-
monic groups in order to problematize hierarchical structures based on
race, ethnicity, class, gender, and sexuality.

MODERNISM

For approximately 100 years many writers and critics have worked to
define the nature of modernism. I am less concerned with applying aspects
of conventional definitions of modernism to Margaret Laurence's Manawaka novels and more interested in looking at a particular instance in
Canadian literary history, an instance when nationalist and feminist movements influenced a generation of women writers who wrote stories that
represented a feminist nationalism using what could arguably be called a
modernist aesthetic. Margaret Laurence's novels are representative of a
Canadian feminist modernism that is interested in exemplifying an unstable social and political climate, a climate that influenced analogous modernist movements in other times and places, present in Canada in the late
1960s and early 1970s. I will, therefore, not engage in an extended summary of the nature of modernism but will identify certain characteristics
and limitations of malestream modernisms as developed and reiterated by
primarily male writers and critics.

Peter Nicholls, in his text *Modernisms: A Literary Guide*, enters the discussion about modernism by drawing attention to the plural form of his
title in an attempt to demonstrate the problems inherent in a modernism
that stands as a "sort of monolithic ideological formation." Nicholls
argues it is important to draw connections between politics and literary
style and to look at the "complex inscription of ideologies in the modernist styles which frequently became their most powerful and ambiguous
vehicle." He is interested in translating "politics into style" in order to
represent the tension between the "social and the aesthetic." Nicholls's
mapping of this tension in literary modernisms demonstrates how a variety of modernist art movements—such as symbolism, dadaism, neo-
classicism, futurism, and surrealism, as well as other avant-garde developments—influenced literary and visual arts.[6]

By looking at the intersection of style, authority, and gender, Nicholls
exposes the falsity of the one-dimensional malestream modernism that to
date still stands as the model for modernism. Nicholls's reworking of

modernism into a "conceptual map of the different modernist tendencies" is helpful because it puts politics in the place of periodicity, drawing attention to traces rather than to "clearly defined historical moments."[7] Nicholls's mapping allows for discussion before and beyond the canonical modernism represented by Ezra Pound, T.S. Eliot, James Joyce, Wyndham Lewis, and D.H. Lawrence, for instance.

Regardless of the work being done by critics such as Nicholls, the term *modernism* is still commonly identified with art made around World War I and is still primarily conceptualized as a male phenomenon, both in terms of the writers of the time and of the more contemporary academic formulators, such as David Lodge, who claims that the Great War created a "climate of opinion receptive to artistic revolution." David Lodge's *The Modes of Modern Writing: Metaphor, Metonymy, and the Typology of Modern Literature* is a key text that represents the critical impulse to develop a singular model of modernism, a "single way of talking about novels, a critical methodology, a poetics or aesthetics of fiction, which can embrace descriptively all the varieties of this kind [modern and modernist] writing."[8] This impulse has contributed to the marginalization of women's modernist literatures because of its primary focus on male-authored texts, with Virginia Woolf and Gertrude Stein being the obvious exceptions, as the model for a modernist aesthetic. However, Lodge's definition of modernist fiction is also helpful in order to demonstrate how the form of Laurence's fiction does fit a conventional model of modernism even while her content challenges the periodicity and place generally assigned to modernism.

Lodge posits two kinds of modern fiction: modern and modernist. Modern literature is still connected to the modern age of realism, while modernist fiction

> is experimental or innovatory in form, displaying marked deviations from preexisting modes of discourse, literary and non-literary. . . . A modernist novel has no real 'beginning', since it plunges us into a flowing stream of experience with which we gradually familiarize ourselves by a process of inference and association; and its ending is usually 'open' or ambiguous, leaving the reader in doubt as to the final destiny of the characters. . . . Modernist fiction eschews the straight chronological ordering of its material, and the use of a reliable, omniscient and intrusive narrator. It employs, instead, either a single, limited point of view, or a method of multiple points of view, all more or less limited and

fallible: and it tends towards a fluid or complex handling of time, involving much cross-reference backwards and forwards across the chronological span of the action.[9]

Lodge's portrait, and especially his focus on the fluidity of time and the multiplicity of voices, will connect my discussion of Laurence's novels to a conventional understanding of the characteristics of modernist fiction.

In addition to being attentive to the stylistic characteristics of modernist fiction, I find it is also important to understand the ways in which modernism has been configured by periodicity and place, especially because a Canadian modernist movement is rarely if ever remarked on in texts dealing with international modernism. Partly, this exclusion exists because 1890 to 1930 is the time period on which critical texts, such as Malcolm Bradbury's and James McFarlane's *Modernism: 1890–1930*, primarily focus. Indeed, Bradbury and McFarlane claim that 1930 is the year when "Modernism, like much else of the world it was born in, came to a kind of end." There is a gap here; modernism did not end, but rather came to a "kind of end." All the world is not on the same developmental timeline. If modernism is an art of "outrage" and "displacement" that occurs in a time of political and cultural disorder,[10] then the 1960s in Canada was an ideal setting for such an occurrence.

Linda Hutcheon claims that the 1960s are generally accepted as years characterized by a flowering of Canadian fiction due to nationalist sentiment, government support for publishers and artists, and a general feeling that Canada had finally ceased to be what Earle Birney calls a "highschool land / deadset in adolescence."[11] This metaphor for Canada's growth supports a position that Canadian identity in the imperial family was one of subordinate adolescent rather than mature adult. The 1960s, however, brought a change in Canadian identity that saw Canada resisting imperial and colonial standards and creating an alternative tradition for itself. Margaret Laurence's Manawaka novels are part of this Canadian literature of change, resistance, re-vision, and re-creation.[12]

This project is also a 'writing back' to imperial and cultural centres that construct a modernism that focusses on a London/Paris/New York triangle. Raymond Williams, in his chapter "When Was Modernism?" from his text *The Politics of Modernism: Against the New Conformists*, theorizes the problematics of a "Modernism" that was constructed as a singular entity "in an act of pure ideology, whose first, unconscious irony is that, absurdly, it stops history dead."[13] He urges resistance to an ideological victory based on metropolitan dominance, which is also connected to new imperialism. Rather than modernism's being an anti-bourgeois, universally unifying condition, Williams sees modernism as becoming complicit in the hegemony. His strategy of subverting this modernism that is based upon "a now dominant and misleading ideology"[14] is to reconsider and rewrite lost histories:

> If we are to break out of the non-historical fixity of post-modernism, then we must search out and counterpose an alternative tradition taken from the neglected works left in the wide margin of the century, a tradition which may address itself not to this by now exploitable because quite inhuman rewriting of the past but, for all our sakes, to a modern *future* in which community may be imagined again.[15]

By strategically recreating a community that combines past and present into new histories, Williams reconfigures modernism in such a way as to make a space for the inscription of a feminist Canadian literary modernism, which critiques imperial centres and destabilizes patriarchal ideologies.

At this point, it might be helpful to briefly summarize the ways in which I will be using the terms *modernism* and *postmodernism*, to demonstrate how Canadian and feminist critics characterize these movements, and to outline how they have considered Laurence's novels to be part of a modernist impulse. Modernism is comprised of cultural movements that use the techniques outlined by David Lodge and that, as Linda Hutcheon in *The Canadian Postmodern* claims, have much in common with postmodern techniques, such as fragmentation and parody. However, modernism is concerned with a search for revolutionary reconstruction (order in chaos), whereas postmodernism is concerned with an urge to question and disturb, "to make both problematic and provisional any such desire for order or truth through the powers of the human imagination."[16] Robert Kroetsch claims that the Canadian writer "must uninvent the word. He [sic] must destroy the homonymous American and English languages that keep him [sic] from hearing his own tongue. But to uninvent the word ... is to uninvent the world."[17] This statement touches on the crucial difference between Canadian modernism and postmodernism: modernism uninvents and then re-creates the word and the world, while postmodernism leaves the word and the world suspended.

While Margaret Laurence's Manawaka novels are not generally defined as modernist novels, several critics compare in varying degrees—from a passing comment to an elaborate comparison—Laurence, her protagonists, and/or her narratives to more generally accepted modernist writers, their protagonists, and/or their narratives. For example, Nancy Bailey in her article "Margaret Laurence, Carl Jung and the Manawaka Women" claims that "Laurence gives new meaning to Rilke's definition of love as two solitudes that 'protect, and touch, and greet each other.'"[18] For Bailey, Laurence's novels expand Rilke's modernist definition to include love of the self, especially a woman's love for her self as she moves from an isolated to a supportive self. In addition, Bailey ends her article by setting Laurence's world against "Fitzgerald's American mythic world."[19] Indeed, F. Scott Fitzgerald ends his modernist classic *The Great Gatsby* with an image of futility that signifies an endless return to the past, an image one might read as a movement both against and with the water's flow: "So we beat on, boats against the current, borne back ceaselessly into the past."[20] As Bailey concludes, Laurence's novels, and especially *The Diviners*, look to the past in order to move into the future, while Fitzgerald's novel does not offer such a hopeful image of a regenerative future. Laurence's river flows both ways; Fitzgerald's Long Island Sound, "the most domesticated body of salt water in the Western hemisphere,"[21] is contained and containing, a body of water that, despite human effort to move forward, restricts movement to one direction. For Bailey to use Rilke and Fitzgerald as the bookends of her article is to name Laurence's novels as modernist works of fiction and is to offer alternatives within modernism so that modernism includes women's subjectivity and a regenerative society.

Other writers who liken Laurence to traditional modernists include Leona M. Gom, who—in her article "Laurence and the Use of Memory"—compares Laurence to Ford Madox Ford, Hagar to Proust's Marcel, and Morag to Woolf's Lily Briscoe.[22] Gayle Greene opens and closes her comparative article "Margaret Laurence's *Diviners* and Shakespeare's *Tempest*: The Uses of the Past" with a quotation from T.S. Eliot: "This is the use of memory: / For liberation—" and she compares Laurence to Woolf in her claim that "In this sense that what matters is process, Laurence more resembles Virginia Woolf than Shakespeare."[23] While each of these examples only gestures towards establishing Laurence as a modernist writer, when read together they can be seen as an indication of a methodology that collectively constructs a readership that looks to generally accepted modernist works as a means of acknowledging the ways in which Laurence is connected to a larger genealogy of modernism.

With the exception of the article by Greene, all the above-cited works were published between 1976 and 1978, within four years of the publication of *The Diviners* and, obviously, the conclusion of the Manawaka cycle (although this conclusion would not have been absolutely certain at the time). It is apparent that immediately following the conclusion of the cycle, critics were interested in firmly establishing Laurence in Canada's literary canon. Furthermore, by comparing aspects of the Manawaka cycle to various established modernist writers and texts, critics not only sought to place Laurence in the Canadian canon, they also sought to put Canadian literature on the international map. For example, Sherrill Grace, in her article "A Portrait of the Artist as Laurence Hero," likens Morag Gunn to Stephen Dedalus in James Joyce's *A Portrait of the Artist as a Young Man* because they are both artists who "forge ... the uncreated conscience of [their] race."[24] In this comparison, Grace states that Laurence, like Joyce, creates a hero who "reflects the national matrix from which the novel springs."[25] By looking to Joyce, Grace establishes Laurence as a writer who is concerned with issues of nation, and although Grace categorizes Laurence as a realist writer, I read Grace's article as part of a critical movement that sets up the Manawaka novels as a modernist cycle.[26]

The most sustained comparison, which firmly establishes the Manawaka novels as a modernist cycle, is David Blewett's article "The Unity of the Manawaka Cycle." His central argument is

> that the Manawaka cycle is unified not only by the centripetal pull of the home town itself, but by the development over the four novels of a vision of the human condition which is not fully rendered until the cycle is complete. This development imparts to the cycle a rhythm of reconciliation in which the fragmentariness of ordinary life, explored in the separate works, is seen against, and so continually absorbed into, a sense of design and purpose in the universe.

Blewett explores this modernist dynamic between the fragmentary and the universal in "an elaborate parallel with Eliot's symbolism of the four elements in *The Wasteland* [sic]."[27]

While each of these critics connects an aspect of the Manawaka cycle to a more generally accepted modernist writer and/or text, none of these critics names Laurence or her fiction as modernist. Therefore, my discussion must expand the commonly accepted definition of modernism in order to include the work of Margaret Laurence in the context of a modern Canada defined by its relation both to its past as a British colony and its present as an economic and cultural colony of the United States. One of the most important characteristics of the aesthetic movement of modernism, for the purposes of this essay, is the sense of tension that exists between the transitional and the eternal. Modernism embraces both the eternal and the fleeting and represents a concern with how to live amidst contradiction and conflict.

One of the ways in which modernism seeks to deal with an overwhelming sense of uncertainty is to break from preceding literary movements and historical conditions in order to create a new art that represents a modern condition. Harvey discusses this break as a dynamic of destruction through the image of "creative destruction" and claims that this image is important to modernism because it calls attention to the dilemma that surrounds the destruction of the old and the simultaneous creation of the new.[28] I suggest reconfiguring this image of creative destruction into one of strategic re-creation. With this reconfiguration comes a regenerative process—a process that finds the protagonist not separate from but connected to the land that surrounds him or her—instead of a tragic ending of futility. This reconfiguration also contains a gendered dynamic because the figures often associated with creative destruction include the mythical Dionysus, the literary Faust, and the painter Picasso.[29] There are few female figures—with the notable exceptions of Salomé and Medusa—in the Western tradition associated with creative destruction, so this version of modernism also needs to be revised.

Laurence's heroines, unlike Goethe's Faust, for example, incorporate their pasts into their presents and are, therefore, able to imagine transformed futures that do not include immediate destruction of themselves or their society. Marshall Berman in *All That Is Solid Melts into Air* speaks of the necessity of Faust's bond to his past and how the rejection of his past leads to a tragic end: "Without that vital bond with his past—the primary source of spontaneous energy and delight in life—he could never have developed the inner strength to transform the present and future. But now that he has staked his whole identity on the will to change, and on his power to fulfill that will, his bond with his past terrifies him."[30]

Instead of being terrified by the past and breaking with it, Laurence's heroines seek ways to incorporate their prairie pasts into their modern presents. Instead of Faust's wasteland being recreated inside the developer, the heroines in Laurence's Manawaka novels imagine their prairie pasts into a regenerative place that is part of their bodies. Their inner geography contains the regenerative prairie, and each heroine is connected to other people through this communal past. With this connection to the past, these heroines are able to acknowledge the complexity of their identities rather than being limited to a homogenous identity that cannot incorporate both the fleeting and the immutable.

One way to acknowledge a complex and diverse identity is to represent such an identity in art. The role of the artist is of primary importance within modernism, especially in post-Nietzschean discourse, thinking, art, and culture. As Harvey explains, when Nietzsche ranked "aesthetics above science, rationality, and politics . . . the exploration of aesthetic experience . . . became a powerful means to establish a new mythology as to what the eternal and immutable might be about in the midst of all the ephemerality, fragmentation, and patent chaos of modern life."[31] If aesthetics become a way to represent and transform the modern experience, then the artist is of paramount importance. The structure that casts the individual artist into the role of tragic hero is problematic because it perpetuates patriarchal ideologies that value the individual over the community. As can be seen in Goethe's Faust, malestream modernism reflects narcissistic individualism in its narratives. Instead, the modern artist needs to represent the world in which s/he exists without erasing the people and places that exist inside and outside the artist. The artist cannot stand alone as individual hero without effectively destroying the community that has helped form the artist.

The artist is central to this reconfiguration because it is the artist who reimagines alternatives that offer a critique of the status quo. It is fitting, therefore, that Morag, the final Manawaka protagonist, is a writer.[32] As Harvey explains, the modernist writer, according to Baudelaire, is "someone who can concentrate his or her vision on ordinary subjects of city life, understand their fleeting qualities, and yet extract from the passing moment all the suggestions of eternity it contains."[33] While Baudelaire suggests that modernism is an urban phenomenon with ordinary city subjects as the focus of the artist's eye, Laurence does not privilege urban peoples over rural peoples as appropriate subjects. This is not to say that the city is not of importance in the Manawaka novels, for the city figures in each of the novels and is especially visible and animate in *The Fire-Dwellers*. Furthermore, while modernism may have begun as an urban phenomenon, it has been transported and reconfigured in ways that may include all subjects regardless of location. What is of primary importance to my argument is the notion that the central challenge to the modernist writer is to create an aesthetic that represents both the transitory and the eternal, the timely and the timeless, the local and the mythic. The writer is able to imagine and represent the spatialization of time through language and form, by experimenting with simultaneity and contradiction, and by exploring the regions of memory and forgetting. In this way, modernism, while a response to historically specific phenomena, also embodies all the experiences leading up to that moment.

THE MANAWAKA NOVELS

The literature of a nation represents people's lived experiences and the places where those experiences occur, and Margaret Laurence's Manawaka novels represent the struggles of many Canadian women to come to voice. By contextualizing the Manawaka novels as works that contribute to a revisionist Canadian literary modernism, the reader sees that the novels are revolutionary in the ways that they reimagine the nation out of repressive social structures through the liberated female individual. Each protagonist struggles to define her own individual identity within her communities. It is not until Morag in *The Diviners*, however, that a protagonist reaches past her individual history to touch several communal histories that strategically reconstruct an imagined community out of complex immigrant and Métis mythologies. When all four novels are considered together, the community of Manawaka becomes visible, even if the individual protagonists are not quite certain of their places in that community. The imagined community that appears is a timeless and timely place grounded in the mythic and the local, a place of both return and regeneration.

The primary protagonists of the Manawaka novels—Hagar, Rachel, Stacey, and Morag—embody different aspects of a feminist modernist struggle to find an identity that represents both individual and collective unity and difference. In order to acknowledge her complex identity, each protagonist must reconcile her contemporary individualism with her communal past to imagine an alternative future. Each protagonist voices feelings of separation and isolation as she contemplates her relationship to the landscape and to the people who are part of her community. One aspect of this past relates to the dynamics between the protagonists' ancestors, the Scots-Irish settlers and townspeople, and their neighbours, the Ukrainians and the prairie Métis peoples. Each protagonist makes visible the conflicts and communities that exist between lower class and middle class, rural and urban, young and aging, desire and regret, women and men, Métis and white.

This essay posits a feminist Canadian modernism that is a revolutionary movement that challenges hegemonic ideologies and represents a society unified in its diversity. I find it is important to mention some of the main historical events that inform the creation of this particular strand of modernism, including the second-wave feminist movement in Canada, the federal policy of multiculturalism, and the nationalist climate surrounding Canada's centennial year. I believe it is also important to note that government strategies, which were implemented to respond to the concerns of the people, did not adequately represent the complex concerns about issues of gender, race, sexuality, ethnicity, class, and region. Recalling Nietzsche's placement of aesthetics above politics, it follows that artists, and especially writers, are the ones to represent the complexity of Canadian identity while offering a critique of the structures on which that identity is based.

The Manawaka novels are revolutionary in how they re-vision Canadian identity beyond a dual French-English identity and beyond patriarchal social structures. Each novel focusses on an individual who struggles to transcend the limitations placed on her by patriarchal society. Together these novels create a community of women who resist the status quo by transgressing the boundaries of past and present, memory and forgetting, reality and imagination. Through these transgressive moments, the women offer subversive strategies that promote social change. The prairie becomes a place of return and regeneration as each protagonist remembers her prairie past and transforms that past into a hopeful future for the nation. Each protagonist's timeless moment contributes to the creation of a fluid historical pattern that is a fleeting and immutable story, which becomes part of an identity.

The Stone Angel

The timeless and fleeting moment of imagination and transcendence for Hagar Shipley in *The Stone Angel* occurs when she runs away from her son Marvin and his wife Doris. Back on the coast again, away from the prairie, Hagar returns to the prairie repeatedly in her memory. For the most part, she does not share these experiences with anyone. It is only at the age of ninety, running away from the seniors' home Silverthreads, and running toward her freedom, that Hagar speaks and weeps and does not regret her actions. Hagar leaves Marvin and Doris in an attempt to construct another house that she can call her own, and her body does not fail her. She returns to an old fish cannery she remembers visiting with Marvin and Doris. She makes her home in "A place of remnants and oddities ... more like the sea-chest of some old and giant sailor than merely a cannery no one has used in years."[34] This place suits her fragmented life, which is made up of its own "remnants and oddities." It is here that she begins to embrace her oddities and her freedom and to let go of her haughty pride.

Before Hagar can perform her fish-cannery transformation, however, she must traverse and conquer a wasteland by the sea. She is a questing hero who needs to survive trials in the wilderness before reaching her destination. In order to make her way back to the fish cannery from the beach, Hagar must climb a forested hill:

> Walking is difficult. I skid and slide on brown pine needles that lie thickly over the ground. Crashing, I stumble through ferns and rotten boughs that lie scattered like old bones. Cedars lash my face, and my legs are lacerated with brambles. . . . And then I do fall. . . . I grow enraged. I curse like Bram, summoning every blasphemy I can lay my hands on, screeching them into the quiet forest. Perhaps the anger gives me strength, for I clutch at a bough, not caring if it's covered with pins and needles or not, and yank myself upright. There. There. I knew I could get up alone. I've done it. Proud as Napoleon or Lucifer, I stand and survey the wasteland I've conquered. (190–191)

Hagar reaches back into both her prairie past with Bram and into a historical and literary past with Napoleon and Lucifer and summons enough strength to conquer the wasteland and stand on her own, both literally and metaphorically. In this moment, Hagar recognizes her individual strength and also realizes that her connection to literal and fictional pasts has helped her be strong in the present.

Significantly, Hagar also alters the role of a male hero, such as Napoleon or Lucifer or Faust. Instead of attempting to conquer the wasteland in order to change it, Hagar sits down and enjoys her time in "this green blue-ceilinged place, warm and cool with sun and shade.... Perhaps I've come here not to hide but to seek" (192). Here, she sees herself as a questing and questioning heroine who changes herself rather than changing the landscape. Indeed, a reciprocal touching occurs between Hagar and the landscape: "Beside me grows a shelf of fungus, the velvety underside a mushroom color, and when I touch it, it takes and retains my fingerprint" (192). She leaves her mark on the wilderness, but this action is not creative destruction. This action is an acknowledgement of her own identity, a simultaneous marking and being marked.

A Jest of God

Rachel Cameron is the only Manawaka protagonist who still lives in Manawaka, so instead of using memory and imagination to incorporate her prairie home into her present, Rachel uses her imagination to take her away from what she believes is a confining space. Rachel is also the only protagonist who reflects on the connection between the train and the water, and this reflection builds community across space because the memory causes her to long for her sister.[35] However, she also takes refuge in places of confinement. As they are with Hagar, for Rachel, the forest and the water are transformative places:

> —A forest. Tonight it is a forest. Sometimes it is a beach. It has to be right away from everywhere. Otherwise she may be seen. The trees are green walls, high and shielding, boughs of pine and tamarack, branches sweeping to earth, forming a thousand rooms among the fallen leaves. She is in the green-walled room, the boughs opening just enough to let the sun in, the moss hairy and soft on the earth. She cannot see his face clearly. His features are blurred as though his were a face seen through water. She sees only his body distinctly, his shoulders and arms deeply tanned, his belly flat and hard. He is wearing only tight-fitting jeans, and his

swelling sex shows. She touches him there, and he trembles, absorbing her fingers' pressure. Then they are lying along one another, their skins slippery. His hands, his mouth are on the wet warm skin of her inner thighs. Now—

I didn't. I didn't. It was only to be able to sleep. The shadow prince. Am I unbalanced? Or only laughable? That's worse, much worse. (25)

Like the landscape that retains Hagar's fingerprint, the skin of Rachel's imaginary lover absorbs Rachel's touch. By touching and being touched, Rachel breaks out of closed systems of thought and action. Rachel's imagination takes her out of her bedroom and into an outer room, a room in the forest that anticipates the place where she will eventually have sex with Nick, where her imaginary lover becomes tangible. In this masturbatory scene, Rachel brings herself to orgasm and then questions her motives as though pleasure cannot be a motive, as though pleasure for a woman without a man makes her laughable.

Rachel's concerns with balance and stability continue throughout the novel as Rachel ruminates on her view of the world:

Nothing is clear now. Something must be the matter with my way of viewing things. I have no middle view. Either I fix on a detail and see it as though it were magnified—a leaf with all its veins perceived, the fine hair on the back of a man's hands—or else the world recedes and becomes blurred, artificial, indefinite, an abstract painting of a world. The darkening sky is hugely blue, gashed with rose, blood, flame pouring from the volcano or wound or flower of the lowering sun. The wavering green, the sea of grass, piercingly bright. Black tree trunks, contorted, arching over the river.

Only Nick's face is clear. Prominent cheekbones, slightly slanted eyes, his black straight hair. Before, it seemed a known face because I knew the feeling of it, the male smell of his skin, the faint roughness along his jaw. Now it seems a hidden Caucasian face, one of the hawkish and long-ago riders of the Steppes.

I'm dramatizing. To make all this seem mysterious or significant, instead of what it is, which is embarrassing, myself standing gawkily here with no words, no charms of either kind, neither any depth nor any lightness. (91–92)

Rachel's vision—her absence of a middle view—reflects her inability to live in the present moment. She questions her way of viewing the world, claiming she has neither words nor charms while she simultaneously creates an apocalyptic modernist aesthetic that is both horrific and beautiful. The wounded sky hovers over a sea of prairie grass. Contorted trees twist over the river. Rachel's internal geography is apparent in the way she translates the prairie landscape. It is in this act of dramatization that she transforms herself from an embarrassed virgin into an imaginative lover.

This landscape in which she stands with Nick is also the landscape of her imagination. Time and space compress as Nick's clear face becomes the blurred and unrecognizable face of a mythical hero, the "shadow prince" who visits her in the night. The forest of her fantasies is the place in which she now sits, and Nick defines this forested space by the river as "neutral territory" that is neither the town nor the farm. Rachel interprets this definition as a place that is "neither one side nor the other" (93), a place that does not follow the division in the town, which the people have created and the train tracks have made visible. The river is the middle space, the neutral territory; it is the transformative place where anything can happen.

The Fire-Dwellers

Time and space compress when Stacey MacAindra's memory takes her to Diamond Lake, first as a ten-year-old and then as an eighteen-year-old. At ten, the voices of loons fascinate Stacey because they are voices "that cared nothing for lights or shelter or the known quality of home."[36] These voices mock the confinement of home and speak to Stacey of alternative ways of living. At eighteen, Diamond Lake is a place where she questions her limits, tentatively with her mind and confidently with her body:

> She was a strong swimmer, and when she reached the place where she could see the one spruce veering out of the rock on the distant point, she always turned back, not really accepting her limits, believing she could have gone on across the lake, but willing to acknowledge this arbitrary place of reference because it was further out than most of her friends could swim.... Stacey, swimming back to shore ... thinking already of the dance she would go to that evening, feeling already the pressure on her lake-covered thighs of the boys. (161)

Stacey places her beliefs beside her actions, using the landscape and her friends as points of reference. She believes she can go beyond the limits, but she does not put this belief into action. Instead of pushing past her self-imposed limits, she nudges against them, always turning back. However, this fleeting moment of memory, which is eternally accessible, enables Stacey to finally "Crash. Out of the inner and into the outer" (161) as she transgresses limits she has internalized.

Stacey finally pushes past her inhibitions, the confinement of both house and society, by returning to her body as a source of pleasure and resistance. Stacey meets Luke Venturi there by the water and he names her "merwoman," confirming that he "look[s] at things from some very different point of view" (164). This point of view, however, is one Stacey understands, although for her it has always meant isolation rather than connection. Luke is someone who understands the importance of speech and imagination to such an extent that Stacey asks him, "You're real? You're not real. I'm imagining" (165). She cannot quite believe that this outer world can contain imagination and conversation. She is "unable for the moment to believe the easiness of his words" (166). Like Hagar's and Rachel's, Stacey's hiding becomes a seeking as Luke encourages her to "Come out. From wherever you're hiding yourself" (167). And Stacey does come out from hiding. This initial accidental visit is one of conversation only. The next time they meet Stacey intentionally seeks Luke.

A transformation occurs when the accidental becomes the intentional, when hiding becomes seeking, when beliefs form actions. When Stacey goes back to see Luke, she is the first one to touch the other. Stacey's body responds to and searches for pleasure through dancing and through sex: "She reacts as she once did to jazz, taking it as it was told to her unverbally, following the beat. Luke takes her hand and puts it on his sex. The surge in her own sex is so great that she presses herself hard against him, urging him" (186). By connecting to dance as the pleasure of her prairie past, which is contained in her body, Stacey reorders time and space through memory and action. This modernist re-creation strategically regenerates Stacey as she returns to eighteen at forty, as she escapes the chaos of the city to find pleasure by the water.

The Diviners

A recognition of the landscape's order and transformative qualities occurs in several places and in many ways in *The Diviners*. The mountain and the valley provide a basis for Pique's identity, while the "river of now and then" orders the novel and serves as an image of both return and regeneration for Morag. This river is an appropriate sign for a feminist Canadian modernism rooted in the prairie because it contains the "apparently impossible contradiction" of being able to exist in both the past and present while simultaneously signifying a geographical space that is both here and there, both McConnell's Landing and Manawaka: "The river flowed both ways. The current moved from north to south, but the wind usually came from the south, rippling the bronze-green water in the opposite direction. This apparently impossible contradiction, made apparent and possible, still fascinated Morag, even after the years of river-watching."[37] By watching the river, Morag returns in memory to the prairie and these memories form the basis of her regeneration and her creation of communal narratives. These narratives interweave memory, history, and story— both Tonnerre and Gunn/Logan family history. As an adult, Morag chooses to live by a river, acknowledging the personal history of the settlers like Catharine Parr Traill, who first lived in her home and her district, and reflecting on the communal present forming around her.

The "river of now and then" flows into the Wachakwa River in Morag's memory. As with Hagar, Rachel, and Stacey, the landscape mirrors Morag's inner conflicts and contains the outer contradictions apparent in a modern condition. The way in which each protagonist interprets the landscape reveals how she views her self in relation to people and place:

> Hill Street, so named because it was on one part of the town hill which led down into the valley where the Wachakwa River ran, glossy brown, shallow, narrow, more a creek than a river. They said "crick," there. Down in the valley the scrub oak and spindly pale-leafed poplars grew, alongside the clumps of chokecherry bushes and wolf willow. The grass there was high and thick, undulating greenly like wheat, and interspersed with sweet yellow clover. But on Hill Street there were only one or two sickly Manitoba maples and practically no grass at all.
>
> I didn't see it in that detail at first. I guess I must have seen it as a blur. (36–37)

As Rachel blurs the features of her imaginary lover, so Morag remembers the vision of her youth to be blurred. In hindsight, Morag acknowledges the difference between the landscape of the valley and the landscape of Hill Street. She sees the valley as a lush place in contrast to the stark street on which she lives. This reflects Morag's inner geography as she constructs her condition as one of lack. Morag's youth is the wasteland she must conquer and re-vision. She achieves this clarity and detail from both spatial and temporal distances when she recognizes that Manawaka and its people are "inside [her] head, for as long as [she] lives" (376). The river of now and then is an analogue to the prairie river that flows timelessly in her blood.

Feminist modernist narratives creatively displace narratives of destruction and replace them with stories of transformation in which the individual, the community, and the landscape are transformed. Laurence makes the connection among novels explicit when she thematically and semantically connects each primary protagonist to another. Communities and cycles, like the ones created in the Manawaka novels, dismantle the hierarchical binary that is part of Canada's founding myth. Canada is not constructed out of two founding nations or languages. The complex construction of Canada as a colonial and arguably post-colonial nation is made more visible when issues about cultural diversity are examined. The divisions in Manawaka between town and farm, between Scots-Irish and Ukrainian, between hill and valley are made visible and then disregarded when Hagar marries Bram, when Rachel and Nick are lovers, and because of the connection between Morag and Jules and Pique. That Stacey embodies this prairie attitude of resistance is apparent when she has an affair with Luke. The English-French identity that is Canada's myth is problematized by making the diversity of the nation visible within the microcosm that is Manawaka. Through memory and imagination, hope and determination, Hagar, Rachel, Stacey, and Morag create a prairie community that extends beyond the confines of space and time and re-visions the nation to include the voices and desires of women.

ENDNOTES

1. Gerald Friesen, *The Canadian Prairies: A History*, student ed. (Toronto: University of Toronto Press, 1987), 23–25.

2. David Harvey, *The Condition of Postmodernity* (Cambridge: Blackwell, 1989), 240.

3. Other articles that note the importance of water and nature in Laurence's fiction include "Quest for the Peaceable Kingdom: Urban/Rural Codes in Roy, Laurence, and Atwood" by Sherrill E. Grace, in *Women Writers and the City: Essays in Feminist Literary Criticism,* ed. Susan Merrill Squier (Knoxville: University of Tennessee Press, 1984), 193–209; and "Laurence's Fiction: A Revisioning of Feminine Archetypes," by Stephanie A. Demetrakopoulos (*Canadian Literature* 93 [Summer 1982]: 42–57). Grace's article focusses primarily on the transformative possibilities that are available when nature is valued. Within this discussion, Grace talks about Stacey's escape to the "shore of saltwater . . . where she will try to heal her wounds sufficiently to keep functioning" (199). Grace's article confirms my argument about Laurence's use of water, although my argument diverges from her discussion because she speaks more generally about nature and not specifically about water. Although Demetrakopoulos's article is largely irrelevant to my discussion because it concentrates on archetypal imagery in *The Fire-Dwellers* and *A Jest of God,* Demetrakopoulos also recognizes the importance of water in Laurence's fiction when she states, "Like all Laurence's women, she [Stacey] goes to a body of water to connect with her own deepest self" (48).

4. Robert Kroetsch, "A Canadian Issue," *boundary* 2, 3 (1974): 1.

5. Only Barbara Godard, in her essay "Ex-centriques, Eccentric, Avant-Garde: Women and Modernism in the Literatures of Canada" (*Room of One's Own* 8, 4 [1983]: 57–75), has articulated a Canadian modernism that includes women's fiction—and especially poetic prose—up to and including the 1960s. While Godard mentions Margaret Laurence's work, she does not discuss it within her genealogy of modernism because she is more interested in reclaiming texts that substitute "the flux of surrealist images for linear narrative" and that have been censored, misread, and/or largely ignored (63). She comments that Laurence's texts have been read "in terms of a national concern with empires and communications" (60), but she disregards Laurence's use of language innovations. My work expands Godard's beginnings and elaborates on the feminist ideologies that contributed to a feminist Canadian modernism as seen in Margaret Laurence's Manawaka novels.

6. Peter Nicholls, *Modernisms: A Literary Guide* (Berkeley: University of California Press, 1995), vii.

7. Ibid., viii, 1.

8. David Lodge, *The Modes of Modern Writing: Metaphor, Metonymy, and the Typology of Modern Literature* (Ithaca: Cornell University Press, 1977), 43, 52.

9. Ibid., 45–46.

10. Malcolm Bradbury and James McFarlane, eds., *Modernism: 1890–1930* (1976; Harmondsworth: Penguin, 1991), 12, 11.

11. Quoted in Linda Hutcheon, *The Canadian Postmodern: A Study of Contemporary English-Canadian Fiction* (Toronto: Oxford University Press, 1988), 1.

12. See George Woodcock, "The Human Elements: Margaret Laurence's Fiction, in *The Human Elements: Critical Essays,* ed. David Helwig (Ottawa: Oberon, 1978), 134–161; Mathew Martin, "Dramas of Desire in Margaret Laurence's *A*

Jest of God, The Fire-Dwellers, and *The Diviners*," *Studies in Canadian Literature* 19, 1 (1994): 58–71; Sherrill E. Grace, "A Portrait of the Artist as Laurence Hero," *Journal of Canadian Studies* 13, 3 (Fall 1978): 64–71; Barbara Hehner, "River of Now and Then: Margaret Laurence's Narratives," *Canadian Literature* 74 (Autumn 1977): 40–57; Diana Brydon, "Sister Letters: Miranda's Tempest in Canada," in *Cross-Cultural Performances: Differences in Women's Re-Visions of Shakespeare*, ed. Marianne Novy (Urbana: University of Illinois Press, 1993), 165–184; Gillian Siddall, "Teaching Margaret Laurence's *The Diviners* as a Postcolonial Text," *Canadian Children's Literature* 79 (1995): 39–46; Neil ten Kortenaar, "The Trick of Divining a Postcolonial Canadian Identity: Margaret Laurence Between Race and Nation," *Canadian Literature* 149 (Summer 1996): 1–33; Gayle Greene, "Margaret Laurence's *Diviners* and Shakespeare's *Tempest*: The Uses of the Past," in *Women's Re-Visions of Shakespeare: On the Responses of Dickinson, Woolf, Rich, H.D., George Eliot, and Others*, ed. Marianne Novy (Urbana: University of Illinois Press, 1990), 165–182; and Laurie Ricou, "Never Cry Wolfe: Benjamin West's *The Death of Wolfe* in *Prochain Episode* and *The Diviners*," *Essays on Canadian Writing* 20 (Winter 1980–81): 171–185 for studies on how Laurence's Manawaka novels resist and subvert traditionally accepted myths and histories about Canadian culture and nationhood.

13. Raymond Williams, *The Politics of Modernism: Against the New Conformists* (1989; New York: Verso, 1994), 34–35.

14. Ibid., 31.

15. Ibid., 35.

16. Hutcheon, *Canadian Postmodern*, 2.

17. Kroetsch, "Canadian Issue," 1.

18. Nancy Bailey, "Margaret Laurence, Carl Jung and the Manawaka Women," *Studies in Canadian Literature* 2 (1977): 307.

19. Ibid., 321.

20. F. Scott Fitzgerald, *The Great Gatsby* (New York: Charles Scribner's Sons, 1925), 182.

21. Ibid., 5.

22. Leona M. Gom, "Laurence and the Use of Memory," *Canadian Literature* 71 (1976): 48, 49, 58.

23. Greene, "The Uses of the Past," 165, 175.

24. James Joyce, *A Portrait of the Artist as a Young Man* (1916; New York: Dover, 1994), 185.

25. Grace, "Portrait," 65.

26. Barbara Hehner in "River of Now and Then" also compares Laurence to Joyce, in passing, when she states, "Mercifully, she did not follow Joyce in returning her protagonist to the crib" (49).

27. David Blewett, "The Unity of the Manawaka Cycle," *Journal of Canadian Studies* 13, 3 (Fall 1978): 31.

28. Harvey, *Condition of Postmodernity*, 16.

29. Ibid., 16–17.

30. Marshall Berman, *All That Is Solid Melts into Air* (1982; New York: Penguin, 1988), 69.

31. Harvey, *Condition of Postmodernity*, 18.

32. See Sherrill Grace's "A Portrait of the Artist as Laurence Hero" and Christian Bök's "Sibyls: Echoes of French Feminism in *The Diviners and Lady Oracle*," *Canadian Literature* 135 (Winter 1992): 80–93 for further analyses on the importance of the writer as a creator, re-creator, and revolutionary.

33. Harvey, *Condition of Postmodernity*, 20.

34. Margaret Laurence, *The Stone Angel* (1964; Toronto: McClelland and Stewart, 1991), 251. All further citations of *The Stone Angel* are from this edition and are given in parentheses in the text.

35. Margaret Laurence, *A Jest of God* (1966; Toronto: McClelland and Stewart, 1989), 173. All further citations of *A Jest of God* are from this edition and are given in parentheses in the text.

36. Margaret Laurence, *The Fire-Dwellers* (1969; Toronto: McClelland and Stewart, 1991), 159. All further citations of *The Fire-Dwellers* are from this edition and are given in parentheses in the text.

37. Margaret Laurence, *The Diviners* (1974; Toronto: McClelland and Stewart, 1993), 11. All further citations of *The Diviners* are from this edition and are given in parentheses in the text.

TIME'S GRIP ALONG THE ATHABASCA, 1920S AND 1930S

by Cam McEachern

The yellowed newspaper photo shows that a few museum supporters turned out, and evidently the press, to welcome this latest and unusual benefactor. He stands vine-like, withered on a tall, erect frame, a dignified octogenarian with liver spots and a well-pressed, white, short-sleeved shirt. Kind smiles all around. His gift now sits on the archive table next to the clipping: three leather-bound volumes typed up a half-century earlier, photographs pasted throughout, and treasured over the decades in his homes in Hawaii and Arizona. They unquestionably belong in this final home tucked just inside the Canadian Rockies, a step removed from the prairies. Yet their cherished story of an adventure just a few kilometres from the little museum is no local story any more. The motives, the language, the gestures in this story are more alien to the mountain town than the European and Asian tourists just outside these windows who arrive daily, crowding streets and shops a block away. The town is Banff, Alberta, home of the Whyte Museum of the Rockies, and the adventure is the old man's success in the mountains to the north when he was an avid, still teenaged, Harvard student and alpinist. The carefully bound volumes record his summer of 1927, when he climbed an amazing thirty peaks in sixty-four days. Hence their cryptic title, *Every Other Day*.

Alfred J. Ostheimer III was an experienced alpine climber when he arrived in Jasper in the summer of 1927 at the end of his third Harvard year, age nineteen. He came with two companions, John DeLaitre, a geologist, and Rupert Maclaurin, a naturalist, packing a pile of gear. The three rendezvoused with five well-known local mountaineers, some of whom Ostheimer had climbed with in previous years. Hans Fuhrer was a licensed Swiss mountain guide, Jean Weber was an amateur Swiss guide, Adam Joachim and Kennie Allen were two local packers, and Don Hoover was a camp cook. The party faced seemingly impossible challenges but they were counting on one other player to aid them. Fifty kilometres southwest of Jasper, at the head of the Athabasca River valley, lay the largest non-polar ice sheet in the world, the Columbia glacier. Half of Ostheimer's climbing would be leveraged by traversing the ice platforms, from shoulder to shoulder, peak to peak. When he stepped from the train that summer to set about his adventure, Ostheimer was aiming to use a distinctive local feature of the Athabasca environment for his own purposes, born almost 4000 kilometres away in an urban environment, that, too, well beyond the prairies. The expedition was both spectacular and very normal. The spectacle, like the water trickling out from beneath the climbers' boots, emits clues about normal human relations that came to bear along the river's course in Ostheimer's generation. Among these relations, people's attitudes to time seem to have influenced events, or, from the standpoint of a developing liberal state, a lack of events. The attitude's effective reach, the Athabasca River, helps map prairie boundaries, not simply as a physical landscape, but as a plateau of national development spanning decades.

Over its 11,000 kilometres, the Athabasca River descends almost 2000 metres from its Rocky Mountain source into north-central Alberta, dipping to within eighty kilometres of Edmonton, and on northward to Lake Athabasca. The lake drains through the Slave River to Slave Lake and on through the Mackenzie River to the arctic. Farther east, in Saskatchewan, the Methye portage links the Churchill River to the Clearwater River, which flows westward and joins the Athabasca at Fort McMurray, midway in its long northward course. The Athabasca's northward leg virtually links the Churchill and Saskatchewan river drainage systems to the Slave and the Mackenzie; the Athabasca uniquely links the prairies and the arctic, and for centuries the people who lived on these terrains. Thus the river is at the centre of western fur trade history, a natural "fifth business" that shaped fur trade companies and lives. Regional boosters in Edmonton, 1912, predicting 50,000 citizens at Fort McMurray within a few years (the population remained under 1000 for decades), were reflecting this historical presence as much as the usual excitement attached to a new railway to northern resources. But today the river is hidden away, mostly unseen by motorists, air travellers, and townspeople, except for the occasional scenic crossing and the ice road it seasonally affords to Fort Chipewyan on Lake Athabasca, Alberta's oldest community. Unseen, the river carries away treated effluent from five pulp mills, two oil-sand companies, and several communities including the city of Fort McMurray. In contrast to its pre-industrial role and reputation, the Athabasca is invisible today.

The story of this river, of its transition from the renowned prairie/arctic fulcrum to oblivion, is an untold, yet significant, story in Canada's modernization. Today's attention is drawn to the fantastic present-day industrial development of the two open-pit mines beside the river, which fuel a quarter of Canada's modern oil needs and soon even more. However, an insight into Canada's development is revealed in that obscure moment between the world wars, along the Athabasca and its tributaries. In that period, with the arrival of a railway, bush planes, and radio, the modern Canadian imagination asserted itself within the region, detecting a corridor for Canadian expansion. The region promised no mere mineral island in the Canadian archipelago,[1] like so many other northern developments, but a funnel for a vast reach of northern wealth toward voracious southern needs. The funnel never formed, despite some vigorous efforts. A long generation separates these efforts from what were still isolated successes in the 1960s onward.

Consequently, this story of a region does not offer a narrative about the place's economic development, as Morris Zaslow ably depicted almost half a century ago,[2] or as Pat McCormack more recently has done,[3] to say nothing of a cultural development or the formation of an identity, as Rob Irwin has recently outlined in the nearby Peace River District.[4] We can borrow lessons from them and from their theoretical streams while we cast an eye to the construction of a larger Canadian identity. Looking at the relation between this time and place, interwar Athabasca, to the rest of Canada, we can take another cue from recent work by Steve High and Chad Gaffield assessing regions' significance in the larger national picture.[5] A popular idea linked this end-of-prairie, the physical space, with economic and cultural attitudes transmitting the idea of the Canadian nation into the space, and the space into the nation. Ostheimer hands us a clue. Liberalism, and more specifically the ideology's implicit, subconscious attitude toward time, percolates in his memoir, and stands out as a regulating influence along the river. Perhaps because we have such wide, conventional agreement about time, we gloss over it as a point of study unless we are physicists or metaphysicists. But time, after all, is a basic component of our physical and cultural environment, and our attitudes toward it shape our ideas about how to dedicate ourselves.

Immediately following his expedition, Ostheimer commenced writing a memoir of events, and he corresponded with a variety of academics and Canadian bureaucrats concerning the identity of plant species, the condition of the mountains and glaciers, and the naming of both lichen and mountain peaks. The memoir displays its author's excitement, energy, eye for detail, and some literary flourish that would satisfy any armchair adventurers, young or young at heart. Another characteristic stands out strikingly three generations later: the account remains a particularly exuberant display of early twentieth-century liberal ideology.

Thus, Ostheimer's first chapter virtually introduces the complex set of human relations that arose along the Athabasca River in the interwar period. "Romance and adventure," he exclaims. "Those two words personified this country which we were entering. They were indigenous to it. They were it. And we modern Voyageurs were to have our share; yes, with all the interest, dividends and bonus which the Power above might add."[6] Any climb, and especially one such as this, is an extraordinary test and reward of individual and group strengths. Self-reliance is paramount for the group to function as a reliable, mutual support, and not a hindrance, and to survive with timely wit and strength, with robust spontaneity, any surprising event that arises. That is "adventure," a word that incidentally was interchangeable in this period with "enterprise." Romance, too, is the celebration of individual spirit and here Ostheimer hints that this Romance stems not only from a human's triumph over a daunting landscape, but also a triumph over other people. No others had taken on this challenge and the scope compares to the role assigned to hardy individuals renowned in national lore for personal determination, strength in adversity, triumph over nature, profit making, and nation building.

Liberal individualism, or more simply, "liberalism," as it was typically spoken of in the period from 1850 to 1950, championed the rights of the individual unfettered by constraints of the state. In liberal states, this ideology has been prized by individuals and governments as they perceive themselves, somewhat ironically, to draw strength from one another. Thus recent literature outlining the morphology of liberalism cites the ideology's propensity to celebrate the making of a liberal state.[7] Fair to say Ostheimer was thinking liberally when he identified so closely with that outstanding brand of individualism typically offered up as a national building block ... or bloc, as Antonio Gramsci would put it. Gramsci postulates "historical blocks" in which groups of people may assert hegemonic power over others.[8]

Like any ideology, liberalism has always had detractors but it has come under scrutiny in the 1980s and 1990s in response to Conservative Thatcherism and Republican Reaganomics, which were perceived as resurgent, "negative," liberalisms.[9] These ideologies contrasted with their predecessor, post-World War II "positive" liberalisms that pursued "freedom to" for citizens, assisted by a relatively wealthy and supportive welfare state. The much older, and seemingly resurgent, negative version of liberalism posited "freedom from" and reduced government reach into social affairs, including welfare supports, while remaining open to some fundamental government intervention such as monetary or broadcast policy. This slender state is prized within "negative" liberalism for the freedom it gives individuals, and for the less costly, more robust and enduring protection it should afford for those freedoms.

The last decades of the millennium coincide with advances in cultural studies techniques, so recent writing on liberalism's morphology has given much more careful attention than in prior decades to the pre-WWII "negative" version of the ideology and its subconscious, cultural estimate of what an "individual" properly is. By reading between the lines what liberals have said and done in the pre-WWII period, and considering hegemonic processes, we understand that the ideology's basic assumptions have been expanded beyond what is explicitly said about individual rights, state limits, uniformity, and so on. In Canada, liberalism's affinity with utilitarian ethics and bureaucratic practice has been exposed[10] and also its intense call for self-development as self-making—the myth of the self-made man.[11] This is made possible by recognizing, as Michael Freeden has, that an ideology massages political concepts to make them less contestable, and liberalism, with its emphasis on liberty, depends also on some common general interest and sociability for the limited state to cohere and be effective.[12] Pursuing this thinking still further, to take a simple example, the more vulnerable, dependent condition of women compared to men's in liberal regimes is seen to mean that, for the liberal, female individualism was not as acceptable as male individualism. Without ever proclaiming itself masculinist, liberalism is seen to have tied individualism closely to masculinity and to ideals of right and good steeped with that.[13]

In addition to being male, the ideal liberal individual was white. Associations with other so-called races—their lassitude (their latitude!), their seemingly less sophisticated heathen ways, their evident lack of independent will or initiative, even their femininity—all pointed to shortcomings that put them outside the set of all self-willed, self-made, nation builders.[14] As a corollary, those characteristics that helped the white, Christian male succeed were viewed by liberals as favourable characteristics.[15] Faith in self and God, a plucky spirit, military and imperial prowess all composed the liberal, male, self-reliant, self-making individual.

Ostheimer's memoir is a testament devoted in three ways to these features of liberal ideology. First, perhaps most interestingly, his writer's subconscious yields fitting imagery. Next, he occasionally consciously reflects on his activities and on his climbing ideology. Lastly, his actions are revealing. A survey of the memoir, alert to each of these readings, certainly helps show 'liberalism' to be a fair characterization of this young man's thinking. In addition, it helps reveal the significance of his attitude to time, which deserves association with this liberalism, with liberal projects such as prairie settlement, and with other, but not all, beholders of the Athabasca.

With fingers that gripped rocky ledges firmly, grasped a pen with flourish so that images poured out upon these pages, although they are not the kind one might at first expect today from an Alpinist, remembering thoughts around the first camp supper in high country, the young man wrote:

> Hans and I were re-baptized, reborn, mysteriously transformed into instruments of war—war the crushing, in total contrast to the peace and solemnity of God's mountain's. Not modern instruments of war, not dreadnoughts, fighting planes, tanks, or deadly gas did we turn. Instead we became—in a figure of speech—the "Light Artillery."(41)

The first ascent, that of Mount Dias, consisted of the usual, extraordinary, climbing conditions:

> The Light Artillery was making fast time … [eventually] we wriggled, straddling the cornice in a sitting position to keep from being blown away. I was in the tail (or lead?). Suddenly, the soft nothing under my feet gave way and I headed toward the Athabasca River, but luckily a protruding rock checked me. A second later Hans started for the Chaba Valley, but the stout mountain rope held us astride the ridge. (43)

> Such a wild crossing that was! Our eye-lids froze together repeatedly; hands were numb, and our clothes a solid mass. (46)

Chapter IV, "The Source of a Great River," opens with their next move to "the head of this valley of the Athabasca, and closer to the Columbia Glacier tongue than anyone had ever camped before" (49). Here Ostheimer paused to give account of the Athabasca's source. "About forty feet distant from the ice tongue, fountains occurred, bubbling vigorously and throwing geysers of water three to eight feet into the air. In this manner practically all the water of the main Athabasca River flows from the glacier." He also notes the epistemological happenstance in physiography, human perception, and naming: "in reality the Columbia Glacier is the Athabasca River, although one is ice and the other water" (56).

Ostheimer enjoyed indulging in military metaphor. Typical dawn-time avalanches surrounded the party. "Cannon to the left of us, Cannon to the right of us, Cannon in front of us, Volleyed and Thundered," writes the young student; "the booming of ice artillery reverberated in the amphitheatre of the Columbia Glacier, and the tiny, white puffs of powdered snow and ice looked, in the half light, all the world like a distant barrage of soixante-quinzes" (61). He represented the rocky hurdles as fortress ramparts and the metaphor seems to have influenced some stylistic choices as well. Mountain features are described as "flying buttresses," "turreted battlements," and "giant towers" (73). For descriptive flourish and superlatives, Ostheimer quotes previous record-setting climbers such as "Mr. H.M.C. Stutfield," "Right Honourable James Bryce," and "Sir James Outram," effectively giving his own adventure and storytelling flying buttresses with this support borrowed from previous accounts. Several days later, waiting for the support party to arrive and hoping for mail: "the Light Artillery awaited news and word of encouragement from General Headquarters at home before commencing the battle upon the western peaks" (179).

Ostheimer wanted to do more than tell a good yarn with bold images. He explicitly remarks upon his climbing ideology in a middle chapter, which is presented as an antidote to a volume he thinks is "becoming dull," where "each day resembles its predecessor," and "times, places, names and adventures" are mounting into a "cataclysmic verbiage." He writes chivalrously, "I ask my wife ... Are not the actors in the play, the scenery, and the humanness horribly in the sloughs and muskegs of a chronological report? In Heaven's name, what does all this clutter of events mean?" (120).

In response, Ostheimer identifies himself and his party as mountaineers and distinguishes this party from other mountaineers such as Sicilians, Basques, Swiss, or Scots. "We have more in common with the Swiss," he writes, "than with any others, yet even they are not our brethren." This group is peerless; "we belong for the time solely to the Canadian Northwest. We are a queer mixture of town and country, Indian and paleface, British, French, Dutch and so on." Ostheimer does not identify himself or others as American or Canadian but cites older, more original national identities. He glosses over the presence of a Métis member who was both Aboriginal and French; the group's hybridity, derived from a sense of democratic, individual sameness, was to be celebrated, but not necessarily genetic hybridity. So, "Nevertheless, despite wide divergences in race and age, we are eight ordinary men in every way absolutely identical with all other men who live in wild and little known parts of the world" (121).

Surveying several motives that can inspire mountain climbing, Ostheimer notices among them that "Real Mountaineers ... love the contact with ice and rock, the nerve-firing rarity of elevation, or the thrill of the never-ceasing battle, a test of ability, keenness, preparedness, and endurance: they are the backbone of the sport." As for those "content to toil up long slopes of scree behind a guide.... They are but poor half-castes among the pure breed of alpinists" (121–122). Ostheimer employs another buttress and adds support to his reflections by quoting A.F. Mummery, "the great English alpinist." The true mountaineer is "a wanderer ... a man who loves to be where no human being has been before, who delights in gripping rocks that have previously never felt the touch of human fingers." The young climber endorses his senior: "The spell of the unknown is the invaluable, progressive stimulus of mountaineering. It is the new country, the unseen valleys, uncrossed glaciers, unclimbed peaks, that beckon the wandering and adventuring spirit within the mountaineer." Ostheimer devotes a few pages to lamenting the disappearance of lands because of encroaching civilization, and he notes the special majesty and harmony of the Rocky Mountains and their environs. "There you have our raison d'etre and our purpose. We came to explore little known and unknown country; we came for first ascents and the acquisition of scientific knowledge" (124).

As for his companions, Ostheimer takes time to speculate about their motivations. "Among the mountains, these two Swiss guides earned their living so that mountaineering was for them and wandering was unknown." In contrast, for the Métis member, Adam Joachim, "It was instinctive and natural … to roam the valleys and hills. They were the home of his race for past centuries unnumbered." The Swiss made a business of climbing, "But the Indian is superstitious and content to linger at lower levels; the higher elevations call him not, so that, although he is a wanderer, he is not a mountaineer" (127).

Ostheimer professed pleasure being in nature, "But this summer I was working for a purpose: the report I should be able to make would so complete my college course that I could embark upon the stream of life a year early." Afterward, he could "the easier settle down to business." His hurry, then, was not just with the immediate conquest in time and space, but with a life stage as well. Thus, "The Light Artillery was fast and accurate: we rarely wasted time." In his ensuing defence of his expedition's speed, and the decision to climb as a pair and not as a larger, safer, number, Ostheimer cites the speed of a pair as an advantage, and the slowness of a larger group as a disadvantage. A tricky, and safe, descent of the Columbia Icefall "hinged on pure, calculated speed" (128). In reckoning with such a challenge, "There is an educative and purifying power in danger that is to be found in no other school, and it is worth much for a man to know that he is not 'clean gone to flesh pots and effeminacy'." He praises the Swiss guide, Hans Fuhrer, for being "a man of absolutely the same temperament in any environment at all: his life and manner were in no way altered by any change in his surroundings" (129). These goals, these personal qualities, and this landscape comprise Ostheimer's adventure. Aptly summarizing his reflections, he concludes: "In our business of mountain climbing we strive for fifty percent efficiency—in other words—a mountain 'Every Other Day.'" On reflection, then, Ostheimer's project most explicitly was an exhibition testing and celebrating racial and masculine purity, the principle of a fundamental sameness of individuals independent of even extreme environments, and the maximally efficient use of time. This efficiency is even capitalization of time, a rush pursued in one venue to hurry and harvest another.

In addition to his imagery, and his conscious reflection, Ostheimer's actions strongly resonate also with period liberal ideology. The climb is a supreme test of individual ability, knowledge, and responsibility for one's self. Such tests have certainly taken place often, and long before there were liberals. But then, they were not embroidered with images, judgements, and actions so regularly supportive of what liberal individualism has so far been assumed to be. This climb was for character building and self-making; it was a masculine climb with rich overtones of militarism and pluck. The instruments of possession, commercial processes, are marshalled as powerful metaphors for describing superior, most meaningful climbing. Meanwhile, Ostheimer's trial is not dedicated to God's works, nor to mere scholarly curiosity, nor to celebration of his race, nor to a token presence on behalf of a larger collective, nor is it disregardful of any audience at all . . . all competing ideologies of his day. This nineteen-year-old climbed with an ideology, a liberal individualist ideology, which he lived out through the climb.

The link between possession and liberalism is strong, since a right to material and to spiritual self-possession enables one to flourish. While he could not own the ranges he climbed, Ostheimer displayed a strong preoccupying interest in possession through three activities. The first of these is the traditional practice of creating mountaintop cairns in which pictures and short notes, sometimes greetings to subsequent visitors, were left. To this day, climbers add messages and tokens to cairns, never removing them, effectively announcing their own membership and indicating the nature of the relatively elite group of people who have shared that unique space, that vista, nature's vastness, and, to some extent, a special personal perspective of individual and human success. Our young alpinist exhibits all these feelings and a whiff of militaristic capture too when he writes, "We climbed the final rock tower, deposited a record in a large cairn that we erected, and crossed to the final snow bench, 11,232 feet high, at two fifteen in the afternoon. His Majesty the Tsar was ours" (219).

More significantly, Ostheimer asserted a sense of possession over great space by naming many previously unnamed places within it. These were not just private names for his use only, or for his expedition's use; this climber wrote to the Geographic Board of Canada attempting to have places named officially, for all others to use the nomenclature also. While naming was clearly a shared, negotiable task and the prerogative of distant bureaucrats, his primordial presence on top of the physical formations was expected to confer some power to name and so impose some control over the meaning imparted to the places—a key ingredient in possession. In this task, Ostheimer was partly successful.[16] The board, as usual, had competing commemorative needs. Nonetheless, Ostheimer's will to name was fully respected.

The suggestion that the act of naming is a possessive act could be construed as overly sensitive. After all, Ostheimer or any such designator was not taking possession of land formations in the manner with which one possesses private property. Yet there is an undeniable possessive significance to the act of naming when one recognizes the intention for the act to continue, not just in space, but in time. Ostheimer did not merely name places for himself, or for his colleagues to joke about or privately venerate. Nor did he simply publish in an alpine journal or newspaper a thought to the effect that "here or there I was moved by this land form to celebrate this or that individual." Rather, his intention was that his named places would signify forever, upon a state-authorized map or in the scientific record, what he wanted them to signify, and he gives over some explanation to this (153).

He occasionally named some landforms, such as Chisel and Brouillard, according to outstanding physical features. Another name type consisted of Mt. Everest Expedition members Odell and Younghusband. Above all, he writes, a "Third class—famous explorers. From the long list available I chose Franklin, Peary, Amundsen, Stanley, Livingston, and Rhodes ... Gray [also Ostheimer's fiancée] I could not resist; nor Lawrence; and Walcott had a special pre-eminence in the history of the Canadian Rockies" (154). He concludes, "So much for our system of names." Ostheimer was taking possession of the historical and geographical record, giving it character and ideals, the veneration of plucky, white, male empire-builders for years to come.

The feminine exception among all the names is Mount Gray and Ostheimer offers a cryptic, riddling explanation: "To E.G.O. is this book dedicated; the G in E.G.O. is Gray" (176). Sitting on the mountaintop, "the fourth and last premier of the day," "we toasted with Danish brandy that we had hoarded in miserly fashion and reserved especially for this occasion 'To the Wife-to-be of the junior member of the Light Artillery' were Hans' words." As usual, a film canister with picture and notes was placed in the summit cairn. "A short letter [lies] therein. Some traveler, I hope, will rescue it in the not too distant future, even though the addressee no longer is known by her maiden name—thank God" (177). Thus Ostheimer chivalrously included his beloved in every aspect of his adventure, including the possessive element of naming.

The expedition's scientific mission furnished another field for discovery and for naming. Early in the climb the party came across a small gully below the Columbia Glacier from which they collected "nearly fifty pounds of trilobites . . . to classify them was a task for a paleontologist" (57–58). These were shipped to a paleontologist at Harvard, who determined that two items among the sample had never been previously discovered. The professor named them "Athabaskia ostheimeri (sp. nov.) and Athabaskia glacialis (sp. nov.)" (66). Ostheimer notes a report was published in the *American Journal of Science*, March 1928. The climber shared ownership of identity with a distinct, primeval, species in a record more enduring and precise than folklore or even a national map: a scientific journal.

Although he never explicitly reflects upon "time," this seemingly natural phenomenon was a significant element in Ostheimer's climbing and liberal individualist thinking. The climbing challenge obviously included a race against time, so much so that this is made more explicit in his memoir's title than the activity of mountain climbing itself. This juxtaposition is a stylistic strategy to represent his climbing feat with understatement, attracting attention to the routine of the ascents. Still, and most evidently, as a liberal individualist, Ostheimer was deeply concerned to fulfill himself, as much as possible, in as little time as possible . . . to have more time afterward to pursue still more. Personally, and even ideologically, Ostheimer anticipated, even husbanded or stewarded, near and mid-future times in which he would achieve something extraordinary himself. In the long term, long after death, he would act vicariously in enduring topographical symbols. The fullest grasp of present time, respect for a selective, liberal-building past, and worthy anticipation of near and distant futures figure immensely in his undertaking and subsequent account of events. Although he never published his memoir, he evidently expected at the time of writing that an audience would read it, understandingly and sympathetically.[17]

This grasp of time doesn't just fit the liberal mould, it helps make the liberal mould, and it deserves some illumination. Liberalism is noted for its preference for white, masculine self-reliance, self-making, and the desire to constrain the state, so that fitting individuals are equally free to judge what is personal fulfillment and pursue that. Liberalism's unique quality lies in its attention to property in that personally judged, self-reliant, pursuit of fulfillment. This draws time uniquely into the centre of the ideological picture. In time, for the duration of a life, say, property may come and go for all manner of reasons, not least a competitive lifestyle, and a successfully self-reliant individual must take care to not get caught out without wealth or property to draw upon if need be. The liberal individual must steward wealth, husband it, accumulate it, anticipating a future day. Capitalization enhances the process and is essentially 'future' gathering, for it endeavours to assure the individual of future income or material property, property that is not presently available but will be.[18] Capitalism operates to reassure the liberal individual that the future is 'in hand' ... or obliges them to notice it is in someone's hand. This is different from period conservatives, communists, or progressives who, for various reasons, also regarded the future and invested collectively, capitalizing, for a future. But these ideologies entertained capitalization in order to assure their respective individuals that they need not worry for the future. Only the liberal individual is, ideologically, so powerfully spurred and unconstrained, so thoroughly oriented to consuming future resources, competitively, in increasing amounts. Only the liberal individual is integrally nurtured or driven by that ideology to reach through time and draw hitherto unavailable resources closer to hand. In assembling his depiction of pre-WWI attitudes to time, Stephen Kern notes that the Liberal-Imperialist Foreign Minister, Lord Rosebury, put things most aptly while promoting late nineteenth-century African colonialism: "the world ... is not elastic, and we are engaged at the present moment, in the language of mining, 'in pegging claims for the future.'"[19]

Today, we typically take 'time' and our everyday practical acquaintance with that to be a universal aspect of human or physical nature. We all watch clocks very closely to proceed through our day as a matter of course, glad of a holiday's respite. We act and plan for future opportunities, trials, and contingencies pretty much like Alfred Ostheimer. This preoccupation does not seem at first glance like a meaningful sign of anything in our history, nor in our relationship with a nondescript mid-north river descending to prairies and then hiding away. A survey of alternative period differences in attitudes to time helps give contour to 'liberal time,' though. It helps us see how a subtle, commonplace concept, one that blanketed prairie life, played out along the Athabasca River of all places in such a way as to make a difference to people in the interwar period.

Five discernable contours help give cultural, philosophical, and psychological dimension to liberal time and show it to be a distinct force in a period and place. It would be easy to look at a completely different culture for different attitudes to time, but even the pre-WWI European attitude to time, for instance, holds some differences. Further, new attitudes were consciously, if vainly, promoted also in Europe about WWI in connection with a widening set of anxieties attached to time. Meanwhile, interwar 'western' philosophy was addressing time quite differently from the mainstream commonsensical view, as did the next-to-last breaths of period, regional, Aboriginal culture. Finally, personal time, a mix of cultural and psychological manifestations, shows still different, poignant, reckoning with 'time.' Whatever time "really" is in our natural environment, a brief survey of these attitudes and some scholarship concerning them underlines how something we can call "liberal time"—now widely and hegemonically taken to be only a natural phenomenon—is largely attitudinal. It carries with it a set of attitudes that may be more or less helpful to people reckoning with nature. We can ask if "liberal time" was a factor in people's relationship to their environment along the Athabasca. (We can also ask if something like it is a factor in our own lives, for better or worse.)

Students of western European culture will concede that few Europeans before the nineteenth century ascribed to time its own properties to respect independent of their lives. The vaguely Augustinian view of time as a gift with creation, for lives to be lived, was widespread. The passing of a task or occasion happened to take time; a quick race, a meal, a harvest, a life ... all took felt time, inseparable from the event. Here, cultural, physical, and personal time were closely wrapped together for, as near as scholars can tell, European culture had not unravelled them yet. E.P. Thompson furnished a remarkable historical summary in the 1960s just when the full measure of the impact of the modern concept of time was about to be taken in the social sciences.[20] This dean of labour history charted how time-pieces, work-discipline, and industrial capitalism slowly introduced regular regard for "clock-time" into people's lives. He takes care to show how, prior to the Napoleonic era, people greatly relied upon tasks, daylight and nightfall, intuitive sense, social needs, the seasons and so on to regard time. Eighteenth-century Europeans regarded time, and especially regular, specific, clock-time, secondarily to matters at hand. Time was a vague clue for all manner of activities. Thompson takes care to underline moralizing puritans' and leisure classes' hypersensitivity toward workers' and poor people's "wasted time." So the scientific and industrial revolutions introduced more precise measures of time, more widely. Increasingly, people saw time as something separate from events, requiring its own management. Stephen Kern picks up where Thompson left off, noting the epitome of time management was reached with schooling, post offices, railways, factories' Taylorism and Fordism, and in WWI with the complex synchronization of large, mechanized, armed forces. With organized schooling, factory, and office life, by 1900 most western Europeans anywhere on the globe respected time separate from their own rhythm. Where once the clock had followed people, people now followed the clock.

Yet relatively new and intense adherence to what was industrial, and linear, 'clock' time of *la belle époque* caused an uneasy reaction, says Kern, from which we see artistic traces today. Several intellectuals consciously addressed time as a subject to treat differently from the prevailing trend and so achieve a different art and, some surmised, a different humanity. Not least to be counted among them, if a local Athabasca history is anything to go by, was a certain "Professor Oswald," who took part in Canada's pre-WWI, pre-radio, circuit of meeting-hall evening entertainments of guest lectures. In 1910 Oswald was making regular Alberta appearances promoting a "Great Plan to Normalize the World," which was basically a metric system of timekeeping.[21] In addition to the high points of social acceleration in activity and information exchange, from industry, to the *Titanic* disaster, to the world war, Kern draws our attention to James Joyce's exploitation of simultaneity, the widespread preoccupation with futuristic novels, and an Italian movement fostering attention to simultaneity in the arts and the ideal of a more federative, democratic age. Kern also sheds light on the stirring debate between philosophy and common sense, a debate between Bergsonian indulgence and acceptance of personal time—and Wyndham Lewis's dismissal of such "time-philosophy" as "anti-physical and pro-mental"[22]: just not realistic.[23] Ostheimer's adventure depended on linear sequencing and the pitting of man against nature. In contrast to these other interests, with the exception of Lewis, the climber reckoned with time in the commonsense fashion of his day, as a natural, linear, physical phenomenon, as real as the mountains.

The period's anxiety with time coincided with renewed efforts in early twentieth-century philosophy to explore the concept and the consequences of time. Modern philosophy's 'softness' on time was indebted to Bergson and Einstein, who, from quite different directions, proposed 'time' to be a personal, relative experience. Between the wars, Heidegger drew heavily on Bergson to describe time in phenomenological terms as a most essential experience enabling perception and enabling senses of being and identity, which were communitarian, not highly individualist separations from others or from nature. With respect to 'time,' twentieth-century philosophy has continued to pursue this avenue, greatly interested in time as a perception, and less as a natural reality. There may be a real time, and certainly an apprehended, perceptual construction of time, but hardly any philosopher will assert that industrial, linear, 'clock' time is an accurate reflection of either the real time or the apprehended one. Interestingly, today, our commonsense attitude to time is very much at broad variance with our culture's best philosophical grasp of it. It takes common sense to harvest 640 or more hectares of monocrop prairie; philosophy gets in the way of that. Or is it the other way around?

Filling the twentieth-century breech between philosophy and everyday practice, with respect to time, stands a generation of anthropologists, sociologists, and geographers concerned with any culture's handling of time and with their own disciplines' sensitivity to that. Again, E.P. Thompson cites several groundbreaking anthropological works, and in subsequent decades helpful surveys have appeared. A good historical overview of attitudes to time is achieved by a number of works drawn together in 1966 by J.T. Fraser in *The Voices of Time*.[24] Another good survey is G.J. Whitrow's *Time in History*,[25] and Donald Wilcox shows various attitudes to time from the Greeks to the Renaissance in *The Measure of Times Past, Pre-Newtonian Chronologies and the Rhetoric of Relative Time*.[26] Stephen Hawking's immensely popular *Brief History of Time* endeavoured to communicate post-Newtonian scientific thinking about time to a wide readership.[27] Huw Price champions a "view from nowhen" in *Time's Arrow and Archimedes' Point*. Price addresses physicists and philosophers but concludes with a message for expert and layman: "We cannot step outside time, but we can try to understand how the way in which we are situated within time comes to be reflected in the ways in which we talk and think and conceptualize about the world around us."[28]

Becoming more sensitive to what are at least elements of social construction in our popular sense of time, certain social scientists have tried to articulate just what difference that makes. Among these, geographer Torsten Hagerstrand stands out for having developed models describing how time's availability and use governed people's negotiation of space and so also daily and longer term lives. Hagerstrand's "Lund" school did pathbreaking work investigating people's navigation of time and space considerations, and noticing how these related to culture.[29] This geographer also influenced sociologist Anthony Giddens.

Giddens felt acutely the need to incorporate the century's philosophical direction respecting "time" within the domain of sociology. This discipline was too strongly pulled in two unhelpful directions, thought Giddens, as he researched and wrote through the 1970s. Too great an attention to structuralism obscured human agency, which was an offence to his discipline's essential subject, an understanding of persons acting in society. Likewise, too great an attention to individual human agency obscured the compelling generalizations and patterns in human behaviour, which the discipline also was reasonably dedicated to elucidating. Giddens proposed his "structuration theory," which relied heavily on the concepts of "positioning" and "routinization" to consider human relations in their oft-repetitive cultural contexts, from dressing in the morning to marrying in one's early twenties.[30] Giddens has very reasonably outlined how our cultural apprehension and handling of time-space runs deep in our lives, helping to build society, but this social adhesive is nonetheless very largely of our own human individual and collective making. In short, the linear, industrial, clock-time we rigorously observe is very much more a cultural construct than, in our culture, we take it to be. Inspired by Giddens, Barbara Adam has more recently explored these implications, pointing to our biological and social dependency upon "rythmicity."[31] She argues for the need to waive disciplinary boundaries in social and even physical science to properly grasp time's role in our lives.

Northwestern Aboriginal attitudes toward time seem to have been fundamentally different from industrial time, just as were pre-nineteenth-century European and non-European attitudes, and this would come as no surprise to the aforementioned generation of scholars. When Thompson speculated that a Mexican, Camerounian, or Bombay "proletariat" living in close proximity to family and friends would only be "partially and temporarily 'committed' to the industrial way-of-life," he was thinking of the struggle to wed factory time with the customary "elastic time-schedules, irregular breaks and meal-times, etc."[32] The linearity and, above all, manageability of a production line is alien to the Aboriginal view. Lives happen in stages and moments happen in days as sets of concentric circles, where a circle, a position, represents personal readiness for the moment in concert with multiple relations.[33] Chipewyan, Cree, and Dene certainly lived with sequences and perceived them as such. But their openness to relate to time in the context of many conditions, not just sequential events, fits into a different metaphysical and epistemological world view, one which entertains a more unified view of people, animals, and the rest of nature than the western European tradition has nurtured.[34] The openness to a less linear view of time endured into the interwar period and beyond, and this is a difference in taste from industrial time, not a difference in kind. European scholars and Aboriginal people mutually declare that both cultures relate to time through reference points that, whether truly past or future, do not presently exist. They are both 'mindsets,' both cultural 'times.' Each apprehension of time has been known to be more or less suitable for different people living their social contexts.

We all know psychological time, how it seems to pass quickly or slowly, depending on our consciousness of it and our preoccupation with something else. Our own biological age or experience with time seems to speed up the sense of its passing. With such feelings, both ancients and moderns have 'sensed' our living with time. Noticing that the pre-WWI-era anxiety about time seems to have yielded broadly to industrial time's embrace, it is interesting to speculate what cultural signs there may be that all is not resolved, that there is a deep public psychosis about time ill-spent.[35] The search for authenticity, connectedness to original, genuine roots, evident in the mid-century folk revival, extreme nationalistic politics, the geneal-ogy boom, beatniks, countercultures—counterculture—are all searches for other 'times.'[36] They are mythical times, perhaps, but each is con-ceived with time subject to people, responsive to their personal and social rhythms, not the other way round. This is not the place to argue the prevalence of this urge or the truth of this representation. Suffice it to say they are plausible human feelings about time and our handling of it, quite at variance with 'industrial time.' Ostheimer was not trying to recover a folkway, nor escape the rat race. He was celebrating a race against linear time, where time was a physical phenomenon outside himself, independ-ent of perception, a resource to be exploited for individual fulfillment. He was climbing frantically and efficiently, to succeed in the industrial time culture, and this matched precisely the requirements of liberal ideology.

These five kinds of attitudes to time, acting in various combinations—some judgement of its physicalness, its social derivation, its philosophical meaningfulness, its cultural and its psychological handling—help us to form a viable commonsense attitude to time. They help to show up Ostheimer's attitude toward time as just that, an attitude, one that played a significant role within the liberal ideology. The attitude is not just an apprehension of linear time, but a vigorous and dominating anticipation of and quest for future time and other favourable future conditions to ensure a liberal individual's prosperity and to celebrate that. 'Liberal time' is a deserving epithet.

From its description, liberal time appears commonplace today. If lib-eral time has become such a widely shared conception of time that it often gets taken for the real, steady thing, a Newtonian physicist's 'time,' it nonetheless is not time itself. It is a powerful hegemonic attitude toward time and its usage, widely agreed upon and indulged in more or less as we function together in industrial society. The attitude functions within our thinking as we anticipate a meeting, some entertainment, building careers, families, homes, industries, and lives. "How am I managing?" addresses an underlying anxiety about limited time and a quest to do better in our future. ("Rat race" is exclusive, unrewarded questing.) Good, liberal use of time means efficient use of resources, not only within a time span but in anticipation of our own future times, disregarding needs of future people—who are non-existent individuals. Liberal time, like all other time views, is an attitude toward a mysterious, little understood part of our natural environment—time—and about our other environmental relations to so-called resources, which become defined as such according to the ease with which they can be processed within the greased liberal timeline. Our selection of this attitude to time over others, and our ability to work with it and to shape things with it, are a shrouded part of the technology we employ, our 'technique,' as Jacques Ellul would say,[37] and a part of our environmental relationships. No doubt part of the shroud is a human perceptual limitation. We countenance space much better than time. Looked at in this light, as the hegemonic slide rule for the capitalizability of our natural resources, liberal time can be exposed as a concept that has mattered in our environmental relations just as much as space and materials and the rest of our culture. It has made a difference in our environmental history.

Liberal time can be seen to be making a difference along the very river originating under Ostheimer's hiking boots, and for good reason. A train, an ice sheet, and an ideology combined to take Ostheimer about as far as technology and nature could take him in 1928 to do what he wanted to do, equipped with his liberal ideology. They would variously help him not only to save time, but to capitalize it and make better personal use of future time. As Athabasca-bound waters dropped from the mountains, scuttled across the northern parkland, set course almost due north, and washed into the world's largest freshwater delta, the river represented, just like its ice origins, the period's outer limits of the sensibility of liberal time. Liberalism, which paved the North American prairies and parkland with township after township of commodity agriculture, could just tenuously reach the river.

The key components in the liberal apparatus, plus some other world views, could reach the Athabasca in the twenties and thirties but liberalism could not yet function nearly so well as it did between Morinville, say, and Selkirk, nor as it did along the river after WWII. Period expansion of self-making pioneers northward into the Peace River district punctured the Athabasca limit uniquely, yet that puncture fell far short of period expectations and later successes. The transport hub and community of Athabasca, a strong contender for provincial capital prior to WWI, was passed over. It declined in the post-WWI period as trans-shipment between roadway and northern water routes yielded to a new railway, which bypassed the town, and pre-war community investment floundered, driving the town into bankruptcy. A nearby community of migrant, self-making, Afro-American farmers presents an interesting marker. This group consciously moved to the farthest fringe of a self-making society around 1911, at once escaping and being driven by a dominant social and bureaucratic view that they could not succeed on Canadian prairies. None of this community's members ever apparently settled northward,[38] yet after WWII their community was decimated from a population outflow southward. From 1911 onward, this group sensed that self-making could not be enhanced within reasonable time beyond the Athabasca River.

The railway embarrassed its sponsoring provincial government, a government ready to invest to promote competitive individualism and infrastructure. Farming townships opened south of the river, closer to the railway. Extraordinary efforts to ship salt and oil-sand products from where the northern stretch of the river traverses vast oil-sands deposits succumbed to every kind of investment failure, from cost overruns, to technology and capital shortfalls, to political bungling. The delta became a haven for depression-era subsistence trappers, a residual commons confined by remoteness and new national park boundaries. In the interwar years, white, Christian, masculine, utilitarian, liberal individualism put a poorly inked stamp on the region again and again, and the ideology's requisite sense of time was the diluent.

Boosters promised that success was just a matter of time, as with prairie frontiers, and it *was* a matter of *time*. Spacial distance did not present a barrier, but the extended related costs of shipping materials did hobnail investments. Those who came with investment capital, counting on technological breakthroughs, ran out of time as much as they did money. Capital financing demanded solutions sooner than available experts and nature could contrive them. Airplanes facilitated speedy travel and their premium cost addressed time, not distance. One could already get where airplanes went, but not nearly so fast. Whether toted across the river at McLeod or trained into Waterways, automobiles were amazing time-savers and work horses limited to the few kilometres of available roadway at the best of times. Certainly, no one went anywhere new or far with them. They saved a few people some time, but not nearly on the scale they increasingly did in other regions. These modes of transportation were new, alien to the region, and marginally effective. An older, pre-modern mode was the boat, and barges still plied the river north of the railhead. It was not uncommon to go aground on the river's shifting sandbars, but it was more common for outsiders, even those who had travelled the river often. The shallow, sandy riverbed constantly shifted in currents upon an underlying smooth limestone shelf. Local Métis pilots considered the newcomers to be in a hurry, not taking time to read the water's signals as they needed to be read.[39]

This string of encounters along the Athabasca constitutes feeble state expansion into the area in the interwar period, and an outstanding hurdle, not the only one, was liberal time. The ideology that drove people to that frontier could not effectively countenance the gap between expectations about that living space and the reality presented along the river. Put another way, the river traversed lands that happened to suit pre-modern life-ways very well so that the fur trade or long-term investment commitments flourished about it prior to WWI. But the post-war economy wanted more, faster, to get ahead, like Ostheimer, while there was really nothing more forthcoming from the region. Three principal encounters or new activities of the period are exemplary.

Since well before the Great War, settlers had migrated into the northwest corner of the new province of Alberta. As usual, much boosterism accompanied them and expectations for community success in these northern plains were high. The new MLA, James Cornwall, would eventually personify the district as 'Peace River Jim' in recognition of his efforts in "preaching the Gospel of Peace River development in Alberta's 'Lost West.'"[40] Early signs of frustration that this country, hundreds of kilometres from its nearest metropolis, hundreds beyond the Athabasca, was being overlooked or underdeveloped would be borne out over the next three decades. R.S. Irwin's recent thesis contends that the prolonged 'pioneer' stage of development in the region contributed substantially to a sense of local identity.[41] Interwar development was far less than expected and hampered by uneven climactic and agricultural conditions, which contrasted with government-regulated land distribution and the market's product demands. Mixed farming worked best in the period but did not facilitate economies of scale in transportation. The ideal monocrop wheat production so well proved upon the pre-war plains had to wait a generation until more early maturing varieties were available. Transportation and resource booms were exciting but short-lived. Meanwhile, since WWI, the eastward-lying Athabasca and a new railway combined to offer a more economical route northward. Oil and gas were more accessible farther south, east, or north. It is easy to hold remoteness, pure distance, responsible for the Peace district's slow development. But one can imagine an earlier period when less capitalization was required to handle less commodification, when a community would develop well on a more self-sufficient basis. The once remote Red River district or the more contemporary Lac St. Jean district come to mind. Nothing integral about geography prevented healthy settlement in the Peace River area. By almost all accounts, it looked most attractive.[42] The dampening factor that stands out in this cultivable land beyond the Athabasca was the critical one of time. Not enough commodity could be produced and shipped quickly enough for modern agricultural enterprise to be viable. And pioneers certainly could not 'prove up' and move on as in Vulcan, the epitome of liberal-individualist farming.[43] The Peace district did not permit competitively fast capitalization. It defied liberal time.

Another outstanding period effort at development in the Athabasca River region was railways. The Edmonton, Dunvegan, and British Columbia railway crawled northwest into the Peace and helped the flow of people and goods, such as that was. The sister railway, the Edmonton and Great Waterways Railway, which chugged northeast from Edmonton to Waterways, on the Clearwater River, three kilometres from its confluence with the Athabasca, really illuminates the geographic hurdle of the Athabasca and the essential problem of time. The railway had only marginal prospects of supporting agricultural communities. The half of its length north of Wandering River was through uncultivable bush and muskeg. Yet of all railways, it was not merely Grand, but Great. What lured this boosterism and investment northward was the prospect of mineral-related traffic through its northern terminus to and fro the Athabasca, Slave, and Mackenzie rivers by barge.

The permanent lack of agricultural produce and the mere future likelihood, no confirmation, of mineral traffic were all that inspired this investment paralleling the river northward. It never returned an interesting profit.[44] Neither the Athabasca corridor, nor especially its confluence with the Clearwater at the railway terminus atop the oil sands, nor any northern Mackenzie River destination, furnished sufficient business for the railroad. The timber was there, the oil, the salt, fish, gas … the railway was a bet against time that the land would 'prove up' in time to support this investment and make its day-long journeys worthwhile. Where the river had carried pre-modern fur traders north into the Athabasca delta area and into the Mackenzie watershed, for good profit, its modern counterpart, a railway dedicated to leveraging transport and time, could do little better; it was an economical medium for post-WWI fur traders but it brought no settlement. It did not noticeably move future prospects, in time and space, any closer to southern community markets as it was intended to do.

It is interesting, then, that one way the railway was at least perceived to have remained viable, until commodities really profitably started to flow, was by spurning 'liberal time.' Customers in the period perceived that they were paying the higher rates, permitted by regulation, on unfinished railway lines. The company denied this, yet pointed to low traffic when explaining rates, and to risky lowlands when resisting expansion. Although most of the line was built from 1913 to 1914 without noticeable lack of progress, it did not reach into the Clearwater River flats for easy transshipment until 1929, when it was extended as a part of the new Northern Alberta Railways. The rails did not reach the last few kilometres into Fort McMurray for over another decade. In short, once laid down, the railway countenanced the critical wait for northern traffic with a wait of its own. Shippers at the proposed, un-built, McMurray railhead were frustrated by the added time and expense of getting materials the few kilometres to Waterways. Most significantly inconvenienced was a local salt plant, which needed to truck or barge materials just a half-dozen kilometres. Small businesses had the manpower, and the time, to live with this inconvenience for twenty years. The community's commodity salt production shut down. Eventually the railway was extended to McMurray to assist the WWII CANOL construction project. (Later it assisted oil-sands plant construction, and in 1992, fallen into disuse, it was torn up for safety's sake to a point over 160 kilometres farther south.) In this manner, and not unlike Alfred Ostheimer, the company negotiated the demands of liberal time and the yields of the Athabasca River and nearby terrain. The railway never covered all its planned ground or tasks. Yet ever since, for all time as far as its directors were concerned, their names remain at wind-blown rail stops strung through the province's northeastern bush lands: Lynton, Quigley, Chard, Leismer, and Boyle.

The penultimate stop on the Great Waterways line was Draper, after Thomas Draper, a Michigan manufacturer who operated the first oil-sands mine in the region. At Draper, the processing plant and employees' houses sat adjacent to the new line through the 1920s. Draper did not produce oil, but asphalt and related products, which he marketed from Alberta to Michigan. Testimonials from a few city works departments indicate that Draper's more or less naturally formed asphalt was of supe-rior quality to competing products. In short, it took less time to produce and less time to maintain and repair. The unique appeal in Draper's prod-ucts, and the reason for his open-faced mine far away from Edmonton, to say nothing of Flint or Detroit, was its apparent fitness for liberal time.

Draper faced four significant hurdles: he was grieved by the Alberta provincial government's lack of support; "ready-made" asphalt contained sand that could usually be found more economically near the paving site; his rail transport costs were high; and the Depression hobnailed municipal investments in infrastructure like paving. But the province did invest in research to establish the asphalt's value as a commodity—a little wary of frontier hucksterism and federal foot-dragging—and municipal engineers did notice the competitive economy in the quality of the product. Under the auspices of Alberta's Scientific and Industrial Research Council, Karl Clark researched the oil sands from 1920 onward, primarily interested in oil recovery but also giving some attention to road surfaces. By 1927 he was disenchanted with paving prospects.[45] In 1926, a short-lived federal-provin-cial Bituminous Sands Committee, consisting of Clark, federal oil-sands geologist Sydney Ells, Alberta's Highway Commissioner C.A Davidson, and the Edmonton City Engineer, A.C. Haddow, seems not to have even produced a report. Haddow told a meeting of provincial municipal lead-ers that the natural asphalt was excellent but slightly more expensive than the customary practice of mixing local sand with imported pure asphalt.[46] Interestingly, Draper's grievance was primarily with how the provincial government consistently ignored his activity in public comments that understated the sands' potential. Draper strongly suspected both from events and from an insider's counsel that the Alberta Research Council was content to pursue development slowly while the province sought control of natural resources from the federal government.[47] The struggle between two governments for economic rents was paralyzing. Through the 1920s, until the plant's end, Draper was frustrated with high transport costs, poor availability of suitable cars for transport, and shipping delays. These are typical business problems in the face of weak infrastructure. But the railway was there; what was missing was sufficient volume of commodity traffic during the post-war decade, and then of course during the Depression. Draper presents an example of the liberal economy's furthest reach into the Canadian interior and, in light of his strong preparedness and viable natural product, he shows up the regime's failure—its inability to do what it proposed to do and enable individuals to flourish. They would have to succeed together.

The Peace River district settlers, the railway proponents, and resource entrepreneurs like Thomas Draper all reached and encountered the Athabasca River just as Alfred Ostheimer did. They anticipated personal success, and measured and demanded this not just in their immediate project, but through capitalizing upon that into future gains at a greater rate. They arrived at the Athabasca dedicated to doing more in less time, driven by social and economic demands of the southerly economies from whence they came. They were conscious their economy would situate them in historical time, their names embedded in the regional map, in the enduring map and record of the national liberal project. And they fell short of their mark. Ostheimer's feat remains inspiring but his motivations are merely quaint today. His raw individualism, his explicit, extraordinary embrace of space and time in the originating Athabasca topography, yielded nothing that a slower, more conventional climb would not also achieve.[48] The Peace district yielded no significant good by contemporary standards, unable to produce either grain or literature that could match its prairie counterpart. Nor did the railway succeed—and even less so when airplanes took prospecting and engineering parties northward. And not Draper.

While the huge Mackenzie district watershed awaited capitalization, activity along this southern boundary shows that period ideology brought people across the prairies and to the river with inappropriate expectations. They strove to achieve results within a short time frame that neither mechanical nor social technology—nor natural environs—could match. This particular grasp of an attitude toward time was the widely held grasp of an idea, one we would commonly call 'gripping' on account of its strong appeal. Though it sounds strange at first, as if some weird, metaphysical netherworld lurked about the river, a special attitude to 'time' nonetheless had a special and unhelpful grip on people along the Athabasca. The idea was liberal time, and the river consequently was a time zone representing the outer limit of Canada's liberal order.

ENDNOTES

1. R. Cole Harris's metaphor is now a generation old and still viable, most recently showcased in a reprint of his article "Regionalism and the Canadian Archipelago," in L. McCann and A. McGunn, eds., *Heartland and Hinterland*, 3rd ed. (Scarborough, ON: Prentice Hall Inc., 1998).

2. Morris Zaslow, "The Development of the MacKenzie River Basin, 1920–1940" (PhD thesis, University of Toronto, 1958).

3. Patricia McCormack, "How the North(West) Was Won" (PhD thesis, University of Alberta, 1986).

4. Robert S. Irwin, "The Emergence of Regional Identity: The Peace River Country, 1910–46" (PhD thesis, University of Alberta, 1996).

5. Steve High, "Imaginative Boundaries: The 'Rust Belt' in the Minds of North Americans, 1969–1984" (paper presented to Canadian Historical Association, Brock University, 1996); and Chad Gaffield, "The New Regional History: Rethinking the History of the Outaouais," *Journal of Canadian Studies* 26, 1 (Spring 1991): 64–81.

6. Alfred J. Ostheimer III, *Every Other Day*, 1929; WMCR M393, file 4, pp. 12–13. All subsequent references to this work are given in parentheses in the text.

7. Stuart Hall helps explain the range of liberalisms in "Variants of Liberalism," in James Donald and Stuart Hall, eds., *Politics and Ideology: A Reader* (Philadelphia: Open University Press, 1986), and their contradictory dedication to a strong state, which is protective of freedoms.

8. Denis Forgacs, ed., *An Antonio Gramsci Reader: Selected Writings 1916–1935* (New York; Schocken Books Inc., 1988). See especially Part Two. For elaborations on the hegemonic operation of power with particular attention to the disclosure of ideas between groups, see Dante Germino, *Antonio Gramsci, Architect of a New Politics* (Baton Rouge: Louisiana State University Press, 1990); and T.J. Jackson Lears, "The Concept of Cultural Hegemony: Problems and Possibilities," *American Historical Review* 90, 3 (June 1985).

9. Will Kymlicka defends the ideology against what he perceives as a too narrow reading of it by late twentieth-century critics reacting to north Atlantic, negative, neo-liberalism. See his *Liberalism, Community and Culture* (Oxford: Clarendon Press, 1989).

10. Ian Radforth, "Sydenham and Utilitarian Reform," in *Colonial Leviathan*, ed. Allan Greer and Ian Radforth (Toronto: University of Toronto Press, 1992). In showing links between utilitarian and liberal thinking, Radforth strongly suggests Canada imported the former together with the latter.

11. Fernande Roy, *Progres, harmonie, liberte: le liberalisme des milieux d'affaires francophone de Montreal au tournant du siecle* (Montreal: Boreal Express, 1988). See also Allan Smith, "The Myth of the Self-made Man in English Canada 1850–1914," *Canadian Historical Review* 59, 21 (1978). Both authors support the close association of the myth, and its contradictions, with nineteenth-century liberalism in Canada.

12. Michael Freeden, "The Family of Liberalisms: A Morphological Analysis," in *The Liberal Political Tradition, Contemporary Reappraisals*, ed. Meadowcraft (Cheltenham: Edward Elgar Pub., 1996), 14–39.

13. The connection is implied in Smith's and Roy's analyses above, for men had the opportunities to capitalize and be self-making, whereas for women, such opportunities were relatively limited. Catherine Cavanaugh makes the connection explicit just a few years later. See her article, "The Limitation of the Pioneering Partnership: The Alberta Campaign for Homestead Dower," *Canadian Historical Review* 74 (1993). In outlining the dower issue, Cavanaugh suggests an enduring affinity between maleness and possessive individualism in nineteenth-century, characteristically liberal, property law.

14. This is captured in Mrinalina Sinha, *Colonial Masculinity: The 'Manly Englishman' and the 'Effeminate Bengali' in the Late Nineteenth Century* (Manchester: Manchester University Press, 1995).

15. Sarah Carter shows how this attitude worked against Aboriginal men in *Lost Harvests, Prairie Indian Reserve Farmers and Government Policy* (Montreal: McGill-Queen's University Press, 1990). See esp. p. 23.

16. Ostheimer, Appendix 1, "Report to Geographical Board of Canada," in *Every Other Day*, lists proposed names, of which a half-dozen appeared on subsequent maps.

17. An excellent study of a key part of Ostheimer's and of Canada's alpinist audience is PearlAnn Reichwein's PhD thesis, "Beyond the Visionary Mountains: The Alpine Club of Canada and the Canadian National Park Idea 1906 to 1969" (Carleton University, 1995). Reichwein shows alpinists at work in nation building, specifically shaping the national parks. A thorough study of the resonance of this sport with national and imperial ideology remains to be done.

18. The process resonates with the consumption generally decried in Tim Flannery's sweeping *The Future Eaters: An Ecological History of the Australian Lands and People* (New York: George Braziller Inc, 1995).

19. Stephen Kern, *The Culture of Time and Space, 1880–1918* (Cambridge: Harvard University Press, 1983), 92.

20. E.P. Thompson, "Time, Work-Discipline, and Industrial Capitalism," *Past and Present*, 36 (1967): 56–97.

21. Dorothy Dahlgren, *People of our Past in Northern Alberta* (1975; Fort McMurray: Bernard Jean Publishing, 1988), 94.

22. Wyndham Lewis, *Time and Western Man*, ed. Paul Edwards (1927; Santa Rosa: Black Sparrow Press, 1993), 421.

23. Kern, *Culture of Time*, chapters 2–4.

24. J.T. Fraser, *The Voices of Time, A Cooperative Survey of Man's View of Time as Expressed by the Sciences and the Humanities*, 2nd ed. (Amherst: University of Massachusetts Press, 1981).

25. G.J. Whitrow, *Time in History, the Evolution of Our General awareness of Time and Temporal Perspective* (Oxford: Oxford University Press, 1988).

26. Donald Wilcox, *The Measure of Times Past, Pre-Newtonian Chronologies and the Rhetoric of Relative Time* (Chicago: University of Chicago Press, 1987).

27. Stephen Hawking, *A Brief History of Time, From the Big Bang to Black Holes* (Toronto: Bantam Books, 1988).

28. Huw Price, *Time's Arrow and Archimedes' Point* (Oxford: Oxford University Press, 1996), 267.

29. See, for example, Nigel Thrift, "Owners' Time and Own Time: The Making of a Capitalist Time Consciousness, 1300–1880," in *Space and Time Geography: Essays Dedicated to Torsten Hagerstrand*, ed. Allan Pred (Lund: CWK Gleerup, 1981); and Allan Pred, "Social Reproduction and the Time-Geography of Everyday Life" in *A Search for a Common Ground*, ed. Peter Gould and Gunnar Olsson (London: Pion Ltd., 1982).

30. Time's role in 'structuration' and the possible link this makes to social organization is most fully laid out in Anthony Giddens, *The Constitution of Society, Outline of the Theory of Structuration* (Berkeley: University of California Press, 1984). See also Philip Cassell, ed., *The Giddens Reader* (Stanford: Standford University Press, 1993).

31. Barbara Adam, *Time and Social Theory* (Philadelphia: Temple University Press, 1990).

32. Thompson, "Time, Work-Discipline," 92–93.

33. Rupert Ross, *Dancing with a Ghost: Exploring Indian Reality* (Markham: Reed Books Canada, 1992), 38–40.

34. In addition to Ross, above, the opinion in this paragraph derives from Colin Scott, "Science for the West, Myth for the Rest?—The Case of James Bay Cree Knowledge Construction," in *Naked Science, Anthropological Inquiry into Boundaries, Power, and Knowledge*, ed. Laura Nadler (New York: Routledge, 1996), and from unfocussed dialogue with several regional elders, college students, and academics during a decade teaching in Fort McMurray. A more formal interview process is underway to probe this plainly informal assessment.

35. Not so deep as to be pathological, the case that Paul Shepard argues, drawing upon our cultural disconnection from nature generally. See his *Nature and Madness* (San Francisco: Sierra Club Books, 1982).

36. Thompson also notes "bohemian or beatnik" as a "form of revolt within Western industrial capitalism" given to "flouting the urgency of respectable time-values." See "Time, Work-Discipline," 95.

37. Jacques Ellul, *The Technological Society* (1954; New York: Vintage Books, 1964), 11.

38. Fred Jamieson, amateur community historian, corres. to archivist, 29 October 1988, ". . . to my recollection no Black family settled north of the Athabasca River." City of Edmonton Archives, MS 386.

39. Interview with retired river pilot, Fort McMurray, 20 April 1999.

40. *Lethbridge Herald*, 3 July 1909.

41. R.S. Irwin, "The Emergence of Regional Identity: The Peace River Country 1910–46" (PhD thesis, University of Alberta, 1995).

42. In addition to Irwin's work, the salutary opinion of the country is borne out in dozens of provincial news stories in the *Calgary Albertan, Edmonton Journal, Medicine Hat News*, and, of course, the *Peace River Record*. These are among hundreds of provincial news items recently collected from earliest Alberta papers until 1929 and they are electronically searchable at the Provincial Archives of Alberta, Edmonton.

43. P. Voisey, *Vulcan: The Making of a Prairie Community* (Toronto: University of Toronto Press, 1988).

44. "Brief History of the Northern Alberta Railways," 27 January 1938; PAA M86.587, file 360a.

45. Letter to Dr. H.M. Tory, in *Oil Sands Scientist, the Letters of Dr. Karl A. Clark, 1920–1949*, ed. Mary Clark Shepard (Edmonton: University of Alberta Press, 1989), 158.

46. A.C. Haddow lists fourteen Edmonton trials over as many years, commenting on the superior quality and durability of the material in *Bituminous Sands of Northern Alberta*, 22nd Annual Convention of Alberta Municipalities, Edmonton, 1 December 1926. He also notes the higher cost and technical limitations of the oil-sand when the sand is already within it.

47. T. Draper to J. Callaghan, 26 November 1923. Provincial Archives of Alberta, Northern Alberta Railway fonds, Box. 31, file 382a.

48. But his energy was conspicuous elsewhere, in a not altogether unrelated pursuit: Ostheimer went on to a brilliant career as a top seller of insurance policies at Northwestern Mutual Co. His cumulative production by 1973, at $145 million, was forty per cent greater than his nearest rival and fourteen times greater than the next half-dozen employees leading a pack of the top 150 who each achieved $10 million in sales (Northwestern Mutual *Report* excerpt, 1974, 85). He also built extraordinary collections of Hawaiian philately and Pacific region native artifacts (*Field Notes* [Northwestern Mutual Co., January-February 1978], 55–63). Special thanks to Mr. Jon Whelan of Banff, Alberta, for locating and sharing these commercial sources.

BIBLIOGRAPHY

Aberhart, William. "God's Great Divisions of the World's History." Lecture 2, in *God's Great Prophecies*. Calgary: Calgary Prophetic Bible Conference, c. 1922, 27–28. Reprinted in *Aberhart Outpourings and Replies*, ed. David R. Elliott. Calgary: Historical Society of Alberta, 1991.

Abrahamson, Una. *God Bless Our Home: Domestic Life in Nineteenth-Century Canada*. Toronto: Burns and MacEachern Limited, 1966.

Adam, Barbara. *Time and Social Theory*. Philadelphia: Temple University Press, 1990.

Allen, Ralph. "Clifford Sifton's Medicine Show." In *Canadian Content*, ed. Nell Waldman and Sarah Norton. Third edition. Toronto: Harcourt Brace, 1996.

Anderson, Ann Leger. "Canadian Prairie Women's History: An Uncertain Enterprise." *Journal of the West* 37, 1 (January 1998): 47–59.

Anderson-Dargatz, Gail. *The Cure for Death by Lightning*. London: Virago, 1997.

Arnason, David. *Marsh Burning*. Winnipeg: Turnstone Press, 1980.

Ashley, Kathleen, Leigh Gilmore, and Gerald Peters, eds. *Autobiography and Post-modernism*. Amherst: University of Massachusetts Press, 1994.

Atwood, Margaret. *Alias Grace*. London: Bloomsbury, 1996.

_____. *Conversations*, ed. Earl G. Ingersoll. Willowdale: Firefly, 1990.

_____. *Second Words: Selected Critical Prose*. Toronto: Anansi, 1982.

_____. *Strange Things, The Malevolent North in Canadian Literature*. Oxford: Clarendon Press, 1995.

_____. *Survival*. Toronto: Anansi, 1972.

Bailey, Nancy. "Margaret Laurence, Carl Jung and the Manawaka Women." *Studies in Canadian Literature* 2 (1977).

Bailyn, B. *On the Teaching and Writing of History*. New Hampshire: Hanover, 1994.

Bakhtin, Mikhail. *Rabelais and His World*, trans. Hélène Iswolsky. Bloomington: Indiana University Press, 1984.

Baring, Anne, and Jules Cashford. *The Myth of the Goddess: Evolution of an Image*. New York: Arkana, 1993.

Barkun, Michael. *Disaster and the Millennium*. New Haven: Yale University Press, 1974.

Barnes, Ruth, and Joanne B. Eicher. "Introduction." In *Dress and Gender: Making and Meaning in Cultural Contexts*, ed. Ruth Barnes and Joanne B. Eicher. New York: Berg, 1992.

Barth, John. *The Friday Book*. New York: Putnam/Perigee, 1984.

Baudrillard, Jean. *L'Échange symbolique et la mort*. Paris: Gallimard, 1976.

Bell, Andrea L. "Creating Space in the Margins: Power and Identity in the cuentos breves of Pía Barros and Cristina Peri Rossi." *Studies in Short Fiction* 33 (1996).

Bennett, Mildred R. *The World of Willa Cather*. 1951; Lincoln: University of Nebraska Press, 1961.

Bennett, Paul W. *Emerging Identities: Selected Problems and Interpretations in Canadian History*. Scarborough: Prentice Hall, 1986.

Benstock, Shari, ed. *The Private Self: Theory and Practice of Women's Autobiographical Writing*. Chapel Hill: University of North Carolina Press, 1988.

Bentley, D.M.R. "Bibliographical Afterword." In *Early Long Poems on Canada*, ed. D.M.R. Bentley. London, ON: Canadian Poetry Press, 1993.

Berger, Carl. *The Writing of Canadian History: Aspects of English-Canadian Historical Writing since 1900*. Toronto: University of Toronto Press, 1976.

Berger, John. *Ways of Seeing*. London: Penguin Books, 1972.

Bergland, Betty. "Postmodernism and the Autobiographical Subject: Reconstructing the 'Other.'" In *Autobiography and Postmodernism*, ed. Kathleen Ashley, Leigh Gilmore, and Gerald Peters. Amherst: University of Massachusetts Press, 1994.

Berman, Marshall. *All That Is Solid Melts into Air*. New York: Penguin, 1988.

Bertens, Hans. *The Idea of the Postmodern: A History*. London: Routledge, 1995.

Bhabha, Homi K. *The Location of Culture*. London: Routledge, 1994.

Billson, Marcus. "The Memoir: New Perspectives on a Forgotten Genre." *Genre* 10, 2 (Summer 1977).

Blaise, Clarke. *Time Lord: The Remarkable Canadian Who Missed his Train and Changed the World*. Toronto: Vintage Canada, 2000.

Blewett, David. "The Unity of the Manawaka Cycle." *Journal of Canadian Studies* 13, 3 (Fall 1978).

Bliss, Jacqueline. "Seamless Lives: Pioneer Women of Saskatoon, 1883–1903." *Saskatchewan History* XLIII, 3 (Autumn 1991).

Blunt, Alison, and Gillian Rose. "Introduction." In *Writing Women and Space: Colonial and Postcolonial Geographies*, ed. Alison Blunt and Gillian Rose. New York: The Guilford Press, 1994.

Bök, Christian. "Sibyls: Echoes of French Feminism in *The Diviners* and *Lady Oracle*." *Canadian Literature* 135 (Winter 1992): 80–93.

Bradbury, Malcolm, and James McFarlane, eds. *Modernism: 1890–1930*. 1976; Harmondsworth: Penguin, 1991.

Braithwaite, Max. *Why Shoot the Teacher*. Toronto: McClelland and Stewart, 1968.

Broadfoot, Barry. *Next-Year Country: Voices of Prairie People.* Toronto: McClelland and Stewart, 1988.

Brook, Barbara. *Feminist Perspectives on the Body.* London: Longman, 1999.

Brooks, Peter. *Reading for the Plot: Design and Intention in Narrative.* New York: Vintage, 1985.

Brown, Russell. "An Interview with Robert Kroetsch." *University of Windsor Review* 7, 2 (1972): 1–18.

_____. "'The Same Old Story Once Again': Making Rain and Making Myth in *The Words of My Roaring,*" *Open Letter* 9th Ser., 5–6 (1996): 129–146.

Bruce, Jean. *The Last Best West.* Toronto: Fitzhenry and Whiteside, 1976.

Bruns, Gerald. *Inventions: Writing, Textuality, and Understanding in Literary History.* New Haven: Yale, 1982.

Brydon, Diana. "Sister Letters: Miranda's Tempest in Canada." In *Cross-Cultural Performances: Differences in Women's Re-Visions of Shakespeare,* ed. Marianne Novy. Urbana: University of Illinois Press, 1993.

Budde, Robert. *Catch as Catch.* Winnipeg: Turnstone Press, 1994.

Burke, P. "History and Social Memory." In *Memory, History, Culture and Mind,* ed. T. Butler. Oxford: Oxford University Press, 1989.

Buss, Helen M. "Memoir with an Attitude: One Reader Reads *The Woman Warrior: Memoirs of a Girlhood among Ghosts.*" *a/b: Auto/Biography Studies* 12, 2 (Fall 1997).

_____. "Settling the Score with Myths of Settlement: Two Women Who Roughed It and Wrote It." In *Great Dames,* ed. Elspeth Cameron and Janice Dickin. Toronto: University of Toronto Press, 1997.

Butala, Sharon. *The Fourth Archangel.* Toronto: HarperCollins, 1992.

_____. *Wild Stone Heart.* Toronto: HarperCollins, 2000.

_____. "Vanishing Species." *West, Globe & Mail* (June 1990): 23–30.

Butler, R. "Literature as an Influence in Shaping the Image of Tourist Destinations: A Review and Case Study." In *Canadian Studies of Parks, Recreation and Tourism in Foreign Lands,* ed. J.S. Marsh. Peterborough: Trent University Press, 1986.

Calder, Alison. "Reassessing Prairie Realism." In *Canadian Fiction,* ed. Christian Riegel and Herb Wyile. Toronto: Oxford University Press, 1988.

Calloway, Colin G. *One Vast Winter Count: The Native American West before Lewis and Clark.* London: University of Nebraska Press, 2003.

Careless, J.M.S. "'Limited Identities' in Canada." *Canadian Historical Review* L, 1: 1–10.

Carrel, Frank. *Canada's West and Farther West.* Toronto: Musson Book Company, 1911.

Carter, Sarah A. *Capturing Women: The Manipulation of Cultural Imagery in Canada's Prairie West*. Montreal: McGill-Queen's University Press, 1997.

_____. *Lost Harvests, Prairie Indian Reserve Farmers and Government Policy*. Montreal: McGill-Queen's University Press, 1990/.

Cassell, Philip, ed. *The Giddens Reader*. Stanford: Stanford University Press, 1993.

Cavanaugh, Catherine A. *Telling Tales: Essays in Western Women's History*. Vancouver: University of British Columbia Press, 2000.

_____. "The Limitations of the Pioneering Partnership: The Alberta Campaign for Homestead Dower." *Canadian Historical Review* 74 (1993).

_____. "'No Place for a Woman': Engendering Western Canadian Settlement." *Western Historical Quarterly* 28, 4 (Winter 1997).

_____, and Randi R. Warne, eds. *Standing on New Ground: Women in Alberta*. Edmonton: University of Alberta Press, 1993.

Clark, Mary, ed. *Oil Sands Scientist, the Letters of Dr. Karl A. Clark, 1920–1949*. Edmonton: University of Alberta Press, 1989.

Climbs and Explorations in the Canadian Rockies. London: Longmans, Green and Co, 1903.

Coleman, Daniel. "Immigration, Nation, and the Canadian Allegory of Manly Maturation." *Essays on Canadian Writing* 61 (Spring 1997).

Colombo, John Robert. *New Direction in Canadian Poetry*. Toronto: Holt, Rinehart and Winston, 1971.

Conner, Ralph. *The Foreigner: A Tale of Saskatchewan*. New York: George H. Doran Company, 1909.

_____. *Gwen, an Idyll of the Canyon*. Toronto: Fleming H. Revell, 1899.

Cook, Blanche Wiesen. "'Women Alone Stir My Imagination': Lesbianism and the Cultural Tradition." *Signs: Journal of Women in Culture and Society* 4 (1979): 718–739.

Cook, Ramsay. "Canadian Centennial Celebrations." *International Journal* XXII: 659–663.

Cooley, Dennis. "David Arnason Interview." *Föstudagur* 20 (March 1981): 2–3, 6.

Cosgrove, D., and S. Daniels, eds. *The Iconography of Landscape: Essays on the Symbolic Representation, Design, and Use of Past Environments*. New Jersey: Prentice Hall, 1988.

Cran, George Marion Dudley. *A Woman in Canada*. London: John Milne, 1910.

Culler, Jonathan. "Poetics of the Lyric." In *Structuralist Poetics: Structuralism, Linguistics, and the Study of Literature*. Ithaca: Cornell, 1975.

Dahlgren, Dorothy. *People of Our Past in North Alberta*. Fort McMurray: Bernhard Jean Publishing, 1988.

Dalley, Stephanie. *Myths from Mesopotamia: Creation, The Flood, Gilgamesh, and Others.* Oxford: Oxford University Press, 1989.

Davey, Frank. "The Language of the Contemporary Canadian Long Poem." In *Surviving the Paraphrase: Eleven Essays on Canadian Literature.* Winnipeg: Turnstone Press, 1983. Based on an earlier publication: *Notes on the Language of the Contemporary Canadian Long Poem, as presented to the Simon Fraser University weekend conference/festival "The Coast Is Only a Line," 25 July 1981.* Lantzville, BC: Island Writing Series, 1983.

——. "A Young Boy's Eden: Notes on Recent 'Prairie" Poetry." In *Reading Canadian Reading.* Winnipeg: Turnstone Press, 1988.

——, and Ann Munton, eds. *The Proceedings of the Long-liners Conference on the Canadian Long Poem.* York University, Toronto, 29 May–1 June 1984. *Open Letter* 6th Ser., 2–3 (1985).

Davis, Angela E. "'Country Homemakers': The Daily Lives of Prairie Women as Seen through the Woman's Page of the Grain Growers' Guide 1908–1928." In *Canadian Papers in Rural History,* ed. Donald H. Akenson. Vol. VIII. Gananoque, ON: Langdale Press, 1992.

De Brou, David, and Aileen Moffat, eds. *"Other" Voices: Historical Essays on Saskatchewan Women.* Regina: Canadian Plains Research Centre, 1995.

de Laurentis, Teresa. "Eccentric Subjects: Feminist Theory and Historical Consciousness." *Feminist Studies* 16, 1 (Spring 1990).

Demetrakopoulos, Stephanie A. "Laurence's Fiction: A Revisioning of Feminine Archetypes." *Canadian Literature* 93 (Summer 1982): 42–57.

Donald, James, and Stuart Hall. *Politics and Ideology: A Reader.* Philadelphia: Open University Press, 1986.

Drucker, Johanna. *The Alphabetic Labyrinth: The Letters in History and Imagination.* London: Thames and Hudson, 1995.

Duncan, J., and N. Duncan. "(Re)reading the Landscape." *Environment and Planning D: Society and Space* 6 (1988): 117–126.

Durkin, Douglas. *The Magpie.* 1923; Toronto: University of Toronto Press, 1974.

Easingwood, Peter. "Margaret Laurence: Prairie Fiction and Prairie History." *Revisions of Canadian Literature* (1984).

Elam, Diane. *Romancing the Postmodern.* London: Routledge, 1992.

Eliot, T.S. "'Ulysses,' Order, and Myth." In *Selected Prose of T.S. Eliot,* ed. Frank Kermode. London: Faber, 1975.

Elliott, David R. "Knowing No Borders." In *Amazing Grace: Evangelicism in Australia, Britain, Canada, and the United States,* ed. George A. Rawlyk and Mark A. Noll. Montreal: McGill-Queen's University Press, 1994.

Ellul, Jacques. *The Technological Society.* New York: Vintage Books, 1964.

Epstein, Daniel Mark. *Sister Aimee: The Life of Aimee Semple McPherson*. New York: Harcourt Brace, 1993.

Fairbanks, Carol. *Prairie Women: Images in American and Canadian Fiction*. New Haven: Yale University Press, 1986.

Faragher, John Mack. *Women and Men on the Overland Trail*. New Haven: Yale University Press, 1979.

Ferguson, Emily. *Open Trails*. London: Cassell and Company, 1912.

Fitzgerald, F. Scott. *The Great Gatsby*. New York: Charles Scribner's Sons, 1925.

Flannery, Tim. *The Future Eaters: An Ecological History of the Australian Lands and People*. New York: George Braziller Inc., 1995.

Fogel, Stanley. *A Tale of Two Countries: Contemporary Fiction in Canada and the United States*. Toronto: ECW Press, 1984.

Forgacs, Denis, ed. *An Antonio Gramsci Reader: Selected Writings 1916–1935*. New York: Schocken Books, Inc., 1988.

Foucault, Michel. "Nietzsche, Genealogy, History." In *Language, Countermemory, Practice: Selected Essays and Interviews*, ed. Donald F. Bouchard. Ithaca: Cornell University Press, 1977.

Fowler, Martin. "Pioneer Memoirs." In *The Oxford Companion to Canadian Literature*, ed. Eugene Benson and William Toye. Second edition. Toronto: Oxford University Press, 1997.

Fox-Genovese, Elizabeth. "Between Individualism and Community: Autobiographies of Southern Women." In *Located Lives: Place and Idea in Southern Autobiography*, ed. J. Bill Berry. Athens, GA: University of Georgia Press, 1990.

Francis, Marvin. *City Treaty*. Winnipeg: Turnstone Press, 2002.

Francis, R. Douglas. *Images of the West: Changing Perceptions of the Prairies, 1690–1960*. Saskatoon: Western Producer Prairie Books, 1989.

_____. "Changing Images of the West." In *The Prairie West: Historical Readings*, ed. R. Douglas Francis and Howard Palmer. Edmonton: University of Alberta Press, 1985.

Fraser, James. *The Golden Bough*. New York: Macmillan Company, 1940.

Fraser, James George. "'The Same Old Story Once Again': Making Rain and Making Myth in *The Words of My Roaring*." *Open Letter* 9th Ser., 5–6 (1996): 129–146.

Fraser, J.T. *The Voices of Time: A Cooperative Survey of Man's View of Time as Expressed by the Sciences and the Humanities*. Second edition. Amherst: University of Massachusetts Press, 1981.

Freeden, Michael. "The Family of Liberalisms: A Morphological Analysis." In *The Liberal Political Tradition, Contemporary Reappraisals*, ed. Meadowcraft. Cheltenham: Edward Elgar Publishers, 1996.

Freud, Sigmund. *Beyond the Pleasure Principle*, trans. James Strachey. New York: Bantam Books, 1963.

Friesen, Gerald. *The Canadian Prairies: A History.* Toronto: University of Toronto Press, 1987.

_____. *Citizens and Nation: An Essay on History, Communication, and Canada.* Toronto: University of Toronto Press, 2000.

_____. *The West: Regional Ambitions, National Debates, Global Age.* McGill Institute Books. Toronto: Penguin, 1999.

_____. "Defining the Prairies: or, why the prairies don't exist." In *Toward Defining the Prairies: Region, Culture, and History*, ed. Robert Wardhaugh. Winnipeg: University of Manitoba Press, 2001.

Friesen, Patrick. *The Shunning.* Winnipeg: Turnstone Press, 1980.

Frye, Marilyn. *The Politics of Reality: Essays in Feminist Theory.* New York: Crossing Press, 1983.

Frye, Northrop. *Anatomy of Criticism.* Princeton: Princeton University Press, 1957.

_____. *The Bush Garden: Essays on the Canadian Imagination.* Toronto: House of Anansi Press, 1971.

_____. "The Narrative Tradition in English-Canadian Poetry." In *The Bush Garden: Essays on the Canadian Imagination.* Toronto: House of Anansi Press, 1971.

Gaffield, Chad. "The New Regional History: Rethinking the History of the Outaouais." *Journal of Canadian Studies* 26, 1 (Spring 1991): 64–81.

Gard, Robert. *Johnny Chinook.* London: Longmans, Green and Company, 1945.

Gayton, Don. *The Wheatgrass Mechanism: Science and Imagination in the Western Canadian Landscape.* Saskatoon: Fifth House, 1990.

Genosko, Garry. *McLuhan and Baudrillard: The Masters of Implosion.* New York: Routledge, 1999.

Germino, Dante. *Antonio Gramsci: Architect of a New Politics.* Baton Rouge: Louisiana State University Press, 1990.

Giddens, Anthony. *The Constitution of Society, Outline of the Theory of Structuration.* Berkeley: University of California Press, 1984.

Gilbert, Sandra, and Susan Grubar. *The Madwoman in the Attic: Women Writers and the Nineteenth-Century Literary Imagination.* New Haven: Yale University Press, 1979.

Gilmore, Leigh. "The Mark of Autobiography: Postmodernism, Autobiography, and Genre." In *Autobiography and Postmodernism*, ed. Kathleen Ashley, Leigh Gilmore, and Gerald Peters. Amherst: University of Massachusetts Press, 1994.

Godard, Barbara. "Ex-centriques, Eccentric, Avant-Garde: Women and Modernism in the Literatures of Canada." *Room of One's Own* 8, 4 (1983): 57–75.

Gom, Leona M. "Laurence and the Use of Memory." *Canadian Literature* 71 (1976).

Gorham, Deborah. "Singing up the Hill." *Canadian Dimension* 10 (June 1975).

Grace, Sherrill E. "A Portrait of the Artist as Laurence Hero." *Journal of Canadian Studies* 13, 3 (Fall 1978): 64–71.

_____. "Quest for the Peaceable Kingdom: Urban/Rural Codes in Roy, Laurence, and Atwood." In *Women Writers and the City: Essays in Feminist Literary Criticism*, ed. Susan Merrill Squier. Knoxville: University of Tennessee Press, 1984.

Graham, Kenneth. "Picaro as Messiah: Backstrom's Election in *The Words of My Roaring*." *Mosaic* 14, 2 (Spring 1981): 177–186.

Granatstein, J.L. *Who Killed Canadian History?* Toronto: HarperCollins, 1998.

Green, Thomas A., ed. "folklife." In *Folklore: An Encyclopedia of Beliefs, Customs, Tales, Music, and Art*. Two volumes. Santa Barbara: ABC-CLIO, 1997.

Greene, Gayle. "Margaret Laurence's *Diviners* and Shakespeare's *Tempest:* The Uses of the Past." In *Women's Re-Visions of Shakespeare: On the Responses of Dickinson, Woolf, Rich, H.D., George Eliot, and Others*, ed. Marianne Novy. Urbana: University of Illinois Press, 1990.

Grierson, John. *Grierson on Documentary*, ed. Forsyth Hardy. London: Faber, 1966.

Grosswiller, Paul. *Method Is the Message: Rethinking McLuhan through Critical Theory*. Toronto: Black Rose Books, 1998.

Guardiani, Francesco. "The Postmodernity of Marshall McLuhan." *McLuhan Studies* 1 (1991): 141–162.

Hall, Stuart. "Variants of Liberalism." In *Politics and Ideology*, ed. J. Donald and S. Hall. Philadelphia: Open University Press, 1986.

Harris, R. Cole. *The Historical Atlas of Canada. From the Beginning to 1800*. Toronto: Toronto University Press, 1987.

_____. "Regionalism and the Canadian Archipelago." In *Heartland and Hinterland*, ed. L. McCann and A. McGunn. Third edition. Scarborough: Prentice Hall, 1998.

Harrison, Dick. *Unnamed Country: The Struggle for a Canadian Prairie Fiction*. Edmonton: University of Alberta Press, 1977.

Hart, Francis Russell. "History Talking to Itself: Public Personality in Recent Memoir." *New Literary History* 11, 1 (Autumn 1979).

Harvey, David. *The Condition of Postmodernity*. Cambridge: Blackwell, 1989.

Hawking, Stephen. *A Brief History of Time, From the Big Bang to Black Holes*. Toronto: Bantam Books, 1988.

Hehner, Barbara. "River of Now and Then: Margaret Laurence's Narratives." *Canadian Literature* 74 (Autumn 1977): 40–57.

Herbison, R. *Deliberate Regression*. New York: Knopf, 1980

Hewison, R. *The Heritage Industry*. London: Methuen, 1987.

Hiemstra, Mary. *Gully Farm*. Toronto: McClelland and Stewart, 1955.

High, Steven. "Imaginative Boundaries: The 'Rust Belt' in the Minds of North Americans, 1969–1984." Paper presented to Canadian Historical Association, Brock University, 1966.

Higonnet, Margaret R. "New Cartographies, an Introduction." In *Reconfigured Spheres: Feminist Explorations of Literary Space*, ed. Margaret R. Higonnet and Joan Templeton. Amherst: University of Massachusetts Press, 1994.

Hildebrandt, Walter. *Sightings*. Dunvegan, ON: Cormorant Books, 1991.

Hill, Douglas. *The Opening of the Canadian West: Where Strong Men Gathered*. New York: The John Day Company, 1967.

Howells, Coral Ann. *Private and Fictional Words: Canadian Women Novelists of the 1970s and 1980s*. London: Methuen, 1987.

Huffer, Lynne. *Maternal Pasts, Feminist Futures: Nostalgia, Ethics, and the Question of Difference*. Stanford: Stanford University Press, 1998.

Huggan, Graham. "Decolonizing the Map: Post-Colonialism, Post-Structuralism and the Cartographic Connection." *Ariel* 20, 4 (October 1989).

Hutcheon, Linda. *The Canadian Postmodern: A Study of Contemporary English-Canadian Fiction*. Toronto: Oxford University Press, 1988.

_____. *Narcissistic Narrative*. 1980; London: Methuen, 1984.

_____. *A Poetics of Postmodernism: History, Theory, Fiction*. New York: Routledge, 1988.

Irving, John A. *The Social Credit Movement in Alberta*. Toronto: University of Toronto Press, 1959.

_____, ed. *Mass Media in Canada*. Toronto: Ryerson, 1962.

Irwin, R.S. "The Emergence of Regional Identity: The Peace River Country 1910–46." PhD thesis, University of Alberta, 1995.

Jackson, Rosemary. *Fantasy: The Literature of Subversion*. London: Methuen, 1981.

Jay, Martin. "Photo-unrealism: The Contribution of the Camera to the Crisis of Ocularcentrism." In *Vision and Textuality*, ed. Stephen Melville and Bill Readings. Durham: Duke University Press, 1995.

Jeffrey, Julie Roy. *Frontier Women: "Civilizing" the West? 1840–1880*. New York: Hill and Wang, 1998.

Johnson, R. "The Story So Far and Further Transformations." In *Introduction to Contemporary Cultural Studies*, ed. D. Punter. London: Longman, 1986.

Jones, D.G. *Butterfly on Rock: A Study of Themes and Images in Canadian Writing*. Toronto: University of Toronto Press, 1970.

_____. "The Mythology of Identity: A Canadian Case." In *Driving Home: A Dialogue Between Writers and Readers*, ed. Barbara Belyea and Estelle Dansereau. Waterloo, ON: Wilfrid Laurier University Press, 1984.

Jones, Manina. *That Art of Difference: 'Documentary-Collage' and English-Canadian Writing*. Toronto: University of Toronto Press, 1993.

Jordan, David. *New World Regionalism: Literature in the Americas*. Toronto: University of Toronto Press, 1994.

Joyce, James. *Finnegan's Wake*. London: Faber, 1975.

_____. *A Portrait of the Artist as a Young Man*. New York: Dover, 1994.

Kagami, Yoshiro. "Edward Byrne: A Life in Ice." *Journal of Alpine Exploration* 2, 6 (1951).

Kamboureli, Smaro. *On the Edge of Genre: The Contemporary Canadian Long Poem*. Toronto: University of Toronto Press, 1991.

Kaye, Frances W., and Robert Thacker. "'Gone Back to Alberta': Robert Kroetsch Rewriting the Great Plains." *Great Plains Quarterly* 14 (1994): 167–183.

Keahey, Deborah. *Making it Home: Place in Canadian Prairie Literature*. Winnipeg: University of Manitoba Press, 1998.

Kern, Stephen. *The Culture of Time and Space, 1880–1918*. Cambridge: Harvard University Press, 1983.

Kinnear, Mary, ed. *A Female Economy: Women's Work in a Prairie Province, 1870–1970*. Montreal: McGill-Queen's University Press, 1998.

_____. *First Days, Fighting Days: Women in Manitoba History*. Regina: Canadian Plains Research Centre, 1987.

Kirby, Kathleen M. "Thinking through the Boundary: The Politics of Location, Subjects, and Space." *boundary 2* 20, 2 (1993).

Kolodny, Annette. *The Lay of the Land: Metaphor as Experience and History in American Life and Letters*. Chapel Hill: The University of North Carolina Press, 1975.

Kreisel, Henry. "The Prairie: A State of Mind." In *Trace: Prairie Writers on Writing*, ed. Birk Sproxton. Winnipeg: Turnstone Press, 1986.

Kristeva, Julia. *Polylogue*. Paris: Seuil, 1977.

_____. "Women's Time." In *The Kristeva Reader*. Oxford: Blackwell, 1986.

Kroetsch, Robert. *Alberta*. Toronto: Macmillan, 1968.

_____. *Badlands*. Toronto: General, 1982.

_____. *Gone Indian.* Toronto: new press, 1973.

_____. *Labyrinths of Voice: Conversations with Robert Kroetsch*, ed. Shirley Neuman and Robert Wilson. Edmonton: NeWest, 1982.

_____. *A Likely Story: The Writing Life.* Red Deer: Red Deer College Press, 1995.

_____. *The Lovely Treachery of Words: Essays Selected and New.* Toronto: Oxford University Press, 1989.

_____. *Seed Catalogue* Winnipeg: Turnstone Press, 1979.

_____. *The Studhorse Man.* Markham: Paper Jacks, 1977.

_____. *What the Crow Said.* Don Mills: General Publishing Company, 1978.

_____. *The Words of My Roaring.* Toronto: Macmillan, 1966.

_____. "Beyond Nationalism: A Prologue." *Mosaic* 14, 2 (1981): v–xi.

_____. "On Being an Alberta Writer." *Open Letter* 5, 4 (1983): 69–80.

_____. "On Being an Alberta Writer: Or, I Wanted to Tell Our Story." In *Towards a Canadian Literature*, ed. D. Daymond and L. Monkman. Volume 2. Ottawa: Tecumseh, 1985.

_____. "A Canadian Issue." *boundary 2: A Journal of Postmodern Literature* 3, 1 (Fall 1974): 1–2.

_____. "A Conversation with Margaret Laurence." In *Trace: Prairie Writers on Writing*, ed. Birk Sproxton. Winnipeg: Turnstone Press, 1986.

_____. "Disunity as Unity: A Canadian Strategy." In *Canadian Story and History 1885–1985*, ed. Colin Nicholson and Peter Easingwood. Edinburgh: Edinburgh University Centre of Canadian Studies, 1985.

_____. "The Fear of Women in Prairie Fiction." *Open Letter* 5th Ser., 4 (1983).

_____. "For Play and Entrance: The Contemporary Canadian Long Poem." Plus "Prologue for the End of an Essay." *Dandelion* 8, 1 (1981): 61–85. "For Play and Entrance" also published in *Open Letter* 5, 4 (1983): 91–110. Reprinted in *Sagetrieb* 7, 1 (1988) 79–97. Reprinted in *The Lovely Treachery of Words: Essays Selected and New.* Toronto: Oxford University Press, 1989. Based on "For Play and Entrance: The Contemporary Canadian Long Poem," original version presented at The Modern Languages Association in Houston, 29 December 1980.

_____. "The Moment of the Discovery of America Continues." In *The Lovely Treachery of Words.* Toronto: Oxford Unversity Press, 1989.

_____. "The Poetics of Rita Kleinhart." In *A Likely Story: The Writing Life.* Red Deer: Red Deer College Press, 1995.

_____. "Stone Hammer Poem." In *Completed Field Notes: The Long Poems of Robert Kroetsch.* Toronto: McClelland and Stewart, 1989.

_____. "Unhiding the Hidden: Recent Canadian Fiction." In *The Lovely Treachery of Words: Essays Selected and New.* Toronto: Oxford Unversity Press, 1989.

_____. "The Veil of Knowing." In *The Lovely Treachery of Words: Essays Selected and New*. Toronto: Oxford University Press, 1989.

_____. "Voice/in prose effing the ineffable." *freelance* 8, 2 (1976): 35–36. Reprinted as "Effing the Ineffable." *Open Letter* 5, 4 (1983): 23–24.

Kymlicka, Will. *Liberalism, Community and Culture*. Oxford: Clarendon Press, 1989.

Lacan, Jacques. *Le Séminaire, livre XI, les quatre concepts fondamentaux de la psychanalyse*. Paris: Seuil, 1973.

Laurence, Margaret. *The Diviners*. Toronto: McClelland and Stewart, 1993.

_____. *The Fire-Dwellers*. Toronto: McClelland and Stewart, 1991.

_____. *A Jest of God*. Toronto: McClelland and Stewart, 1989.

_____. *The Stone Angel*. Toronto: McClelland and Stewart, 1991.

Lears, T.J. Jackson. "The Concept of Cultural Hegemony: Problems and Possibilities." *American Historical Review* 90, 3 (June 1985).

Lecker, Robert. *Robert Kroetsch*. Boston: Twayne, 1986.

Lefebvre, Henri. *The Production of Space*, trans. Donald Nicholson-Smith. Oxford: Basil Blackwell, 1991.

Leick, Gwendolyn. *A Dictionary of Ancient Near Eastern Mythology*. London: Routledge, 1991.

Leitch, Vincent B. *Deconstructive Criticism: An Advanced Introduction*. New York: Columbia University Press, 1983.

Lejeune, Philippe. *Le Pacte Autobiographique*. Paris: Seuil, 1975.

Lenoski, Daniel S., ed. *a/long prairie lines: an anthology of long prairie poems*. Winnipeg: Turnstone Press, 1989.

Lewis and Clark. Lincoln: University of Nebraska Press, 2003. Reviewed by Pekka Hämäläinen, Department of History, Texas A&M University, and University of Helsinki Collegium for Advanced Studies. Published by H-AmIndian (March, 2004).

Lewis, Wyndham. *Time and Western Man*, ed. Paul Edwards. 1927; Santa Rosa: Black Sparrow Press, 1993.

Lewthwaite, Elizabeth. "Women's Work in Western Canada." In *The Fortnightly Review* LXX (1901).

Livesay, Dorothy. "The Documentary Poem: A Canadian Genre." In *Contexts of Canadian Criticism: A Collection of Critical Essays*, ed. Eli Mandel. Chicago: University of Chicago Press, 1971.

Lodge, David. *The Modes of Modern Writing: Metaphor, Metonymy, and the Typology of Modern Literature*. Ithaca: Cornell University Press, 1977.

Lowenthal, D. *Possessed by the Past*. New York: Free Press, 1995.

Luftig, V. "Literary Tourism and Dublin's Joyce." In *Joyce and the Subject of History*, ed. M. Wollenger. Ann Arbor: University of Michigan Press, 1996.

Maher, Susan Naramore. "Deep Mapping the Great Plains: Surveying the Literary Cartography of Place." *Western American Literature* 36, 1 (2001).

Mair, Charles. "The New Canada." In *The Search for English-Canadian Literature: An Anthology of Critical Articles from the Nineteenth and Early Twentieth Centuries*, ed. Carl Ballstadt. Toronto: University of Toronto Press, 1975.

Malin, James C. *History and Ecology: Studies of the Grassland*, ed. Robert P. Swierenga. Lincoln: University of Nebraska Press, 1984.

Mallinson, Jean. "John Robert Colombo: Documentary Poet as Visionary." In *Brave New Wave*, ed. Jack David. Windsor: Black Moss, 1978.

Mandel, Ann. "Uninventing Structures: Cultural Criticism and the Novels of Robert Kroetsch." *Open Letter* 5, 8 (Spring 1978): 52–71.

Mandel, Eli. *Another Time*. Erin, ON: Press Porcépic, 1977.

_____. *The Family Romance*. Winnipeg: Turnstone Press, 1986.

_____. *Out of Place*. Erin, ON: Press Porcépic, 1977.

_____. "Authentic Speech: Eli Mandel in Conversation with Pat Krause." *freelance* (1979): 9–14.

_____. "Introduction." In *Eight More Canadian Poets*. Toronto: Holt, Rinehart and Winston, 1972.

_____. "Writing West: On the Road to Wood Mountain." In *Another Time*. Erin, ON: Press Porcépic, 1977. Also published in *Canadian Forum* LVII.

Martin, Mathew. "Dramas of Desire in Margaret Laurence's *A Jest of God, The Fire-Dwellers*, and *The Diviners.*" *Studies in Canadian Literature* 19, 1 (1994): 58–71.

Martin, Paul. "The Discovery of America." *Science* 179 (1973): 969–973.

Martineau, Joel. "Landscapes and Inscape in Thomas Wharton's *Icefields.*" *Open Letter* 10, 2 (Spring 1998): 41–49.

Martinet, Jeanne. "Le paysage: signifiant et signifié." In *Lire le paysage—lire les paysages, C.I.E.R.E.C. Travaux XLII*. Saint Etienne: Presses de l'Université de Saint Etienne, 1982.

Mathews, Robin. *Canadian Literature: Surrender or Revolution*. Toronto: Steel Rail Educational Publishing, 1978.

McClung, Nellie L. *Sowing Seeds in Danny*. Toronto: Ryerson Press, 1922.

McCourt, Edward. *The Canadian West in Fiction*. 1949; Toronto: Ryerson Press, 1970.

McKinnon, Barry. *I Wanted to Say Something*. Red Deer: Red Deer College Press, 1990.

McLuhan, Marshall. *The Gutenberg Galaxy*. Toronto: University of Toronto Press, 1962.

_____. *Understanding Media: The Extensions of Man*. New York: McGraw-Hill, 1964.

_____. "Myth and Mass Media." *Daedalus* 88, 2 (Spring 1959): 339–348. Reprinted in *Media Research: Technology, Art, Communication*, ed. Michel A. Moos. Amsterdam: G+B Arts, 1997.

_____, with Gerald Emanuel Stearn. "The Hot and Cold Interview." In *McLuhan: Hot and Cool: A Critical Symposium*, ed. Gerald Stearn. New York: Dial, 1967.

McCormack, Patricia. "How the North(West) Was Won." PhD thesis, Unversity of Alberta, 1986.

Meine, Curt. "Reimagining the Prairie: Aldo Leopold and the Origins of Prairie Restoration." In *Recovering the Prairie*, ed. Robert F. Sayre. Madison: University of Wisconsin Press, 1999.

Mellor, Winnifred. "'The Simple Container of Our Existence': Narrative Ambiguity in Carol Shields' *The Stone Diaries*." *Studies in Canadian Literature* 20, 2 (1995): 96–110.

Mitchell, Elizabeth B. *In Western Canada Before the War: Impressions of Early Twentieth Century Prairie Communities*. 1915; Saskatoon: Western Producer Prairie Books, 1981.

Momaday, N. Scott. *The Way to Rainy Mountain*. Albuquerque: University of New Mexico Press, 1968.

Morris, Elizabeth Keith. *An Englishwoman in the Canadian West*. London: Simpkin, Marshall, 1913.

Mouat, Jeremy, and Catherine Cavanaugh, eds. *Making Western Canada: Essays on European Colonization and Settlement*. Toronto: Garamond Press, 1996.

Neuman, Shirley. "Autobiography: From Different Poetics to a Poetics of Difference." In *Essays on Life Writing: From Genre to Critical Practice*, ed. Marlene Kadar. Toronto: University of Toronto Press, 1992.

_____, ed. *Autobiography and Questions of Gender*. London: Frank Cass, 1991.

New, William H. *Land Sliding: Imagining Space, Presence, and Power in Canadian Writing*. Toronto: University of Toronto Press, 1997.

Newby, P.T. "Literature and the Fashioning of Tourist Taste." In *Humanistic Geography and Literature: Essays on the Experience of Place*, ed. D.C. Pocock. London: Croom Helm, 1981.

Nicholls, Peter. *Modernisms: A Literary Guide*. Berkeley: University of California Press, 1995.

Nicholson, N. *The Lakers: The First Tourists*. London: Robert Hale, 1972.

Norris, Kathleen. *Dakota: A Spiritual Geography*. New York: Ticknor & Fields, 1993.

O'Hagan, Howard. *Tay John*. 1939; Toronto: McClelland and Stewart, 1989.

O'Leary, Stephen D. *Arguing the Apocalypse: A Theory of Millennial Rhetoric*. New York: Oxford University Press, 1994.

Omhovère, Claire. "Aritha van Herk's Tesselated Territory." *Etudes canadiennes / Canadian Studies* 47 (1999): 177–190.

Ostheimer, Alfred J. III. *Every Other Day*. WMCR M393, file 4, 1929.

Palmer, Howard. "Strangers and Stereotypes: The Rise of Nativism, 1880–1920." In *The Prairie West: Historical Readings*, ed. R. Douglas Francis and Howard Palmer. Second edition. Edmonton: Pica Pica Press, 1992.

Parker, Seymour. "Rituals of Gender: A Study of Etiquette, Public Symbols, and Cognition." *American Anthropologist* 90, 2 (1988).

Paterson, Janet. *Postmodernism and the Quebec Novel*, trans. David Homel and Charles Phillips. Toronto: University of Toronto Press, 1994.

Perkin, Joan. *Women and Marriage in Nineteenth-Century England*. Chicago: Lyceum Books, 1989.

Pical, Michel. "Lecture(s) du paysage." In *Lire le paysage—lire les paysages*, *C.I.E.R.E.C. Travaux XLII*. Saint Etienne: Presses de l'Université de Saint Etienne, 1982.

Pickering, Jean, and Suzanne Kehde. "Introduction." In *Narratives of Nostalgia, Gender, and Nationalism*, ed. Jean Pickering and Suzanne Kehde. New York: New York University Press, 1997.

Pocock, D.C. *Humanistic Geography and Literature*. London: Croom Helm, 1981.

_____. "Haworth: The Experience of Literary Place." In *Geography and Literature: A Meeting of the Disciplines*, ed. W. Mallory and P. Simpson-Housley. Syracuse: Syracuse University Press, 1987.

_____, and S. Squire. "The Cultural Values of Literary Tourism." *Annals of Tourism Research* 21: 103–120.

Pred, Allan. "Social Reproduction and the Time-Geography of Everyday Life." In *A Search for a Common Ground*, ed. Peter Gould and Gunnar Olsson. London: Pion Limited, 1982.

Price, Huw. *Time's Arrow and Archimedes' Point*. Oxford: Oxford University Press, 1996.

Quantic, Diane Dufva. *The Nature of the Place: A Study of Great Plains Fiction*. Lincoln: University of Nebraska Press, 1995.

Quinby, Lee. "The Subject of Memoirs: The Woman Warrior's Technology of Ideographic Selfhood." In *De/Colonizing the Subject: The Politics of Gender in*

Women's Autobiography, ed. Sidonie Smith and Julia Watson. Minneapolis: Minnesota University Press, 1992.

Radforth, Ian. "Sydenham and Utilitarian Reform." In *Colonial Leviathan*, ed. Allan Greer and Ian Radforth. Toronto: University of Toronto Press, 1992.

Rasmussen, Linda., et al. *A Harvest Yet to Reap: A History of Prairie Women*. Toronto: The Women's Press, 1976.

Reaney, James. "Editorial." *Alphabet* 1 (1960).

Rees, Roberta. *Eyes Like Pigeons*. London, ON: Brick Books, 1992.

Reid, Monty. *Karst Means Stone*. Edmonton: NeWest Press, 1979.

Renov, Michael, ed. *Theorizing Documentary*. London: Routledge, 1993.

Ribeiro, Aileen. *Dress and Morality*. London: B.T. Batsford, 1986.

Rice, Bruce. *Daniel*. Dunvegan, ON: Cormorant Books, 1988.

Richler, Mordecai. *Solomon Gursky Was Here*. Toronto: Viking, 1989.

Richter, David H., ed. *The Critical Tradition: Classic Texts and Contemporary Trends*. Second edition. Boston: Bedford, 1998.

Ricou, Laurie. *Vertical Man/Horizontal World: Man and Landscape in Canadian Prairie Fiction*. Vancouver: University of British Columbia Press, 1973.

_____. "The Long Poem." *Canadian Literature in English* 4 (1990): 26–38.

_____. "Never Cry Wolfe: Benjamin West's The Death of Wolfe in *Prochain Episode* and *The Diviners*." *Essays on Canadian Writing* 20 (Winter 1980–81): 171–185.

Reichwein, PearlAnn. "Beyond the Visionary Mountains: The Alpine Club of Canada and the Canadian National Park Idea 1906 to 1969." PhD thesis, Carleton University, 1995.

Riegel, Christian, and Herb Wyile, eds. *A Sense of Place: Re-Evaluating Regionalism in Canadian and American Writing*. Edmonton: University of Alberta Press, 1977.

Ringwood, Gwen Pharis. *The Rainmaker*. Toronto: Playwrights Co-op, 1975.

Ritchie, J. Ewing. *To Canada with Emigrants: A Record of Actual Experiences*. London: T. Fisher Unwin, 1885.

Rose, Gillian. "The Geographical Imagination: Knowledge and Critique." In *Feminism and Geography: The Limits of Geographical Knowledge*. Cambridge, Oxford: Polity Press, 1993.

Ross, Rupert. *Dancing with a Ghost: Exploring Indian Reality*. Markham: Reed Books Canada, 1992.

Ross, Sinclair. *As for Me and My House*. Toronto: McClelland and Stewart, 1957.

Roy, Fernande. *Progres, harmonie, liberte: le liberalisme des milieux d'affaires francophone de Montreal au tournant du siecle*. Montreal: Boreal Express, 1988.

Rukszto, Katarzyna. "Representing Canada: Heritage, History and the Politics of Belonging." In *Nationalism, Citizenship and National Identity Conference.* Mount Allison University, Sackville, New Brunswick, November 11–13, 1999.

Scobie, Stephen. "Amelia Or: Who Do You Think You Are? Documentary and Identity in Canadian Literature." *Canadian Literature* 100 (1984): 264–285.

Sconce, Jeffrey. *Haunted Media: Electronic Presence from Telegraphy to Television.* Durham: Duke University Press, 2000.

Scott, Colin. "Science for the West, Myth for the Rest?—The Case of James Bay Cree Knowledge Construction." In *Naked Science, Anthropological Inquiry into Boundaries, Power, and Knowledge,* ed. Laura Nadler. New York: Routledge, 1996.

Shelley, Mary. *The Last Man.* London: Henry Colburn, 1826.

Shepard, Paul. *Nature and Madness.* San Francisco: Sierra Club Books, 1982.

Shields, Carol. *The Stone Diaries.* Toronto: Vintage, 1993.

Siddall, Gillian. "Teaching Margaret Laurence's *The Diviners* as a Postcolonial Text." *Canadian Children's Literature* 79 (1995): 39–46.

Silverman, Eliane Leslau. *The Last Best West: Women on the Alberta Frontier, 1880–1930.* Montreal: Eden Press, 1984.

_____. "Writing Canadian Women's History, 1970–82: An Historiographical Analysis." *Canadian Historical Review* LXIII, 4 (1982).

Sinclair, David, ed. *Nineteenth-Century Narrative Poems.* Toronto: McClelland and Stewart, 1972.

Sinha, Mrinalina. *Colonial Masculinity: The "Manly" Englishman and the "Effeminate Bengali" in the Late Nineteenth Century.* Manchester: Manchester University Press, 1995.

Smith, Allan. "The Myth of the Self-made Man in English Canada 1850–1914." *Canadian Historical Review* 59, 21 (1978).

Smith, Arthur James Marshall. *Towards a View of Canadian Letters: Selected Critical Essays 1928–1971.* Vancouver: University of British Columbia Press, 1973.

Smith, Paul. *Discerning the Subject.* Minneapolis: Minnesota University Press, 1988.

Smith, Sidonie. *A Poetics of Women's Autobiography: Marginality and the Fictions of Self-Representation.* Bloomington: Indiana University Press, 1987.

_____. "Performativity, Autobiographical Practice, Resistance." *a/b: Auto/Biography Studies* 10, 1 (Spring 1995): 21.

Sproxton, Birk. *Headframe:.* Winnipeg: Turnstone Press, 1985.

Spry, Irene. "The Tragedy of the Loss of Commons in Western Canada." In *As Long as the Sun Shines and the Water Flows: A Reader in Canadian Native Studies*, ed. Ian A.L. Getty and Antoine S. Lussier. Vancouver: University of British Columbia Press, 1983.

Squire, S. "Wordsworth and Lake District Tourism: Romantic Reshaping of the Landscape." *The Canadian Geographer* 32.

_____, and J. Corner. "Codes and Cultural Analysis." In *Media, Culture, and Society: A Critical Reader*, ed R. Collins, J. Curran, N. Garnham, et al. London: Sage, 1986.

Stadler, Eva Maria. "Addressing Social Boundaries: Dressing the Female Body in Early Realist Fiction." In *Reconfigured Spheres: Feminist Explorations of Literary Space*, ed. Margaret R. Higonnet and Joan Templeton. Amherst: University of Massachusetts Press, 1994.

Stanzel, Frank K. "Texts Recycled: 'Found' Poems Found in Canada." In *Gaining Ground: European Critics on Canadian Literature*, ed. Robert Kroetsch and Reingard M. Nischik. Edmonton: NeWest Press, 1985.

Stegner, Wallace. *Wolf Willow: a history, a story, and a memory of the last plains frontier*. New York: Penguin, 2000.

Stein, Gertrude. *The Autobiography of Alice B. Toklas*. New York: Vintage, 1933.

Strange, Kathleen. *With the West in Her Eyes: The Story of a Modern Pioneer*. Toronto: Macmillan, 1945.

Stringer, Arthur. *The Mud Lark*. Indianapolis: Bobbs-Merrrill, 1931.

_____. *The Prairie Wife*. New York: A.L. Burt Company, 1915.

Taylor, R.S. "How New Salem Became an Outdoor Museum." *Historic Illinois* 2 (1979): 256–268.

ten Kortenaar, Neil. "The Trick of Divining a Postcolonial Canadian Identity: Margaret Laurence Between Race and Nation." *Canadian Literature* 149 (Summer 1996): 1–33.

Thacker, Robert. *The Great Prairie Fact and Literary Imagination*. Albuquerque: University of New Mexico Press, 1989.

Thesen, Sharon, ed. *The New Long Poem Anthology*. Toronto: Coach House Press, 1991. Second edition, Vancouver: Talonbooks, 2001.

Thomas, Joan. "'The Golden Book': An Interview with Carol Shields." *Prairie Fire* 14, 4 (Winter 93–94): 56–62.

Thomas, Peter. *Robert Kroetsch*. Vancouver: Douglas and McIntyre, 1980.

Thompson, E.P. "Time, Work-Discipline, and Industrial Capitalism." *Past and Present* 36 (1967): 56–97.

Thompson, John Herd. *Forging the Prairie West: The Illustrated History of Canada*. Don Mills: Oxford University Press, 1998.

Thrift, Nigel. "'Owners' Time and Own Time: The Making of a Capitalist Consciousness, 1330–1880." In *Space and Time Geography: Essays Dedicated to Torsten Hagerstrand*, ed. Allan Pred. Lund: CWK Gleerup, 1981.

Tierney, Frank M., and Angela Robbeson, eds. *Bolder Flights: Essays on the Canadian Long Poem*. Ottawa: University of Ottawa Press, 1998.

Urry, J. *The Tourist Gaze*. London: Sage, 1993.

Van Herk, Aritha. *Places far from Ellesmere, a geografictione, explorations on site*. Red Deer: Red Deer College Press, 1990.

_____. "CrowB(e)ars and Kangaroos of the Future: The Post-Colonial Ga(s)p." *World Literature Written in English* 30, 2 (Fall 1990): 42–54.

_____. "Prairie as Flat as . . ." In *A Frozen Tongue*. Sydney: Dangaroo, 1992.

_____, and Brian Stanko. "De-binarizing the Erotic Kroetsch." *The New Quarterly: New Directions in Canadian Writing* 18, 1 (Spring 1998).

Vauthier, Simone. "Ruptures in Carol Shields's *The Stone Diaries*." *Anglophonia: French Journal of English Studies* 1 (1997): 177–192.

Vipond, Mary. "The Image of Women in Canadian Mass Circulation Magazines in the 1920s." *Modernist Studies* 1, 3 (1974–75).

Voisey, P. *Vulcan: The Making of a Prairie Community*. Toronto: University of Toronto Press, 1988.

Wainwright, J.A. *A Very Large Soul: Selected Letters from Margaret Laurence to Canadian Writers*. Dunvegan, ON: Cormorant Books, 1995.

Wardhaugh, Robert, ed. *Toward Defining the Prairies: Region, Culture, and History*. Winnipeg: University of Manitoba Press, 2001.

Wasson, Richard. "Marshall McLuhan and the Politics of Modernism." *Massachusetts Review* 13 (1972): 567–580.

Weir, Allison. *Sacrificial Logics: Feminist Theory and the Critique of Identity*. New York: Routledge, 1996.

Weiss, R. *The Renaissance Discovery of Classical America*. Oxford: Oxford University Press, 1959.

Welter, Barbara. "The Cult of True Womanhood: 1820–1860." *American Quarterly* 18 (1966): 151–174.

Wharton, Thomas. "The Country of Illusion." In *Fresh Tracks: Writing the Western Landscape*, ed. Pamela Banting. Victoria: Polestar Book Publishers, 1998.

Wharton, Thomas. *Icefields*. Edmonton: NeWest Press, 1995.

White, Hayden. *Tropics of Discourse: Essays in Cultural Criticism*. Baltimore: Johns Hopkins University Press, 1978.

White, Richard. "The Cultural Landscape of the Pawnees." *Great Plains Quarterly* 2 (1982).

Whitrow, G.J. *Time in History, the Evolution of Our General Awareness of Time and Temporal Perspective*. Oxford: Oxford University Press, 1988.

Whyte, Jon. *Homage, Henry Kelsey*. Winnipeg: Turnstone Press, 1981.

Wilcox, Donald. *The Measure of Times Past, Pre-Newtonian Chronologies and the Rhetoric of Relative Time*. Chicago: University of Chicago Press, 1987.

Williams, Raymond. *The Politics of Modernism: Against the New Conformists*. New York: Verso, 1994.

Willmott, Glenn. *McLuhan, or Modernism in Reverse*. Toronto: University of Toronto Press, 1996.

Wilson, Milton. "Introduction." In *Recent Canadian Verse*. Kingston: Jackson Press, 1959.

Winston, Brian. "The Documentary Film as Scientific Inscription." In *Theorizing Documentary*, ed. Michael Renov. London: Routledge, 1993.

Winston, Elizabeth. "The Autobiographer and Her Readers: From Apology to Affirmation." *Women's Autobiography: Essays in Criticism*, ed. Estelle Jelinek. Bloomington: Indiana University Press, 1980.

Woodcock, George. "The Human Elements: Margaret Laurence's Fiction." In *The Human Elements: Critical Essays*, ed. David Helwig. Ottawa: Oberon, 1978.

Zaslow, Morris. "The Development of the Mackenzie River Basin, 1920–1940." PhD thesis, University of Toronto, 1958.

CONTRIBUTORS

RUSSELL BROWN is a professor at the University of Toronto and the co-editor of *A New Anthology of Canadian Literature in English* and of *Canadian Short Stories*. His recent critical essays have dealt with the history of the debate over Canadian thematic criticism, with Alice Munro, and with the visionary tradition in Canadian writing.

ALISON CALDER teaches Canadian literature and creative writing at the University of Manitoba. She has published articles on Canadian prairie literature and culture, including gophers; and on authors ranging from Guy Vanderhaeghe to Sky Lee. She is currently editing a forthcoming selection of poetry by Tim Lilburn. Her critical edition of F.P. Grove's novel *Settlers of the Marsh* is also forthcoming.

DENNIS COOLEY teaches creative writing, literary theory, and Canadian literature at St. John's College at the University of Manitoba. He has taught Prairie literature for many years, edited two anthologies of prairie poetry, helped to organize three conferences on the Prairies, published a collection of essays, and written several volumes of poetry, the latest being *country music*, from Kalamalka Press.

DEBRA DUDEK has published articles on Margaret Laurence, Fred Wah, and Aboriginal literature and post-colonial identity. She is currently a Canadian Studies Fellow at the Centre for Canadian-Australian Studies at the University of Wollongong.

FRANCES W. KAYE is Professor of Great Plains Studies and English at the University of Nebraska-Lincoln. She also occasionally teaches at the University of Calgary. For many years she was editor of the interdisciplinary journal *Great Plains Quarterly*. Her most recent book is *Hiding the Audience: Viewing Arts and Arts Institutions on the Prairies*.

HEIDI SLETTEDAHL MACPHERSON is Reader in North American Literature at the University of Central Lancashire. She is the author of *Women's Movement: Escape as Transgression in North American Feminist Fiction* and the co-editor of *Transatlantic Studies, New Perspectives in Transatlantic Studies* and *Britain and the Americas: Culture, Politics, and History*.

S. LEIGH MATTHEWS, who is teaching at Thompson Rivers University in Kamloops, BC, completed a PhD at the University of Calgary in 2001. Her study titled "'Bound to Improve': Canadian Women's Prairie Memoirs and Intersections of Culture, History and Identity" focusses on how women settlers represent themselves both in alignment with and over against dominant cultural narratives of prairie settlement. She specializes in nineteenth- and twentieth-century Canadian literature, children's literature, and theories of life writing, and is currently researching in the areas of eco-criticism and the representation of animals in literature.

CAM McEACHERN is completing his doctoral thesis on the interwar Athabasca River region for the history department at Queen's University. He lives and teaches in Saskatoon, Saskatchewan.

CLAIRE OMHOVÈRE is a lecturer in English at the Université Nancy 2 (France). She specializes in Canadian literature with a specific interest in the connections between the fiction and geography of western Canada.

SARAH PAYNE completed her doctoral dissertation in Geography at York University, Toronto.

NINA VAN GESSEL teaches English Literature at the Vrije Universiteit in Amsterdam. Her special research interests are the Canadian postmodern novel, American modernism, travel writing, and women's autobiography. She has published articles about American women publishers in interwar Paris, including Sylvia Beach, Caresse Crosby, and Margaret Anderson.

ROBERT WARDHAUGH is Assistant Professor of History at the University of Western Ontario. He has written *Mackenzie King and the Prairie West* (2000), edited *Toward Defining the Prairies: Region, Culture, and History* (2001), and is continuing work on national politics and Prairie regional society.